Beiträge zum
ausländischen öffentlichen Recht und Völkerrecht

Edited by

the Max Planck Society
for the Advancement of Science
represented by Prof. Dr. Armin von Bogdandy
and Prof. Dr. Anne Peters

Volume 313

Kevin Li

# Reconceiving Extraterritorial Jurisdiction

From Formality to Function

Nomos

Gefördert durch die Deutsche Forschungsgemeinschaft (DFG) – 499582385
funded by the Deutsche Forschungsgemeinschaft (DFG, German Research Foundation) – 499582385

**The Deutsche Nationalbibliothek** lists this publication in the Deutsche Nationalbibliografie; detailed bibliographic data are available on the Internet at http://dnb.d-nb.de

a.t.: München, Univ., Diss., 2020

ISBN 978-3-8487-8984-9 (Print)
978-3-7489-3321-2 (ePDF)

**British Library Cataloguing-in-Publication Data**
A catalogue record for this book is available from the British Library.

ISBN 978-3-8487-8984-9 (Print)
978-3-7489-3321-2 (ePDF)

**Library of Congress Cataloging-in-Publication Data**
Li, Kevin
Reconceiving Extraterritorial Jurisdiction
From Formality to Function
Kevin Li
368 pp.
Includes bibliographic references.

ISBN 978-3-8487-8984-9 (Print)
978-3-7489-3321-2 (ePDF)

1st Edition 2022



Published by
Nomos Verlagsgesellschaft mbH & Co. KG
Waldseestraße 3–5 | 76530 Baden-Baden
www.nomos.de

Production of the printed version:
Nomos Verlagsgesellschaft mbH & Co. KG
Waldseestraße 3–5 | 76530 Baden-Baden

ISBN 978-3-8487-8984-9 (Print)
ISBN 978-3-7489-3321-2 (ePDF)
DOI https://doi.org/10.5771/9783748933212

Onlineversion
Nomos eLibrary

# Preface

The present thesis was accepted as inaugural dissertation at the Faculty of Law of LMU Munich on 8 December 2020. With the permission of the Faculty, parts of this thesis were slightly abridged and updated prior to publication.

A doctoral thesis is never written alone. Of all the people who accompanied me on this long journey, I am most grateful to my doctoral supervisor Professor Christian Walter: Not only did he inspire and encourage me to pursue this work in the first place, but he also offered invaluable, timely and kind support during the research and writing of this thesis. Most importantly, he was always open to listen to my struggles and ideas and in turn responded with profound criticism and thoughtful advice.

I also wish to thank Professor Martin Burgi for providing a speedy and favourable second examiner's report. Further, I am indebted to Professor Jens Kersten for serving as examiner during a particularly lively oral examination.

Many of the ideas and inspirations contained in this work are the fruits of discussions at the LMU Chair of Public International Law and Public Law and for that I would like to express my gratitude to my colleagues at the Chair. At various times, I worked with, among others, Maria Monnheimer, Stefan Herrmann, Markus Vordermayer-Riemer, Stefan Schäferling, Charlotte Mölter, Cathrine Crämer and Philip Nedelcu. Thanks are also due to the other academic and administrative staff at the Faculty of Law with whom I had the pleasure of working with over the years.

Furthermore, I wish to thank Professor Anne Peters and Professor Armin von Bogdandy of the Max Planck Institute for Comparative Public Law and International Law for including this work into the book series 'Contributions on Comparative Public Law and International Law'. I couldn't have asked for a more appropriate place to publish this thesis.

This research has been generously supported by the *Stiftung der Deutschen Wirtschaft* (sdw, Foundation of German Business). The publication is funded by the *Deutsche Forschungsgemeinschaft* (DFG, German Research Foundation). I am grateful for the support provided by both organisations. I also wish to thank the anonymous reviewer for the

*Deutsche Forschungsgemeinschaft*, who offered constructive comments and suggestions.

I am deeply grateful to my parents and my brother Enno who have continuously encouraged and supported me in this endeavour.

But above all, Nicole: This work has been a journey for me as much as it has been for you and if I have learned one thing during this time, then it is that you are an infinitely better person than me. Nothing that I could write here would do justice to your patience, trust and sacrifice. Thank you.

Spring 2022 *Kevin Li*

# Inhaltsverzeichnis

# A. Introduction

## I. Purpose and Scope of the Study

The concept of extraterritorial jurisdiction evokes very different emotions. Some may be fearful because it reminds them of imperialism and hegemonic claims. Others may be alarmed, because they view extraterritorial jurisdiction as a desperate response by States to the forces of globalization chipping away at their regulatory capacities. Others again may be hopeful, because extraterritorial jurisdiction provides a timely answer to pressing global challenges without the need for the dreaded international consensus.

This diversity of perspectives is certainly remarkable, given that at first glance, extraterritorial jurisdiction is merely an inconspicuous technical legal concept. The exercise of extraterritorial jurisdiction is subject to rules of international law. In fact, according to Hans Kelsen, it is one of the 'essential functions' of international law to limit the spheres of validity of national legal orders.[1] The limits to the competences of States have been traditionally drawn by the principle of sovereign equality of States. Therefore, according to this model, State power is generally territorially bounded and the exercise of extraterritorial jurisdiction as an exception should only be valid when some other legitimizing principle in international law is satisfied. The functionality of this system depends on two separate but intertwined premises that lie at the heart of the system: First, that it is possible to precisely locate the limits of territorially bounded State power, that is, the boundary between territoriality and extraterritoriality, and second, that it is possible to define such other principles, as exceptions to territoriality, that reasonably establish the legitimacy of extraterritorial jurisdictional assertions.

1 Hans Kelsen, *Principles of international law* (Rinehart and Co 1952), 94; Very similar language can be found in the seminal treatise by Frederick A Mann, 'The Doctrine of Jurisdiction in International Law' (1964) 111 Recueil des Cours 1, 15, who states that '[j]urisdiction, it thus appears, is concerned with what has been described as one of the most fundamental functions of public international law, viz. the function of regulating and delimiting the respective competences of States'.

For a very long time, States and international law scholars believed they had found satisfactory determinations with regard to both of these premises. There was of course debate regarding the details, in particular in relation to the first question. In the field of criminal law, arguments around the proper geographical reach of law may be traced back at least to medieval Europe.[2] And even in the area of law, which may be termed commercial regulation,[3] issues of extraterritorial jurisdiction have featured prominently as early as the 1909 Supreme Court case in *American Banana*.[4] Despite these debates, the international law doctrine on jurisdiction has remained surprisingly resilient and its underlying assumptions have only undergone small changes.[5] Even in 2006, the International Law Commission felt that the law was settled enough to propose the elaboration of a draft instrument on extraterritorial jurisdiction.[6]

This draft instrument never materialized. To be fair, it is almost certain that any draft instrument elaborated in 2006 would have become obsolete by now. In fact, it does not take a tremendous amount of fantasy to see that the tectonic shifts occurring around the world must eventually impact the international law on jurisdiction. Without getting into terminological debates, what has happened in the meantime can be aptly described with the word 'globalization'. Globalization is not a purely economic phenomenon, although the globalization of markets, including the increased movement of capital and labour across borders and the consolidation of multinational corporations, is one important manifestation of the process.[7]

---

2 Cedric Ryngaert, *Jurisdiction in International Law* (Oxford Monographs in International Law, Second edition), 52 – 53.

3 There seems to be no internationally accepted term to describe the body of law concerned with the regulation of business enterprises with the purpose to uphold the public order and certain public values. Different States have different historical practices in this regard. The term commercial regulation was adopted from the International Law Commission, *Report of the International Law Commission on the Work of its Fifty-eighth Session* (UN Doc A 61/10, 2006), at 526.

4 *American Banana Co. v United Fruit Co.*, 213 US 347 (1909).

5 The arguably most ground-breaking contribution within these debates may have been the *Restatement (Third) of the Foreign Relations Law of the United States* (American Law Inst. Publ 1987), which was largely prompted by US jurisprudence on the reach of US antitrust regulation.

6 International Law Commission (n 3), at 517.

7 On the term of 'globalization', see Günther Handl, 'Extra-Territoriality and Transnational Legal Authority' in Günther Handl, Joachim Zekoll and Peer Zumbansen (eds), *Beyond Territoriality: Transnational Legal Authority in an Age of Globalization* (Queen Mary studies in international law. Martinus Nijhofff Publishers 2012), 3.

However, this process has led to new challenges as well, such as the rise of transnational criminal activities and perhaps even more acute, the climate crisis as a truly global threat to humanity. All of these phenomena have been enabled, amplified and shaped through the relentless technological progress and in particular, the advent of the internet.[8]

This study focuses on a related aspect, namely that globalization as a *de facto* development has also caused a globalization of regulation.[9] This is to be understood as the process, by which powerful States advance a particular domestic moral or political stance through the use of unilateral regulation.[10] This is not an entirely new phenomenon, as already the development of extraterritorial antitrust regulations could be regarded as the 'exportation' of a particular ideal of competition. However, in this instance, the regulations remedied the economic order within domestic territory, which was under threat from external conduct.[11] Increasingly however, States also resort to regulation when the primary objective is

---

8 The internet in particular has posed difficult challenges to the allocation of jurisdiction in international law and prompted a sometimes radical discourse, see David R Johnson and David. Post, 'Law and Borders: The Rise of Law in Cyberspace' (1996) 48 Stanford Law Review 1367.

9 See for the relevance of this globalization of regulation: John Braithwaite and Peter Drahos, *Global Business Regulation* (Cambridge Univ. Press 2000), 8.

10 William Magnuson, 'Unilateral Corporate Regulation' (2016) 17 Chicago Journal of Interanational Law 521, 524. Unilateral extraterritorial jurisdiction is sometimes praised as a possible solution to some of the most pressing global problems of our time, see: Nico Krisch, 'The Decay of Consent: International Law in an Age of Global Public Goods' (2014) 108 AJIL 1; Joanne Scott, 'Extraterritoriality and Territorial Extension in EU Law' (2013) 62 AJCL 87; Cedric Ryngaert, *Unilateral Jurisdiction and Global Values: Oratie in verkorte vorm uitgesproken bij de aanvaarding van het ambt van hoogleraar Internationaal Publiekrecht aan de Faculteit Recht, Economie, Bestuur en Organisatie van de Univ. Utrecht op maandag 30 maart 2015* (Eleven International 2015). However, this position is forcefully criticized by B. S Chimni, 'The international law of jurisdiction: A TWAIL perspective' (2022) 35(1) Leiden Journal of International Law 29; Furthermore, some authors also view extraterritorial jurisdiction as a threat to consent-based international efforts undermining a progressive development of the international community, see Austen L Parrish, 'Reclaiming International Law from Extraterritoriality' (2009) 93 Minnesota Law Review 815.

11 The United States realized that in a wholly integrated market, it was not enough to simply regulate conduct within US territory but that conspiracies between third State companies could also cause significant adverse effects on domestic competition; see further: Karl M Meessen, 'Antitrust Jurisdiction under Customary International Law' (1984) 78 AJIL 783; David J Gerber, 'The Extraterritorial Application of the German Antitrust Laws' (1983) 77(4) AJIL 756.

not to mitigate adverse domestic effects. States have met these more demanding regulatory objectives with the design of more complex regulatory mechanisms.

Under these circumstances, this study seeks to answer two research questions: First, this study intends to establish whether the territoriality-based system of jurisdiction is still capable of providing order in international relations by delimiting regulatory competences between States. The answer to this question depends on whether the first premise laid out in the second paragraph above still holds true in light of globalization: Is it possible to define normatively consistent boundaries of territoriality to be respected by States? Or are States, in their pursuit of political and legal goals, exploiting and disregarding the system? Second, this study also seeks to answer how, in light of the necessary progressive development of the law, extraterritorial jurisdiction can be adequately reconceptualised to account for the increasing importance of interests beyond State sovereignty. Because considering the normative upheaval brought about by globalization, this study questions the validity of the second premise laid out above, that the recognized exceptions to the principle of territoriality can reasonably legitimize extraterritorial jurisdiction.

There has been an impressive amount of writing on the topic of extraterritorial jurisdiction in recent years.[12] In relation to the first research question, other scholars have doubted the effectiveness of the territoriality-based system of jurisdiction in light of modern technological developments.[13] However, this study is novel because its results will be derived from a strict analysis of actual practice of States and certain regional organizations such as the European Union (**EU**) in four diverse regulatory areas, economic sanctions, export control, transnational anti-corruption and business and human rights. If, with regard to these reference areas, the territoriality-based system of jurisdiction is found to provide no consistent

---

12 See for instance: International Bar Association, *Report of the Task Force on Extraterritorial Jurisdiction* (International Bar Association 2008).

13 Dan J B Svantesson, *Solving the Internet Jurisdiction Puzzle* (Oxford University Press 2017); see also: Paul S Berman, *Global Legal Pluralism: A Jurisprudence of Law beyond Border* (1. publ, Cambridge Univ. Press 2012), at 44 compares the, in his view, futile efforts of law academics to solve the jurisdictional challenges posed by the internet to the *streetlight* effect:
'[...] a police officer sees a drunk man searching in vain under a streetlight for his keys and asks whether he is sure he lost them there. The drunk replies, no, he lost them across the street. The officer, incredulous, asks then why he is searching here, and the drunk replies, "the light is so much brighter here."'.

allocation of regulatory competences between States, a general conclusion may be drawn to answer the first research question. In relation to the second research question, a number of studies have argued that State jurisdiction should be receptive to considerations apart from State sovereignty.[14] However, this study advances a novel perspective by highlighting the hybrid nature of extraterritorial jurisdiction in that it also concerns the exercise of public authority *vis-à-vis* individuals.

Therefore, this study argues that although the territoriality-based system of jurisdiction seems to be a logical way of allocating regulatory competences between States, in practice, it now fails to deliver on its main promise: order. The formal boundaries of territoriality are not normatively consistent and States either exploit or disregard the system in their pursuit of political and legal interests. However, the necessary progressive development of the law provides a chance to reconceive extraterritorial jurisdiction not only as a function of State sovereignty, but more broadly as an exercise of public authority, the legitimacy of which also depends on the relationship between the regulating State and the addressee and the international community at large.

## II. Structure of the Argument

To arrive from the two research questions to the thesis proposed, this study necessarily has to engage with the current rules of jurisdiction in international law. On the one hand, the first part of the thesis claims that the formal, territoriality-based system of jurisdiction has become increasingly unsustainable because it is not possible to define, in a normatively consistent way, the boundaries of territoriality. On the other hand, the second part of the thesis argues that within the traditional system, it is not possible to account for certain interests which are relevant in determining the legitimacy of jurisdictional assertions.

Therefore, this study needs to ascertain how currently under international law, territoriality is separated from extraterritoriality and in the latter case, which principles, exceptionally, allow for the exercise of jurisdiction. According to Art. 36 (2) Statute of the International Court of Justice (**ICJ**), this task requires an analysis of relevant legal sources, i.e., treaties, customary international law and general principles. Treaty law in

14 See in this regard: Ryngaert, *Jurisdiction in International Law* (n 2); Alex Mills, 'Rethinking Jurisdiction in International Law' (2014) 84 BYIL 187.

the field of jurisdiction is scarce: No generally binding instrument exists and only few rules about the scope of jurisdiction are included in treaties dealing with specific areas of international law.[15] Therefore, customary international law will serve as the most important authority. However, establishing customary international law would require the proof of both a general practice[16] and *opinio iuris* in a comprehensive manner that far exceeds the scope of this research.[17] Thus, this research can only analyse exemplary practice and will recourse to the academic work of other commentators to establish the content of the international law rules on jurisdiction.

In a next step, in order to argue that the rules just ascertained do not deliver normatively consistent results in practice, actual exercises of jurisdiction by States and the EU in the selected research areas will be examined. To determine the general practice, this research reviews a large number of official documents, ranging from legislation, administrative determinations, court decisions and other judicial documents including *amicus curiae* briefs to verbal acts such as protests and affirmations through diplomatic notes as well as other communications.[18] The case studies chosen for research are among the most outrageous claims of extraterritorial jurisdiction or those that elicited the greatest reaction by other States and academic commentators. Precisely these cases put the traditional doctrine to a breaking test, while also highlighting the host of interests that should be taken into account when exercising jurisdiction. This focus explains why this research is primarily (though by no means exclusively[19]) con-

---

15 See for instance Art. 42 of the United Nations Convention against Corruption (adopted 11 December 2003, entered into force 14 December 2005) 2349 UNTS 41 ('UNCAC').

16 The requirement of a 'general practice' for the establishment of customary international law refers primarily to State practice. In this regard, the practice of the European Union may be equated to the practice of its member States in those subject matters in which the member States have transferred exclusive competence to the European Union, see International Law Commission, *Draft Conclusions on Identification of Customary International Law, with Commentaries* (UN Doc A/73/10, 2018), Conclusion 4 para. 2 and Commentary (6) thereto. For the sake of simplicity, any reference to 'State practice' in this study also includes practice of the European Union.

17 ICJ, *North Sea Continental Shelf Cases (Fed Rep of Germany v Netherlands)* [1969] ICJ Rep 3, 44.

18 James Crawford and Ian Brownlie, *Brownlie's Principles of Public International Law* (Eighth edition, Oxford University Press 2012), at 24.

19 In particular, China is just beginning to exercise extraterritorial jurisdiction, e.g. through the Chinese Anti-Monopoly Law, see Michael Faure and Xinzhu Zhang,

cerned with studying US law and the law of a number of European States as well as of the EU, as it is generally powerful States or trading blocs that have acted at the forefront of transnational regulation.[20] This analysis will provide insight into the legal bases, practical instruments and arguments relied upon by States in justifying their exercises or rejections of certain exercises of jurisdiction. To prove the argument, these State actions are to be normatively assessed under the jurisdictional rules of international law already ascertained. In doing so, two phenomena dominate: First that States deliberately resort to exercises of jurisdiction, which, although they may formally rely on a territorial basis, allow States to unilaterally set regulations with a global reach contrary to the ordering purpose of the territoriality-based system of jurisdiction; and second, that States disregard the system entirely: They promote or contest such measures not based on considerations of territoriality, but on political convenience.

Finally, in the necessary search for an alternative to that dysfunctional system, the study advocates for a change in perspective: While traditionally, the legitimacy of exercises of jurisdiction has been solely mediated by considerations of State sovereignty, the specific hybrid nature of extraterritorial jurisdiction, in that it also directly affects individual interests, brings it functionally much closer to domestic public regulation. This realization has normative ramifications, because domestic public law knows other bases of legitimacy and establishes other limits on the exercise of public authority than State sovereignty. These bases of legitimacy and limits are to be transferred to the transnational context of extraterritorial jurisdiction. Finally, it has always been my hope that this study will have actual application beyond the immediately studied cases and areas of reference. Therefore, this study will translate these considerations of legitimacy and limits into practically applicable variables and tests.

Thus, the structure of this research is as follows:

The remainder of this part A will clarify some definitions of the terms and concepts most commonly used in this study. Part B ascertains the current rules of international law on State jurisdiction. It does so by reviewing scholarly commentary as well as some influential practice, beginning inevitably with the seminal judgment of the Permanent Court

'Towards an Extraterritorial Application of the Chinese Anti-Monopoly Law that Avoids Trade Conflicts' (2013) 45 The George Washington International Law Review 101.

20 Ryngaert, *Jurisdiction in International Law* (n 2), 3.

of International Justice (**PCIJ**) in *Lotus*,[21] before turning to the classical bases of jurisdiction accepted under general international law. Part C, the bulk to this research, is dedicated to analysing the relevant practice of States and the EU and assessing this practice against the norms of international law just ascertained. This part concludes that in the face of modern regulatory efforts, it is not possible to define, in a normatively consistent way, the boundaries of territoriality. Finally, part D proposes a functional perspective to extraterritorial jurisdiction as an alternative to the territoriality-based system and for that, draws upon domestic public law concepts of legitimacy and limits, before translating these considerations into a new practical framework. Part E concludes.

## III. Concepts and Definitions

### 1. State Jurisdiction and State Sovereignty

So far, this study has pretended that concepts such as jurisdiction, territoriality and extraterritoriality or State sovereignty are self-explanatory. They are certainly not. However, in a first attempt at definition, jurisdiction, as referred to in this research, means the 'the lawful power of a State to define and enforce the rights and duties, and control the conduct, of natural and juridical persons'.[22] How a State chooses to exercise this power is primarily a domestic issue. It may be subject to constitutional rules such as the division of power into a legislative, executive and judicial branch. Jurisdiction only becomes a concern of international law when, in exceptional cases, its exercise may affect the relationship between multiple sovereigns. This relationship is affected when a State projects its legal authority to a situation, which is (also) connected to or in the interest of another State. In these cases, jurisdiction becomes an international law inquiry about the requirements and the scope of the power of a State to regulate conduct in relation to other interested States.

---

21 PCIJ, *S.S. Lotus (France v Turkey)* [1927] PCIJ Rep Series A No 10.

22 Bernard H Oxman, 'Jurisdiction of States' in R. Wolfrum (ed), *The Max Planck Encyclopedia of Public International Law* (Oxford University Press), para. 3. It is difficult to provide an exact definition of 'jurisdiction', see for instance Ryngaert, *Jurisdiction in International Law* (n 2) at 5, who notes that although most international lawyers have an inkling of its meaning, the definition is not self-evident.

There is no easy answer to this inquiry. As indicated, most commentators agree that the fundamental principle of State sovereignty provides an apt starting point of analysis. Sovereignty is expressed both in the independence and authority of States to act internally and in the entitlement of a State to freedom from external interventions.[23] The exercise of jurisdiction is a function of sovereignty. At the same time however, it is also limited by sovereignty, in the sense that assertions of jurisdiction have to respect the equal sovereignty of other States, that is, they must not unduly encroach on such sovereignty.[24] This international law principle of non-intervention, the prohibition to interfere with the domestic affairs of another State, therefore forms one of the outer limits to exercises of jurisdiction. It is important to note however, that while plenty of domestic assertions of jurisdiction affect other sovereigns, only few of them actually conflict with the legal principle of non-intervention.

Under the currently dominant account of jurisdiction in international law, the principles of sovereignty and non-intervention are more than just the doctrinal basis. Correct understanding of these principles may have practical consequences as well. On the one hand, the paramount importance of territorial sovereignty for ordering modern State relations is reflected in the equally powerful jurisdictional basis of territoriality. The exercise of regulatory power was historically confined exclusively to persons, property and conduct within the territory of the State.[25] Today still, it serves as the primary reference to exercises of authority. On the other hand, however, principles of sovereignty and non-intervention are also reflected in the exceptional bases of jurisdiction. In fact, there are some exercises of jurisdiction that, even though they do not concern an entirely territorial situation within the regulating State, are nonetheless not exclusively domestic affairs of another State. This is the case when a State exercises jurisdiction in relation to its own nationals or to protect a vital national interest, particularly the functioning of government. These aspects, just like territoriality, are equally connected to the very core of

23 John H Jackson, 'Sovereignty – Modern: A new Approach to an Outdated Concept' (2003) 97(4) AJIL 782, 786; Eyal Benvenisti, 'Sovereigns as Trustees of Humanity: On the Accountability of States to Foreign Stakeholders' (2013) 107(2) AJIL 295 characterizes sovereignty as traditionally conceived as 'akin to owning a large estate separated from other properties by rivers or deserts'.

24 Mann (n 1), 30; Markus Volz, *Extraterritoriale Terrorismusbekämpfung* (Tübinger Schriften zum internationalen und europäischen Recht Bd. 86, Duncker & Humblot 2007), 40.

25 See International Law Commission (n 3), at 516.

statehood, namely the existence of a State population and an independent government.[26] When a State exercises jurisdiction based on one of these principles, even if doing so affects interests of another State, there will be no *prima facie* violation of the principle of non-intervention.

### 2. Extraterritoriality and Extraterritorial Jurisdiction

It has already been noted that the exercise of jurisdiction generally becomes controversial under international law only when it affects the relationship between multiple sovereigns. In diplomatic exchanges between States, this potentially contentious exercise of authority is frequently referred to as 'extraterritorial jurisdiction'.[27] We have already drawn some considerations with regard to the term 'jurisdiction', so that this section seeks to shed some light on the 'extraterritorial' part. A report by the International Law Commission defines 'extraterritoriality' as 'the area beyond [the] territory [of a State], including its land, internal waters, territorial sea as well as the adjacent airspace'.[28] However, when international law scholars speak about extraterritoriality, they are rarely interested in the physical dimensions of 'extraterritoriality', but rather, they want to know whether a certain act of a State constitutes an exercise of 'extraterritorial jurisdiction'.[29]

Historically, a clear example for the exercise of extraterritorial jurisdiction was provided by the practice of Western States in maintaining consular courts abroad. Here, all the elements involved were 'extraterritorial'. There was a domestic authority located abroad, which was defining and enforcing the rights and duties, and controlling the conduct of certain persons within the territory of another State.[30] The situation becomes much

---

26 Charlotte Beaucillon, 'Practice Makes Perfect, Eventually? Unilateral State Sanctions and the Extraterritorial Effects of National Legislation' in Natalino Ronzitti (ed), *Coercive Diplomacy, Sanctions and International Law* (Brill Nijhoff 2016), 16.

27 Marko Milanovic, 'From Compromise to Principle: Clarifying the Concept of State Jurisdiction in Human Rights Treaties' (2008) 8(3) HRLRev 411, at 421 remarks that 'practically the entirety of the law of (prescriptive) jurisdiction is about the exceptions to territoriality'.

28 See International Law Commission (n 3), 518.

29 Scott (n 10), notes at 89 that, 'There is uncertainty and disagreement about what counts, and what should count, as a territorial connection for the purpose of distinguishing between the exercise of territorial and extraterritorial jurisdiction'.

30 Eileen P Scully, *Bargaining with the State from Afar: American Citizenship in Treaty Port China, 1844-1942* (Columbia University Press 2012), 6 – 7.

more difficult, however, when not all the elements of an assertion of jurisdiction are so clearly 'extraterritorial'. Take the example of a cross-border shooting, is it the State, where the perpetrator is located, or the State where the victim is located, that is exercising 'extraterritorial jurisdiction', or is it possibly both, or none of them? This depends on whether 'extraterritorial jurisdiction' requires that all of the elements involved are 'extraterritorial' such as in the case of consular jurisdiction, or whether it is enough that one of the elements is 'extraterritorial'. And if only the 'extraterritoriality' of one element suffices, which element is the relevant one? In the situation of the cross-border shooting, is it the location of the perpetrator or the location of the victim? How should international law determine which element is the relevant one?

It is easy to realize that in our modern, globalized world, where any action taken anywhere could have repercussions anywhere else, answering these crucial questions is immensely difficult. In fact, these are essentially normative questions with possibly more than one set of reasonable answers. Thus, when States, but also academic commentators, employ the term 'extraterritorial jurisdiction', unless they explicitly explain their particular understanding, they may be, and in fact often are, referring to wholly different circumstances. There is a second, related issue with the term 'extraterritorial jurisdiction'. The concept itself does not imply any normative consequences under international law: Depending on the circumstances, the exercises of jurisdiction by a State *vis-à-vis* persons or conduct abroad may even be generally permissive, for instance if a State prescribes rules for its own nationals.[31]

Despite this normative fuzziness, the term 'extraterritorial jurisdiction' in practice almost always carries a negative connotation. States generally use this term to describe situations, in which one State feels that the action of another State infringes on its domestic interests.[32] Thus, 'extraterritorial jurisdiction' in these instances is often used as a political statement and a hardly concealed claim for arguing that some assertion of authority is deemed excessive in scope or illegal under international law. This is unfortunate because, as was just argued, 'extraterritorial jurisdiction' is in itself a normatively neutral concept. However, particularly in contested cases, 'extraterritorial jurisdiction' is almost never meant to describe such other-

31 See on this principle below at B.I.2c) Active Personality.

32 Hannah L Buxbaum, 'Territory, Territoriality, and the Resolution of Jurisdictional Conflict' (2009) 57(3) AJCL, 635; Ryngaert, *Jurisdiction in International Law* (n 2), 7.

wise permissive assertions of authority, but is used solely to demarcate the political fault line between territoriality and extraterritoriality.

Two observations can be made already at this point: First, in an attempt to strengthen terminological clarity, for the remainder of this research, the term 'extraterritorial jurisdiction' will be used in a broad and politically neutral sense, which in itself does not allow any conclusions about its normative permissibility. Rather, 'extraterritorial jurisdiction' is a shorthand statement that simply describes all exercises of jurisdiction, which (not necessarily exclusively) affect the rights and duties, or incentivize or regulate the conduct of natural and juridical persons outside the territory of the State. Second, the study of 'extraterritorial jurisdiction' is a task requiring immense precision. Any successful argument on jurisdiction under international law must move beyond labels – these should be used as sparingly as possible – and instead look behind the façade of the measures in question. This research intends to do so.

### 3. The Concept of Jurisdiction in International Human Rights Treaties

Jurisdiction, as a concept under general international law to negatively delimit the spheres of authority between States must not be confused with the equally controversial notion of jurisdiction in international human rights law. Human rights treaties regularly include clauses that limit their reach to situations 'within their jurisdiction'[33] or 'within its territory and subject to its jurisdiction'.[34] As a first reflex, it would not be far-fetched to think that 'jurisdiction' in this respect refers to the same concept of 'jurisdiction' under general international law that was just discussed above. Thus the scope of international human rights treaties would coincide with the lawful authority of States to define and enforce rules. However, the treaty bodies nowadays largely follow a different interpretation for the concept of jurisdiction for the purpose of international human rights protection (although the matter is still in flux and the treaty bodies themselves have not devised a coherent line of interpretation yet).[35]

The distinction between the two concepts was of course deliberate and, to a certain degree, necessary. After all, jurisdiction as referred to in international human rights treaties fulfils a different function than jurisdiction

33 Art. 1 ECHR.
34 Art. 2 (1) ICCPR.
35 Milanovic (n 27), 417.

under general international law. If a person is found to be within the jurisdiction of a State, then that State is obliged to extend the human rights guaranteed in the treaty to that person, less it will incur international responsibility.[36] Put simply, jurisdiction in international human rights law is a concept to delimit the spheres of State legal *obligation* while jurisdiction in general international law delimits the spheres of State *competence*. However, despite the seemingly bright-line distinction put out here, the two notions have been confused by even the most eminent judges of the European Court of Human Rights (**ECtHR**).[37] What makes this matter particularly difficult is that both conceptions of jurisdiction take 'territoriality' as their default, but also allow for 'extraterritoriality' in exceptional circumstances.

In international human rights law, the extraterritoriality inquiry concerns whether certain 'extraterritorial' State acts trigger the application of human rights treaties and extension of obligations under these treaties to persons or circumstances located abroad. There are two categories of circumstances that are generally accepted in this regard and they are both related to factual power: Either, the State exercises effective control over foreign territory (such as in the case of occupation) or the State exercises effective control over an individual person abroad.[38] On the other hand, in general international law, the inquiry concerns something different, namely, whether a State has the authority to exercise extraterritorial jurisdiction, i.e. whether certain 'extraterritorial' acts are lawful in the first place. The answer to this question depends on the kind of State action and on the existence of certain connections between the State and the subject matter in question. Therefore, for instance in the case of detaining an individual on foreign territory, it is possible that jurisdiction exists for the purpose of triggering the applicability of an international human rights treaty, while at the same time, the acting State cannot claim the lawful exercise of jurisdiction under general international law. While this result may seem strange at the first moment, it becomes comprehensible when one remembers that the concept of jurisdiction under international human rights law is concerned with factual power while the concept under general interna-

36 Ryngaert, *Jurisdiction in International Law* (n 2), 22.

37 See on this Milanovic (n 27), 417 discussing the relevant passages of ECtHR, *Banković and others v Belgium and others*, App No 52207/99, Decision of 12 December 2001, paras. 59–61.

38 See also Barbara Cooreman, *Global Environmental Protection through Trade: A Systematic Approach to Extraterritoriality* (Edward Elgar Publishing 2017), 116 – 117.

tional law refers to lawful authority.[39] Since this research is concerned with determining the scope of legal authority of States the concept of jurisdiction under international human rights law will generally not be further addressed.[40]

### 4. Categories of State Jurisdiction

For purposes of international law, the traditional doctrine distinguishes between different categories of jurisdiction depending on the nature of the underlying State act to be analysed. Typically in Anglo-Saxon literature, three categories are defined, which, at first sight, roughly resemble the separation of governmental powers into legislative, judicial and executive aspects.[41] These are termed jurisdiction to prescribe, i.e. the power of a State 'to make law applicable to persons, property or conduct', jurisdiction to adjudicate, i.e. the power 'to apply law to persons or things, in particular through the process of its courts or administrative tribunals', and jurisdiction to enforce, i.e. the power 'to compel compliance with law'.[42]

In this sense, jurisdiction to prescribe encompasses not only rules through legislation or executive regulations, but also through a determination of a court or an order of the executive branch, typically by the administration.[43] Thus, jurisdiction to prescribe is engaged when a new antitrust law is enacted as well as when the European Commission finds the behaviour of an individual corporation to be abusive. However, in these cases, the distinction between jurisdiction to prescribe and jurisdiction to enforce may become controversial. This is particularly the case, when a foreigner is fined or subjected to other non-forcible sanctions by a domestic administrative body or court for engaging in prohibited conduct.

39 Milanovic (n 27), 417.

40 An exception hereto will be discussed in the area of business and human rights, where a trend has emerged which seeks to merge the two notions, see below at C.V.3b) Extraterritorial Jurisdiction as a Matter of Obligation.

41 *Restatement (Third) of the Foreign Relations Law of the United States* (n 5), comment *a*) to § 401.

42 *Restatement (Fourth) of the Foreign Relations Law of the United States* (American Law Inst. Publ 2018), § 401; see also Oxman (n 22); Michael B Akehurst, 'Jurisdiction in International Law' (1972-73) 46 BYIL 145, 145.

43 Werner Meng, *Extraterritoriale Jurisdiktion im öffentlichen Wirtschaftsrecht: Extraterritorial Jurisdiction in Public Economic Law* (Beiträge zum ausländischen öffentlichen Recht und Völkerrecht vol 119, Springer 1994), 6.

Here, it could be argued that these sanctions are levied in order to compel the foreigner to comply with a certain rule and thus, that these acts should be properly seen as an exercise of enforcement jurisdiction. On the other hand, one may view the imposition of a fine as yet another prescriptive rule, non-compliance of which may eventually trigger the use of forcible measures by a State, for instance, the seizure of domestic property and only that seizure should be categorized as an actual exercise of enforcement jurisdiction.

This issue is far from purely academic as the requirements for the assertion of prescriptive and enforcement jurisdiction under international law are quite different. In particular, it is widely accepted that, absent express consent of the affected State for instance through a treaty, enforcement outside State territory is generally prohibited by the principle of non-intervention. This consequence has led some commentators to view enforcement jurisdiction more narrowly to only encompass acts that directly bring about a change in the physical or legal situation concerned, typical examples may be the seizure of assets, the search of an apartment or the imprisonment of an individual.[44] However, as will be seen in later parts, even this seemingly bright-line rule may not bring about ultimate clarity in distinguishing between the two categories of jurisdiction. There is a second well accepted rule in relation to enforcement jurisdiction apart from strict territoriality, namely that the enforcement of a rule is only legal under international law if the enforcing State could lawfully prescribe the underlying rule in the first place.[45] Thus, even when a State undoubtedly has the authority of enforcement, for instance by imprisoning an individual present within domestic territory, the exercise of jurisdiction may still be illegal if the imprisonment is based on a law for which the State cannot claim prescriptive jurisdiction.[46]

---

44 In this sense: Ryngaert, *Jurisdiction in International Law* (n 2), 9; Akehurst (n 42), 145 – 151; see also OLG Rostock, Order of 29 February 2008, I Ws 60/08: the court held that summoning the accused living abroad to trial under threat of sanctions does not violate international law if the sanctions will only be enforced domestically.

45 Oxman (n 22), para. 5.

46 *The Restatement (Fourth) of the Foreign Relations Law of the United States* (n 42), § 401, Reporters' notes 3 follows a different approach: 'A state may exercise jurisdiction to enforce although it lacks jurisdiction to prescribe and to adjudicate. For instance, it is common for one state to arrest and extradite a criminal defendant for trial under the substantive law of another state.'.

Adjudicative jurisdiction, as already mentioned, is equivalent to the jurisdiction of courts over persons, in the United States also known as *in personam* jurisdiction. In continental European literature, the status of adjudicative jurisdiction as a stand-alone category is sometimes doubted as the activity of courts may usually be subsumed either as prescription, i.e. when a court makes a legal determination *vis-à-vis* a certain situation, or enforcement, for instance when an individual is sentenced to imprisonment.[47] However, even though the activity of courts thus follows the same rules of prescriptive and enforcement jurisdiction as other State action, there is still some value in acknowledging the particularities of adjudicative jurisdiction. In this regard, it is important to understand that establishing procedure over persons or a certain situation may not necessarily entail the application of domestic law to these persons or the situation. Thus, a court may decide that it has judicial jurisdiction to try a case with one or more foreign parties, but it may still, based on choice-of-law rules, apply foreign law more appropriate to the case. Here, the reach of prescriptive jurisdiction may be intertwined with the choice-of-law problem. This is a particularly pertinent issue in US-style regulatory litigation, where private parties may sue each other for the infringement of what is essentially public administrative law. Thus, even though a US court may exercise judicial jurisdiction over foreign litigants, it may nonetheless determine that the reach of the domestic securities fraud legislation is limited by international law rules on prescriptive jurisdiction and therefore, that it may only apply foreign law to the situation.[48]

The value of the distinction between the three types of jurisdiction is sometimes doubted in general.[49] However, with regard to the traditional doctrine of jurisdiction, it seems necessary to uphold the distinction because the general prohibition of enforcement action on foreign territory is one of the more solid rules in this area. The remainder of this research is thus overwhelmingly concerned with questions of prescriptive jurisdiction and will refer to issues of enforcement only when it is necessary for overall understanding or when distinguishing between the two categories poses particular challenges.

47 See for instance Meng, *Extraterritoriale Jurisdiktion im öffentlichen Wirtschaftsrecht* (n 43), 9 – 10; Volz (n 24), 43 – 44; Cooreman (n 37), 85 – 86.

48 Antony J Colangelo, 'Spatial Legality' (2012) 107 Northwestern University Law Review 69, 73; Ryngaert, *Jurisdiction in International Law* (n 2), 16.

49 Oxman (n 22), para. 6.

### 5. Regulation, Public Law and Jurisdiction

This research is fundamentally concerned with using the lens of jurisdiction within the normative framework of international law to study particular phenomena and mechanisms of 'regulation'. At this point, one might already question whether 'jurisdiction', with its three different facets of prescription, enforcement and adjudication, is, within the context of international law, actually synonymous with 'regulation'. Several commentators at least seem to use the terms 'extraterritorial jurisdiction' and 'extraterritorial regulation' interchangeably.[50] It seems therefore necessary, on the one hand, to distinguish 'regulation' from other acts of States as well as from other types of governance, and on the other hand, to examine whether certain types of 'regulation' are outside the scope of jurisdictional rules under international law.

On a highly abstract level, 'regulation' may be defined as 'any process or set of processes by which norms are established, the behaviour of those subject to the norms monitored or fed-back into the regime, and for which there are mechanisms for holding the behaviour of regulated actors within the acceptable limits of the regime (whether by enforcement action or by some other mechanism)'.[51] Within domestic legal systems for instance, norms may be set by a representative public body and monitored through some administrative agency. Finally, the monitored behaviour and the standard set by the norm are re-aligned by sanctioning breaches of the norms through the police and court system. For domestic legal systems therefore, regulation generally entails the 'creation of public authoritative obligations on private parties to act or to refrain from acting in certain

50 See in particular, Austen L Parrish, 'Evading Legislative Jurisdiction' (2012) 87 Notre Dame Law Review 1673, 6: 'Legislative jurisdiction refers to Congress's authority to prescribe or regulate conduct'; Vaughan Lowe and Christopher Staker, 'Jurisdiction' in Malcolm D Evans (ed), *International Law* (5th ed. Oxford University Press 2018), 289: 'States regulate conduct in this sense in a variety of ways […]. Thus, the legislature may lay down rules by statute […]. States also regulate conduct by means of the decisions of their courts, which may order litigating parties to do or abstain from doing certain things. So, too, may the State's administrative bodies, which may apply rules concerning, for example, the issuance of licences […]. All of these activities are in principle regulated by the rules of international law concerning jurisdiction'.

51 Colin Scott, 'Analysing Regulatory Space: Fragmented Resources and Institutional Design' [2001] PL 329, 331.

ways or the establishment or facilitation of authoritative measures to enforce such duties'.[52]

However, the creation and enforcement of norms is not the only instrument for a State to shape society. In large parts, States also intervene into the daily life of private citizens by directly providing services and goods, (re-)distributing benefits (characteristic for the welfare State), information, or the adoption of public policies short of binding law. As these examples already illustrate there is much 'governance', steering and directing a particular society, outside of regulation.[53] More fundamentally however, ordering through governance may involve more, in particular private, actors (though they play an increasingly important role in traditional regulation as well), and instruments apart from law such as private contracts.

The considerations above explain why the terms jurisdiction and regulation are so closely intertwined. In fact, while States may also be offended by, say, the non-recognition of a legal foreign marriage, protests have mostly ensued over foreign overreach in the form of command-and-control. Questions of jurisdiction are so essential to international relations between States because they concern a fundamental issue, the allocation of regulatory, that is, public authority between sovereigns. This characterisation also explains why in the last decades, jurisdictional conflicts have been mostly confined to the area of public law, which is precisely the body of law within domestic systems concerned with the (not necessarily only hierarchical) relationship between the State and the individual.

Because of this relationship between regulation and public law, and between regulation and jurisdiction under international law, the question might arise whether international law is also relevant for other areas of law, in particular private law. For instance, it has been strongly argued that public and private matters follow two different set of rules because one is concerned with issues of private fairness while the other deals with the allocation of regulatory authority between States.[54] However, this strict division between the two areas of jurisdictional law has come under some critique in recent years for being artificial as different legal systems draw

---

52 Jacob Katz Cogan, 'The Regulatory Turn in International Law' (2011) 52(2) HarvIntlLJ 322, 324.

53 Eric L Windholz, *Governing through Regulation: Public Policy, Regulation and the Law* (Routledge critical studies in public management, Routledge Taylor & Francis Group 2018), 5.

54 Akehurst (n 42), at 177: 'It is hard to resist the conclusion that [...] customary international law imposes no limits on the jurisdiction of municipal courts in civil trials'.

the line between private law and public law differently and it may come down to cultural peculiarities whether one State chooses to adopt tort law or criminal law as instrument in order to enforce regulatory standards. Moreover, private law also increasingly reflects considerations of public policy.[55] Finally, even ordinary civil jurisdiction is ultimately reinforced through public sanctions so that there should be no great difference in treatment, a point acknowledged by Crawford.[56] The better arguments thus support the view that in principle, international law also poses limits to exercises of jurisdiction in private, non-regulatory law.

It should be noted however, that this conclusion may not mean that domestic legal systems need to set precisely the same limits for the exercise of jurisdiction within all bodies of law.[57] Indeed, as will be demonstrated throughout this research, the precise jurisdictional limits may differ according to the particular subject matter and design of the regulatory mechanism. For instance, US practice indicates that States may treat the extraterritorial scope of 'true' regulatory law different than the scope of criminal law. Stigall, examining the jurisprudence of US courts, observes that considerations of reasonableness and comity feature prominently in the regulatory context of antitrust regulation whereas individual due process provides an additional yardstick for criminal trials.[58] As a starting point however, even though they may vary to a certain extent in their precise application between areas and bodies of law, there are some common principles handling the exercise of prescriptive jurisdiction in general. It is to these principles that the next part of this research turns.

55 *Restatement (Fourth) of the Foreign Relations Law of the United States* (n 42), § 407, reporters' notes 5; Svantesson (n 13), 84 – 85.

56 Crawford and Brownlie (n 18), 471 – 472.

57 *The Restatement (Fourth) of the Foreign Relations Law of the United States* (n 42), § 407, reporters' notes 5 argues that indeed the limitations under customary international law are different for public and private matters.

58 Stigall (n 58), 372.

# B. Prescriptive Jurisdiction in Public International Law

## I. General Approaches

### 1. The Case of the S.S. Lotus

To whom may a State extend its laws and conversely, when does a State asserting authority exceed its jurisdictional limits? It is fair to suggest that this question has been the subject of scholarly debate for centuries as it arguably touches the core of the sovereignty of States.[59] Given the status and practical relevance of this issue, it may be surprising that judicial guidance in the form of decisions by the PCIJ or the ICJ remain scarce. Thus, almost a hundred years later, the case of reference for the question of jurisdiction in public international law remains the *Lotus* judgment of the PCIJ in 1927. Factually, the well-known case concerned a collision on the high seas between a French and a Turkish vessel, causing the death of eight Turkish nationals on board the Turkish ship. After the French ship had put into a port in Istanbul, Turkish authorities prosecuted and detained the responsible French officer on board the French ship. France heavily protested the Turkish actions on the ground that under international law, Turkey was not entitled to extend its criminal law to an occurrence on a foreign ship on the high seas.

In relation to jurisdiction, the Court's first proposition, that the enforcement jurisdiction of a State is in principle limited to its own territory, is uncontroversial and widely accepted.[60] However, the same cannot be said about its second proposition with regard to the core issue of the case at hand, that of prescriptive jurisdiction. On this issue, France contended that, for the Turkish courts to have jurisdiction, Turkey must point to some title recognized under international law in its favour. Conversely, Turkey argued the exact opposite view, that unless a contradicting princi-

---

59 See for a summary of the historical development: Hans-Jörg Ziegenhain, *Extraterritoriale Rechtsanwendung und die Bedeutung des Genuine-Link-Erfordernisses: Eine Darstellung der deutschen und amerikanischen Staatenpraxis* (Zugl.: München, Univ. Diss. 1991/92. Münchener Universitätsschriften Reihe der Juristischen Fakultät vol 92, Beck 1992), 28.

60 *S.S. Lotus (France v Turkey)* (n 20), 18 – 19.

ple of international law existed, it could exercise jurisdiction as it saw fit.[61] Both arguments are rooted in the sovereignty of States, the French one emphasizing the principle of sovereign equality of the affected State while the Turkish one reaffirming the sovereign independence of the State prescribing rules for extraterritorial conduct. In principle, these arguments of the two parties before the Court laid the foundation for the two possible approaches to State jurisdiction in international law. As is well known, the PCIJ decided in an 8 to 7 vote in favour of the Turkish standpoint. Recalling the voluntary nature of international law, the court held:

> 'It does not, however, follow that international law prohibits a State from exercising jurisdiction in its own territory, in respect of any case which relates to acts which have taken place abroad, and in which it cannot rely on some permissive rule of international law. Such a view would only be tenable if international law contained a general prohibition to States to extend the application of their laws and the jurisdiction of their courts to persons, property and acts outside their territory, and if, as an exception to this general prohibition, it allowed States to do so in certain specific cases. But this is certainly not the case under international law as it stands at present. Far from laying down a general prohibition to the effect that States may not extend the application of their laws and the jurisdiction of their courts to persons, property and acts outside their territory, it leaves them in this respect a wide measure of discretion which is only limited in certain cases by prohibitive rules; as regards other cases, every State remains free to adopt the principles which it regards as best and most suitable.'[62]

Commentators have generally interpreted this statement as indicating that the reach of a State's prescriptive jurisdiction is presumed to be unlimited, unless a positive rule of international law to the contrary exists.[63] Under this reading, the PCIJ decision in *Lotus* has been on the receiving end of heavy criticism.[64] From a theoretical perspective, it has been argued that the judgement concedes the sovereign independence of the State exercising jurisdiction too much weight. Considering the equally important

---

61 Ibid., 18.
62 Ibid., 19.
63 Lowe and Staker (n 50), 295; however, see for an alternative reading of the judgement: An Hertogen, 'Letting Lotus Bloom' (2015) 26(4) EJIL 901.
64 Mann (n 1), 35 and Hertogen, 'Letting Lotus Bloom' (n 63), 903, both indicating further critiques in the literature and jurisprudence.

principle of sovereign equality, it would make no sense if in the case of concurrent jurisdiction between two sovereign States, one of the two was generally given primacy over the other.[65] In addition, from a practical point of view, States objecting the assertion of excessive jurisdiction by another State have rarely pointed to a specific prohibition against that assertion but rather simply disputed the existence of a right of the other State. In relation to this argument, it should also be noted that the establishment of a customary prohibitive norm before any concrete assertion of jurisdiction would be difficult in practice, as States would have to engage in abstract declarations of *opinio iuris* in order to do so.[66]

However, as one author has pointed out, the opposite view, that a State has to demonstrate a precise rule allowing the exercise of jurisdiction in any given case would be equally unworkable in practice. Under this assumption, a State would have to violate international law every time a new extraterritorial threat requiring regulation comes into existence.[67] Academic opinion has thus led to the development of something of a middle way, in that the State exercising jurisdiction has to demonstrate the existence of a sufficient connection or a genuine link between the State and the person or conduct it seeks to regulate through one of the permissive principles.[68] This view also closely aligns with actual State practice although States that rely on controversial exercises of jurisdiction still often fall back on *Lotus* as the only judgement in this matter by a major international court.[69] In this respect therefore, *Lotus* is still of lasting influence for the doctrine in international law as it stands today.

### 2. The Permissive Principles Approach under Customary International Law

As already indicated, for practical reasons, States did not follow the presumed freedom to act approach of the *Lotus* judgment and instead generally exercised their prescriptive jurisdiction based on the existence of certain permissive principles that mediate a sufficient connection between the

65 Volz (n 24), 49; Lowe and Staker (n 50), 295.
66 Volz (n 24), 50.
67 Ryngaert, *Jurisdiction in International Law* (n 2), 29 – 30.
68 Lowe and Staker (n 50), 295 – 296; Crawford and Brownlie (n 18), 457.
69 ICJ, *Arrest Warrant of 11 April 2000 (Democratic Republic of the Congo v Belgium)* [2002] ICJ Rep 3 (2002) Counter Memorial of the Kingdom of Belgium, 28 September 2001, 94 – 95.

State and the circumstances to be regulated.[70] Naturally, this prompted the question, which principles can be considered strong enough to legitimize an exercise of extraterritorial jurisdiction. The Harvard Research Draft Convention on Jurisdiction with Respect to Crime (hereinafter: Harvard Research Draft) provided the most influential answer to this inquiry.[71] It established and defined five such links, which are now interchangeably called 'bases of jurisdiction' or 'principles of jurisdiction', namely territoriality, nationality, the protective principle, universality and passive personality, in this order. Although these principles of jurisdiction are not entirely static, they currently form the widely accepted framework for the allocation of regulatory power between States.[72] Any normative assessment of certain jurisdictional assertions is conducted against this background.

However, despite the dominance of these principles in theory and practice, their exact scope and contours, and sometimes their status under customary international law are to some extent subject to debate. The following sections are therefore dedicated to shed some light on the content of each of these principles and the more contentious issues around them. However, one more principle has made it into this brief theoretical overview, which has to do with the steady expansion of the territorial principle through the acceptance of merely territorial effects as a legitimate connection. Because this modern effects doctrine brings with it issues distinct from those identified under the territoriality principle, it seemed appropriate to discuss these developments under a separate heading.

#### a) Territoriality

If jurisdiction is an aspect of sovereignty, then territorial sovereignty, as an aspect of statehood, must necessarily manifest itself in jurisdiction over all persons, property and conduct within that territory.[73] This principle, territoriality, is generally considered the most common and least controversial basis of jurisdiction. The territory of a State includes its land, its internal waters, its territorial sea, which extends up to 12 nautical miles from its

---

70 Mann (n 1), 49; Volz (n 24), 57 – 60.

71 'Harvard Research Draft Convention on Jurisdiction with Respect to Crime' (1935) 29 Supp AJIL 439.

72 On the lasting influence oft he Harvard Research Draft, see Svantesson (n 13), 24 – 29.

73 In similar language, Mann (n 1), 30; Buxbaum (n 32), 631 – 632; see already above at A.III.1. State Jurisdiction and State Sovereignty.

coast, and its airspace. Within this area, a State's jurisdiction is plenary and it may impose the entirety of its laws, be they criminal, economic, social or other laws, not only on its citizens, but also on anyone else found within the State.[74] With regard to its coastal sea however, a State's jurisdiction is somewhat limited by the rules of the law of the sea. In particular, foreign vessels enjoy a right to innocent passage, which may only be regulated for certain purposes.[75]

#### aa) The Territoriality Principle and Cross-border Criminal Offenses

The application of the territoriality principle becomes more complicated in practice when the conduct to be regulated occurs partially within the territory of one State and partially within another, that is, when the conduct straddles multiple territorial jurisdictions. For instance, in the famous 1988 *Lockerbie* incident, it was suspected that the bomb was loaded aboard the aircraft in Malta while the eventual explosion took place in the skies over Lockerbie, Scotland.[76] Here, and in similar cases, both the State where the conduct was initiated and the State where it was completed may have legitimate claims to territorial jurisdiction. In Anglo-Saxon scholarship, the terms subjective territoriality and objective territoriality are frequently used in the context of international criminal law. While subjective territoriality denotes a State's jurisdiction over an offense which occurred or was initiated within its territory but has consequences in another State, objective territoriality refers to the exercise of jurisdiction over an offense that was initiated abroad, but where the result of the offense is felt within domestic territory.[77] The Harvard Research Draft combined the two theories and proposed that a State may assert territorial jurisdiction

---

74 Lowe and Staker (n 50), 296.

75 *Restatement (Fourth) of the Foreign Relations Law of the United States* (n 42), § 408, comment b. More recently, in an interesting intersection between the law of the sea and the customary international law on State jurisdiction, the issue of port State jurisdiction, exercised to influence conditions extraterritorially, has garnered increased scholarly attention; see on this issue Cedric Ryngaert and Henrik Ringbom, 'Introduction: Port State Jurisdiction: Challenges and Potential' (2016) 31(3) The International Journal of Marine and Coastal Law 379.

76 High Court of the Justiciary at Camp Zeist, *Her Majesty's Advocate v Abdelbaset Ali Mohmed Al Megrahi and Al Amin Khalifa Fhimah* (Case No. 1475/99), Opinion of 31 January 2001, para. 82.

77 Christopher Blakesley, 'Extraterritorial Jurisdiction' in M. C Bassioni (ed), *International Criminal Law* (3rd ed. Martinus Nijhoff Publishers 2008), 96 – 108.

if a crime is committed either 'in whole or in part' within the territory, which requires, more specifically, that any essential constituent element of the crime is consummated domestically.[78] This constituent elements approach is well established beyond the Harvard Research Draft so that in practice, multiple States may legitimately assert jurisdiction over cross-border offenses such as the one forming the basis of the *Lockerbie* incident.[79]

### bb) The US Presumption against Extraterritoriality

Because US State practice, which forms a significant part of the analysis of case studies below, frequently includes aggressive assertions of extraterritorial jurisdiction, it seems worth to take a closer look at how the territoriality principle is interpreted in US domestic law. The guiding consideration in this regard is the presumption against extraterritoriality, a domestic principle that has its roots in the canon of statutory construction that 'an act of Congress ought never to be construed to violate the law of nations if any other possible construction remains'.[80] Because international law on jurisdiction was rather territoriality-centred around the eighteenth and nineteenth century, courts in the United States were supposed to interpret federal statutory provisions to apply only within US territorial jurisdiction. Later however, the presumption was detached from its international law roots and instead found justification in the notion that Congress primarily legislates with domestic conditions in mind.[81] Therefore, the presumption could be rebutted if there is a clear indication of congressional intent that a certain statute should apply extraterritorially.[82] If such an intent is found, courts have to defer to Congress even if the application of law in question would exceed the limits of jurisdiction under customary international law.[83] With particular relevance to our first case study below, the presump-

78 Harvard Research Draft (n 71), 495.

79 Akehurst (n 42), 152; Lowe and Staker (n 50), 297.

80 *Murray v Schooner Charming Betsy*, 6 US 2 Cranch 64, 118, 2 L Ed 208 (1804).

81 See on this: *Restatement (Fourth) of the Foreign Relations Law of the United States* (n 42), § 404, reporters' notes 1.

82 *EEOC v Arabian American Oil Co.*, 499 US 244, 248 (1991).

83 A question different from the courts' application of the presumption against extraterritoriality is whether Congress has authority to legislate for extraterritorial circumstances in the first place. Under US Constitution, Congress has such powers in a number of areas, see Antony J Colangelo, 'A Unified Approach to Extraterritoriality' (2011) 97 Virginia Law Review 1019, 1047 – 1050.

tion may be rebutted with regard to laws imposing foreign policy based economic sanctions, where the legislator's main concern is interpreted as to defend the United States against foreign behaviour.[84]

If the presumption against extraterritoriality is not rebutted, then a court may still apply the statute if it determines that the application of the provision to the specific set of facts at hand is actually to be considered domestic and not extraterritorial under US law. According to recent jurisprudence on the presumption, courts have to look to the 'focus' of a statutory provision, and if that 'focus' occurs within the United States, then application of this statute would be considered domestic. The 'focus' in this sense might consist of the transaction, the conduct, or the injury.[85] For instance, in *RJR Nabisco, Inc. v European Community*, the EC sued RJR Nabisco, Inc. under the Racketeer Influenced and Corrupt Organizations Act (**RICO**), alleging that RJR had engaged in a global money-laundering conspiracy. However, the Supreme Court ultimately ruled against the European Community (**EC**) on the grounds that the presumption against extraterritoriality was not rebutted in the first step and that the focus of the RICO was the injury sustained by the plaintiff. However, because the EC suffered no US domestic injuries to its business or property, application of the provision to these facts would be impermissibly extraterritorial.[86] On the other hand, when the 'focus' of a statutory provision is on the injuries or effects suffered, it may allow for extraterritorial application even if the conduct occurred completely abroad, which is precisely the US standpoint in relation to the effects principle in competition law.

#### b) The Effects Principle

According to the effects principle, a State may exercise jurisdiction with respect to conduct occurring outside its territory, but which has an effect, subject to certain qualifications, within its territory.[87] While continental European scholars tend to interpret the effects doctrine as a variation of objective territoriality,[88] it is treated as a separate basis of jurisdiction

84 *United States v Zarrab*, No. 15-cr-867, 2016 WL 6820737 (SDNY 2016), 18.

85 *Morrison v National Australia Bank Ltd.*, 561 US 247, 261 – 265 (2010).

86 *RJR Nabisco, Inc. v European Community*, 136 S Ct 2090, 2108 – 2111 (2016).

87 Austen L Parrish, 'The Effects Test: Extraterritoriality's Fifth Business' (2008) 61 Vanderbilt Law Review 1455, 1457 – 1458.

88 See for instance the categorization in Volz (n 24), 74; Cooreman (n 38), 92; Ryngaert, *Unilateral Jurisdiction and Global Values* (n 10), 82 – 84.

particularly in the United States.[89] The PCIJ, in its judgement in *Lotus*, referred interchangeably either to 'effects' or 'territoriality' when discussing the Turkish assertion of jurisdiction over the collision on the high seas leading to deaths on board the Turkish ship (which was then assimilated to Turkish territory).[90] The differing views have no implication for the content of this principle. However, it is clear that the legitimacy of the effects principle is often discussed by comparing its application to the more obvious applications of objective territoriality, such as when the State of the victim exercises jurisdiction over the offender in the case of a cross-border shooting. Historically, it has been most controversial whether anticompetitive behaviour that caused detrimental domestic effects are comparable to the situation such as the one presented in *Lotus*.

#### aa) The Effects Principle in Competition Law

Typically, the 1945 US decision in *Alcoa* is identified as the starting point of the debate. In that case, the question was whether US law extended to the conduct of a group of foreign companies that had agreed on an aluminium production quota, which caused a shortage of production and thus might have affected the level of aluminium imports to the United States. In response, the court famously held that: 'it is settled law [...] that any state may impose liabilities even upon persons not within its allegiance, for conduct outside its borders that has consequences within its borders which the state reprehends, and these liabilities other states will ordinarily recognize.'[91] While the detailed facts of the case and the judgement were complicated, the basic principle set out in this decision is clear: At least in the area of antitrust, the exercise of jurisdiction does not necessarily depend on the commission of physical acts within domestic territory, but rather, effects or possibly the intent to produce effects would suffice.[92]

---

89 *Restatement (Fourth) of the Foreign Relations Law of the United States* (n 42), § 409, reporters' notes 5: 'By addressing effects jurisdiction in a separate section from territorial jurisdiction, this Restatement reflects the evolution of the effects principle into a distinct basis for jurisdiction to prescribe under customary international law'.

90 *S.S. Lotus (France v Turkey)* (n 20), 23.

91 *United States v Aluminum Corp of America* 148 F 2d 416, 443 (2d Cir 1945).

92 For a more detailed analysis of the case including its factual background, see Florian Wagner-von Papp, 'Competition Law and Extraterritoriality' in Ariel

While the effects principle has gained widespread recognition in US jurisprudence since then, its precise scope is yet unsettled. For instance, it is unclear how qualified the effects have to be to trigger the application of the principle. Logic dictates that not any effect, however miniscule, should lead to the assertion of jurisdiction against foreign companies as the progressive integration of global commerce means that anything happening anywhere possibly results in effects everywhere else.[93] For instance, the Foreign Trade Antitrust Improvements Act of 1982 requires that effects be 'direct, substantial, and reasonably foreseeable'.[94] The US Supreme Court in *Hartford Fire*[95] as well as the Third Restatement on Foreign Relations Law only relied on the qualification 'substantial',[96] while the Fourth Restatement uses the somewhat cryptic formulation that the effects have to be 'substantial' in a way that 'creates a genuine connection between the conduct and the prescribing state'.[97]

Another somewhat contentious issue relates to the subjective component to trigger the application of the effects doctrine: Is the intent to produce effects alone sufficient or must there have been actual effects? The decisions in *Aloca* and *Hartford Fire* at least seem to suggest that the two requirements need to be satisfied cumulatively.[98] If both intent and effects need to be present, it is equally unsettled whether intent refers to 'subjective' intent, which encompasses an element of volition or desire to cause effects, or 'objective' intent, which may only require that the effects were 'reasonably foreseeable'.[99]

Outside of the United States, the application of the effects doctrine has initially been met with scepticism and outright protest. In particular,

---

Ezrachi (ed), *Research handbook on international competition law* (Elgar 2012), 23 – 26 and Akehurst (n 42), 193 – 194.

93 See for instance Wagner-von Papp (n 92), 28; Akehurst (n 42), 198.

94 Foreign Trade Antitrust Improvements Act of 1982, Title IV of Pub.L. 97–290, 96 Stat 1246, § 402, codified at 15 U.S.C. § 6a.

95 *Hartford Fire Insurance v California* 509 US 764, 796 (1993).

96 *Restatement (Third) of the Foreign Relations Law of the United States* (n 5), § 402 comment d.

97 *Restatement (Fourth) of the Foreign Relations Law of the United States* (n 42), § 409, comment a.

98 In *Hartford Fire Insurance v California* 509 US 764, 796 (1993), the Supreme Court stated that: 'it is well established by now that the Sherman Act applies to foreign conduct that was meant to produce and did in fact produce some substantial effect in the United States'. However, contrast this approach to *Restatement (Third) of the Foreign Relations Law of the United States* (n 5), § 402 comment d.

99 See on this Wagner-von Papp (n 92), 27 – 28.

the United Kingdom, partly as a response to a private suit initiated by a US company against an international cartel in the *Uranium Antitrust Litigation*, adopted the Protection of Trading Interests Act of 1980, intended to block US exercise of extraterritorial jurisdiction in commercial matters.[100] Other nations including Canada, Australia and Japan have voiced their opposition through diplomatic protests and *amicus curiae* briefs.[101] However, the exercise of jurisdiction in competition matters against foreign companies based on effects has gained ground and many countries have since then adopted regulations similar to the ones in the United States, including countries that originally opposed this principle.[102] Of the major economies, at least China,[103] Japan,[104] and Germany[105] have explicitly endorsed effects based jurisdiction in legislation.

The position of the EU *vis-à-vis* the effects principle has been somewhat more complicated: The Commission has supported the application of the effects principle at least since 1969 in the famous *Dyestuffs* case, in which it commenced proceedings against a company based outside the European Economic Community (**EEC**) for alleged price-fixing through its Belgian subsidiary.[106] However, the jurisprudence of the Court of Justice of the

---

100 For a detailed analysis of the background and provisions of this Act, see A.V Lowe, 'Blocking Extraterritorial Jurisdiction: The British Protection of Trading Interests Act, 1980' (1981) 75 AJIL 257.

101 Cf the State practice listed in *Restatement (Fourth) of the Foreign Relations Law of the United States* (n 42), § 409, Reporters' Notes 2.

102 See Wagner-von Papp (n 92), 41.

103 Anti-Monopoly Law of the People's Republic of China, Art. 2, available at http://www.gov.cn/flfg/2007-08/30/content_732591.htm, last accessed on 13 April 2022; see also the analysis provided by Zhenguo Wu, 'Perspectives on the Chinese Anti-Monopoly Law' (2008) 75(1) Antitrust Law Journal 73, 102 – 103. For an application of the Law to foreign companies, see MOFCOM Announcement No. 46 of 2014 on Decisions of Anti-monopoly Review to Prohibit Concentration of Undertakings by Prohibiting Maersk, MSC and CMA CGM from Establishing a Network Center, http://english.mofcom.gov.cn/article/policyrelease/buwei/201407/20140700663862.shtml, last accessed on 13 April 2022.

104 See for a discussion of the situation in Japan, Marek Martyniszyn, 'Japanese Approaches to Extraterritoriality in Competition Law' (2017) 66(03) ICLQ 747.

105 Act Against Restraints on Competition, § 185 para 2, English translation available at https://www.gesetze-im-internet.de/englisch_gwb/index.html, last accessed on 13 April 2022; for a prominent discussion of the limits of the effects principle, see Kammergericht, Order of 1 July 1983, Kart. 16/82, reported in WuW/E OLG 3051 (*Philip Morris Inc. v Bundeskartellamt*) and the analysis by Buxbaum (n 32), 658.

106 *Dyestuffs*, (Case IV/26278) Commission Decision 69/243/EEC [1969], OJ L 195/11; the EEC later became the European Community.

European Union (**CJEU**) has been more ambiguous. Without outright rejecting the Commission's arguments (which were also supported by Advocate General Mayras[107]), the court chose to establish jurisdiction not through the effects principle but instead to rely on an economic entity theory by attributing the (territorial) actions of the EEC subsidiary to its non-EEC parent company.[108] Similarly, in its next significant decision on the extraterritorial reach of EU competition law, the *Wood Pulp* case, the court failed to endorse the effects principle explicitly. Instead, the CJEU argued that the violation of competition law at hand consisted of two elements, namely the formation of an agreement and its implementation. Therefore, as long as the implementation of the concerted action occurred on EU territory through agents, branches and subsidiaries, it was immaterial that the agreement itself was formed outside the EU.[109]

Commentators have long observed that the decision in *Wood Pulp* and the wide interpretation of conduct with the 'implementation doctrine' brought the position of the EU much closer to the effects principle than the name suggested.[110] However, it was only in 2017 in *Intel v Commission* that the CJEU formally recognized effects, qualified by the triad foreseeable, immediate and substantial, as an alternative to the implementation doctrine for establishing jurisdiction.[111] While the CJEU did not clarify the precise contours of the test, the new approach significantly aligns EU and US positions on the effects principle in competition law.[112] Thus, given the widespread support for and application of this doctrine by practically all major economies, the Fourth Restatement's claim that the effects principle

107 CJEU, C-48/69, *Imperial Chemical Industries Ltd. v Commission of the European Communities* [1972] ECR 619, Opinion of AG Mayras, Part II.

108 CJEU, C-48/69, *Imperial Chemical Industries Ltd. v Commission of the European Communities* [1972] ECR 619, paras. 129 – 142.

109 CJEU, C-89/85, *Ahlström Osakeyhtiö and others v Commission of the European Communities* [1988] ECR 5193, paras. 16 – 17.

110 Alexander Layton and Angharad M Parry, 'Extraterritorial Jurisdiction: European Responses' (2004) 26 Houston Journal of International Law 309, 318; Wagner-von Papp (n 92), 44 – 46.

111 CJEU, C-413/14 P, *Intel Corp. v European Commission* [2017] ECLI:EU:C:2017:632, paras. 40 – 60.

112 Luca Prete, 'On Implementation and Effects: The Recent Case-law on the Territorial (or Extraterritorial?) Application of EU Competition Rules' [2018] Journal of European Competition Law & Practice 1, 6.

forms part of customary international law is most likely correct at least in the area of competition law.[113]

bb) The Effects Principle in Other Areas of Substantive Law

Although the effects principle has been extensively developed and used in the context of competition law, since *Alcoa*, its application has also diffused into other substantive areas of regulation. For instance, multiple judicial opinions and academic commentators have considered the principle as a possible basis for extraterritorial environmental protection. The leading decision in this regard may be the US *Trail Smelter* case, which concerned a factory in Canada located approximately 10 miles from the US-Canadian border. Over some time, the operator of the factory, Teck Cominco, discharged hazardous waste into the Columbia River, which was eventually carried downstream across the border into the United States. Subsequently, private members of a tribe inhabiting the area filed suit against Teck Cominco, seeking to compel the company to conduct an investigation and feasibility study with regard to clean-up actions according to US environmental protection law.[114] The district court gave judgement for the plaintiff and the circuit court affirmed on appeal.[115] The reasoning of the district court is of particular salience for the purposes of this study. Clarifying that US laws generally are meant to apply only within the territorial jurisdiction of the United States, it finds precedent for an exception to this rule where such a limitation of the scope of the statute would result in adverse effects within the United States. With this

---

113 *Restatement (Fourth) of the Foreign Relations Law of the United States* (n 42), § 409; Jack L Goldsmith, 'Against Cyberanarchy' (1998) 65(4) The University of Chicago Law Review 1199, 1208; Wagner-von Papp (n 92), 41; Volz (n 24), 80 – 82. Meng, *Extraterritoriale Jurisdiktion im öffentlichen Wirtschaftsrecht* (n 43), at 479 – 482 argues that at least the States participating in the practice have formed particular customary international law among them. However, other commentators are more cautious: Cooreman (n 38), 101 – 102; Danielle Ireland-Piper, *Accountability in Extraterritoriality: A Comparative and International Law Perspective* (Edward Elgar Publishing 2017), 36 – 37; Ryngaert, *Jurisdiction in International Law* (n 2), 82 – 84; Lowe and Staker (n 50), 298; Menno T Kamminga, 'Extraterritoriality' in R. Wolfrum (ed), *The Max Planck Encyclopedia of Public International Law* (Oxford University Press), para. 15.

114 *Pakootas v Teck Cominco Metals, Ltd.*, CV-04–256-AAM, 2004 WL 2578982 (ED Wash. 8 November 2004).

115 *Pakootas v Teck Cominco Metals, Ltd.*, 452 F 3d 1066 (9th Cir 2006).

argumentation, the district court clearly embraced the application of the effects principle to transboundary environmental harms.[116]

The possible ramifications of transferring the effects doctrine to environmental regulation are significant. As Advocate General Kokott has pointed out in her opinion on the CJEU case *Air Transport Association of America and Others*, 'pollution knows no boundaries and [...] greenhouse gases contribute towards climate change worldwide irrespective of where they are emitted; they can have effects on the environment and climate in every State and association of States, including the European Union.'[117] Some academic commentators have adopted this line of reasoning and highlighted the potential of the effects principle to legitimize unilateral interventions in the face of the global challenge climate change.[118] However, there are serious doubts about this line of interpretation in relation to both its normative foundation and its possible ramifications. Can it really be said that the emission of each ton of CO2 anywhere in the world causes a direct, substantial and foreseeable environmental harm everywhere else? And if one accepts this proposition, is it truly desirable that any State can regulate emissions occurring anywhere in the world unilaterally?

116 However, although the appellate court followed the decision on appeal, it did so on rather convoluted grounds and rejected extraterritoriality altogether. According to the 9th Circuit, because the waste came to be accumulated in the Columbia River in the US, and because waste sites could qualify as 'facilities' under the applicable law, the fact that the hazardous material was discharged in Canada did not matter at all. The issue was thus interpreted as purely domestic in nature, see *Pakootas v Teck Cominco Metals, Ltd.*, 452 F 3d 1066, 1074 – 1075 (9th Cir 2006). For a more detailed discussion of the judgements, see Jonathan R Nash, 'The Curious Legal Landscape of the Extraterritoriality of US Environmental Laws' in Günther Handl, Joachim Zekoll and Peer Zumbansen (eds), *Beyond Territoriality: Transnational Legal Authority in an Age of Globalization* (Queen Mary studies in international law. Martinus Nijhofff Publishers 2012).

117 CJEU, C-366/10, *Air Transport Association of America and Others v Secretary of State for Energy and Climate* Change [2011] ECR I-13755, Opinion of AG Kokott, para. 154.

118 Eckard Rehbinder, 'Extra-Territoriality of Pollution Control Laws from a European Perspective' in Günther Handl, Joachim Zekoll and Peer Zumbansen (eds), *Beyond Territoriality: Transnational Legal Authority in an Age of Globalization* (Queen Mary studies in international law. Martinus Nijhofff Publishers 2012), 158 – 159; Natalie L Dobson and Cedric Ryngaert, 'Provocative Climate Protection: EU "Extraterritorial" Regulation of Maritime Emissions' (2017) 66(02) ICLQ 295, 327 – 330.

### c) Active Personality

States may extend their prescriptive jurisdiction to their own nationals abroad. This principle is firmly established under international law and in fact, it is arguably the oldest type of jurisdiction, developed before rulers had managed to consolidate their control over territory to a degree where it was possible to assert jurisdiction based on territoriality.[119] Active personality jurisdiction has particular importance in the area of criminal law, where many States (especially from a civil law tradition) prohibit the extradition of their own nationals,[120] and thus, without the assertion of extraterritorial jurisdiction, offenders may be able to evade any possible prosecution by returning to their home country after committing a crime abroad and before local authorities take enforcement actions.[121] In practice however, States often limit the exercise of nationality-based jurisdiction, for instance to serious crimes which carry a minimum punishment of a certain level or to crimes that are subject to extradition. Other States may require the satisfaction of dual criminality, which means active personality jurisdiction for crimes abroad is only exercised if the conduct concerned is considered criminal also in the place of commission. However, these limitations seem not to stem from a legal obligation but rather reflect considerations of international comity, and indeed, the practice among States in this regard differs widely.[122]

Although the exercise of nationality-based jurisdiction is almost universally recognized, international law itself is generally neutral towards the grant of nationality to natural persons. Rather, this determination is in the discretion of each nation's own laws, despite the fact that the ICJ has

---

119 For more on this: Ryngaert, *Jurisdiction in International Law* (n 2), 107; Richard T Ford, 'Law's Territory (a History of Jurisdiction)' (1999) 97 Michigan Law Review 843, 873.

120 Blakesley (n 77), 117.

121 Ibid.

122 For the dual criminality criterion, see for instance: BGH, Order of 26 March 2009, StB 20/08, reported in NJW 2010, 385; See further Tobias Dietrich, *Die Erstreckung der Strafbarkeit auf Auslandssachverhalte nach § 35 AWG: Die Vereinbarkeit von § 35 AWG mit dem Völkerrecht* (Zugl.: München, Univ. Diss. 2013. Schriftenreihe Studien zum Völker- und Europarecht vol 121, Kovač 2014); However, Klaus Pottmeyer, 'Die Strafbarkeit von Auslandstaten nach dem Kriegswaffenkontroll- und dem Außenwirtschaftsrecht' [1992] Neue Zeitschrift für Strafrecht 57, 59 – 60 argues that dual criminality is required under international law principles.

recognized certain limitations to this freedom in the *Nottebohm* case.[123] Apart from nationals *stricto sensu*, the active personality principle has been gradually expanded to cover also (permanent) resident aliens as a result of increased mobility.[124] While laws in private matters, such as succession, divorce and in some cases torts have long recognized residency as an alternative connecting factor, this principle is also increasingly applied in criminal and regulatory laws. By way of example, both the US Foreign Corrupt Practices Act (**FCPA**) and the UK Bribery Act 2010 apply to citizens as well as to residents. Such expansions have not caused protests by other States and now seem to be rather firmly established in international law.[125]

Of particular importance to international economic regulations, the active personality principle also applies to corporations, although how their nationality is determined is more controversial under international law. The two most widely accepted criteria for this purpose are (1) the corporation's place of incorporation and (2) its centre of control or seat of management.[126] However, the United States in particular has at times included subsidiaries and branches abroad that are controlled by US shareholders into the category of corporate nationals and thus extended its jurisdictional reach based on active personality. Subjecting foreign branches to active personality jurisdiction seems to have caused little diplomatic backlash, presumably because branches are not distinct juridical entities and it is thus plausible to attach the nationality of the corporate parent to them.[127] On the other hand, the same rationale does not apply to subsidiaries, as the incorporation in a foreign State creates more legal distance between the domestic shareholders and the subsidiary. Thus, US assertions of juris-

---

123 ICJ, *Nottebohm, Second Phase (Liechtenstein v Guatemala)* [1955] ICJ Rep 4; The two most common bases are to grant nationality to anyone born in the territory (ius soli) or to anyone who descended from nationals of that State (ius sanguinis); in addition, most States allow for naturalization, see Lowe and Staker (n 50), 299.

124 Ibid., 325.

125 However, Ireland-Piper, *Accountability in Extraterritoriality* (n 113), at 26 correctly observes that this extension is not without problems, given that residents, unlike nationals, have no right to vote for parliament and are disadvantaged in other areas of law. Thus, the legitimacy of asserting extraterritorial jurisdiction over mere residents is questionable.

126 ICJ, *Barcelona Traction Light and Power Co, Ltd. (Belgium v Spain)* [1970] ICJ Rep 3 (1970), para. 70.

127 *Restatement (Third) of the Foreign Relations Law of the United States* (n 5), § 414, comment a.

diction based on this principle have prompted critical responses by the countries where the subsidiaries were incorporated.[128] Commentators have also largely rejected this sort of 'control doctrine' and either regarded it as generally incompatible with international law[129] or subjected its exercise to a number of criteria to reflect its exceptional character.[130]

### d) Passive Personality

Unlike the active personality principle, jurisdictional assertions on the basis that the victim of an offense carries a certain nationality are more controversial under international law.[131] The rationale for this caution is that ordinarily, the perpetrator of a crime will not be able to know the victim's nationality and thus cannot anticipate that the laws of a certain State will apply to his conduct. In an increasingly diverse world, someone committing a crime in an urban centre would thus need to be familiar with the laws of potentially all nations or risk being subjected to wholly unexpected enforcement measures.[132] Despite these theoretical concerns, State practice has increasingly featured the assertion of jurisdiction based on the passive personality principle, at least for particular categories of offenses. For instance, this is the case for acts of terrorism, where victims are often specifically chosen for their nationality as well as attacks on diplomatic representatives and other officials of the State. While one of the earliest international protests against the assertion of extraterritorial jurisdiction, the 1886 *Cutting* case, had passive personality as its central matter, States today have largely acquiesced to such exercise.[133] Thus, in

---

128 For conflicts in the field of economic sanctions, see below at C.II.2. The Extension of Personality-based Jurisdiction to Foreign Subsidiaries.

129 Ryngaert, *Jurisdiction in International Law* (n 2), 108; Beaucillon (n 26), 116 – 118.

130 *Restatement (Third) of the Foreign Relations Law of the United States* (n 5), § 414 (2) (b).

131 Mann (n 1), 92 considered passive personality an 'excess of jurisdiction'.

132 This example is drawn from *S.S. Lotus (France v Turkey)* (n 20), Dissenting Opinion of Judge Moore, 92.

133 In the *Cutting* case, the US national Cutting had allegedly libelled a Mexican citizen in a paper published in Texas and was subsequently seized by Mexican authorities when he was visiting that country. The US Secretary of State strongly protested this assertion arguing that international law did not recognize this basis for jurisdiction. In particular, it would expose US citizens to indefinite criminal responsibility with regard to foreigners on domestic territory, see the

principle, the literature and jurisprudence now accept passive personality as a valid basis of jurisdiction though its precise scope is still unclear.[134]

Similar to the active personality principle, jurisdiction based on the victim's nationality is often accompanied by a number of requirements limiting its exercise. For instance, the criminal law of Germany only extends its scope of application to extraterritorial cases based on passive personality if dual criminality is satisfied.[135] This requirement does indeed refute some of the concerns argued above, as the perpetrator may be expected to know the laws of the place where he is currently residing.[136] Other restrictions may require the territorial presence of the offender or executive consent for prosecutions based on this principle. However, just as with active personality, those limitations seem to be applied out of international comity rather than a sense of legal obligation.[137]

### e) The Protective Principle

Applying the protective principle, States may exercise jurisdiction over conduct occurring abroad that poses a danger to the State's fundamental interests, including its security, integrity, sovereignty or important governmental functions.[138] In theory, the protective principle differs from the effects doctrine in that the prescribing State does not need to show actual or even intended effects on domestic territory as long as the conduct is directed against the above-mentioned interests.[139] In practice however, the distinctions may be blurry, in particular because what precisely constitutes a fundamental national interest satisfying the protective principle is uncer-

---

reports of this case in the 1887 Papers relating to the Foreign Relations of the United States (1888), 751, https://history.state.gov/historicaldocuments/frus1887/d491, last accessed on 13 April 2022; see also Blakesley (n 77), 123.

134 For this jurisprudence, see *Arrest Warrant of 11 April 2000 (Democratic Republic of the Congo v Belgium)* (n 69), Joint Separate Opinion of Judges Higgins, Kooijmans and Buergenthal, 77, para. 47.

135 German Criminal Code (Strafgesetzbuch), § 7.

136 Oxman (n 22), para. 33.

137 *Restatement (Fourth) of the Foreign Relations Law of the United States* (n 42), § 411 reporters' notes 2.

138 Blakesley (n 77), 108; Ireland-Piper, *Accountability in Extraterritoriality* (n 113), 33.

139 *Restatement (Fourth) of the Foreign Relations Law of the United States* (n 42), § 412 reporters' notes 1; Blakesley (n 77), 109.

tain and up to the definition of each individual State.[140] Still, there seems to exist a consensus at least over certain crimes such as treason, espionage and counterfeiting of State documents or currency. Equally uncontroversial has been the extension of the protective principle to conspiracies to evade the State's immigration or customs laws as well as perjury against consular officials.[141]

In US jurisprudence, the principle is also invoked frequently in cases related to narcotics trafficking by foreigners or other crimes on the high seas. The jurisprudence in this area is complex as the factual circumstances vary and there seems to be no consensus among the different Circuits about the role of international law in the normative analysis regarding the jurisdictional assertions against foreigners outside US territory.[142] However, the decisions that do mention international law frequently resort to the protective principle to establish the required nexus between the conduct on the high seas and the United States. For instance, *Peterson* argues that drug trafficking presented so severe a threat to the ability of the nation to properly function that the protective principle could be applied in this instance.[143] The protective principle is preferred over objective territoriality or the effects doctrine in these cases '[...]because it is often difficult to prove beyond a reasonable doubt that a vessel seized on the high seas carrying contraband was headed for the United States.'[144] Despite the possibly very extensive reach of US jurisdiction in these matters, foreign States have largely acquiesced to this practice, as enforcement is frequently directed against vessels which are either stateless or where the flag State has consented to the exercise of jurisdiction.[145] Additionally, the status of large-scale narcotics trafficking as an almost universally condemned practice may also bolster US jurisdictional claims.[146]

---

140 On this point, Volz (n 24), 93 – 94; See also the examples provided by Akehurst (n 42), 158 – 159; Philip Uecker, *Extraterritoriale Regelungshoheit im Datenschutzrecht* (Frankfurter Studien zum Datenschutz vol 52, 1. Auflage, Nomos 2017), 57 – 60 argues that the protective principle may also serve as a possible basis for extraterritorial data protection legislation.

141 See for instance Blakesley (n 77), 108 – 109; *Restatement (Fourth) of the Foreign Relations Law of the United States* (n 42), § 412.

142 See the lengthy analysis by Stigall (n 58), 347 – 368.

143 *United States v Peterson*, 812 F 2d 486, 493 – 494 (9th Cir 1987); See also *United States v Angola*, 514 F Supp 933, 935 – 936 (SD Florida 1981).

144 *United States v Gonzales*, 776 F 2d 931 (11th Cir 1985), para. 42.

145 See the practice in Stigall (n 58), 347 – 368.

146 *United States v Gonzales*, 776 F 2d 931 (11th Cir 1985), para. 42.

Finally, it is contentious whether the protective principle serves as a possible jurisdictional basis for extraterritorial trade restrictions, boycotts and embargoes premised on foreign policy or national security issues. Among others, this point has been argued (albeit briefly) by the German Federal Court of Justice in a case concerning material supplies for the Iranian nuclear programme.[147] It is also regularly invoked by the United States in relation to its export control and economic sanctions measures.[148] The literature has viewed the exercise of extraterritorial jurisdiction based on the protective principle critically and accepted this extension only in cases, in which sufficient evidence of a direct threat to national security through the regulated transaction could be proven.[149] Indeed, this limitation seems to be necessary to prevent an abuse of the principle as a tool to advance convenient economic objectives.[150] Thus, while particular contributions to known terrorist organizations or programmes of weapons of mass destruction may be accessible to the protective principle, the vast amount of export control and economic sanctions policies seem to fall short of this quality.[151]

f) The Universality Principle

It has been argued that the principles of jurisdiction are derivatives of the definition of statehood. Territoriality, active and passive personality as well as the protective principle mirror the fact that a State under international law must necessarily possess a territory, a population and an independent

---

147 See BGH, Order of 26. 3. 2009 StB 20/08, reported in NJW 2010, 385.

148 For US secondary boycotts, see below C.II.4. Secondary Trade Boycotts.

149 Ryngaert, *Jurisdiction in International Law* (n 2), 118; Dieter Holthausen, 'Die Strafbarkeit von Auslandstaten Deutscher und das völkerrechtliche Interventionsverbot' [1992] NJW 214, 215 with regard to the extraterritorial support of programmes of weapons of mass destruction; in this sense also Akehurst (n 42), 159.

150 See on this point Akehurst (n 42), 158 with regard to US re-export controls targeting the Soviet Block.

151 See for instance Jeffrey A Meyer, 'Second Thoughts on Secondary Sanctions' (2009) 30(3) University of Pennsylvania Journal of International Law 905, 909: 'The United States itself is prone to exaggerated claims that secondary sanctions measures can be justified by the protective or effects jurisdictional principles, even when these measures aim to redress [...] conduct that occurs in distant lands and that has no real prospect of jeopardizing the safety of or causing any substantial effect in the United States.'.

government that may exercise its international law personality.[152] Under this conception, the status of the universality principle has always been somewhat dubious as it allows for the exercise of jurisdiction based solely on the nature of the conduct in question, without the presence of any aspect related to State sovereignty, such as the nationality of the perpetrator, the place of commission or whether the conduct is directed against a fundamental interest of the State.[153] Therefore, controversies and a certain doctrinal fuzziness regarding the legitimacy and scope of this principle under international law still exist, a fact that is exacerbated by the dearth of State practice in the actual exercise of universal jurisdiction.[154] In addition, while the domestic legislation of a growing number of States establishes universal jurisdiction over certain types of crimes, this may not provide conclusive evidence over the status of universality under customary international law since these laws are often based (also) on treaties.[155] Since 2009 therefore, the scope and application of the principle of universal jurisdiction has featured annually on the agenda of the General Assembly of the United Nations (**UN**) and the Secretary General is tasked with collecting information and observations on State practice of this principle.[156] The possible outcome of this project is yet unclear.

The principle of universal jurisdiction is best established, and most commonly applied in criminal law. Because of its atypical nature – it does not require any connection between the conduct and the State exercising

152 Armand L de Mestral and T. Gruchalla-Wesierski, *Extraterritorial application of export control legislation: Canada and the USA* (Research study/ Canadian Council of International Law vol 1, Nijhoff 1990), 18.

153 Roger O'Keefe, 'Universal Jurisdiction: Clarifying the Basic Concept' (2004) 2(3) JICJ 735, at 745 defines universal jurisdiction as 'prescriptive jurisdiction over offenses committed abroad by persons who, at the time of commission, are non-resident aliens, where such offenses are not deemed to constitute threats to the fundamental interests of the prescribing state or, in appropriate cases, to give rise to effects within its territory'; a similar definition is provided by the Institut de droit international, Universal Criminal Jurisdiction with regard to the Crime of Genocide, Crimes against Humanity and War Crimes, Resolution of 26 August 2005.

154 See Ryngaert, *Jurisdiction in International Law* (n 2), 129 – 132.

155 This is argued by Sienho Yee, 'Universal Jurisdiction: Concept, Logic, and Reality' (2011) 10(3) Chinese Journal of International Law 503; however, the *Restatement (Fourth) of the Foreign Relations Law of the United States* (n 42), § 413 reporters' notes 2 points out that these treaties may indirectly support universal jurisdiction in customary international law.

156 See for instance: General Assembly, The scope and application of the principle of universal jurisdiction, Resolution of 20 December 2018, A/Res/73/208.

jurisdiction – the list of crimes amenable to universality is necessarily limited.[157] Precisely which specific offences trigger the application of this principle is subject to debate within jurisprudence and literature, but most commentators seem to agree that at least piracy, war crimes (consisting of grave breaches of provisions of the Geneva Conventions) and crimes against humanity including genocide belong to this category.[158] This is also reflected in the domestic legislation of a growing number of States.[159] However, there is great controversy surrounding the question whether under international law, universal jurisdiction covers terrorism or at least specific acts of terrorism. With regard to the former, problems already arise because no prevailing definition of the concept of terrorism as such exists.[160] Nonetheless, US commentators in particular have applied univer-

157 Multiple theories have been offered to justify the raison d'être of the universality principle: The most common explanation suggests that some types of conduct are so morally reprehensible that every State has a legitimate interest in their repression, see Lowe and Staker (n 50), 302; Ryngaert, *Jurisdiction in International Law* (n 2), 127; Ireland-Piper, *Accountability in Extraterritoriality* (n 113), 29. However, this theory may not explain why one of the most established crimes subject to universal jurisdiction is piracy, an act, which may involve relatively minor use of force and may not be more morally reprehensible than for instance common murder. This anomaly is often explained by the fact that it was easy for pirates to evade the jurisdiction of any State and that therefore, universal jurisdiction was *necessary* in order to bring these persons to justice, see Lowe and Staker (n 50), 302 and Yee (n 155), para. 4.

158 ICJ, *Arrest Warrant of 11 April 2000 (Democratic Republic of the Congo v Belgium)* (n 69), Joint Separate Opinion of Judges Higgins, Kooijmans and Buergenthal, paras. 61 – 65; *Israel v Eichmann*, 36 International Law Reports 277, 289 – 304, Isr. S. Ct. (1962); Principle 2(1) of the Princeton Principles on Universal Jurisdiction (2001), https://lapa.princeton.edu/hosteddocs/unive_jur.pdf, last accessed on 13 April 2022; Lowe and Staker (n 50), 302; Stephen G Coughlan and others, *Law Beyond Borders: Extraterritorial Jurisdiction in an Age of Globalization* (Irwin Law; Canadian Electronic Library 2014), 37 – 38; Ilias Bantekas, 'Criminal Jurisdiction of States under International Law' in R. Wolfrum (ed), *The Max Planck Encyclopedia of Public International Law* (Oxford University Press), paras. 23 and 28.

159 See for instance 18 U.S.C. § 1091 (genocide); 18 U.S.C. §§ 1583 – 1584, 1596 (slavery); German Code of Crimes against International Law 2002, § 1; Canadian Crimes Against Humanity and War Crimes Act (S.C. 2000, c. 24), § 6(1); Australian Criminal Code Act 1995, §§ 15.4 with 238.117.

160 This was the main argument of the Second Circuit for rejecting the application of the universality principle to an act of terrorism, *United States v Yousef*, 327 F 3d 56 (2d Cir 2003) at 108.

sality to certain specific terrorist acts, among others hijacking of aircrafts and hostage taking.[161]

Another source of great controversy or at least misunderstanding relates to whether universal jurisdiction may be exercised *in absentia*, that is, in relation to an accused who is not territorially present. The origin of this debate was laid down in the *Arrest Warrant* case before the ICJ, where the various separate and dissenting opinions of the members of the Court found different answers to the normative permissibility of universal jurisdiction *in absentia*.[162] While there is little practice of States explicitly exercising universal jurisdiction without the accused being present in domestic territory, this is not necessarily an indication that such exercises are prohibited under customary international law.[163] Rather, as is pointed out by a number of commentators, there seems to be no logical need for a distinct concept of universal jurisdiction *in absentia* and the members of the ICJ analysing this issue have most likely conflated prescriptive, adjudicative and enforcement jurisdiction. The principle of universality only relates to jurisdiction to prescribe, where, as the principle suggests, it is irrelevant whether the accused is within domestic territory or not at the time of the commission of the crime. However, whether the accused is within domestic territory for the purposes of a trial or the execution of an arrest warrant only concerns the legitimate exercise of adjudicative or enforcement jurisdiction, an issue distinct from that of prescription.[164] Thus, as O'Keefe has correctly pointed out, 'as a matter of international law, if universal jurisdiction is permissible, than its exercise *in absentia* is logically permissible also'.[165]

The true reason for the international scepticism with regard to the initiation of criminal proceedings, such as issuing an arrest warrant or

161 *Restatement (Fourth) of the Foreign Relations Law of the United States* (n 42), § 402 reporters' notes 10; Blakesley (n 77), 124 – 136.

162 See for instance: *Arrest Warrant of 11 April 2000 (Democratic Republic of the Congo v Belgium)* (n 69), Separate Opinion of Judge Guillaume, para. 12 ('Universal jurisdiction *in absentia* as applied in the present case is unknown to international law.'); Joint Separate Opinion of Judges Higgins, Kooijmans and Buergenthal, para. 59 ('[…] a State may choose to exercise a universal criminal jurisdiction *in absentia* […]); Dissenting Opinion of Judge Van den Wyngaert, paras. 54 – 56.

163 Ryngaert, *Jurisdiction in International Law* (n 2), 133 – 134; *Restatement (Fourth) of the Foreign Relations Law of the United States* (n 42), § 413 reporters' notes 1.

164 *Restatement (Fourth) of the Foreign Relations Law of the United States* (n 42), § 413 reporters' notes 1; Colangelo, 'Spatial Legality' (n 48), 92.

165 O'Keefe (n 153), 750.

conducting a trial *in absentia*, against persons not present in domestic territory is likely that it potentially raises delicate questions of international stability.[166] Since these proceedings are based on universal prescriptive jurisdiction, in theory, a large number of States may decide to concurrently initiate criminal proceedings over the same person. Additionally, assertions of universal jurisdiction at times target high-ranking State officials and are thus often politically sensitive.[167] However, the better solution to these issues would be not to create an artificial jurisdictional category of universal jurisdiction *in absentia*, but rather to limit such exercises based on established principles of restraints or through other domestic mechanisms.[168]

Lastly, with regard to the principle of universality, it is contentious whether this jurisdictional basis has any application outside of the field of criminal law. In particular, this issue is debated in the closely related area of tort law where universality may function as a vehicle to redress victims of international wrongs who may otherwise not be able to initiate suit in the State where such crimes were committed. However, these questions have gained practical relevance almost only in relation to the US Alien Tort Statute (**ATS**) and its application to corporate wrongdoing, so that they are best discussed jointly with other issues in the area of business and human rights.[169]

### 3. Treaty-based Extensions of Jurisdiction

In practice, customary international law principles of State jurisdiction are complemented by an increasing net of treaties allowing or requiring the parties to exercise jurisdiction with respect to certain conduct of common concern. Generally, these treaties define and criminalize certain offenses, such as the financing of terrorism[170] or bribery[171], before setting out the

---

166 See on this point, *Arrest Warrant of 11 April 2000 (Democratic Republic of the Congo v Belgium)* (n 69), Dissenting Opinion of Judge Van den Wyngaert, para. 56.

167 However, Ryngaert, *Jurisdiction in International Law* (n 2), 131 notes that the conflict potential is overblown.

168 See for suggestions: ibid., 134 – 135.

169 See below at C.V.5c) Comparative Normative Analysis.

170 International Convention for the Suppression of the Financing of Terrorism (adopted 9 December 1999, entered into force 10 January 2000) 2178 UNTS 197, Resolution A/RES/54/109 ('Terrorist Financing Convention').

171 UNCAC (n 15).

circumstances, in which State parties shall or may establish jurisdiction. Typically, these situations reflect the ordinary basis under customary international law such as territoriality and nationality, including when the offense is committed in the territory of the State, on board a vessel flying the flag of the State or an aircraft registered under the laws of the State, or when a national of the State commits the offense. Some treaties also allow for jurisdiction based on variations of the protective principle, such as when the offense is directed against a State or government facility abroad or when the offense is committed in order to compel the State to do or abstain from doing something.[172]

More importantly however, such treaties also often contain a provision that allows a State to establish jurisdiction over anyone, regardless of the location where the offense was committed, the nationality of the perpetrator or the direction of the offense, if the individual is found within domestic territory and the State does not extradite this person to another State claiming jurisdiction.[173] This concept is known as *aut dedere aut iudicare* (extradite or prosecute) and serves to ensure that the alleged offender may not escape prosecution anywhere. Because this basis allows a State to exercise jurisdiction without any connection to the facts of the underlying offense, it is sometimes termed 'conditional'[174] or 'quasi'-universal jurisdiction.[175] While in principle, such treaty-based obligations only apply *inter partes*, States have often implemented these provisions in domestic law without differentiating between nationals of party and non-party States.[176] Theoretically, a State that relies on such a provision to prosecute a national of a foreign State which is not a party to the convention at issue could thus possibly face diplomatic protests. In reality however, there have been no such protests to date,[177] which may bolster the argument that such treaties indeed often deal with issues of common concern to which even non-party States generally subscribe. As will be seen, the existence of a treaty regulating a certain set of conduct makes the assertion of extraterri-

172 Terrorist Financing Convention, Art. 7(2)(b) and (c).
173 Ibid., Art. 7(4); Convention for the Suppression of Unlawful Acts against the Safety of Civil Aviation (adopted 23 September 1971, entered into force 26 January 1973) 974 UNTS 177, Art. 5(2).
174 Coughlan and others (n 158), 38.
175 Volz (n 24), 100; Crawford and Brownlie (n 18), 469.
176 *Restatement (Fourth) of the Foreign Relations Law of the United States* (n 42), § 413, reporters' notes 2.
177 Lowe and Staker (n 50), 304.

torial jurisdiction in this area much less contentious, even if the treaty does not have universal adoption.

### 4. Territoriality-based Jurisdiction and the Internet

This study argues that the boundaries of territoriality as the cornerstone of the traditional doctrine in international law are not capable of providing order with regard to complex mechanisms of modern commercial regulation. However, the growing complexity of regulatory design is not the only significant challenge to the currently dominant jurisdictional framework. In the last few decades, giant leaps in internet technology, from e-commerce to social media to cloud computing have posed another formidable challenge. While cross-border information flows and transactions have long existed, there is no doubt that the rise of the internet has exacerbated the issue. First, it is only through the internet that every person connected to it is able to communicate simultaneously to anyone else in the world. Second, these communications, information and data may be 'located' in or 'transiting' through servers in one or more third countries distinct from the location of the sender and the (intended receiver). Because of its stark contrasts to the physical world, early commentators had thus occasionally argued for the recognition of a 'Cyberspace' that required a distinct set of rules different from traditional territorial legal authority.[178] However, States had (as expected) little interest in such conceptions.[179] Quite the opposite, actual practice shows that States are undertaking immense efforts across different substantive areas to tame the internet so that the question, which State is entitled to regulate which online activity, has become increasingly salient.[180]

One of the earliest cases that rose to prominence by highlighting the conflict potential of asserting jurisdiction over cross-border internet matters was the *Yahoo* case.[181] In that case, two French Jewish organizations

---

178 Johnson and Post (n 8).

179 Paul S Berman, 'The Globalization of Jurisdiction' (2002) 151 University of Pennsylvania Law Review, 315 – 316.

180 Uta Kohl, 'Jurisdiction in Cyberspace' in Nikolaos K Tsagourias and Russell Buchan (eds), *Research Handbook on International Law and Cyberspace* (Research handbooks in international law, Paperback edition 2017. Edward Elgar Publishing 2015), 35.

181 Tribunal de Grande Instance de Paris, Ordonnance de référé, 22 May 2000, *UEJF et Licra v Yahoo! Inc. et Yahoo France*, and Tribunal de Grande Instance de Paris,

sued Yahoo! Inc., a US corporation and its French subsidiary for permitting French internet users access to Yahoo's auction site, which allowed these users to purchase Nazi artefacts contrary to France's prohibition on the sale and distribution of Nazi-memorabilia. In its decision, the Paris Court ordered that Yahoo! Inc. and its French subsidiary to undertake all necessary measures to prevent any access of French users to Yahoo auction sites that sell artefacts sympathetic to Nazism or that might amount to Holocaust denial. While this order was uncontroversial with regard to yahoo.fr, which was dedicated to French users, its extension to yahoo.com, which arguably had a much stronger connection to the United States, proved problematic. Yahoo! Inc. argued that the court order was impermissibly extraterritorial and that to comply with the order, it needed to remove such content from its servers altogether, an action, which may run afoul of the First Amendment of the US Constitution. The French court, on the other hand, considered relevant the fact that French users could potentially access yahoo.com in addition to yahoo.fr, so that the site also had to comply with French law.

Normatively, this assertion of jurisdiction based on the mere accessibility of a website within the State may be interpreted as a variation of the objective territoriality or the effects principle.[182] However, this interpretation seems to be very expansive, as, in fact, the majority of websites are retrievable all over the world and jurisdiction based on accessibility would thus come close to universality.[183] These concerns also have likely guided the California Court petitioned by Yahoo! Inc. in the case mentioned above, which declared the French order unenforceable in the United States.[184] However, decisions like *Yahoo* are far from being an anomaly and several States have exercised jurisdiction under this wide effects theory despite the possible ramifications, in particular in morally highly loaded cases.[185]

---

Ordonnance de référé, 20 November 2000, *UEJF et Licra v Yahoo! Inc. et Yahoo France*.

182 Kohl, 'Jurisdiction in Cyberspace' (n 180), 47; Stefanie Schmahl, 'Zwischenstaatliche Kompetenzabgrenzung im Cyberspace' (2009) 47 Archiv des Völkerrechts 284, 305; Stefano Battini, 'Globalisation and Extraterritorial Regulation: An Unexceptional Exception' in Gordon Anthony, Jean-Bernard Auby and Morison John (eds), *Values in Global Administrative Law* (Hart 2011), 70.

183 This is also noted by Ryngaert, *Jurisdiction in International Law* (n 2), 80.

184 *Yahoo! Inc v La Ligue Contre Le Racisme et l'Antisémitisme*, 169 F Supp 2d 1181, 1186 (ND Cal 2001).

185 See for instance, for Germany, BGH, Judgment of 12 December 2000, 1 StR 184/00, reported in NJW 2001 (*Töben*), 624 and for the UK, *R v Perrin* (2002)

Nonetheless, similar to the development in competition law, States have at times tried to limit the application of their laws in internet matters through the additional requirement of intention. Under this variation, jurisdiction may not be premised solely upon the accessibility of a website in a certain State, but rather, the website must have been specifically targeting users in that State.[186] This is arguably the approach taken in the new EU General Data Protection Regulation (**GDPR**), the territorial scope of which is extended to foreign enterprises only if they process data in relation to the offering of goods and services to residents in the Union or to the monitoring of the behaviour of such residents within the Union.[187] This test sometimes also provides the yardstick in US jurisprudence on finding jurisdiction over defendants based on contact over the internet. Thus, in a case concerning prohibited online gambling in the State of New York, the court repeatedly alluded to the fact that the foreign defendants actively targeted residents within the State and undertook no efforts to exclude identifiable New Yorkers from their advertising efforts.[188] However, even this reference to intention or targeting may in the end prove unworkable in practice, as there are no reliable criteria for assessing this question. For instance, one commonly cited requirement, that the website appears in the language of the target user, is increasingly less meaningful, given the development of automatic translation tools.[189]

The second possible issue with jurisdiction in the internet era is that not only is data accessible anywhere in the world, but it may be stored in or transiting through States that have no connection to the sender, the receiver or the content of the communication. In the context of export control regulation, one could thus imagine a Swedish engineer sending an email containing sensitive technical data to a researcher in Russia, using a service where the email is stored on a US based server. While this action

---

EWCA Crim. 747 (22 March 2002); see also Schmahl (n 182), 299 – 304 and Kohl, 'Jurisdiction in Cyberspace' (n 180), 38 – 44.

186 See for more on this: Thomas Schultz, 'Carving up the Internet: Jurisdiction, Legal Orders, and the Private/Public International Law Interface' (2008) 19(4) EJIL 799, 816 – 819.

187 Regulation (EU) 2016/679 of the European Parliament and of the Council of 27 April 2016 on the protection of natural persons with regard to the processing of personal data and on the free movement of such data, and repealing Directive 95/46/EC (General Data Protection Regulation) [2016] OJ L 119/1, Art. 3.

188 *People v World Interactive Gaming Corp*, 714 NYS 2d, 844 (1999); See also Kohl, 'Jurisdiction in Cyberspace' (n 180), 47; Berman, 'The Globalization of Jurisdiction' (n 179), 412 – 420.

189 Berman, 'The Globalization of Jurisdiction' (n 179), 420.

may be innocuous in Sweden, the content of the email may be illegal in the United States.[190] In these cases, the question arises whether the State, where such data is located in or transiting through, in our case the United States, may claim jurisdiction, even though it has only a marginal connection to the facts and the Swedish engineer possibly may not even know that his or her email would pass through the United States.[191] That strict territoriality would lead to potentially arbitrary results in these cases was also recognized by the predecessor of the GDPR, the jurisdictional provision of which explicitly excluded foreign operators when they use 'equipment' within the EU solely for the purpose of a transit through Union territory.[192]

The geographically arbitrary storage of data, an increasingly important problem in the age of cloud computing and, most recently, blockchain, has potential ramifications for the exercise of enforcement jurisdiction as well. This issue is best illustrated through the *Microsoft Ireland* saga, in which US prosecutors, in a drug-trafficking related investigation, obtained a warrant directing Microsoft to produce the content of the email account of one of its customers. While Microsoft turned over information stored in the United States, it refused to provide (the more relevant) communications stored in its datacentres in Ireland, arguing that these were outside the jurisdictional reach of US law enforcement.[193] However, the magistrate judge deciding on the warrant did not follow this reasoning. On the issue of extraterritoriality, the judge pointed out that the warrant 'does not criminalize conduct taking place in a foreign country; it does not involve the deployment of American law enforcement personnel abroad; it does not require even the physical presence of service provider employees at the location where data are stored. At least in this instance, it places

190 See also the similar example provided by Svantesson (n 13), 33.

191 Compare this to the very similar problem posed by international wire transfers denominated in US dollars examined below at C.II.3. Territoriality and US Dollar Transactions by non-US Financial Institutions.

192 Directive 95/46/EC of the European Parliament and of the Council of 24 October 1995 on the protection of individuals with regard to the processing of personal data and on the free movement of such data, Art. 4(1)(c).

193 *In re Warrant to Search a Certain E-Mail Account Controlled and Maintained by Microsoft Corp.*, 15 F Supp 3d 466, 470 (SDNY 2014): 'Microsoft's argument is simple [...]. Federal courts are without authority to issue warrants for the search and seizure of property outside the territorial limits of the United States. Therefore, Microsoft concludes, to the extent that the warrant here requires acquisition of information from Dublin, it is unauthorized and must be quashed.'.

obligations only on the service provider to act within the United States.'[194] This decision was reversed on appeal, in which the Second Circuit found the domestic presumption against extraterritoriality to apply to the legislation at issue while also considering the possible Irish and EU interests in the case at hand.[195] The case was then set to be argued in front of the Supreme Court. However, in the meantime the United States passed a law explicitly including extraterritorial communication into the scope of such warrants,[196] so that at least from the perspective of US domestic law, the issue was rendered moot.[197]

Examining this case under the lens of public international law, the crucial question is whether the original warrant ordering Microsoft to produce communication stored in Ireland engaged the United States' (strictly prohibited) extraterritorial jurisdiction to enforce. There seems to be some divergence on this issue. While both Ireland and the EU protested the warrant by way of *amicus curiae* briefs,[198] several European States as well as Australia and Canada allow domestic law enforcement to compel the production of data stored abroad.[199] It is important to remember here that, as a matter of law, enlisting Microsoft as an intermediary to perform the actual production of the communications in question should be treated no differently than if US agencies had decided to directly access the servers in Ireland themselves, as Microsoft would simply be acting as a proxy to these agencies. Having established this, the question turns to whether governmental access of communication located abroad constitutes exterritorial enforcement. Even here, State practice is diverse as it could be argued that no State agent has to physically enter foreign territory when accessing foreign equipment and thus that no enforcement happens on foreign soil.[200] However, it would certainly be doctrinally more correct

---

194 *In re Warrant to Search a Certain E-Mail Account Controlled and Maintained by Microsoft Corp*, 15 F Supp 3d 466, 475 – 476 (SDNY 2014).

195 *In re Warrant to Search a Certain E-Mail Account Controlled and Maintained by Microsoft Corp*, 829 F 3d 197, 221 (2d Cir 2016).

196 Clarifying Lawful Overseas Use of Data Act, Pub. L. 115–141, s 103(a)(1).

197 *United States v Microsoft Corp.*, 138 S Ct 1186 (2018).

198 *United States v Microsoft Corp.*, 138 S Ct 1186 (2018), Brief of the European Commission on Behalf of the European Union as *amicus curiae* in Support of neither Party and Brief for Ireland as *amicus curiae* in Support of neither Party.

199 Reference is made to the table included in Robert J Currie, 'Cross-Border Evidence Gathering in Transnational Criminal Investigation: Is the Microsoft Ireland Case the "Next Frontier"?' (2017) 54 Canadian Yearbook of international Law 63, 93.

200 Ryngaert, *Jurisdiction in International Law* (n 2), 82.

to assume the opposite, that remote data access is essentially the digital version of the case when police officers physically seize a letter located in a foreign State. Support for this notion can also be found in Art. 32 of the Cybercrime Convention,[201] which allows for trans-border access outside of mutual legal assistance only if the information is publicly available or if the information holder gives its consent. While these principles define international law *de lege lata*, this is not to say that they may not change in the near future due to technological advances: At about the same time as the *Microsoft Ireland* case, Google found itself in a similar dispute. However, unlike Microsoft, Google uses dynamic cloud technologies that constantly 'move' the data around different datacentres worldwide so that it might be impossible to precisely predict the physical location of any communication at any given time.[202] In these cases, where mutual legal assistance is close to impossible, States may feel the urge to redefine the boundaries of extraterritorial enforcement jurisdiction to allow for more efficient transnational criminal investigations.

## II. Principles Restraining the Exercise of Jurisdiction

As the analysis above has shown, it is not only possible but also permitted under principles of international law that multiple States assert jurisdiction over the same behaviour by the same actor, i.e. concurrent jurisdiction. For instance, this would be the case if a national of State A residing in State B perpetrated a crime, over which State B exercised jurisdiction based on the territoriality principle and State A based on the active nationality principle. Similarly, concurrent jurisdiction would also be possible in the case of anti-competitive behaviour, which is initiated in one State, but which has effects in another State. The solution to these situations may be found in substantive harmonization efforts or mutual cooperation, which

---

201 Convention on Cybercrime, (adopted 23 November 2001, entered into force 1 July 2004) ETS No. 185 ('Cybercrime Convention').

202 *In re Search Warrant No. 16–1061-M to Google*, 232 F Supp 3d 708, 712 (ED Pa. 2017): 'Google operates a state-of-the-art intelligent network that, with respect to some types of data, including some of the data at issue in this case, automatically moves data from one location on Google's network to another as frequently as needed to optimize for performance, reliability, and other efficiencies. As a result, the country or countries in which specific user data, or components of that data, is located may change.'.

may prevent such conflicts in the first place.[203] However, beyond that, several authors have studied whether specific rules of customary international law or general principles exist that require States to moderate their exercises of jurisdiction in light of possible conflicts with other States.[204] For instance, in the first example above, a satisfactory solution could involve one State deferring its jurisdictional claim to the claim of the other State.[205] To reframe the issue, this chapter looks at whether under international law, *after* a jurisdictional link for prescriptive jurisdiction has been established, other restraining principles exist to avoid or to arbitrate provocative, excessive or conflicting exercises of jurisdictions.

The result of this investigation will necessarily influence the normative analysis to be carried out in part C. However, it should already be noted here that while there is no dearth of proposals in this regard, none of the principles examined below, with the possible exception of the principle of genuine link, has found general acceptance in the international law on jurisdiction. In practice therefore, there are currently no adequate mechanisms to limit assertions of jurisdiction once it can be shown that these assertions are based on one of the permissive principles.

Theoretically however, international law knows a number of general principles to restrain exercises of power. Three of these are examined in section 1: the requirement of a genuine link, the prohibition of abuse of rights and the concept of proportionality. While the two latter concepts are somewhat established in other areas of international law, they are rarely applied within the context of extraterritorial jurisdiction. In addition to these general principles, international comity has featured as a nebulous but prominent concept on arbitrating conflicting exercises of jurisdiction since the seventeenth century. Closer analysis, however, reveals the limited usefulness of comity in practice, particularly because of its discretionary status (section 2). Finally, this chapter looks at the principle of 'reasonableness', which in a way was the rediscovery of comity by US Courts in the area of antitrust litigation in the 1970s. The development culminated in the Restatement on Foreign Relations Law (Third), which included a 'rule of reason', requiring States asserting jurisdiction

---

203 International Bar Association (n 12), 22.

204 For example: Meng, *Extraterritoriale Jurisdiktion im öffentlichen Wirtschaftsrecht* (n 43), 648; Ryngaert, *Jurisdiction in International Law* (n 2), 145.

205 It is no coincidence that this issue bears resemblance to conflict-of-laws and several proposals to solve this issue draw heavily from conflict-of-laws principles, Buxbaum (n 32), 631, 647.

to balance their interests against other possibly conflicting interests.[206] According to the Restatement, application of this rule of reason was not only morally desirable, but truly mandated by customary international law. However, the pronunciation of such a reasonableness test has been vehemently criticized and it is doubtable, whether it actually forms part of international law *de lege lata* (section 3).

## 1. Limitations according to General Principles in International Law

### a) Genuine Link

In international law, the test of a 'genuine link' or 'genuine connection' is most commonly associated with the ICJ judgment in the *Nottebohm* case, which dealt with the requirements for a State to exercise diplomatic protection for one of its citizens abroad. According to *Nottebohm*, this power may be limited if the naturalized citizen has no real links with the State exercising diplomatic protection.[207] Deciding whether Mr Nottebohm retained sufficient connections with Liechtenstein for this purpose, the Court looked to a variety of factors, including his habitual residence, the centre of his interest and his family ties.[208] From there, the test of genuine connection has found its way into the rules regarding prescriptive jurisdiction, which is not surprising considering that both bodies of laws concern the legitimacy of certain acts of a State outside its territory, be it the exercise of diplomatic protection or extraterritorial jurisdiction.[209] In both of these instances, the existence of a genuine connection between the subject and the State may serve as a useful yardstick.

This requirement, though it operates differently than the one discussed in *Nottebohm*, is now widely interpreted as a fundamental notion behind the customary international law framework of prescriptive jurisdiction.[210] While assertions of jurisdiction are generally measured against the permissive principles explored above, such as territoriality and nationality, the

206 *Restatement (Third) of the Foreign Relations Law of the United States* (n 5), § 403 (1).

207 *Nottebohm, Second Phase (Liechtenstein v Guatemala)* (n 122), 22; see on this interpretation, Lowe and Staker (n 50), 300.

208 *Nottebohm, Second Phase (Liechtenstein v Guatemala)* (n 122), 22.

209 Gunnar Schuster, *Die internationale Anwendung des Börsenrechts* (Beiträge zum ausländischen öffentlichen Recht und Völkerrecht, Springer 1996), 41.

210 See already above at B.I.1. The Case of the S.S. Lotus.

test of 'genuine connection' always lurks behind every jurisdictional analysis. Hypothetically therefore, it may function as an additional principle of restraint when it can be shown that a particular exercise of *prima facie* permissible jurisdiction does not satisfy that requirement or that another State applying its laws to the same situation can also rely on a (possibly more) genuine connection.[211] Ryngaert for instance argues that this criterion may provide a useful restraint to reject some of the most egregious forms of extraterritorial jurisdiction based on particularly fleeting connections.[212] This principle may prove particularly useful in relation to the ephemeral territorial connections and effects in internet jurisdiction.[213] In practice however, it may be difficult to dismiss exercises of extraterritorial jurisdiction for a lack of 'genuine connection', because the application of this test presupposes that one of the recognized jurisdictional bases has been satisfied, which necessarily indicates some sort of connection between the State and the regulated circumstance.

#### b) Abuse of Rights

Several authors have suggested that the principle of abuse of rights may serve as a general limitation on States in their exercise of jurisdiction.[214] Abuse of rights is generally well established in the domestic legal systems of civil-law countries. For instance, German private law recognizes and prohibits a variety of instances where the exercise of an existing right solely causes detriment to another party or where such exercise does not advance

---

211 In this sense in particular: Bernhard Grossfeld and C. P Rogers, 'A Shared Values Approach to Jurisdictional Conflicts in International Economic Law' (1983) 32(4) ICLQ 931, 945.

212 Ryngaert, *Jurisdiction in International Law* (n 2), 157.

213 Schultz (n 186), at 815 claims that in the case of internet jurisdiction, '[t]he [required] genuine link between the state and the activity needs to be taken to a higher threshold'; see also *Restatement (Fourth) of the Foreign Relations Law of the United States* (n 42), § 409, comment a, which, for the establishment of effects based jurisdiction, requires a 'genuine connection between the conduct and the prescribing state'; see also above at B.I.4. Territoriality-based Jurisdiction and the Internet.

214 Akehurst (n 42), 188 – 190; Ryngaert, *Jurisdiction in International Law* (n 2), 160 – 161; Meng, *Extraterritoriale Jurisdiktion im öffentlichen Wirtschaftsrecht* (n 43), 589 – 595; Ireland-Piper, *Accountability in Extraterritoriality* (n 113), 56 – 64.

any legitimate interest of the acting party.[215] It is less well-known in common-law systems, although Ireland-Piper argues that in fact, a number of common-law legal concepts serve essentially the same function or are based on the same basic notion.[216] Given the divergence in recognition in different legal systems, the status of abuse of rights as a 'general principle of law' according to Art. 38(1)(c) of the Statute of the ICJ is somewhat contested.[217] Nonetheless, the principle has found its way into multiple international law documents: Its clearest expression is included in Art. 300 United Nations Convention on the Law of the Sea, which obliges States to 'exercise the rights, jurisdiction and freedoms recognized in this Convention in a manner which would not constitute an abuse of right.'[218] Moreover, the Word Trade Organization (**WTO**) Appellate Body has interpreted Art. XX of the General Agreement on Tariffs and Trade (**GATT**) as an expression of good faith, including a prohibition on *abus de droit*.[219] Several judgments of the PCIJ have equally considered this principle.[220]

While the principle thus has some application at least in the law of the sea and international trade law, its status and content in relation to the law of jurisdiction is unclear. According to Akehurst, abuse of rights could serve to limit jurisdiction in two instances. First, even when a State satisfies some basis of prescriptive jurisdiction, it is not entirely free with regard to the content of the regulation, as it would be contrary to international law if the legislation is designed solely to produce mischief in another country without advancing any legitimate State interest. He gives the example of a hypothetical law that requires all UK citizens to drive on the left-hand side of the road in foreign countries, which, although it could be based on the active personality principle, would violate the principle of abuse of

215 See in particular, German Civil Code (Bürgerliches Gesetzbuch), § 226 and § 242.

216 Ireland-Piper, *Accountability in Extraterritoriality* (n 113), 60 – 62.

217 Alexandre Kiss, 'Abuse of Rights' in R. Wolfrum (ed), *The Max Planck Encyclopedia of Public International Law* (Oxford University Press), paras. 9 – 10; Meng, *Extraterritoriale Jurisdiktion im öffentlichen Wirtschaftsrecht* (n 43), 589 – 595.

218 United Nations Convention on the Law of the Sea (adopted 10 December 2082, entered into force 16 November 1994) 1833 UNTS 3.

219 WTO Appellate Body, *United States – Import Prohibition of Certain Shrimp and Shrimp Products*, WTO Doc WT/DS58/AB/R (1998), para. 158.

220 PCIJ, *Free Zones of Upper Savoy and the District of Gex, Second Phase (France v Switzerland)* [1930] PCIJ Rep Series A No 24, 12 and *Certain German Interests in Polish Upper Silesia (Germany v Poland)* (Merits) [1926] PCIJ Rep Series A No 7, 30 and 37 – 38.

rights.[221] While this hypothetical example certainly has some charm, it is hard to imagine that States in practice would actually adopt such obviously abusive laws. More realistic in practice is Akehurst's second proposition that an abuse of rights also exists when a regulation, although it advances some legitimate interest of the State, does so illegitimately at the expense of other States.[222] In this second variation, the doctrine of abuse of rights closely resembles the principle of proportionality, which is discussed in more detail below.[223]

*De lege ferenda*, Ireland-Piper proposes the application of the principle of abuse of rights to extraterritoriality in the area of criminal law, where the specific content of the principle is linked to requirements of the rule of law. In her view, both principles are connected by the common objective of restraining the arbitrary exercise of power and discretion.[224] Accordingly, when an exercise of extraterritorial jurisdiction is inconsistent with the rule of law, which in her specific perspective on criminal law has a strong focus on the protection of individual rights, such exercise may also amount to an abuse of rights.[225] This approach is commendable as it highlights the important positions of individuals, which, as we will see, are often neglected in the discourse on State jurisdiction.

#### c) Proportionality

Similar to the principle of abuse of rights, proportionality is a concept widely established in the domestic legal systems of civil-law countries, which has also gained a wide range of applications in international law. This principle is invoked among others in the context of countermeasures and self-defence, international humanitarian law, international and regional arrangements of human rights protection, international trade law and

---

221 Akehurst (n 42), 188 – 190.
222 Ibid., 188 – 190.
223 Ryngaert, *Jurisdiction in International Law* (n 2), 161; See below at B.II.1c) Proportionality.
224 Ireland-Piper, *Accountability in Extraterritoriality* (n 113), 70.
225 Ibid., at 67 – 70 proposes three basic criteria for the rule of law that (1), '[t]he law must be readily knowable, and certain and clear', (2), '[t]he law should be applied to all people equally, and operate uniformly in circumstances that are not materially different' and (3), '[t]here must be some capacity for judicial review of executive action'.

investment arbitration.[226] For instance, the ECtHR has made proportionality one of the cornerstones of the analysis of possible breaches of human rights, stating that any restriction 'imposed in this sphere must be proportionate to the legitimate aim pursued'.[227] Similarly in international humanitarian law, proportionality provides the yardstick for determining whether an attack is illegally indiscriminate, which is the case when the incidental loss of civilian life 'would be excessive in relation to the concrete and direct military advantage anticipated'.[228] Finally, a WTO panel has regarded the proportionality of countermeasures as a general principle of international law, which also finds application in the specific context of the suspension of trade concessions.[229]

It is not surprising therefore, that this principle has also been discussed as a possible restraint against the excessive exercise of extraterritorial jurisdiction. This has happened particularly in Germany, where constitutional law doctrine puts a strong focus on proportionality. According to doctrine, this principle encompasses four different elements, the pursuit of a legitimate objective, the general suitability of the measure to achieve this objective, that the measure is necessary (i.e. the least restrictive measure) in order to achieve this objective and that the measure is properly related in size or degree to that objective.[230] Under this conception, proportionality has proved a useful starting point to restrain the exercise of jurisdiction in German law for at least two reasons. First, it offers a clear structure for identifying and rationalizing the underlying competing interests to any jurisdictional assertion, which is a prerequisite for a successful balancing between those interests. For instance, this may involve the regulatory interest of the State asserting jurisdiction on the one hand and the interest of non-interference by the affected State as well as the interest of the affected individual on the other hand. And second, proportionality draws the atten-

---

226 Anne Peters, 'Verhältnismäßigkeit als globales Verfassungsprinzip' in Björnstjern Baade and others (eds), *Verhältnismässigkeit im Völkerrecht* (Jus Internationale et Europaeum vol 116. Mohr Siebeck 2016), 2 – 3.

227 ECtHR, *Handyside v United Kingdom,* App No 5493/72, Judgment of 7 December 1976, paras. 46–49.

228 Additional Protocol I to the Geneva Conventions (adopted 8 June 1977, entered into force 7 December 1978) 1125 UNTS 3, Art. 51(5)(b).

229 WTO, Decision by the Arbitrators, *EC – Regime for the importation, sale and distribution of bananas, Recourse to arbitration by the EC under Article 22.6 of the DSU*, WT/DS27/ARB (1999), para. 6.16.

230 Alec S Sweet and Jud Mathews, 'Proportionality Balancing and Global Constitutionalism' (2008) 47(1) Columbia Journal of Transnational Law 72, 75.

tion not only to *what* objective a measure is pursuing (which is also the main test under the principle of abuse of rights), but also to *how* this is done, i.e. to the degree of intrusiveness of the extraterritorial measure and to the question, whether less restrictive measures may be designed in a given case.[231]

The decision of the German Kammergericht in *Philip Morris/Rothmans* provides a brilliant example of how these aspects function in practice. In this case, the Court had to consider an order of the Federal Cartel Office preventing the merger of two global companies. The Court reasoned that principles of jurisdictional restraint, either based on reasonableness or on the principle of abuse of rights, may apply here. However, following domestic tradition, it then essentially indulged in a proportionality analysis. Accordingly, it had to consider and balance the domestic interest of upholding competition on the one hand against the interest not to interfere in foreign affairs on the other hand.[232] The key aspect in this case was then found to be the test of necessity, which requires the State, among measures equally effective to reach the objective, to choose the one that is least restrictive to the competing interest. Based on this test, the Court rejected the order of the Federal Cartel Office as excessive because it would have been sufficient to limit the order solely to the German subsidiaries of these two companies.[233] However, the Court drew on domestic, not international, doctrine to reach its conclusion and to date, this decision remains an outlier in the jurisprudence on merger control.[234] Rather, similar to the principle of abuse of rights, there is no indication that proportionality has found acceptance in international law as a concept restraining exercises of jurisdiction legitimized by one of the permissive bases.

### 2. Comity

Historically, the roots of the concept of comity can be traced back to seventeenth century Holland. Originally, comity referred to the discretionary act of a State to recognize the laws of another State in the forum, which

231 This point is also made by Dobson and Ryngaert (n 118), 331.

232 Kammergericht, Order of 1 July 1983, Kart. 16/82, reported in WuW/E OLG 3051 (*Philip Morris Inc. v Bundeskartellamt*), 3058.

233 Ibid., 3057; see on this also: Meng, *Extraterritoriale Jurisdiktion im öffentlichen Wirtschaftsrecht* (n 43), 417.

234 For more examples on how the principle of proportionality might function in practice, see: ibid., 614 – 616.

was treated as a matter of courtesy.[235] This was also the meaning given to comity by the US Supreme Court in its decision in *Hilton v Cuyot*, which considered the recognition and enforcement of awards rendered in France.[236] Thus, comity was less a principle of restraint upon a State exercising extraterritorial jurisdiction, but rather one of expansion in relation to the exercise of jurisdiction by another State.[237] In any event, even back then, the doctrine of comity was attributed the capability to resolve conflicts of laws in the absence of treaty provisions. With regard to civil and commercial disputes, the subsequent development of complex rules of private international law largely supplanted the application of comity. In the sphere of regulatory antitrust disputes however, US courts rediscovered comity in the 1970s as a principle to solve conflicts of laws not within the territorial State, but because of the extraterritorial application of domestic laws.[238]

Nonetheless, comity remains a somewhat difficult concept for solving issues of concurrent prescriptive jurisdiction. The main reason is the ambiguous nature and status of the principle. According to *Hilton v Cuyot* and a number of commentators, comity is no hard rule of law, but at the same time, it is also more than mere courtesy and goodwill.[239] More precisely, it seems to denote an objective custom, but undertaken out of a moral conviction rather than *opinio iuris*, which would turn it into customary international law. This interpretation is in line with some passages of the Restatement (Fourth), which categorizes different US jurisprudential techniques to limit the scope of extraterritorial jurisdiction as not required by

235 Harold G Maier, 'Jurisdictional Rules in Customary International Law' in Karl M Meessen (ed), *Extraterritorial Jurisdiction in Theory and Practice* (Kluwer Law Internat 1996), 64, 70.

236 *Hilton v Guyot*, 159 US 113, 163 – 4 (1895).

237 Reuven S Avi-Yonah, 'National Regulation of Multinational Enterprises: An Essay on Comity, Extraterritoriality, and Harmonization' (2003) 42(1) Columbia Journal of Transnational Law 5, at 12 uses comity in a similar sense when he discusses the exercise of extraterritorial jurisdiction *vis-à-vis* multinational enterprises: Under his conception of comity, certain instances would require the extension of jurisdiction beyond the local entity of the corporation to the entire global enterprise.

238 See below at B.II 3. Reasonableness.

239 Ryngaert, *Jurisdiction in International Law* (n 2), 148; Crawford and Brownlie (n 18), 485; Jörn A Kämmerer, 'Comity' in R. Wolfrum (ed), *The Max Planck Encyclopedia of Public International Law* (Oxford University Press), paras. 5 – 6; Ireland-Piper, *Accountability in Extraterritoriality* (n 113), 40 – 41; Coughlan and others (n 158), 43.

customary international law, but rather as matters of domestic comity.[240] Thus, the usefulness of this concept in international law is rather limited as its precise content is unclear and in any case, its application is subject to the discretion of the legislator or court.[241]

In this regard, Mestral and Gruchalla-Wesierski have made an interesting observation: In retaining the original purpose of comity as a tool to solve issues of conflicts of laws, the principle may encourage States, when they design regulations with extraterritorial application, to prescribe not domestic law, but the forum law of the addressees of the regulation.[242] This is for example the approach taken by the EU Timber Regulation, which prohibits the placement into the EU market of illegally harvested timber, whereas illegality is to be defined according to the law of the exporting country.[243] While it is unclear whether this provision was inspired by considerations of comity, in practice, it certainly does mitigate the potential for jurisdictional conflicts between States as well as the burden on affected individuals. Interpreted this way, comity as a choice-of-law doctrine may retain some significance.

### 3. Reasonableness

One of the most contested issues surrounding the traditional doctrine of State jurisdiction concerns the question whether the exercise of jurisdiction is subject to an overarching restraint of 'reasonableness', what the content of such a principle may be and whether this principle forms part of customary international law. Judge Fitzmaurice, in his separate opinion in *Barcelona Traction*, hinted at the existence of such rule of reason when he argued

> 'that, under present conditions, international law does not impose hard and fast rules on States delimiting spheres of national jurisdiction [...]. It does however (a) postulate the existence of limits [...] and (b) involve for every State an obligation to exercise moderation and

240 *Restatement (Fourth) of the Foreign Relations Law of the United States* (n 42), § 402, reporters' notes 3.

241 Ireland-Piper, *Accountability in Extraterritoriality* (n 113), 40 – 41.

242 Mestral and Gruchalla-Wesierski (n 152), 39.

243 Regulation (EC) No 593/2008 of the European Parliament and of the Council of 20 October 2010 laying down the obligations of operators who place timber and timber products on the market, Art. 2(g).

> restraint as to the extent of the jurisdiction assumed by its courts in cases having a foreign element, and to avoid undue encroachment on a jurisdiction more properly appertaining to, or more appropriately exercisable by, another State.'[244]

The most audacious and certainly most controversial proposal, however, has been formulated by the previous Restatement (Third) of Foreign Relations Law. According to its infamous § 403(1), even if one of the traditional bases of jurisdiction has been satisfied, States have to, through the evaluation of a number of factors, determine whether the exercise of jurisdiction would be unreasonable in the specific case, and, if it so determines, decline to exercise such unreasonable jurisdiction.[245] § 403(2) then goes on to provide a (non-exhaustive) list of eight such criteria, including the link of the activity to be regulated to the territory of the State, the connections between the regulating State and the person principally responsible for the activity, the character of the activity, the existence of justified expectations that might be hurt by the regulation and the likelihood of conflict with regulation by another State.[246] Finally, according to § 403(3), in the case that two States may concurrently exercise jurisdiction reasonably and the two prescriptions conflict with each other, each State has the obligation to balance its own interest against that of the other State, and defer its own jurisdiction if the interest of the other State is clearly greater.[247]

This principle of reasonableness as articulated in the Restatement (Third) and its specific operationalization through a multi-factor balancing test were inspired by a limited number of court decisions in US antitrust law in the 1970s. In the wake of the expanding effects principle and its potential to cause international discord, the Ninth Circuit in *Timberlane* argued that as a matter of international comity and fairness, showing an effect on US commerce alone was not in itself sufficient for the exercise of jurisdiction. Rather, a more comprehensive approach was necessary, which the Ninth Circuit summarized as a case-by-case interest balancing drawn from the field of conflict of laws, which included a list of factors similar to that contained in the Restatement (Third).[248] This approach was

---

244 *Barcelona Traction Light and Power Co, Ltd. (Belgium v Spain)* (n 126), Separate Opinion of Judge Fitzmaurice, para. 70.

245 *Restatement (Third) of the Foreign Relations Law of the United States* (n 5), § 403(1).

246 Ibid., § 403(2).

247 Ibid., § 403(3).

248 *Timberlane Lumber Co. v Bank of America NT & SA*, 549 F 2d 597, 611 – 615 (9th Cir 1976).

later repeated in the case concerning *Mannington Mills*[249] and finally found its way into the Restatement (Third), however, not only as a matter of international comity, but as a true principle of customary international law.

Commentators have criticized both the content of the principle of reasonableness and its characterization as a rule of customary international law. Interest balancing, it has been argued, is futile without the existence of an objective standard against which the conflicting interests of the States exercising jurisdiction may be assessed.[250] Moreover, the open formulation of § 403(2) of the Restatement (Third) makes the results of its application wholly unforeseeable and diminishes its value in solving conflicts of concurring jurisdiction.[251] In relation to its status as a rule of customary international law, multiple authors have correctly pointed out that the Restatement (Third) almost exclusively examined US State practice in the area of antitrust regulation.[252] However, even in the United States, that practice is not uniform,[253] while there is even less support for the application of reasonableness as a principle of jurisdictional restraint in other States.[254] For these reasons, the recent Restatement (Fourth), departing from the previous edition, also rejected such an interest-balancing test as a requirement of customary international law.[255]

However, rejecting reasonableness as a rule of customary international law as embodied in the Restatement (Third) does not entail the non-existence of that principle as such. Meng, for instance, describes reasonable-

---

249 *Mannington Mills v Congoleum Corp*, 595 F 2d 1287, 1297 (3d Cir 1979).

250 Meng, *Extraterritoriale Jurisdiktion im öffentlichen Wirtschaftsrecht* (n 43), 623; similarly, Rain Liivoja, 'Review of "Jurisdiction in International Law" by Cedric Ryngaert' (2008) 19 Finnish Yearbook of International Law 397, 400.

251 Ryngaert, *Jurisdiction in International Law* (n 2), 185: 'The problem with the reasonableness factors set forth for instance in § 403 of the Restatement as legal grounds under international law is that they are so malleable as to render them non-criteria in practice. Indeed, almost any jurisdictional assertion could be defended or opposed by invoking one or more reasonableness factors'; Ireland-Piper, *Accountability in Extraterritoriality* (n 113), 45; Volz (n 24), 55 – 56.

252 Meng, *Extraterritoriale Jurisdiktion im öffentlichen Wirtschaftsrecht* (n 43), 629 – 630; Ryngaert, *Jurisdiction in International Law* (n 2), 167.

253 See *Hartford Fire Insurance Co v California*, 509 US 764, 798 (1993).

254 However, for one significant example of a non-US court applying the rule of reason as a matter of customary international law, see Kammergericht, Order of 1 July 1983, Kart. 16/82, reported in WuW/E OLG 3051 (*Philip Morris Inc. v Bundeskartellamt*).

255 *Restatement (Fourth) of the Foreign Relations Law of the United States* (n 42), § 407, reporters' notes 6.

ness as a methodological requirement for the interpretation and construction of norms, on par with other methodological aspects such as logic. In his view, the principle limits the discretion of States in the exercise of their rights in light of the purposes of those rights. In other words, an exercise of jurisdiction may be unreasonable, if the objective of such exercise is inappropriate. Defined as such, this principle seems to reflect a case of abuse of rights.[256] In a similar vein, Ryngaert argues that a more specific rule of reason for the exercise of jurisdiction may be informed by certain general principles of international law, such as non-interference, proportionality and equity.[257] *De lege ferenda*, he imagines that a new rule of reason could put the interests of the international community centre stage and allow for the 'subsidiary' exercise of extraterritorial jurisdiction if doing so furthers those interests.[258] However, as customary international law currently stands, the existence of such a specific rule of reason requiring interest balancing for the exercise of jurisdiction seems doubtful. Rather, as both Meng and Ryngaert argue, and as this study will show in the next part, restraints on extraterritorial jurisdiction *de lege lata* may be rather scarce.

256 Meng, *Extraterritoriale Jurisdiktion im öffentlichen Wirtschaftsrecht* (n 43), 597.
257 Ryngaert, *Jurisdiction in International Law* (n 2), 182.
258 Ibid., 230.

## C. Case Studies

### I. Focus and Structure

There is, of course, no room to consider every possible substantive area of law in which exercises of extraterritorial jurisdiction have occurred. Therefore, this study necessarily had to focus on a selection of reference areas, from which a general conclusion as to the state of the territoriality-based system of jurisdiction may be synthesized. Such selection is naturally not completely objective. This study has settled on cases within the regulation of economic sanctions (chapter **II**) and export control (chapter **III**), transnational corporate bribery (chapter **IV**) and the prevention of and redress for corporate violations of human rights (chapter **V**). In each of these areas, sufficient practice in extraterritorial jurisdiction exists to conduct a meaningful assessment. These reference areas also have in common that States frequently utilise extraterritorial jurisdiction to unilaterally set regulations with a global reach. This is because the objectives and State interests within these areas often have an outward orientation, meaning that States seek to promote their municipal policies and regulatory standards to third countries. This is to be contrasted to substantive areas with a stronger inward orientation, where the primary interest of the State is the immediate protection of the domestic territory, its inhabitants or the domestic market.[259] This study expects that in relation to such outward-looking regulation, States have a stronger need to resort to complex regulatory mechanisms exploiting the traditional jurisdictional system.

However, these reference areas also fundamentally differ in the kind of interests they seek to realize. While the regulation of transnational corporate bribery and to a certain degree also export control concern objectives almost universally accepted in the international community, the same cannot be said about the enactment of economic sanctions. Rather, States resort to economic sanctions to 'enforce' a host of different moral, legal and political interests. Finally, prevention of and redress for corporate

259 Examples include competition law, the law of data protection and certain parts of securities law and environmental law. Extraterritoriality in these inward-looking regulatory areas may often be justified by an expanding view of the effects doctrine.

violations of human rights adds another dimension to the picture, in that regulations in this area not only seek to vindicate State interests, but also, in a triangular relationship, the rights of the victims of human rights violations. This study expects that even though States rely on comparable regulatory mechanisms of unilateral extraterritorial jurisdiction across some or all of these areas, the acceptance or rejection of such assertions by other States will depend on the nature of these interests.

The presentation of each regulatory area follows a similar structure. A brief introduction sets out the context of each substantive area, including which legal and political interests are at stake or need to be balanced. In particular, it will be investigated whether and what kind of an international framework exists to support the objectives of each area. The next sections in each chapter determine the practice in both the United States and in Europe in the respective subject matter by reviewing documents ranging from legislation, administrative acts, court decisions and other judicial documents including *amicus curiae* briefs to verbal acts such as protests and affirmations through diplomatic notes as well as other communications. The data gained through this analysis will be evaluated against the normative framework of jurisdiction under international law as set out in part B of this research.

Across all substantive areas, this part of the study reveals the deficiencies of the traditional, territoriality-based system of jurisdiction in international law (chapter **VI**). These inadequacies are twofold and they align with the two research questions set out in the introduction: First, this part establishes that the territoriality-based system of jurisdiction does not provide sufficient limits on the competences of States in practice. In fact, States are able to draw on a host of regulatory mechanisms to unilaterally set regulations with a global reach by exploiting the inconsistencies of territoriality. Second, the traditional system of jurisdiction also conflicts with actual practice because it does not allow for consideration of other important interests besides State sovereignty, in particular, the relationship between the regulating State and the addressee and the international community at large.

## II. Economic Sanctions

### 1. Introduction

Economic sanctions 'have become a fact of international life'.[260] For instance, the EU alone has 45 regimes of restrictive measures in place at present.[261] While economic sanctions were historically related to situations of warfare – one may remember the early Greek example when Athens under Pericles sought to embargo the Spartan-allied state Megara during the Peloponnesian War[262] – they have morphed into versatile political tools and are now used to pursue a multiplicity of goals. According to the EU's Service for Foreign Policy Instruments for instance, the overarching objectives include promoting international peace and security, preventing conflicts, supporting democratic principles, the rule of law and human rights and defending the principles of international law.[263]

In achieving these objectives, economic sanctions become arguably more effective the more States implement identical measures. Unilateral sanctions are particularly prone to failure because in our globally interconnected market, targets of economic sanctions may easily thwart or circumvent such efforts by turning to other trading partners willing to fill in the economic vacuum caused by the sanctioning State. To mitigate this issue, the United States in particular has sought to adopt measures that not only affect the direct sanctioning target, but also third parties engaged in commercial relationships with the primary target. For instance, in its ongoing standoff with Russia, the United States is also targeting persons and companies, particularly in Germany, for their involvement in the construction of the Nord Stream 2 pipeline.

These measures form the focus of the subsequent analysis. They are especially controversial because of their perceived extraterritoriality: While

260 Barry E Carter, 'Economic Sanctions' in R. Wolfrum (ed), *The Max Planck Encyclopedia of Public International Law* (Oxford University Press), para. 33.

261 See for an overview: EU Sanctions Map, available at https://sanctionsmap.eu/#/main, last accessed on 17 December 2020.

262 Bert Chapman, *Export Controls: A Contemporary History* (University Press of America 2013), 1 referring to Charles Fornara, 'Plutarch and the Megarian Decree' in Donald Kagan (ed), *Studies in the Greek historians: In memory of Adam Parry* (Yale classical studies vol 24. Cambridge University Press 1975), 213 – 220.

263 European Commission https://ec.europa.eu/info/business-economy-euro/banking-and-finance/international-relations/restrictive-measures-sanctions_en, last accessed on 17 December 2020.

the adoption of unilateral economic sanctions in itself always entails a subjective moral and political judgment, imposing this evaluation on unconcerned foreign individuals or entities of third States raises particularly delicate questions of legitimacy. Given the outright egregiousness of some of the US sanctions, it often seems that these measures 'have to be' violating international law, particularly the customary international law rules of jurisdiction. Conversely, if there is one area of law for which the doctrine on prescriptive State jurisdiction should offer clear limits it would seem to be that of extraterritorial economic sanctions.

However, this chapter argues that customary international law principles of jurisdiction are not able to regulate these measures because they do not make a clear statement about when extraterritorial economic sanctions violate international law. On the one hand, there is no consistent practice, even within the EU, rejecting sanctions with extraterritorial effects. Rather, EU reactions to these jurisdictional assertions by the United States are grounded in political expediency and remain in the realm of inter-subjectivity. On the other hand, a legal doctrinal analysis with the customary international law principles of jurisdiction as the reference point equally offers no conclusive answer to the (il-)legality of extraterritorial economic sanctions. These two aspects are mutually reinforcing: The normative uncertainty allows States to pursue their individual political objectives while claiming the legal high-ground. At the same time, the inconsistent practice contributes to and fuels the controversy around the international legality of extraterritorial economic sanctions.

This chapter starts out with an overview of economic sanctions including the distinction between primary and secondary sanctions and an introduction into the framework of US sanctions in section 1. Sections 2 – 4 of this chapter analyse economic sanctions regulations with extraterritorial implications structured according to the principle of jurisdiction invoked to justify them. Among these measures are some of the most controversial economic sanctions ever imposed, including those targeting domestic controlled foreign subsidiaries and those intending to control financial services based on correspondent account banking. Section 5 puts the protection of foreign individuals into focus and asks how sanctioning States provide due process protection to the affected before section 6 offers some preliminary conclusions.

### a) Economic Sanctions under International Law

Economic sanctions, according to a commonly cited definition by Lowenfeld, are 'measures of an economic – as contrasted with diplomatic or military – character taken to express disapproval of the acts of the target state or to induce that state to change some policy or practices or even its governmental structure.'[264] Carter adopted this definition but broadened its personal scope to include not only States, but also international organizations and non-State actors as potential senders and targets of economic sanctions.[265] Modern economic sanctions may span a wide variety of different measures, including limits on existing benefits, imports, exports, financial transactions or other activities.[266]

Depending on the originator of the measures, economic sanctions are commonly categorized as multilateral or unilateral. In this regard, collective measures authorized under chapter VII of the UN Charter occupy a special status in the architecture of economic sanctions as they are binding upon all member States and supersede other treaty obligations according to Arts. 25 and 103 of the UN Charter.[267] It follows that UN mandated sanctions prove rather unproblematic from a normative point of view as long as the Security Council acts pursuant to its authorities as set out in the Charter.[268] On the other end of the spectrum are unilateral or autonomous sanctions, imposed by individual States or regional organizations against third States or non-State targets.

Before we dive into the main argument of the chapter, it is essential to note that there is no clear rule of customary international law *against* unilateral economic sanctions *per se*.[269] This is important, because if unilateral economic sanctions – or at least certain categories thereof – were clearly incompatible with other, easier identifiable, legal principles, there would

---

264 Andreas F Lowenfeld, *International Economic Law* (International Economic Law Series, 2nd ed. Oxford University Press 2008), 850.

265 Carter (n 260), para. 1.

266 Ibid., para. 6.

267 Matthew Happold, 'Economic Sanctions and International Law: An Introduction' in Matthew Happold and Paul Eden (eds), *Economic Sanctions and International Law* (Studies in international law volume 62. Hart Publishing 2016), 1.

268 Ibid., 2; Nigel D White and Ademola Abass, 'Countermeasures and Sanctions' in Malcolm D Evans (ed), *International Law* (5th ed. Oxford University Press 2018), 543 – 544.

269 Carter (n 260), para. 29; Omer Y Elagab, *The Legality of Non-Forcible Counter-Measures in International Law* (Oxford Monographs in International Law, Clarendon Press 1988), 212 – 213.

be less need to discuss the specific problem of extraterritorial sanctions with regard to rules of jurisdiction. There are, of course, voices to the contrary who argue that economic sanctions are incompatible with the principle of non-intervention because they are measures of a coercive nature that seek to induce change within a target State regarding its political, economic or social system.[270] Notably the Charter of the Organization of American States and numerous General Assembly Resolutions suggest that economic sanctions may be illegal under customary international law.[271] However, as is rightly pointed out, State sovereignty includes the freedom to trade and accordingly, to also not trade with other States as long as no international (treaty) obligations are breached.[272] The extensive State practice strongly suggests that unilateral economic sanctions are generally accepted under customary international law, a view that is also supported by the ICJ opinion in *Nicaragua*.[273]

Depending on the scope of the measures, economic sanctions may be categorized as comprehensive, sectoral or targeted. At least at the UN level, comprehensive sanctions have somewhat fallen out of favour after

---

270 White and Abass (n 268), 536; Natalino Ronzitti, 'Sanctions as Instruments of Coercive Diplomacy: An International Law Perspective' in Natalino Ronzitti (ed), *Coercive Diplomacy, Sanctions and International Law* (Brill Nijhoff 2016), 13.

271 Art. 20 of the Charter of the OAS provides: 'No State may use or encourage the use of coercive measures of an economic or political character in order to force the sovereign will of another State and obtain from it advantages of any kind.' See also: UNGA Resolution 2131 (21 Dec 1965) A/RES/20/2131 (XX), Declaration on Principles of International Law concerning Friendly Relations and Cooperation among States in accordance with the Charter of the United Nation, UNGA Resolution 2625 (24 Oct 1970) UN Doc A/RES/2625 (XXV), Charter of Economic Rights and Duties of States, UNGA Resolution 3281 (12 Dec 1974) UN Doc A/RES/3281(XXIX).

272 Sarah H Cleveland, 'Norm Internalization and U.S. Economic Sanctions' (2001) 26(1) YaleJIntLaw 1, 53; Daniel H Joyner, 'International Legal Limits on the Ability of States to Lawfully Impose International Economic/Financial Sanctions' in Ali Z Marossi and Marisa R Bassett (eds), *Economic Sanctions under International Law* (T.M.C. Asser Press 2015), 86; In reality, of course, modern States are often restrained in their economic conduct by bilateral and multilateral treaties, in particular by investment treaties and the WTO framework. However, despite the fact that economic sanctions disrupt trade and investment flows, the compatibility of unilateral economic sanctions with these regimes remains largely 'untested'. See on this, Tom Ruys and Cedric Ryngaert, 'Secondary Sanctions: A Weapon out of Control? The International Legality of, and European Responses to, US Secondary Sanctions' [2020] BYIL, 30.

273 ICJ, *Case concerning military and paramilitary activities in and against Nicaragua (Nicaragua v United States of America)* [1986] ICJ Rep 14 (1986), 126.

the humanitarian catastrophe caused by the Iraq sanctions regime, which has ignited the discussion whether human rights limitations existed regarding the effects of coercive economic measures.[274] To avoid collateral damage, States and international organizations have subsequently moved away from such sweeping sanctions and began to target more specifically the individuals and organizations responsible for or associated with a reprehensible situation.[275]

Where the sanctions seek to induce change in the behaviour of a State, these 'smart' sanctions are often levied against the governing elite and leaders within the country, including the individuals designing or implementing the opposed policy. Indeed, all active UN and EU sanctions as of 2016 have had some sort of targeted component.[276]

However, targeted sanctions have also found broader usage distinct from economic sanctions in State-to-State relations, as they may also be levied against non-State actors, including terrorist networks and other criminal organizations.[277] Technically, smart sanctions usually involve the freezing of assets of the affected individuals and a broad prohibition on engaging with them, including travel bans.[278]

---

274 Marc Bossuyt, 'The Adverse Consequences of Economic Sanctions on the Enjoyment of Human Rights' (2000); Michael Reisman and Douglas L Stevick, 'The Applicability of International Law Standards to United Nations Economic Sanctions Programmes' (1998) 9 EJIL 86, 103; see also for a moe extensive Analysis of this and related issues: Cleveland (n 272).

275 Lowenfeld (n 264), 875 – 876 describes the shift from comprehensive to smart sanctions during the Iraq regime.

276 Happold (n 267), 8.

277 See for instance UNSC Resolution 1382 (29 Nov 2001), UN Doc S/RES/1382 (2001).

278 Since smart sanctions are a relatively recent development, it is yet unclear whether they are capable of achieving their high objectives, inducing change in the behaviour of the responsible targets while alleviating the suffering of the general population, see White and Abass (n 268), 543; However, in a somewhat ironic twist, these 'smart' sanctions themselves have become subjects of legal scrutiny in relation to the protection of individual rights. On multiple occasions, courts have (albeit indirectly) found deficiencies in UN collective sanctions in particular with regard to procedural rights for the affected to effectively contest a wrongful targeting by the competent authority, see CJEU, C-402/05 P, *Kadi and Al Barakaat International Foundation v Council and Commission* [2008] ECR I-06351; For these cases see also below, at C.II.5b) Practice in Europe.

### b) Primary and Secondary Sanctions

As already indicated, the effectiveness of unilateral sanctions is severely curtailed by third actors willing to step in and take up commercial relationships in the place of the sanctioning country. For instance, while the United States imposed sanctions on Sudan and thus prohibited its own citizens from dealing with the government accused of genocide, China has swept in and become Sudan's largest trading partner, thus weakening the US policy.[279] In these cases, States have sometimes sought to strengthen their primary economic sanctions against the direct target and to prevent sanctions 'busting' through third countries by also disrupting commercial relationships between Sudan and China. These measures, which seek to deter third parties (in our case China) from engaging with the actual sanctions target (Sudan) are sometimes referred to as 'secondary sanctions', as opposed to the primary sanctions solely concerning the target State.

Secondary sanctions can therefore be defined as any measure that regulates the economic relationship between two foreign actors. They may come in different forms, as there are multiple ways on how a regulation may 'persuade' a third party to uphold the primary sanction. Sometimes, the crucial fact may be that the third party is a subsidiary of a domestic parent company, thus the secondary sanction is based on a parental-control doctrine. Other times, third State companies are targeted because they make use of domestic means of communication, such as interbank monetary transfer mechanisms.

In academic literature, the term 'secondary sanctions' is used unevenly. Some authors restrict the concept to measures in which the sanctioning State imposes economic penalties – such as restrictions to market access – on third State actors that engage in commercial relationships with the primary target.[280] In our example above for instance, this may entail the United States prohibiting domestic persons from trading with Chinese companies that in turn deal with Sudan. However, in line with the broader concept adopted above, these measures are really only one specific category of secondary sanctions.[281] To avoid confusion, this chapter will use the term 'secondary trade boycott' for these particular regulations.[282]

---

279 Meyer, 'Second Thoughts on Secondary Sanctions' (n 151), 906.

280 See e.g., Perry S Bechky, 'Sanctions and the Blurred Boundaries of International Economic Law' (2018) 83 Missouri Law Review 1, 10 – 11.

281 A similar definition is used by Ruys and Ryngaert (n 272), 7.

282 See e.g. Meyer, 'Second Thoughts on Secondary Sanctions' (n 151), 926.

### c) Overview of US Economic Sanctions

Unilateral US economic sanctions and the reactions of other States thereto form the core of the following analysis on extraterritoriality. Thus, it is worth to provide an overview of the complex legal framework governing this area of regulation, as it includes broadly framed and sometimes overlapping legislation, executive orders and implementing regulations.[283]

During the Cold War era, the Trading with the Enemy Act 1917 (**TWEA**)[284] provided the most important statutory basis for the imposition of economic restrictions. Among others, this authority was invoked for measures targeting China, North Korea and Cuba of which some are still in force today. In an effort to restrain the excessive powers granted to the President under TWEA, Congress limited the application of the act to times of war (though existing sanctions were to remain in place) and adopted a new statute, the International Emergency Economic Powers Act 1977 (**IEEPA**),[285] which subsequently became the core statutory authority for most economic sanctions in place today.[286] Sec. 203 of the act provides that, upon the declaration of a national emergency with respect to a foreign threat to the national security, foreign policy or economy, the president may impose a wide range of transaction restrictions, typically through executive orders. For instance, the first sanctions against Iran following the occupation of the Teheran embassy in 1979 were implemented through executive orders based on the IEEPA.[287] Although the declaration of national emergency may in principle only remain effective for the duration of one year, they can be, and in fact have been, renewed continuously.

Apart from the IEEPA and executive orders based on the statute, the US Congress has enacted a number of independent pieces of legislation codifying economic sanctions that may or may not interact with the executive orders. For instance, The internationally strongly criticized Iran and Libya Sanctions Act of 1996 (**ISA**) as amended by the Comprehensive Iran

283 For a more comprehensive overview over U.S. economic sanctions, see Meredith Rathbone, Peter Jeydel and Amy Lentz, 'Sanctions, sanctions everywhere: Forging a path through complex transnational sanctions laws' (2013) 44(3) Georgetown Journal of International Law 1055.

284 Trading with the Enemy Act, Pub. L. No. 65–91 (40 Stat 411), 12 U.S.C. §§ 95a – 95b and 50 U.S.C. App. §§ 1–44.

285 International Emergency Economic Powers Act 1977, Pub. L. No. 95–223 (91 Stat 2626), 50 U.S.C. §§ 1701 ff.

286 Lowenfeld (n 264), 892 – 893.

287 E.O. 12170 of November 14, 1979.

Sanctions, Accountability, and Divestment Act of 2010 (**CISADA**) and other statutes provided for entirely new kinds of restrictions on business with Iran.[288] On a lower level, these statutes and executive orders are mainly administered by the Office of Foreign Asset Control (**OFAC**), an agency within the US Treasury, which issues and updates regulations based on these measures. The core of the Iran sanctions for instance is codified in the Iranian Transactions and Sanctions Regulations (**ITSR**) and the Iranian Financial Sanctions Regulations (**IFSR**).[289] OFAC is also responsible for maintaining various sanctions lists, which contain the names of individuals and companies subject to targeted sanctions and with whom US persons are prohibited from dealing.[290]

OFAC is also the agency primarily responsible for the enforcement of economic sanctions. However, depending on the type of offense and the regulation violated, the US Department of Justice (**DoJ**), the Bureau of Industry and Security (**BIS**) and even individual State authorities may be involved.[291] While the IEEPA foresees both civil regulatory and criminal penalties for violation of executive orders based on the statute,[292] most cases against corporate offenders are settled through a variety of measures, including deferred prosecution agreements and guilty pleas. Importantly therefore, US enforcement actions based on sanctions violations, including their often controversial jurisdictional reach, are rarely argued and decided in court. While the United States maintains some sort of economic sanctions against a whole range of countries, non-State actors and individuals, the most controversial and economically significant programmes include those against Cuba, Iran and Russia.

---

288 Iran and Libya Sanctions Act of 1996, §§ 4, 5, Pub. L. No. 104–172, 50 U.S.C.§ 1701 (1996 & Supp. III 1997); Comprehensive Iran Sanctions, Accountability, and Divestment Act of 2010, Pub. L. No. 111–195 (2010).

289 31 C.F.R. Part 560 and 31 C.F.R. Part 561.

290 See for instance the Specially Designated Nationals And Blocked Persons List, available at https://home.treasury.gov/policy-issues/financial-sanctions/specially-designated-nationals-and-blocked-persons-list-sdn-human-readable-lists, last accessed on 13 April 2022.

291 Bruce Zagaris, *International White Collar Crime: Cases and Materials* (2. ed. Cambridge University Press 2015), 214.

292 IEEPA, Sec. 206, 50 U.S.C. § 1705.

aa) US Sanctions against Cuba

Sanctions against Cuba, in particular in the form of the Cuban Asset Control Regulation (**CACR**),[293] have been in place since the early 1960s. Their scope is comprehensive as they prohibit virtually all transactions with Cuba or Cuban nationals as well as all transactions involving 'blocked' property, that is property in which Cuba or a Cuban national has any interest. Additionally, unlike many other sanctions programmes, the jurisdiction of the Cuban regulations explicitly extends to foreign incorporated subsidiaries of domestic companies.[294] However, the most significant development of the sanctions regime since its initial promulgation has been the adoption of the widely controversial Helms-Burton Act in 1996. In particular, the statute created a private claim of recovery against any person worldwide who was 'trafficking' in property, in which the claimant had an interest, if the property had before been 'confiscated' by the Castro government in Cuba.[295] In essence, this strongly extraterritorial provision meant that any foreign investor in Cuba could potentially be sued in US courts for transacting with Cuba or Cuban nationals if the transaction concerned property previously owned by the United States or its citizens.

bb) US Sanctions against Iran

Similar to its policy on Cuba, the United States also maintains a comprehensive embargo on Iran. While primary sanctions have existed since the Tehran hostage crisis in 1979, sanctions with extraterritorial implications have only been enacted through the aforementioned ISA. The ISA was intended to complement the previously existing executive orders as Congress feared that foreign investors engaging in Iran would diminish the effectiveness of US sanctions.[296] Thus, Sec. 5 (a) of the ISA prohibits investment by anyone, wherever located, into the Iranian petroleum sector, thought to be the country's major financial lifeline. Individuals and companies failing to comply with this provision could face a number of different sanctions, subject to executive discretion, including denial of assistance by

293 31 C.F.R. Part 515, Cuban Asset Control Regulation (CACR).

294 31 C.F.R. § 515.329.

295 Sec. 301 – 306, Cuban Liberty and Democratic Solidarity Act, Pub. L. No. 104–114, 12 (1996), 110 Stat. 785, 22 U.S.C. §§ 6021–6091.

296 Rathbone, Jeydel and Lentz (n 283), 1084.

the US Export-Import Bank, the denial of export licenses to that person, a prohibition for US financial institutions to grant loans to that person and a prohibition for US government agencies to procure goods from that person.[297] Similar to the Helms-Burton-Act, the ISA irritated other US trading partners because of its strong extraterritorial effects. However, in reaction to the growing nuclear threat posed by Iran, restrictive measures, applicable to both US and foreign persons and entities, were subsequently even tightened and expanded to other economic areas through CISADA, various executive orders and other pieces of standalone legislation over the years.[298]

Consequently, the adoption of the Joint Comprehensive Plan of Action (**JCPOA**)[299] between the P5+1 (China, France, Germany, Russia, the UK, and the United States), the EU, and Iran on 14 July 2015 marked a turning point in US sanctions policy. Under the JCPOA, colloquially known as the Iran Nuclear Deal, Iran committed to limit its nuclear activities in return for relief from certain economic sanctions maintained by the United States, the EU and the UN Security Council. While the EU lifted significant parts of its restrictive measures targeting Iran, the United States still maintained most of its primary sanctions even after the implementation of the JCPOA. However, presumably to coordinate action with the EU, the United States eased its extraterritorial sanctions directed towards non-US persons. Among others, under the JCPOA, the United States waived the application of the above-mentioned Sec. 5 (a) ISA.[300] Moreover, the adoption of the JCPOA led to the issuance of a new General License H by OFAC, which authorized most Iran transactions for domestic controlled foreign subsidiaries.[301]

However, less than three years after the implementation of the Iran Nuclear Deal, the US Government under President Trump claimed that Iran had violated the agreement and subsequently decided to withdraw from the JCPOA and to re-install lifted extraterritorial sanctions against Iran.[302]

297 Sec. 5 (a) and Sec. 6 of ISA.

298 For an overview of the different legal authorities: Dianne E Rennack, 'Iran: U.S. Economic Sanctions and the Authority to Lift Restrictions' (May 2018) https://fas.org/sgp/crs/mideast/R43311.pdf.

299 Annex A to UNSC Resolution 2232 (20 Jul 2015), UN Doc S/RES/2231 (2015).

300 See Sec. 4 and Sec. 4.3.2. of Annex II of the JCPOA.

301 See Sec. 17.5 of Annex V with Sec. 5.1.2 of Annex II of the JCPOA.

302 See Presidential Memorandum (8 May 2018), 'Ceasing U.S. Participation in the JCPOA and Taking Additional Action to Counter Iran's Malign Influence and Deny Iran All Paths to a Nuclear Weapon', available at https://trumpwhitehous

Since the other parties to the Nuclear Deal, in particular the European nations, are still committed to preserve the agreement and by extension their economic interest in Iran, the recent US action has been strongly condemned.[303]

cc) US Sanctions against Russia

In response to the 2014 annexation of Crimea and the ensuing unrest in other parts of Eastern Ukraine, the United States, together with the EU and other States, imposed economic sanctions against the Russian Federation. The initial executive orders were based again on the IEEPA and targeted those individuals and companies deemed responsible for the Ukraine situation. Subsequently, standalone legislation was adopted to complement these measures. Of particular interest for the present research is the Ukraine Freedom Support Act (**UFSA**)[304] as the statute contained provisions similar to those of the ISA. They required the President to impose ISA-style sanctions on foreign investors involved in Russian crude oil projects, including the withdrawal of sanctioned persons from Export-Import Bank assistance, the prohibition of public procurement through sanctioned persons, as well as a ban on banking and property transactions with these persons. However, the UFSA's strong extraterritorial implications were somewhat mitigated by US President Obama, who, at the time of signing the bill, stated that he did not intend to impose the sanctions under UFSA at that time.[305]

US economic sanctions intensified significantly when it became clear that Russia had attempted to interfere in the 2016 US elections. In June 2017, the United States passed the Countering America's Adversaries

e.archives.gov/presidential-actions/ceasing-u-s-participation-jcpoa-taking-additional-action-counter-irans-malign-influence-deny-iran-paths-nuclear-weapon/, last accessed on 13 April 2022.

303 See Joint statement from Prime Minister Theresa May, Chancellor Angela Merkel and President Emmanuel Macron following President Trump's statement on Iran, https://www.gov.uk/government/news/joint-statement-from-prime-minister-may-chancellor-merkel-and-president-macron-following-president-trumps-statement-on-iran, last accessed on 13 April 2022.

304 Ukraine Freedom Support Act of 2014, H.R. 5859, Pub. L. No. 113–272 (2014).

305 The White House, Statement by the President on the Ukraine Freedom Support Act, available at https://obamawhitehouse.archives.gov/the-press-office/2014/12/18/statement-president-ukraine-freedom-support-act, last accessed on 13 April 2022.

Through Sanctions Act (**CAATSA**),[306] which strengthened existing sanctions by codifying a number of executive orders, cutting back presidential discretion in the imposition of sanctions and widening their scope of application to cover even more Russian energy, intelligence and defence projects. Similar to ISA and UFSA, CAATSA contained provisions that allowed the imposition of sanctions against foreign economic operators. Sec. 232 of the CAATSA drew particularly hostile response from some European nations as it prohibited the investment by anyone into Russian pipeline projects, ostensibly targeting the Nord Stream 2 Pipeline.[307] Nord Stream 2 is a controversial project running from Russia through the Baltic Sea to Western Europe and would potentially allow Russia to cut off gas supply to the Ukraine without threatening supply of other European States. Therefore, the pipeline is politically strongly opposed by the United States but was initially supported by Western European nations, in particular, Germany and Austria. CAATSA has subsequently drawn strong criticism from these countries.[308]

### 2. The Extension of Personality-based Jurisdiction to Foreign Subsidiaries

#### a) Practice in the United States

With some notable exceptions, the personal scope of application of modern US economic sanctions is generally restricted to US persons, defined as 'any United States citizen, permanent resident alien, entity organized under the laws of the United States or any jurisdiction within the United States (including foreign branches), or any person in the United States'.[309] This rule already provides for a rather broad interpretation of the personality principle as it extends to both permanent resident aliens and foreign branches of US entities. Especially the assertion of jurisdiction over foreign

306 Countering America's Adversaries Through Sanctions Act, H.R. 3364, Pub. L. No. 115–44 (2017).
307 CAATSA, Sec. 232.
308 Federal Foreign Office, Press Release, Foreign Minister Gabriel and Austrian Federal Chancellor Kern on the imposition of Russia sanctions by the US Senate, https://www.auswaertiges-amt.de/en/newsroom/news/170615-kern-russland/290666, last accessed on 13 April 2022.
309 See for example 31 C.F.R. § 560.314.

branches has at times led to conflict of jurisdiction situations with the State in which the branch operated.[310]

More controversially however, the United States also has a long tradition of extending its sanctions legislation to foreign subsidiaries incorporated abroad that are 'controlled' by US nationals. In 1942 for instance, Treasury issued an order under the TWEA that broadened the definition of the term 'persons subject to jurisdiction of the United States' to include 'any corporation or other entity, wherever organized or doing business, owned or controlled by [US] persons'.[311] As already mentioned above, even today, US economic sanctions contain jurisdictional extensions covering foreign incorporated subsidiaries of US companies, in particular the programmes targeting both Cuba and Iran.[312]

Even though the issue remains controversial, State practice suggests that US authorities see no legal barriers in enforcing these provisions. In 2014 for instance, OFAC initiated proceedings directly against the foreign subsidiary of a US corporation for violation of the CACR. The government agency alleged that CWT B.V. (**CWT**), a Dutch incorporated company, breached Cuban sanctions 'when its business units mostly outside the United States provided services related to travel to or from Cuba'.[313] It is certainly questionable why a Dutch company, which, by the own admission of OFAC, conducted business mostly outside of the United States, should be subject to US jurisdiction. The enforcement information by OFAC takes no issue with that, reasoning that under the TWEA and the CACR, CWT was brought under the jurisdiction of the United States after it became majority-owned by US persons in 2006. As with other similar allegations, the jurisdictional assertions were never contested in court: the case was settled, this time for the payment of almost USD 6 million.[314]

Apart from the Cuban sanctions, amendments of the Iran sanctions enacted in 2012 also affect foreign incorporated subsidiaries. Sec. 218 of

310 *Libyan Arab Foreign Bank v Bankers Trust Co* [1989] 1 QB 728.

311 TWEA, Sec. 5(b); US Treasury Public Circulary No. 18, 30 March 1942, 7 Fed. Reg. 2503 (1 April 1942).

312 See for instant, 31 C.F.R. § 515.329, Cuban Asset Control Regulation (CACR).

313 OFAC, Enforcement Information for April 18, 2014, https://home.treasury.gov/system/files/126/20140418_cwt.pdf, last accessed on 13 April 2022.

314 Ibid.

the Iran Threat Reduction and Syria Human Rights Act of 2012 (**ITRA**),[315] implemented through 31 C.F.R. § 560.215, provides that any

> 'entity that is owned or controlled by a United States person and established or maintained outside the United States is prohibited from knowingly engaging in any transaction, directly or indirectly, with the Government of Iran or any person subject to the jurisdiction of the Government of Iran that would be prohibited pursuant to this part if engaged in by a United States person or in the United States'.[316]

In effect, the provision prohibits US-controlled, foreign subsidiaries from engaging in businesses with Iran. Unlike the Cuban sanctions however, enforcement actions such as the imposition of fines are not to be directed against the foreign controlled subsidiary but restricted to the parent company, which is strictly liable for any violation of its subsidiaries.[317]

As already briefly mentioned, US economic sanctions against Iran targeting foreign subsidiaries of domestic corporations were lifted with the issuance of the General Licence H following the implementation of the JCPOA. However, this development did not suggest a change in US government attitude in the sense that it was rejecting jurisdictional assertions regarding controlled foreign subsidiaries. Rather, the explicit language of the JCPOA that the United States 'will license non-U.S. entities that are owned or controlled by a U.S. person' to engage in activities with Iran leads to the conclusion that the US government still claimed legal authority over controlled foreign subsidiaries, but simply decided to permit their transactions for political expedience.[318] The sanctions relief was necessary, as otherwise, EU based companies, now being encouraged to re-establish trade with Iran, could have found themselves bound by contradicting US rules. This conclusion is also supported by action from the Trump administration, which revoked the General License on 27 June 2018 after previously withdrawing from the Iran Nuclear Deal.[319] Thus, foreign companies controlled by US nationals are again obliged to comply with US

---

315 Iran Threat Reduction and Syria Human Rights Act of 2012, Pub. L. No. 112–158.

316 See ITRA, Sec. 218, 31 C.F.R. § 560.215 from December 26, 2012; See also similar rules in Sec. 4 E.O. 16328 of October 12, 2012 and 31 C.F.R. § 561.202.

317 See 31 C.F.R. § 560.701 (a) (3).

318 See Sec. 5.1.2 of Annex II of the JCPOA.

319 See OFAC, Revocation of JCPOA-Related General Licenses, https://home.treasury.gov/policy-issues/financial-sanctions/recent-actions/20180627, last accessed on 13 April 2022.

economic sanctions. In sum therefore, the short-lived sanctions relief does not support the conclusion that the US government will refrain from using control-based jurisdiction anytime soon, a fact that is also evidenced by its continued attitude towards the Cuban sanctions.

### b) Practice in Europe

#### aa) The Personal Scope of EU Restrictive Measures

More often than not, the EU and its member States have viewed US jurisdictional assertions based on parental control with suspicion. Consequently, they have also refrained from exercising jurisdiction over non-EU subsidiaries. Since the Treaty of Lisbon, the authority to impose sanctions, in the EU termed restrictive measures, is vested in the Union under the Common Foreign and Security Policy in Art. 215 of the Treaty on the Functioning of the European Union. Since 2008, regulations implementing restrictive measures have a more or less unified scope of application. With regard to the personality principle, they apply to any person inside or outside the territory of the Union who is a national of a member State and to any legal person, entity or body which is incorporated or constituted under the law of a member State.[320]

Although the provision mentions neither controlled branches nor subsidiaries, the dominant view is that EU restrictive measures extend to branches as they are legally dependent parts of an EU company and thus 'incorporated or constituted under the law of a member State'.[321] Consequently, the wording suggests that subsidiaries incorporated in foreign nations are excluded.[322] This finding is confirmed by a systematic argument:

---

320 E.g. Art. 29 Council Regulation (EU) No 961/2010 of 25 October 2010 on restrictive measures against Iran and repealing Regulation (EC) No 423/2007; See further Tobias Schöppner, *Wirtschaftssanktionen durch Bereitstellungsverbote* (Zugl.: Münster, Univ. Diss, 2013. Schriftenreihe des Europäischen Forums für Aussenwirtschaft, Verbrauchsteuern und Zoll e.V. an der Westfälischen Wilhelms-Universität Münster vol 51, Mendel 2013), 110 ff.

321 Bastian Mehle and Volkmar Mehle, 'Die notwendige Einhaltung von EU-Embargoregelungen durch Unternehmen mit Sitz in Drittstaaten' (2015) 61(7) Recht der internationalen Wirtschaft 397, 398; see also FAQ of the Ministry of Foreign Affairs of Finland, https://um.fi/sanctions-questions-and-answers, last accessed 13 April 2022.

322 Ibid., 398.

Certain provisions of the EU regulations concerning Iran explicitly refer to control and ownership as criteria in determining whether a person is an Iranian entity and therefore a sanctioned target.[323] *E contrario*, one can infer that the Council of the European Union was aware of the difference between corporate branches and subsidiaries and thus deliberately excluded the latter. Along these lines, several member State authorities have stated that the scope of application of restrictive measures does not extend to foreign owned subsidiaries.[324] Similarly, the General Court (**EGC**) has held, in an *obiter dictum*, that restrictive measures do not affect the conduct of foreign financial institutions 'established in a non-member State and constituted under the law of that State.'[325] Exceptions to this general rule may exist if the foreign subsidiary is in fact an *alter ego* of the EU parent company or if the parent company is acting through its subsidiary precisely to evade restrictive measures, contrary to the prohibition of circumvention.[326] Still, the EU's approach firmly differs from the control-based jurisdiction employed by OFAC.

#### bb) Diplomatic Protest against US Assertions of Control-based Jurisdiction

While the EU does adhere to this more restrictive interpretation of the personality principle in its own sanctions regulations, it has failed to maintain the same consistency in protesting US prescriptive jurisdiction regarding controlled foreign subsidiaries.

---

323 Art. 1 (m) Council Regulation (EU) No 961/2010 of 25 October 2010.

324 See FAQ of the Ministry of Foreign Affairs of Finland, https://um.fi/sanctions-questions-and-answers, last accessed 13 April 2022 and of the Belgian Foreign Public Service, http://diplomatie.belgium.be/en/policy/policy_areas/peace_and_security/sanctions, last accessed 13 April 2022.

325 CJEU, T-35/10, *Bank Melli Iran v Council of the European Union* [2013] ECLI:EU:T:2013:397, paras. 132.

326 See Art. 41 Council Regulation (EU) No 267/2012 of 23 March 2012 concerning restrictive measures against Iran and repealing Regulation (EU) No 961/2010; See also Marian Niestedt, 'Die Geltung des EU-Sanktionsrechts für Tochtergesellschaften und Niederlassungen' in Arnold Wallraff, Dirk Ehlers and Hans-Michael Wolffgang (eds), *Recht der Exportkontrolle: Bestandsaufnahme und Perspektiven: Handbuch zum Exportkontrollrecht.* zugleich Festgabe für Dr. Arnold Wallraff zum 65. Geburtstag (Schriften zum Aussenwirtschaftsrecht 2015), 262 – 264.

To be sure, the EC most notoriously did condemn the 1982 'Soviet Pipeline Regulations' by articulating a clear legal position regarding the control theory. The affair concerned the construction of a pipeline running from Western Siberia to Germany with the participation of various Western European firms. Following a crackdown in Poland, President Reagan, fearing that the pipeline project would strengthen Western European dependency on the Soviet Union, signed executive orders to prevent the realization of the project. Among others, the executive orders prohibited European companies to supply pipeline equipment to the Soviet Union if the equipment in question contained components of US origin, if it contained non-US origin components produced under US licences, or if the transaction involved any person subject to the jurisdiction of the United States, defined in the executive order to also include subsidiaries of US companies.[327]

Specifically, with regard to the assertion of jurisdiction over US controlled foreign subsidiaries, the EC argued that this measure could be based neither on the territoriality nor on the personality principle. According to the EC, territoriality was clearly not applicable because companies in the EC were not subject to the territorial competence of the United States.[328] The EC also rejected the personality principle because the EC based subsidiaries of US companies did not possess US nationality. In this regard, the EC argued that the nationality of corporations could not be determined based on control. Rather, according to *Barcelona Traction,* only two criteria were generally accepted to determine corporate nationality, i.e. the place of incorporation and the place of the registered office.[329] Thus, because the US executive orders lacked any recognized jurisdictional basis, it was illegal under international law.[330]

---

327 15 C.F.R. §§ 376, 379 and 385, Amendment of Oil and Gas Controls to the U.S.S.R of 24 June 1982, 21 ILM (1982) 853, 865 – 866; For an analysis of the executive order with regard to the control of US origin components and components produced under US licenses, see below at C.III.3. Jurisdiction Based on the 'Nationality' of Goods.

328 European Community: Note and Comments on the Amendments of 22 June 1982 to the Export Administration Act, Presented to the United States Department of State on 12 August 1982, 21 ILM (1982) 891, 893.

329 See *Barcelona Traction Light and Power Co, Ltd. (Belgium v Spain)* (n 126), 36.

330 European Community: Note and Comments on the Amendments of 22 June 1982 to the Export Administration Act, Presented to the United States Department of State on 12 August 1982, 21 ILM (1982) 891, 893 – 894.

Likewise, the EU has reacted strongly against the re-instalment of Iran sanctions, including those targeting controlled foreign subsidiaries, after the failure of the JCPOA. In fact, the EU has currently reactivated Council Regulation (EC) No 2271/96, the EU blocking statute originally adopted in response to the ISA and the Helms-Burton Act.[331] To this end, the Commission has adopted Commission Delegated Regulation (EU) 2018/1100 to nullify the US regulations that currently extraterritorially affect EU companies.[332] In the explanatory memorandum to Commission Delegated Regulation (EU) 2018/1100, the Commission argues that the US measures, 'in so far as they unduly affect the interests of natural and legal persons established in the Union […]' are contrary to international law. However, the broadly framed explanatory memorandum does not distinguish between different sanctions measures so that it is unclear whether the Union took particular issue with control-based jurisdiction.[333]

Despite the examples mentioned above, the rejection of US jurisdictional claims based on the control theory does not seem to be a principled stance. Most notably, the EU did not react to the adoption of the ITRA in 2012 – implemented through 31 C.F.R. § 560.215 – even though these sanctions explicitly targeted controlled foreign subsidiaries. The lack of protest is significant because this was indeed the first time that any measure against Iran was extended to cover controlled companies abroad. The inconsistency of the EU's response is even more glaring because the EU currently protests Iran sanctions that were previously adopted through the ITRA in 2012, which were dropped after the implementation of the JCPOA, and then finally restored after the United States withdrew from the JCPOA. Thus, as far as the EU's rejection rests on international law, it could have raised the same reasons against the measures adopted through the ITRA in 2012, which the EU, however, did not react to.

331 Council Regulation (EC) No 2271/96 of 22 November 1996 protecting against the effects of the extra-territorial application of legislation adopted by a third country, and actions based thereon or resulting therefrom, [1996] OJ L 309/1.

332 Commission Delegated Regulation (EU) 2018/1100 of 6 June 2018 amending the Annex to Council Regulation (EC) No 2271/96 protecting against the effects of extra-territorial application of legislation adopted by a third country, and actions based thereon or resulting therefrom, [2018] LI 199/1.

333 Explanatory Memorandum to Commission Delegated Regulation (EU) …/… amending the Annex to Council Regulation (EC) No 2271/96 of 22 November 1996 protecting against the effects of extra-territorial application of legislation adopted by a third country, and actions based thereon or resulting therefrom, C(2018) 3572 final; For an explanation of General Licence H, see above at C.II.1c)bb) US Sanctions against Iran.

### cc) Jurisprudence with regard to US Assertions of Control-based Jurisdiction

European courts have also not formed a consistent position denouncing US regulation based on parental control even though they have frequently decided cases involving such practice. Typically, the decisions concern the non-performance of contracts or the non-satisfaction of other claims by US controlled subsidiaries or branches, allegedly because US embargo regulations bar them from fulfilling the claims. However, such lawsuits involving conflicts between US extraterritorial sanctions and host State contract law are regularly not decided using public international law arguments. Rather, the cases are usually resolved through conflict-of-law principles or the rule to not apply foreign public law provisions.[334]

The often-cited *Fruehauf* case in the 1960s constitutes an early example: Fruehauf was a French incorporated, US owned company that entered into a sales contract with goods eventually destined for China. Based on the control theory (and on the nationality of the company directors), the US Treasury ordered the American parent company to prohibit the execution of the contract due to economic sanctions on China. The French minority board members of Fruehauf sued in France and requested the court to give them leave to fulfil the contract. The Court eventually did decide in favour of the French board members; however, it reached its conclusion not by relying on international law grounds but rather on a balancing between the interests of the American shareholders and the imminent unemployment of 600 employees should Fruehauf not execute the contract.[335]

In contrast, only few court judgments explicitly refer to public international law: During the *Pipeline* incident, a private claim for performance was litigated before a Dutch court. In its opinion, the court gave judgment for the plaintiff, stating explicitly that the US regulation violated international law according to traditional principles of jurisdiction.[336] Considerations of public international law were also (partly) decisive in a 2011 German court case involving a bank transfer that was to be halted according to both US and EU regulations concerning the nuclear proliferation

334 See e.g. Art. 9 Regulation (EC) No 593/2008 of the European Parliament and of the Council of 17 June 2008 on the law applicable to contractual obligations (Rome I).

335 *Société Fruehauf Corp. v Massardy*, 1968 D.S. Jur. 147, 1965, 5 ILM 476 (1966).

336 *Compagnie européenne des Pétroles S.A. v Sensor Nederland B.V.*, The Hague District Court (17 September 1982), 22 ILM (1983) 66, 72.

activities of Iran. While the transaction was covered by similar US and EU regulations, the parties where disputing whether the defendant had to transfer the blocked funds to the German Central Bank, which was the required action for asset freezes in the EU. Even though the reasoning of the judgment is somewhat imprecise, it is clear that the court considered the extraterritorial US regulation as a potential violation of the sovereignty of other States and ruled that the EU regulation therefore had priority in this case.[337]

In more recent times, courts in Germany,[338] France[339] and the UK[340] have decided comparable cases with different outcomes. German courts have regularly ruled against giving effect to extraterritorial US sanctions. For instance, one case concerned a claim against an insurance company based on transportation damages sustained by Iranian goods. While the insurer admitted the damage was covered by the insurance contract in question, it refused to satisfy the claim as it has, in the meantime, become part of a US corporate group and fulfilling the claim would have contradicted US sanctions regulations. The insurer thus requested the court to give effect to US sanctions by voiding the contract. The court, however, was not persuaded and instead demanded satisfaction by the US insurer contrary to US embargoes.[341]

In contrast, the UK High Court of Justice recently ruled that a UK borrower may deny paying interest on a loan provided by an entity owned by a sanctioned person. The court argued that applicable US secondary sanctions constituted 'mandatory provisions of law' allowing for non-payment. This decision is particularly significant because the UK borrower in question was not even subject to US sanctions at the time of the judgment

---

337 OLG Frankfurt am Main, Judgment of 9 May 2011, 23 U 30/10.

338 LG Hamburg, Judgment of 3 December 2014, 401 HKO 7/14.

339 Cour d'appel de Paris (pole 5, ch 4), 25 February 2015, n° 12/23757.

340 *Lamesa Investments Ltd v Cynergy Bank Ltd* [2019] EWHC 1877 (Comm).

341 LG Hamburg, Judgment of 3 December 2014, 401 HKO 7/14; This decision is in sharp contrast to a more dated decision from the 1960s: There, the Federal Court of Justice rendered null and void contracts that violated US sanctions against the East bloc based on § 138 of the German Civil Code, the provision concerning legal transactions contrary to public policy and morals. Specifically, the court stated that: 'It is undisputed that the American embargo regulations are designed to uphold the peace and freedom of the West. The measures, therefore, were taken not only in the interest of the United States, but in the interest of the entire free Western World and therefore also in the interest of the FRG.' See BGH, Judgment of 21 December 1960, VIII ZR 1/60, reported in BGHZ 34, 169; translation in Lowenfeld (n 264), 910.

but would only potentially be sanctioned in case of performance.[342] The different outcomes in these cases suggest that even courts have not found a consistent approach to US sanctions.

### c) Comparative Normative Analysis

The above analysis of relevant State practice has demonstrated that the United States frequently utilises the corporate relationship between domestic parent companies and foreign subsidiaries to extend its economic sanctions regulations. In particular, US sanctions against Cuba assume that all US-controlled foreign subsidiaries are unconditionally subject to US jurisdiction. Even though US sanctions against Iran similarly claim control-based jurisdiction, the situation is more nuanced here. Indeed, while the wording of 31 C.F.R. § 560.215 directly addresses foreign incorporated subsidiaries, the enforcement of this provision is restricted to the domestic parent company. It was further demonstrated above that the EU has failed to mount a consistent response rejecting US jurisdictional assertions *vis-à-vis* foreign subsidiaries. I will argue here that there are two reasons for this development: First, EU reactions to US sanctions are grounded in political expediency and remain in the realm of inter-subjectivity and second, the legality of assertions of jurisdiction over controlled foreign subsidiaries remains contentious under customary international law principles.

The EU has frequently voiced the most vehement protest against US sanctions when it disagreed with the United States not only in its legal analysis, but also more fundamentally in its economic and foreign policy position. This is particularly clearly illustrated with regard to Iran. Most notably, the EU has mounted no objection against the adoption of the ITRA in 2012, even though the act introduced, for the first time, sanctions against Iran targeting controlled subsidiaries. Conversely, the EU has voiced vocal opposition against the re-instalment of the same sanctions after the Trump administration withdrew from the Iran Nuclear Deal. Comparing the two episodes, it becomes clear that the different political landscape and the EU's willingness to protect its own businesses against US interference were likely the main drivers of EU action. While in 2012, both EU and US economic sanctions had largely aligned and companies on both sides of the Atlantic were winding down their Iran engagement,

342 *Lamesa Investments Ltd v Cynergy Bank Ltd* [2019] EWHC 1877 (Comm); however, see also *Libyan Arab Foreign Bank v Bankers Trust Co* [1989] 1 QB 728.

the interests were diametrically different after the US withdrawal from the JCPOA: Here, EU businesses had just started to re-invest in Iran, an engagement that was now threatened after the Trump administration broke away from the JCPOA.[343]

However, political alignment with the United States may not completely explain the EU's inconsistent reaction. In fact, the EU sometimes also failed to protest US control-based jurisdiction despite the existence of a fundamental policy disagreement. This was most notably the case in relation to the highly publicized CWT incident, where neither the Netherlands (where CWT is incorporated) nor France (where CWT has its global headquarters) protested against the heavy fine levied by OFAC for violation of US sanctions against Cuba. This is even more astonishing when taking into account the personal repercussions of this incident: Specifically, CWT France had previously directed its staff to comply with the US embargo and subsequently let go of two regional directors involved in the breach.[344] It seems, therefore, that a consistent response to US jurisdictional claims over controlled foreign subsidiaries is also complicated by normative reasons: In fact, whether these measures actually violate customary international law has remained controversial.

To be sure, there is indeed a strong position in academic commentary arguing that control-based jurisdiction should be generally considered a violation of international law: According to this position, exercises of jurisdiction have to satisfy either the territoriality principle or one of the exceptional bases legitimizing extraterritorial jurisdiction. Both are not the case here. On the one hand, measures such as the US sanctions against Cuba cannot be based on territoriality because the regulations strictly apply to foreign subsidiaries. On the other hand, this position also rejects the argument that extending jurisdiction to controlled subsidiaries can

343 See on this: European Commission, Press Release of 18 May 2018, 'European Commission acts to protect the interests of EU companies investing in Iran as part of the EU's continued commitment to the Joint Comprehensive Plan of Action', https://ec.europa.eu/commission/presscorner/detail/en/IP_18_3861, last accessed on 13 April 2022. Note, 'Developments in the Law – Extraterritoriality' (2011) 124 HarvLRev 1226 at 1252 ff. also sees the EU's unified trading strength, which makes it more sympathetic to extraterritorial trade measures of its own, as a possible explanation for the lack of reaction against the extension of Iran sanctions by the United States.

344 Fabrice Bugnot, 'Carlson Wagonlit Travel: les dessous de l'affaire cubaine', *L'echo touristique*, http://www.lechotouristique.com/article/carlson-wagonlit-travel-les-dessous-de-l-affaire-cubaine,68314, last accessed on 13 April 2022.

be legitimized through the active personality principle: As was stated in *Barcelona Traction*, corporate nationality under international law (bar certain exceptions) does not follow the control theory.[345] Therefore, because jurisdiction over foreign subsidiaries can be neither based on territoriality nor on an exceptional principle, it violates customary international law.

While this position does seem to be sound at first glance, it may in fact be an oversimplification. Specifically, it could be argued that jurisdiction based on the control-theory is in fact just a variation of territoriality. For instance, 31 C.F.R. § 560.215, a regulation typically cited as an example of jurisdiction based on the control theory,[346] provides that any

> 'entity that is owned or controlled by a United States person and established or maintained outside the United States is prohibited from knowingly engaging in any transaction, directly or indirectly, with the Government of Iran or any person subject to the jurisdiction of the Government of Iran […]'.[347]

This measure strictly addresses foreign incorporated subsidiaries. Therefore, applying the same logic as above, it can be justified neither by the territoriality nor by the active personality principle.

However, we could compare 31 C.F.R. § 560.215 to this fictitious regulation:

> 'A US-based corporation is subject to penalties if any foreign entity that it owns or controls knowingly engages in any transaction, directly or indirectly, with the Government of Iran or any person subject to the jurisdiction of the Government of Iran'.

Such a provision would only address companies based within the United States. At first glance, therefore, this rule seems like a perfectly valid exercise of territorial jurisdiction. Crucially, however, it could be argued that this fictitious rule is in fact substantially identical to 31 C.F.R. § 560.215. Because even though the fictitious regulation does not explicitly prohibit foreign subsidiaries from business with Iran, these subsidiaries will refrain from engaging with the sanctioned target to not jeopardize the

345 For this conclusion see Cedric Ryngaert, 'Extraterritorial Export Controls (Secondary Boycotts)' (2008) 7 Chinese Journal of International Law 625, 633; Beaucillon (n 26) 116 – 118; see already above at C.II.2 b)bb) Diplomatic Protest against US Assertions of Control-based Jurisdiction.

346 See Meyer, 'Second Thoughts on Secondary Sanctions' (n 151), 966; Ruys and Ryngaert (n 272), 19.

347 31 C.F.R. § 560.215.

parent company. The domestic US parent company will also direct all its controlled subsidiaries to stop any businesses with the sanctioned target. In effect therefore, both regulations should achieve the same substantial result.

In fact, every direct assertion of jurisdiction over a foreign subsidiary could be rephrased as a territorial regulation addressing the domestic parent company and holding it strictly liable for the conduct of its foreign subsidiaries abroad. However, when we are confronted with two substantially identical regulations, why should we consider one regulation a prohibited exercise of control-based jurisdiction and the other a perfectly valid example of territoriality? Would it not be more consistent to consider both 31 C.F.R. § 560.215 and our fictitious rule an exercise of territorial jurisdiction or to consider them both illegal assertions of control-based jurisdiction?

It could be argued that the actual and the fictitious regulation presented above are not completely identical because the fictitious rule seems to limit enforcement actions to domestic companies whereas 31 C.F.R. § 560.215 would – in principle – also allow for enforcement directly against the foreign subsidiary. However, this (potential) difference only concerns the possible target of enforcement actions and thus the scope of *enforcement* jurisdiction. The behaviour giving rise to such enforcement actions, i.e., the behaviour that is regulated through both the actual and the fictitious regulation, is the conduct of the foreign subsidiary abroad. The *prescriptive* reach of both regulations is thus the same. In reality, 31 C.F.R. § 560.215 is identical to our fictious rule even from an enforcement perspective because the provision actually restricts enforcement actions to the domestic parent companies. Nonetheless, 31 C.F.R. § 560.215 is widely considered as a prohibited exercise of control-based jurisdiction by the literature.[348]

Because the *prescriptive* reach of both the actual and the fictitious regulation is the same, consistency demands that they be treated the same way under international law. This is a point which has also been acknowledged by the widely regarded Restatement Third.[349] Accordingly, the Re-

348 Meyer, 'Second Thoughts on Secondary Sanctions' (n 151), 966; Ruys and Ryngaert (n 272), 19; additionally, the scope of enforcement jurisdiction is ultimately identical for both the actual and the fictitious regulation. In fact, for both regulations, physical enforcement is limited to the territorially-based corporate parents. This follows from the international law principle prohibiting extraterritorial enforcement.

349 *Restatement (Third) of the Foreign Relations Law of the United States* (n 5), § 414, Comment a).

statement argues that this kind of jurisdictional assertion cannot solely be assessed based on whether the regulation formally addresses the domestic parent company or the foreign subsidiary. Rather, the Restatement suggests that the legality of such assertions of jurisdiction can only be judged by considering a host of material circumstances, with the formal addressee being only one relevant factor. This seems to be the right approach as otherwise, the legality of extraterritorial sanctions would be reduced to a question of smart wording. Thus, not all assertions of jurisdiction targeting foreign subsidiaries should be regarded as illegal, and not all assertions of jurisdiction targeting domestic parent companies as legal, under customary international law.

To sum up this section, three conclusions may therefore be drawn. First, the normative status of control-based assertions of jurisdiction such as 31 C.F.R. § 560.215 remains unresolved; in fact, if the United States wanted to avoid criticism that 31 C.F.R. § 560.215 was violating customary international law, it could simply reformulate the regulation as a strict liability criterion in relation to the domestic corporate parent and achieve the same substantial result. Second, EU reactions to these regulations remain inconsistent and are largely determined by converging or diverging foreign policy objectives and the desire to protect domestic businesses against extraterritorial foreign regulations. Finally, the unclear legal status may also explain why courts in Europe deciding on those issues have generally eschewed public international law arguments and rather resorted to private conflict-of-law rules to handle these cases.[350]

### 3. Territoriality and US Dollar Transactions by non-US Financial Institutions

#### a) Practice in the United States

The United States not only adheres to a wide interpretation of the personality principle, which is extended to include domestic controlled foreign subsidiaries, but it also has a broad view of the territoriality principle, which serves as the doctrinal justification to bring most of the world's financial transactions within US jurisdiction. OFAC and other US agen-

350 For a US case using private international law, see *Chase Manhattan Bank v State of Iran*, 484 F. Supp. 832 (SDNY 1980) where the court had to decide on a preliminary injunction to stop a lawsuit in the UK.

cies have used this jurisdictional hook to successfully pursue numerous foreign financial institutions including the French Crédit Agricole[351] and BNP Paribas as well as the Dutch ING Bank[352] for sanctions violations. All of these cases have in the end led to settlement agreements between OFAC and the affected banks, often resulting in the banks paying fines in the hundreds of millions or even billions. Up to now, the banks have readily paid those expensive prices and refrained from challenging OFAC's jurisdictional assertions in court, presumably to avoid being cut off the important US financial market.[353]

The statutory basis for these far-reaching legal actions seems innocent enough: On the one hand, most embargo programs directed against a country as a whole (as in the case of Iran, Sudan and Cuba) contain a prohibition of direct or indirect exportation and re-exportation of goods, technology or services *from the United States* to the designated countries.[354] On the other hand, US targeted sanctions against individual subjects typically require the blocking of all economic resources of a designated person and the prohibition extends to 'all property and interests in property [...] that are in the United States [or] that hereafter *come within the United States*'.[355] This asset block (sometimes also termed freeze) does not only prevent any move or transfer of existing funds that would result in a change thereof but also prohibits any kind of business transaction in which the designated person has an interest.

The United States interprets these two rules as encompassing almost any (physical or financial) transaction with or on behalf of sanctioned subjects even if the transaction merely passes through US territory. Specifically, OFAC has interpreted the facilitation of US dollar payments from or to sanctioned countries, individuals and entities as both a prohibited exporta-

---

351 See Press Release, DoJ, 'Crédit Agricole Corporate and Investment Bank Admits to Sanctions Violations, Agrees to Forfeit $312 Million' (20 October 2015), http://www.justice.gov/opa/pr/cr-dit-agricole-corporate-and-investment-bank-admits-sanctions-violations-agrees-forfeit-312, last accessed on 13 April 2022.

352 See Press Release, DoJ, 'ING N.V. Agrees to Forfeit $619 Million for Illegal Transactions with Cuban and Iranian Entities' (12 June 2012), http://www.justice.gov/opa/pr/ing-bank-nv-agrees-forfeit-619-million-illegal-transactions-cuban-and-iranian-entities-0, last accessed on 13 April 2022.

353 Suzanne Katzenstein, 'Dollar Unilateralism: The New Frontline of National Security' (2015) 90 Indiana Law Journal 293, 312 f.

354 E.g. 31 C.F.R. § 560.204 (ITSR) and 31 C.F.R. § 538.205 (Sudanese Sanctions Regulations).

355 See e.g., Sec. 1 (b) E.O. 13382 of 1 July 2005; Sec. 1 E.O. 13599 of 5 February 2012.

tion or re-exportation of services *from the United States* and as dealing with property and interests in property that have *come within the United States*.[356] Therefore, the office claims jurisdiction over practically all money transfers worldwide, as long as they involve US dollars.

To understand OFAC's legal analysis in relation to payments in US dollars, it is very helpful to take a closer look at the mechanisms and operations of wire transfers. In its simplest form, both the sending party (originator) and the receiving party (beneficiary) of the funds have accounts at the same bank. In this case, the bank can settle the claims by debiting the originator's account and crediting the beneficiary's account (book transfer). However, if the involved parties have accounts at different banks, the process becomes more complicated. To move the money, the banks may maintain a correspondent relationship, which means that they operate correspondent accounts of each other. In this case, the sending bank will debit the originator's account and credit the correspondent account of the receiving bank. The receiving bank will in turn credit the beneficiary's account. Finally, if the involved banks do not maintain such a relationship, they may still transfer the funds if both banks have established accounts at a third, intermediary bank, which then settles the transaction.[357]

For US dollar transactions, banks have gone one-step further and established two centralized clearing systems, CHIPS (Clearing House Interbank Payment System) and Fedwire (Federal Reserve Wire Network), to communicate and to settle money transfers. In essence, both CHIPS and Fedwire are connected to the Federal Reserve Banks in the United States, which therefore have become something of intermediary banks for almost all US dollar transactions.[358] Thus, even when a French bank sends money to an Iranian bank, the funds will be technically crossing US banks as long as they involve US dollars. Similarly, when foreign financial institutions omit reference to sanctioned parties in their payment messages (also

356 See e.g., Department of the Treasury, Settlement Agreement between OFAC and BNP Paribas SA of 30 June 2014, COMPL-2013–193659, paras. 18 ff. https://home.treasury.gov/system/files/126/20140630_bnp_settlement.pdf, last accessed on 13 April 2022.

357 Barry E Carter and Ryan M Farha, 'Overview and Operation of the Evolving U.S. Financial Sanctions, Including the Example of Iran' (2013) 44(3) Georgetown Journal of International Law 903, 905 ff.

358 Sebastian v Allwörden, *US-Terrorlisten im deutschen Privatrecht: Zur kollisions- und sachrechtlichen Problematik drittstaatlicher Sperrlisten mit extraterritorialer Wirkung* (Studien zum ausländischen und internationalen Privatrecht v.313, Mohr Siebeck 2014), 55.

referred to as 'stripping') and thus cause US banks to clear the transaction, the United States claims jurisdiction based on the effects doctrine where the effect is a violation of US sanctions by the deceived US bank.[359]

As already mentioned, US enforcement actions of economic sanctions regulations based on correspondent banking accounts located in the United States are rarely litigated in court as the cases are often settled. Thus, the legally and politically controversial case *United States v Zarrab et al* offers a rare judicial opinion on the issue. The case revolved around a criminal prosecution against several Turkish businesspersons and government officials concerning an elaborate multibillion-dollar scheme to evade Iran sanctions during the period 2010 through 2015. The case had received immense public attention across the Atlantic and even led to a diplomatic standoff between the United States and Turkey. In essence, the allegations claimed that Reza Zarrab and his associates facilitated payments on behalf of the Iranian government, which were processed by the US financial system.[360] Among others, Zarrab was charged with conspiracy to violate the IEEPA and 31 C.F.R. § 560.204 of the ITSR, which prohibits 'the exportation, reexportation [...] directly or indirectly, from the United States [...] of any [...] services to Iran [...]'.

Several times, the defence raised the issue of extraterritorial jurisdiction: For instance, Zarrab, in a motion to dismiss before the US District Court for the Southern District of New York, argued that the acts, transferring funds from a Turkish to an Iranian bank, only touched the United States *en route* when the funds passed through US banks and that they were thus overwhelmingly, if not entirely foreign. Therefore, the case had to be dismissed because the allegedly violated US statutes did not cover extraterritorial conduct.

The court, however, was not convinced and denied the motion to dismiss: Mirroring OFAC's interpretation, it found that Zarrab's conduct amounted to an exportation of services from the United States and that therefore, there was a sufficient domestic nexus.[361] In establishing the territorial nature of Zarrab's conduct, the court discussed several precedents supporting its conclusion. For instance, the court argued that the Second Circuit had previously held in *Licci v Lebanese Canadian Bank* that wiring

359 Susan Emmenegger, 'Extraterritorial Economic Sanctions and Their Foundation in International Law' (2016) 33 Arizona Journal of International & Comparative Law 631, 654 ff.

360 Superseding Indictment, *United States v Zarrab*, No. 15-cr-867, (SDNY 2016).

361 *United States v Zarrab*, No. 15-cr-867, 2016 WL 6820737 (SDNY 2016), 17.

funds from a Lebanese bank to Hezbollah through correspondent accounts established at a New York bank constituted aiding and abetting of terrorist activities within US jurisdiction.[362] Additionally, however, the court argued that even if Zarrab's alleged conduct were to be considered extraterritorial, it could still apply the IEEPA and the ITSR to such conduct because any presumption against extraterritoriality would be overcome by the United States' interest in defending itself.[363]

The district court's position on the IEEPA was later also confirmed by the Second Circuit.[364] Taken together, these judicial opinions suggest that there is at least some support within the judiciary for OFAC's theory that the United States may exercise territorial jurisdiction over money transfers between two foreign countries clearing through US correspondent accounts.

#### b) Practice in Europe

The US interpretation of territorial jurisdiction in relation to US dollar transfers 'passing through' US-based correspondent accounts has remained a singular practice in the world. Specifically, the EU and its member States, despite the Euro being the world's second largest reserve currency, have not endorsed such a wide view of territoriality. However, there is some indication that the UK is taking an equally broad stance towards jurisdiction based on money transfers. In any case, the above-mentioned US theory has not seen any explicit rejection by States in Europe and has even been (tacitly) accepted in the practice of certain States.

According to the standard jurisdictional clause, EU sanctions regulations apply within the territory of the Union, including its airspace, on board any aircraft or any vessel under the jurisdiction of a member State and more broadly, to any legal person, entity or body in respect of any business done in whole or in part within the Union.[365] Even though the wording 'in whole or in part within the Union' seems broad enough to cover the transfer of funds between two foreign banks if the money at some

---

362 *Licci v Lebanese Canadian Bank*, No. 15–1580 (2d Cir 2016), at 25; See below for extensive analysis of ATS litigation, at C.V.5a) Practice in the United States.

363 *United States v Zarrab*, No. 15-cr-867, 2016 WL 6820737 (SDNY 2016), 18.

364 *United States v. Atilla*, No. 18–1589 (2d Cir. 2020), 16 – 18.

365 E.g. Art. 29 Council Regulation (EU) No 961/2010 of 25 October 2010 on restrictive measures against Iran and repealing Regulation (EC) No 423/2007, [2010] OJ L 281/1.

point also traverses EU financial institutions, which would precisely be the position of the United States,[366] in practice, member State authorities have up to now refrained from pursuing foreign individuals and institutions the same way OFAC has done.

The situation is somewhat different in the UK: According to guidance issued by the Office of Financial Sanctions Implementation (**OFSI**), a new government agency created in 2016 specifically tasked with overseeing the implementation and enforcement of financial sanctions, the agency claims 'authority' over any breach with a UK nexus, which may explicitly 'be created by such things as […] transactions using clearing services in the UK'.[367] This interpretation seems to closely mirror OFAC's playbook on jurisdictional reach. In fact, the agency's powers seem to have been generally inspired by OFAC: For instance, OFSI may impose 'civil' monetary penalties of up to £ 1 Million or 50 % of the value of the sanctioned transaction, whichever is greater. Similarly, financial sanctions are now one of the offences for which a deferred prosecution agreement can be made, reminiscent of the practice of OFAC.[368] It seems therefore reasonable to expect that the OFSI may take a similarly broad view on territoriality in relation to money transfers through correspondent accounts.

At this point, one might question whether the apparently different jurisdictional scope assumed by OFAC and OFSI on the one hand and EU member State authorities on the other hand is really nothing more than a criminal law / administrative law divide. While both OFAC and OFSI rely on administrative or civil penalties, sanctions enforcement in EU member States is predominantly in the hand of criminal authorities.[369] Possibly, criminal authorities view themselves bound to a stricter interpretation of jurisdictional rules as potential infringements of individual rights and due

---

366 According to at least one commentator, the sanctions apply to a transaction between two third country institutions if they conducted part of their negotiation in a hotel located within the Union, see Mehle and Mehle (n 321), 399.

367 OFSI, Monetary penalties for breaches of financial sanctions: Guidance of April 2021, paras. 3.6 – 3.7.

368 OFSI, UK Financial Sanctions: General Guidance, available at https://assets.publishing.service.gov.uk/government/uploads/system/uploads/attachment_data/file/685308/financial_sanctions_guidance_march_2018_final.pdf, last accessed on 13 April 2022.

369 See for instance for a German prosecution of an Iranian citizen for alleged sanctions violations: BGH, Order of 23 April 2010, AK 2/10, reported in BGHSt 55, 94, paras. 24, 25.

process may weigh heavier in criminal processes.[370] However, from the perspective of international law, such considerations generally do not affect the scope of State jurisdiction. Rather, it should be irrelevant whether jurisdiction is asserted by an administrative or a criminal authority (or by civil courts for that matter).[371] For the specific area of economic sanctions, the IEEPA provides for both administrative and criminal penalties and the court in *United States v Zarrab* similarly did not consider a different jurisdictional doctrine because it was handling criminal charges.[372]

Although enforcement levels in Europe are substantially lower, the EU as well as its member States have not voiced any substantial critique against the actions of US authorities.[373] This comes even more as a surprise considering that European banks have been one of the major targets of OFAC's activity. Only in the case of BNP Paribas with its record 8.9 billion USD fine has France, the company's home State, sent a letter of protest to President Obama. However, the letter apparently did not mention any jurisdictional issues but solely criticized the fine for being disproportionate.[374] Considering that subsequently, the *French Autorité de contrôle prudentiel et de résolution*, BNP Paribas' regulator at home, has found no violation of the company against French, EU or UN sanctions, one might expect that the issue of extraterritoriality or at least conflicting legal requirements would have been brought up in the letter.[375] Whether this restraint was due to a belief that US authorities had indeed acted compliant to international law jurisdictional limits and whether it reflected *opinio iuris* is unclear. Again, it could simply have been a converging foreign policy view at that time between the United States and the EU regarding States such as Iran and Sudan that prompted European countries to tread lightly.

---

370 However, issues of due process may also arise in civil matters Colangelo, 'Spatial Legality' (n 48), 94 – 104; *Societe Internationale pour Participations Industrielles et Commerciales, S.A. v Rogers* 357 US 197, 211 (1958).

371 See Samuel L Hatcher, 'Circuit Board Jurisdiction: Electronic Payments and the Presumption against Extraterritoriality' (2020) 48 Georgia Journal of International and Comparative Law 591, 598; See also above at A.III.5. Regulation, Public Law and Jurisdiction.

372 See above at C.II.3a) Practice in the United States.

373 This has also been noted by Ruys and Ryngaert (n 272), 23.

374 M Rochan, 'French President Hollande Defends BNP Paribas in Letter to President Obama', *International Business Times*, http://www.ibtimes.co.uk/french-president-hollande-defends-bnp-paribas-letter-president-obama-1451262, last accessed on 13 April 2022.

375 See Emmenegger (n 359), 634 – 635 citing the French press.

There is also at least one instance in which a European regulator has tacitly accepted US territorial jurisdiction in relation to US dollar transfers. In particular, the Swiss financial authority FINMA specifically investigated whether BNP Paribas (Suisse) SA had adequate risk management in place for compliance with *US sanctions*. It found that the bank had in various ways violated US regulation and thus failed the requirements for adequate organization under Swiss supervisory law.[376] FINMA has likewise reprimanded Credit Suisse in 2009 for similar conduct. In a more detailed report about this case, FINMA stated that it regarded OFAC regulations as '*extra-territorial*' but seemingly accepted OFAC's legal analysis and did not question OFAC's jurisdictional authority. FINMA further elaborated that it would not enforce US regulations as a matter of principle, but still demanded from the violating banks that they adhere to US sanctions in the future.[377]

### c) Comparative Normative Analysis

While OFAC's assertion of territorial jurisdiction in relation to financial transactions 'passing through' US bank accounts has remained a specific feature of 'American Exceptionalism', the preceding section has shown that it has not caused widespread State protest so far and that at least the UK is pondering a similar practice. As with the extension of US sanctions to foreign subsidiaries based on the control doctrine, I will argue here that analysing these measures according to the traditional framework of jurisdiction yields no unambiguous result: In fact, while there are strong arguments against the legality of correspondent account jurisdiction under international law, there are equally convincing arguments to the contrary.

---

376 Press Release, Swiss Financial Markets Supervisory Authority, 'Inadequate Risk Management of US Sanctions: FINMA Closes Proceedings Against BNP Paribas (Suisse)' (1 July 2014), https://www.finma.ch/en/news/2014/06/mm-abschluss-verfahren-bnp-paribas-suisse-20140701/, last accessed on 13 April 2022.

377 FINMA, 'Processing of USD payments for countries and persons sanctioned under the OFAC-Rules', (16 December 2009), https://www.finma.ch/en/~/media/finma/dokumente/dokumentencenter/8news/medienmitteilungen/2009/12/20091216-bericht-cs-usbehoerden.pdf?la=en, last accessed on 13 April 2022.

In academic commentary, OFAC's theory that correspondent account jurisdiction can be justified either through territoriality or the effects principle is overwhelmingly rejected.[378]

I concur with this opinion as far as the effects principle is concerned. OFAC argues that it may assert jurisdiction based on the effects principle because through the act of 'stripping', i.e., the practice of concealing identification data of sanctions targets from payment messages, European financial institutions cause prohibited payments to pass the US financial system undetected which in turn causes the involved US banks to (unknowingly) violate economic sanctions. However, it is doubtful whether this practice satisfies the requirements of the effects principle, in particular considering the limitations of this doctrine. First, outside the field of antitrust regulation, using effects to justify jurisdiction is heavily controversial in international law.[379] Second, even proponents of the doctrine usually require that the effects to be qualified by characteristics such as *direct or substantial* in order to trigger jurisdiction.[380]

The practice of stripping does not seem to result in such direct or substantial effects.[381] Specifically, since the US banks involved in the clearing process supposedly did not know about the scheme, they are not at risk of civil or criminal enforcement measures themselves and suffer no reputational damage. Likewise, there is no quantifiable damage to the US economy: The domestic banking and payment system did not become less reliable or more expensive to use. Even if the practice of stripping did incur additional costs for US banks, as they had to maintain more complex compliance systems, this effect seems to be indirect at best. The only party that undoubtedly suffers a direct and substantial damage is OFAC itself,

378 See Emmenegger (n 359), 654 ff; Thilo Rensmann, 'Völkerrechtliche Grenzen extraterritorialer Wirtschaftssanktionen' in Arnold Wallraff, Dirk Ehlers and Hans-Michael Wolffgang (eds), *Recht der Exportkontrolle: Bestandsaufnahme und Perspektiven: Handbuch zum Exportkontrollrecht.* zugleich Festgabe für Dr. Arnold Wallraff zum 65. Geburtstag (Schriften zum Aussenwirtschaftsrecht 2015), 104 – 106; For the FCPA see also: Natasha Wilson, 'Pushing the Limits of Jurisdiction Over Foreign Actors Under the Foreign Corrupt Practices Act' (2014) 91 Washington University Law Review 1063, 1079.

379 Crawford and Brownlie (n 18), 463; see also above at B.I.2b)bb) The Effects Principle in Other Areas of Substantive Law.

380 See Beaucillon (n 26), 120 – 121; *Restatement (Third) of the Foreign Relations Law of the United States* (n 5), § 402 Comment d); Akehurst (n 42), 154; For a statute that requires a qualified effect for its application see: Foreign Trade Antitrust Improvements Act of 1982, 15 U.S.C. § 6a(I)(A).

381 Emmenegger (n 359), 656; Rensmann (n 378), 105 – 106.

whose ability to control US dollar transactions to embargoed destinations is seriously impaired.[382] However, it is exactly the question whether OFAC has authority over these transactions that needs to be answered in the first place, which means this argument is circular and not particularly helpful.[383]

While OFAC's jurisdictional claims are not covered under the effects doctrine, I am much less convinced that they cannot be simply based on plain-old territoriality. In this regard, some commentators point out that the clearing of US dollar banking transactions through correspondent accounts in New York provides such a minute territorial nexus that it is insufficient to sustain the exercise of territorial jurisdiction: In today's globalized economy, transactions regularly pass through the territories of multiple nations due to modern communication systems, sometimes even without the participants' knowledge. In the case *United States v Zarrab* for instance, defendants claimed that the wire transfer did not actually move any goods, but that, much like data in cyberspace, the only thing that is physically happening is a change of accounting entries within banks.[384] Indeed, the objections against OFAC's interpretation of territoriality are similar to those offered against jurisdictional claims founded on internet-based data processing.[385]

However, this position cannot convincingly explain precisely *why* the clearing of financial transactions in New York is insufficient for assuming territoriality. According to most authoritative interpretations of the territoriality principle, this basis is satisfied when at least one constituent element of the conduct to be regulated occurred in the territory of the State.[386] Moreover, the question which elements are to be considered constituent for a crime is not answered by international law, but rather by domestic law.[387] In this regard, the sanctioned money transfer in *United States v*

382 This point is further illustrated by the fact that most criminal complaints relating to sanctions violations through US dollar transfers also allege the defendant to have conspired to defraud an agency of the United States.

383 See Emmenegger (n 359), 656.

384 See above at C.II.3a) Practice in the United States.

385 Paul S Berman, 'Global Legal Pluralism' (2007) 80 Southern California Law Review, 1182: 'In an electronically connected world the effects of any given action may immediately be felt elsewhere with no relationship to physical geography at all.'.

386 *Restatement (Fourth) of the Foreign Relations Law of the United States* (n 42), § 408 comment c; Harvard Research Draft (n 71), 495; International Law Commission (n 3), p. 521, para. 11.

387 Ryngaert, *Jurisdiction in International Law* (n 2), p. 78.

*Zarrab* could be considered a typical cross-border offence. The funds are first sent from a Turkish bank to a US counterpart, are then transferred to a different US bank account before they continue to their destination somewhere in Iran. According to the constituent elements doctrine, the United States is in principles free to determine that the part of the offence taking place in the United States is a constituent element giving rise to US jurisdiction.[388]

That indeed a crucial part of the offence is committed under US jurisdiction is furthermore confirmed by a related consideration: There is no doubt that in those moments where these funds – *en route* to the sanctioned destination – are booked onto a US account, OFAC would have jurisdiction over these funds.[389] However, if that is the case, there is no reason why OFAC should not also have jurisdiction over the conduct that brought the funds within its reach in the first place as well as over the conduct that causes the funds to eventually leave the United States.

Another way to look at OFAC's jurisdictional claims is through the theory of innocent agency: For instance, German courts have assumed territorial jurisdiction over a perpetrator abroad if he had acted through an innocent third party within Germany: Because the third party's conduct is attributed to the perpetrator abroad, the territoriality of the conduct is also attributed.[390] It seems arguable that we are faced with a substantially similar situation here as the US banks operating the correspondent accounts could be regarded as innocent agents of the sending and receiving party of the sanctioned money transfer. In this case, the territorial acts of the innocent US banks would be attributed to the perpetrators abroad, bringing them under the jurisdiction of the United States.

The problem with accepting correspondent account jurisdiction thus seems to be less of a doctrinal one, but more of a practical one: It simply

388 In this case therefore, Turkey, Iran and the United States could claim jurisdiction, see also the related example by Akehurst (n 42), 152, in which X in State A writes a fraudulent to Y in State B who then sends money to X in State C, giving rise to jurisdiction in State A, B and C over the fraudulent conduct.

389 See for instance Michael Gruson, 'The U.S. Jurisdiction over Transfers of U.S. Dollars between Foreigners and over Ownership of U.S. Dollar Accounts in Foreign Banks' [2004] Columbia Business Law Review 721, 734: 'If a dollar transfer is cleared […] at a Federal Reserve Bank in the United States, there is little doubt that the dollars being transferred are under the control of a U.S. person and that the transferor and the transferee have an interest in the funds being transferred. Thus, the executive orders apply and do not have any extraterritorial effect.'.

390 Federal Court of Justice, BGH, Order of 27 August 2019, 5 StR 196/19.

seems outrageous that the United States could claim almost limitless jurisdiction as long as the dollar is still the world's leading currency.[391] In this regard, commentators frequently reject the notion that correspondent accounts may sustain territoriality because in their view, the US nexus is not 'sufficiently strong', 'substantial' or 'reasonable'.[392] What is certainly correct about this line of thought is the argument that jurisdictional assessments should take into account substantial aspects such as the materiality of the connection, the content of the regulations at issue, the personal circumstances of the affected natural or juridical persons and the consequences of jurisdictional assertion. What is much less clear, however, is whether such considerations fit into the doctrine of constituent elements or whether a solution is rather to be found outside the traditional framework *de lege lata*.

#### 4. Secondary Trade Boycotts

Secondary trade boycotts, as mentioned above,[393] refer to measures in which the sanctioning State imposes economic penalties – such as restrictions to market access – on third State actors that engage in commercial relationships with the primary target of the sanctions. The rationale behind these sanctions is to induce change in the behaviour of the third State actors towards the primary target. The third State actor is forced to either abandon its relationships with the primary target, or risk being cut off the market of the sending State.[394] As with other economic sanctions with extraterritorial effects, it is primarily the United States that utilises this type of regulation (see below **a**)). Even though European States have at times sharply criticized US secondary trade boycotts, certain targeted sanctions enacted by the EU may in effect achieve quite similar results (see below **b**)). While a growing number of commentators regard secondary trade boycotts as permitted under international law, the doctrinal status of these measures remains unresolved (see below **c**)).

391 Emmenegger (n 359), 656.
392 Ruys and Ryngaert (n 272), 22; Rensmann (n 378), 105; Emmenegger (n 359), 655; see also Berman, 'The Globalization of Jurisdiction' (n 179), 330.
393 See above at C.II.1b) Primary and Secondary Sanctions.
394 See e.g., Bechky (n 280), 10 – 11.

### a) Practice in the United States

The United States has been a strong proponent of secondary trade boycotts, often to the irritation of its allies: In 1996, the United States passed the Helms-Burton Act to almost universal condemnation. In Title III, the Helms-Burton Act created a private right of action for US citizens allowing them to claim damages from any person who was 'trafficking' in property, in which the claimant had an interest, if the property had before been 'confiscated' by the Castro government in Cuba.[395] Additionally in Title IV, the Helms-Burton Act allowed the denial of entrance into the United States of officers or controlling shareholders of companies that 'traffic' in property, which was previously owned by US citizens. The act was especially targeting foreign investors who were active in Cuba. For instance, shortly after its promulgation, a Canadian cooperation was sanctioned under the Act for operating a nickel mine in Cuba, which before had belonged to a New Orleans company.[396] To mitigate the effects of the Helms-Burton Act, US presidents have continuously waived the application of Title III (the private right of action) since its entry into force. This suspension was ended for the first time in 2019 by former President Trump.[397]

The United States seemed to have grounded the Helms-Burton Act and especially its controversial Title III on both the effects doctrine[398] and the protective principle.[399] However, as in the case of US dollar transactions passing through correspondent accounts, it is difficult to imagine how

---

395 Sec. 301 – 306, Cuban Liberty and Democratic Solidarity Act, Pub. L. 104–114 (110 Stat. 785), 22 U.S.C. §§ 6021–6091 (1996).

396 The Irish Times, 'US bans Canadian mining executives over company's investments in Cuba', https://www.irishtimes.com/news/us-bans-canadian-mining-executives-over-company-s-investments-in-cuba-1.66468, last accessed on 13 April 2022.

397 Secretaría de Relaciones Exteriores, Position of the Mexican Government on Ending Suspension of Title III of the Helms-Burton Act, https://www.gob.mx/sre/prensa/position-of-the-mexican-government-on-ending-suspension-of-title-iii-of-the-helms-burton-act, last accessed on 13 April 2022.

398 Sec. 301 (9) of the Helms-Burton Act states:
'International law recognizes that a nation has the ability to provide for rules of law with respect to conduct outside its territory that has or is intended to have substantial effect within its territory'.

399 Sec. 2 (28) of the Helms-Burton Act states:
'[f]or the past 36 years, the Cuban government has posed and continued to pose a national security threat to the U.S.'.

dealing in confiscated property has a *direct* and *substantial* effect in the United States: Should the expropriation undertaken by Cuba have been illegal under international law, then further 'trafficking' would not alter or diminish the claims of the United States or its citizens. It is true that the subsequent use or transfer of the confiscated property in some cases might complicate its return to the original owner, but this can hardly be characterized as a direct or substantial effect.[400] As for the protective principle, commentators point out that the United States has failed to demonstrate a direct threat posed by Cuba to the security, integrity or other fundamental interests of the United States.[401]

Shortly after the Helms-Burton Act, the United States passed the ISA, which, as already mentioned, prohibited anyone, wherever located, from making investments exceeding USD 40,000,000 into the Iranian petroleum sector.[402] Failure to comply with this provision could lead to different penalties, including a possible prohibition for US financial institutions to grant loans to and a prohibition for US government agencies to procure goods from that person.[403] As with the Helms-Burton Act, the President may waive sanctions if it is in the national interest. Indeed, in 1998, the French company Total was granted a waiver to develop the Iranian South Pars gas field and in subsequent years, no determination has been made against any European company.[404] However, starting from 2010, ISA and its successor legislations have been enforced on multiple occasions against other third State persons, including Chinese, Singaporean, Israeli and Venezuelan companies.[405] The ISA sanctions have been subsequently amended and tightened through other legislative acts, which lowered the value bar of USD 40,000,000, increased the number of sanctions to be imposed and added new sanctions to the catalogue, the most significant

400 See for this result also Beaucillon (n 26), at 122; See also Werner Meng, 'Wirtschaftssanktionen und staatliche Jurisdiktion – Grauzonen im Völkerrecht' (1997) 47 ZaöRV 269, at 301.

401 Ryngaert, 'Extraterritorial Export Controls (Secondary Boycotts)' (n 345), 642; Meng, 'Wirtschaftssanktionen und staatliche Jurisdiktion – Grauzonen im Völkerrecht' (n 400), 305.

402 See above at C.II.1c)bb) US Sanctions against Iran.

403 See above at C.II.1c)bb) US Sanctions against Iran.

404 Ryngaert, 'Extraterritorial Export Controls (Secondary Boycotts)' (n 345), at 649.

405 Fact Sheet, Office of the Spokesman of 24 May 2011,https://2009-2017.state.gov/r/pa/prs/ps/2011/05/164132.htm, last accessed on 13 April 2022; Press Release of 31 July 2012, https://home.treasury.gov/news/press-releases/tg1661, last accessed on 13 April 2022.

one may be a general prohibition for US financial institutions to transact with sanctioned parties.[406] As already discussed, ISA style sanctions have also been adopted more recently to target Russia, specifically through the above-mentioned UFSA and CAATSA.[407]

Given the US record of extending domestic law to situations with only questionable ties to its territory, one might be surprised to find that the United States is less than shy to react when it finds itself on the receiving end of allegedly extraterritorial regulation. However, this was precisely the case when the United States, in 1977, started to adopt formal measures protesting the Arab boycott of Israel.[408] The Arab boycott of Israel, just like the ISA, is a typical example of a secondary trade boycott: The Arab League Council not only prohibited any transaction with persons in Israel, of Israeli nationality and of persons working on behalf of Israel, but it also demanded that foreign firms complied with these rules if they wanted to continue business with the Arab world.[409] Moreover, non-compliant foreign firms could be blacklisted themselves so that the Israel boycott also extended to these companies.[410]

### b) Practice in Europe

As in the 1982 *Pipeline* case, the promulgation of the Helms-Burton Act and the ISA has prompted strong negative responses across the Atlantic Ocean, which resulted in the initial adoption of the EC/EU blocking statute, Council Regulation (EC) No 2271/96 of 22 November 1996. The regulation, explicitly stating that a third country had enacted laws that intended to influence the conduct of EC persons and thus violated in-

406 Sec. 102 of CISADA; Sec. 201 of ITRA.

407 See above, at C.II.1c) Overview of US Economic Sanctions.

408 Ribicoff Amendment to the Tax Reform Act of 1976, Pub. L. 94–455 (90 Stat 1649), 26 U.S.C. § 999 (2005); Export Administration Amendments of 1977, Pub. L. 95–52 (91 Stat 242), § 117 (1977).

409 Mestral and Gruchalla-Wesierski (n 152), 151.

410 Ryngaert, 'Extraterritorial Export Controls (Secondary Boycotts)' (n 345), 640; James Friedberg, 'The Arab League Boycott of Israel: Warring Histories, International Trade, and Human Rights' in Jena Martin and Karen E Bravo (eds), *The Business and Human Rights Landscape: Moving Forward, Looking Back* (Cambridge University Press 2015), 56.

ternational law, sought to nullify those extraterritorial effects.[411] Persons subject to the EC regulation were prohibited from complying with the Helms-Burton Act and the ISA as well as related orders. In addition, EC entities shall have the right to recover damages suffered because of those acts. The UK for their part had already passed a blocking statute in 1980, the British Protection of Trading Interests Act, which mainly aimed at US antitrust enforcement, but which was also invoked in the case of US Cuba sanctions.[412] At the same time, the EC initiated proceedings against both the Helms-Burton Act and the ISA according to the Dispute Settlement Understanding of the WTO. The cases were suspended in 1997 after both parties reached an understanding in which the United States agreed to suspend the application of the two acts against EU member State persons.[413] EU protest against both acts continued into the 2000s: For instance, in an official statement in 2001, the Commissioner for External Relations regretted the extension of ISA by the United States for another five years.[414] Equally, EU member States have constantly criticized the US embargo against Cuba in the UN, referring among others to the extraterritorial effects and the undue interference it created for EU citizens.[415]

Similarly, the EC protested a selective purchasing law from the state of Massachusetts, which barred the state from buying goods or services from any person doing business with Burma as identified on a 'restricted purchase list' maintained by Massachusetts. In an *amicus curiae* brief supporting a legal action against this legislation, the EC described the

---

411 Council Regulation (EC) No 2271/96 of 22 November 1996 protecting against the effects of the extra-territorial application of legislation adopted by a third country, and actions based thereon or resulting therefrom.

412 Harry L Clark, 'Dealing with U.S. Extraterritorial Sanctions and Foreign Countermeasures' (1999) 20 University of Pennsylvania Journal of International Economic Law, 87; On the Protection of Trading Interests Act 1980, see also Lowe (n 100).

413 European Union and the United States, 'Memorandum of Understanding concerning the U.S. Helms-Burton Act and the U.S. Iran and Libya Sanctions Act', 36 ILM (1997) 529.

414 Statement by Commissioner for External Relations, Chris Patten, https://ec.europa.eu/commission/presscorner/detail/en/IP_01_1162, last accessed on 13 April 2022.

415 European Union, 'Explanation of Vote at the at the 74th Session of the United Nations General Assembly on the Necessity of ending the economic, commercial and financial embargo imposed by the United States of America against Cuba', https://www.eeas.europa.eu/eeas/eu-explanation-vote-united-nations-general-assembly-resolution-embargo-imposed-usa-against_en, last accessed on 13 April 2022.

Massachusetts Burma Law as a 'secondary boycott' as well as 'extraterritorial' and contended that the regulation 'constitutes a direct interference with the ability of the EU to cooperate and carry out foreign policy with the United States.'[416] While the Union submitted that the US and EU positions on Burma aligned because of the nation's human rights and democracy record, the EU has explicitly refrained from imposing sanctions on Burma at that time and rather opted to withdraw Burma's access to generalized tariff preferences. The US Supreme Court finally struck down the state legislation, though on grounds unrelated to extraterritoriality and thus ended this direct confrontation between the EU and the United States on this issue.[417]

However, as in the case of the extension of personality-based jurisdiction to controlled foreign subsidiaries, the European reaction to US sanctions has been far from consistent. Specifically, the EU has protested neither against the expansion of ISA through CISADA in 2010 and ITRA in 2012 nor against UFSA and related Russia sanctions in 2014. Conversely, some member States have reacted strongly to the technically similar CAATSA in 2017.[418] Germany and Austria sent a formal note of protest after the US Senate adopted the proposed sanctions bill.[419] They particularly deplored the inclusion of gas pipeline projects into the scope of activities that give rise to possible sanctions as companies of both countries were heavily invested in the Nord Stream 2 pipeline.[420] According to the diplomatic note, Germany and Austria viewed the CAATSA as 'illegal extraterritorial sanctions', which were primarily motivated by the economic objective of maintaining sales of American liquefied natural gas into the European

---

416 See *National Foreign Trade Council v Baker*, 26 F Supp 2d 287 (D Mass 1998), *amicus curiae* Brief in support of Plaintiff.

417 See *Crosby v National Foreign Trade Council* 530 US 363 (2000).

418 The act was first introduced into Congress as S. 722 – Countering Iran's Destabilizing Activities Act of 2017.

419 Federal Foreign Office, Press Release, Foreign Minister Gabriel and Austrian Federal Chancellor Kern on the imposition of Russia sanctions by the US Senate, https://www.auswaertiges-amt.de/en/newsroom/news/170615-kern-russland/290666. Apart from political expedience, a different reading highlights the growth of the EU's own institutional capacity due to successive integration as the driving factor behind the EU's reaction (or rather inaction), see Note, 'Developments in the Law – Extraterritoriality' (n 343), at 1255. This argument claims that the modern EU with one of the largest 'single market' in the world has a tremendous self-interest to influence foreign behaviour, thus leading to restraint in critique of other nation's supposedly 'extraterritorial' regulation.

420 CAATSA, Sec. 232 and Sec. 235.

market by preventing European nations from diversifying their energy supply network.

Finally, certain targeted sanctions of the EU itself may in fact achieve quite similar effects to US secondary trade boycotts. This is the case when EU targeted sanctions are not imposed on the primary sanctions target, but instead on third State entities that merely assist a primary target. For instance, while Council Implementing Regulation (EU) No. 503/2011 implementing the restrictive measures against Iran mostly included Iranian persons and entities on its sanctions list, it also sanctioned a number of UAE and Malaysian entities for the explicit reason that they have procured items for sanctioned Iranian programmes.[421] As mentioned above, the objective of secondary trade boycotts is to induce change in the behaviour of third State actors towards the primary target.[422] In this regard, it could be argued that adding third State entities to a sanctions list for assisting a primary target achieves a similar effect: Because third State entities now have to fear that their assistance of a primary target of the economic sanctions may result in their addition to the sanctions list, they may be persuaded to abandon their ties with the primary sanctions target to preserve their relationship with the EU.

#### c) Comparative Normative Analysis

As demonstrated in the preceding section, the practice in relation to secondary trade boycotts has been wildly inconsistent. For instance, this is evidenced by the actions of the United States, which has condemned the Arab boycott of Israel even though it is adopting very similar measures against targets such as Cuba and Iran. While the EU has so far refrained from explicitly enacting secondary trade boycotts, some of its primary sanctions may in fact exert comparable influence on third-State targets. Furthermore, the EU and its member States have protested US secondary trade boycotts only selectively. As is the case with control-based jurisdiction as well as correspondent account jurisdiction, this inconsistent practice is rather a reflection of subjective political motives than normative analysis.

---

421 Annex I B Council Implementing Regulation (EU) No 503/2011 of 23 May 2011 implementing Regulation (EU) No 961/2010 on restrictive measures against Iran [2011] OJ L 136/26.

422 See above at C.II.4. Secondary Trade Boycotts.

When the EU failed to protest US secondary trade boycotts, the reason is likely to be found in a general conformity of EU and US foreign policy with regard to Iran from 2010 – 2012 and with regard to Russia in 2014. It is submitted that in both cases, the transatlantic partners have closely coordinated their efforts, aligned their timetables and largely targeted the same industries and individual targets, leading to legal cohesion.[423] This needs to be contrasted with the harshly worded diplomatic note that Germany and Austria filed with the United States during the CAATSA episode. While the two States also did condemn the measures on international law grounds, it is more likely that the diplomatic note was mainly driven by foreign policy, particularly when considering that both countries did not protest similar secondary trade boycotts in the same bill targeting other economic areas outside of energy supply.

However, secondary trade boycotts are not only heavily controversial from a policy standpoint, their normative status under the international law rules of jurisdiction is also far from clear. In fact, a strong legal position has re-emerged which claims that secondary trade boycotts like the ISA or the CAATSA do not raise any *jurisdictional* issues. According to these commentators, the crucial part about the ISA is not that it seeks to prohibit business relationships of anyone in the world with Iran, but rather that acting contrary to these rules may result in restricted or denied access to the US domestic market and economic benefits. Thus, they claim that the ISA and subsequent legislation in fact contain trade restrictions addressing domestic operators: Domestic companies and government agencies are prohibited from certain dealings with third State persons, if these third State persons in turn conduct business with the primary sanctions targets.[424] Therefore, the ISA should rather be likened to, for instance, a restriction for domestic companies on the importation of goods that have been produced abroad adhering to subpar environmental standards. One author summarized these thoughts in a remark about the Arab Boycott when he commented, 'there was, in fact, nothing extraterritorial about their acts. All they said was "We in this country will not deal

423 Note, 'Developments in the Law – Extraterritoriality' (n 343), at 1254.

424 See Meyer, 'Second Thoughts on Secondary Sanctions' (n 151), 951; Meng, 'Wirtschaftssanktionen und staatliche Jurisdiktion – Grauzonen im Völkerrecht' (n 400), 292 – 293; regarding the ISA, see Vaughan Lowe, 'US Extraterritorial Jurisdiction: The Helms-Burton and d'Amato Acts' (1997) 46 ICLQ 378 at 386 who admits that although the sanctions do not raise 'legal' issues, they are 'inappropriate'.

with you if you do these things abroad."'[425] Of course, if one understands Sec. 5 (a) of the ISA as a territorial trade condition, the EU restraint is easily explained given the fact that the Union is one of the largest proponents of such restrictions worldwide.[426]

Related to this argument is Meyer's observation that secondary trade boycotts should not be treated with great difference to traditional primary sanctions because both types of measures bar domestic entities from dealing with a foreign individual or country to induce certain changes in policy or otherwise. He argues that were secondary trade boycotts incompliant with international law because of jurisdictional issues, then all economic sanctions would have to be illegal.[427] In relation to this argument, the normative difference between primary and secondary sanction may be especially blurred with regard to those EU targeted sanctions that 'blacklist' third State individuals and entities because of their affiliation with the primary target of the economic sanctions. While these measures are directly imposed against the intended target (and thus 'primary') they are 'secondary' in that the choice of the individual target is related to its dealings with the principal State or entity sanctioned.

To be sure, a possible normative distinction may be established as these targeted sanctions enacted by the EU do not actually have the purpose to 'regulate' foreign behaviour in a strict sense: Unlike US measures, they do not provide the 'if you engage in illegal activities with the primary sanctions targets, we will sanction you' kind of legal obligation that characterizes secondary trade boycotts.[428] In this regard, it has been argued

425 Harold G Maier at the Second Annual International Business Law Symposium, 'Trading with Cuba: The Cuban Democracy Act and Export Rules' (1993) 8 Florida Journal of International Law 335 at 374.

426 See more generally Anu Bradford, 'The Brussels Effect: The Rise of a Regulatory Superstate in Europe' (2012) 107 Northwestern University Law Review 1.

427 Meyer, 'Second Thoughts on Secondary Sanctions' (n 151), at 955 and 958; see already above at C.II.1b) Primary and Secondary Sanctions; In this regard, most authors do not consider primary economic sanctions problematic under international law rules of jurisdiction even though they seek to achieve change abroad. It is argued that technically, sanctions are only regulating the behaviour of domestic persons, barring them from dealing with the sanctioned targets, see also Judson Bradley, 'The Legality of Executive Orders 13628 and 13645: A Bipartite Analysis' (2015) 29 Emory International Law Review 705 709; Lorand Bartels, 'Article XX of GATT and the Problem of Extraterritorial Jurisdiction: The Case of Trade Measures for the Protection of Human Rights' (2002) 36(2) Journal of World Trade 353, 385.

428 Sec. 1 (a) (iii) of the Executive Order 13382 of June 28, 2005 Blocking Property of Weapons of Mass Destruction Proliferators and Their Supporters.

above that it is the quintessence of regulation to command private parties, through the application of rules, to act or to refrain from acting in certain ways and to enforce such duties in case of breaches.[429] Secondary trade boycotts attempt to regulate (third State) persons to perform a specific conduct through market access conditions. In contrast, the targeted sanctions by the EU do not carry a legal obligation for third State actors. It seems that the – at most – implicit threat of economic consequences does not transform these targeted sanctions against third State actors into secondary trade boycotts.

The fact that secondary trade boycotts attempt to impose legal obligations onto third State actors is also the reason that the (still) mainstream literature considers these measures to be illegal under international law. According to this position, one cannot argue that secondary trade boycotts such as Sec. 5 (a) of the ISA are simply territorial measures, which only regulate the behaviour of domestic persons. In their opinion, this argument confuses prescriptive and enforcement jurisdiction: It is true that a denial of export licenses, a prohibition for domestic banks to maintain accounts with a foreign party or the restriction of participation in public procurement are domestic measures. But – and this is the essence of the argument – these territorial measures constitute the *enforcement* of a prescriptive norm, in our case the prohibition for a foreign commercial entity to conduct business with the primary sanctions target. However, it is precisely this prescriptive rule imposed onto a third State actor that cannot be justified under international law: As we have seen for the Helms-Burton Act, it is hard to ground the prohibition of maintaining business relationships between two foreign entities on either the effects principle or the protective principle.[430] Therefore, because there is no prescriptive jurisdiction under international law, the enforcement of these regulations, even through territorial measures, would be illegal.[431]

However, let us assume for argument's sake that the denial of an export license or the limitation of trade engages *enforcement jurisdiction* under international law.[432] The problem is obviously that this would put *any* market access regulation that is contingent on extraterritorial behaviour

429 Katz Cogan (n 52), 324; see above at A.III.5. Regulation, Public Law and Jurisdiction.

430 See above at C.II.4a) Practice in the United States.

431 Bradley (n 427), at 727; Carlos M Vázquez, 'Trade Sanctions and Human Rights: Past, Present and Future' (2003) 6 JIEL 797, 814; Rensmann (n 378), 103 – 104.

432 *Restatement (Third) of the Foreign Relations Law of the United States* (n 5) seems to follow this approach as well.

under severe international law pressure. Consider for example a regulation that restricts the import of t-shirts produced abroad using child labour: Using the above logic, one could claim that denying the import is merely an enforcement measure complementing the prescriptive norm that requires companies abroad to refrain from using child labour. However, even this regulation would likely be incompliant with international law as there is no jurisdictional basis allowing for the prohibition of child labour abroad (unless one finds that the prohibition of child labour warrants universal jurisdiction).[433]

Some commentators have therefore put forward more sophisticated proposals to conceptualize whether and when market access conditions should be regarded as raising issues of jurisdiction. Bartels for instance suggests that trade measures should not be considered purely territorial (with the implication that they would have to satisfy principles of extraterritorial jurisdiction under international law) if the measures are defined by something located or occurring abroad.[434] In relation to Sec. 5 (a) of the ISA and similar secondary trade boycotts, this is easily shown as the application of domestic sanctions such as a restriction on public procurement is defined by the relationships of the third State actor with Iran. Meng on the other hand suggests a somewhat stricter criterion and argues that trade measures (or any measure really) should only be considered extraterritorial if they produce (intended) coercive effects, as contrasted to mere factual effects.[435] However, while it could be argued that Sec. 5 (a) of the ISA and similar secondary trade boycotts produce intended coercive effects, he has denied in later writings that this provision raises issues of jurisdiction, signalling a somewhat inconsistent application of his criterion.[436]

While Bartels and Meng seek to establish formal frameworks to determine when domestic market access conditions raise issues of jurisdiction under international law, Vazquéz follows a different strategy. While he considers such measures as generally extraterritorial, they may nonetheless be justified if the conduct they seek to influence is regulated by internationally recognized norms because in this case, the enacting State does

433 Lowe and Staker (n 50), at 308 consider that '[i]t is quite possible to redraft every offence so as to make it a crime to enter the State having done *x*, *y*, or *z* before entry' and that '[t]here is no theoretical answer to this problem'.

434 Bartels, 'Article XX of GATT and the Problem of Extraterritorial Jurisdiction' (n 427), 381.

435 Meng, *Extraterritoriale Jurisdiktion im öffentlichen Wirtschaftsrecht* (n 43), 86.

436 Meng, 'Wirtschaftssanktionen und staatliche Jurisdiktion – Grauzonen im Völkerrecht' (n 400), 292 – 293.

not unilaterally impose its own standards on behaviour abroad.[437] This approach has some appeal as regulations such as Sec. 5 (a) of the ISA that merely seek to advance domestic foreign policy goals would not pass muster while the regulation restricting the import of t-shirts produced using child labour would not raise jurisdictional issues. However, even this view may be unduly restrictive: The point of setting trade restrictions is often to surpass internationally recognized norms or to influence conduct where a binding international norm has not yet emerged.[438] Vazquéz' position would thus severely limit the options of States to protect their fundamental values in the face of international commerce.

In conclusion, the normative question surrounding secondary trade boycotts such as Sec. 5 (a) of the ISA remains unresolved. While the EC has historically rejected them as outright impermissible under the doctrine of jurisdiction under international law, a growing group of academic commentators likens them to other domestic trade conditions. However, this argument has equally come under attack as the status of such domestic trade conditions remains contested. Especially in relation to Sec. 5 (a) of the ISA, some argue that withholding domestic market access and economic benefits concerns the enforcement of an extraterritorial rule, for which one of the bases of prescriptive jurisdiction must be present. While other authors follow a more nuanced approach to trade measures and acknowledge that they should be legitimate in certain circumstances, they are not in agreement regarding the precise formal or substantive requirements. Therefore, both practice and academic opinion remain divided on the issue of secondary trade boycotts particularly when they are analysed in light of other trade measures with extraterritorial implications. In this regard, it seems that the rather formal criteria of the currently dominant jurisdictional framework offer no satisfactory answer.

### 5. Protection of Individual Rights

Being powerful coercive measures, economic sanctions have always been viewed with suspicion by international lawyers with a strong focus on the protection of individual rights. As already mentioned, the recent shift at the UN level from comprehensive sanctions to 'smart' sanctions targeting specific individuals and entities was prompted in part by the humanitar-

437 Vázquez (n 431), 817.
438 Scott (n 10), at 114.

ian disaster that the Iraq sanctions inflicted on the local population.[439] In recent years however, these targeted measures themselves have been subject to vehement critique that they violate the human rights of the affected individuals. This debate has cast doubt on the legitimacy of these regulations, even though they emanate from the high authority of the UN Security Council. Commentators and courts have criticized that these regimes provided only limited procedures for individuals to challenge the measures taken against them, that the measures and their extensions did not provide any notice and that the measures were taken on the basis of classified information to which the affected had no or at best limited access.[440] Within the EU, the discussion eventually culminated in the highly publicized judgments of the EGC and CJEU in *Kadi I* and *Kadi II*.[441]

It is outside the scope of this section to retrace the debate as a whole. However, it is clear that States employing targeted economic sanctions against individuals may face similar scrutiny related to the protection of fundamental rights as the UN Security Council. Under traditional doctrine, this issue is not strictly connected with the competence of States to exercise extraterritorial jurisdiction under international law. Whether a State offers mechanisms of judicial review and redress to affected persons has no bearing on the prescriptive reach of its laws. However, this section demonstrates that this issue indeed does have an extraterritorial dimension. Specifically, this section shows that whether affected persons have recourse to certain individual rights may also depend on whether these individuals are located within or outside of the State's territory. We will return to these findings in later chapters when we discuss in more detail the normative relationship between the scope of individual protection and the scope of State jurisdiction.

---

439 See above C.II.1a) Economic Sanctions under International Law.

440 See Bardo Fassbender, 'Targeted Sanctions Imposed by the UN Security Council and Due Process Rights' (2006) 3 International Organizations Law Review 437; Iain Cameron, 'UN Targeted Sanctions, Legal Safeguards and the European Convention on Human Rights' (2003) 72(2) Nordic Journal of International Law 159.

441 CJEU, C-402/05 P, *Kadi and Al Barakaat International Foundation v Council and Commission* [2008] ECR I-06351 and CJEU, C-584/10 P, *Commission and Others v Kadi,* [2013] ECLI:EU:C:2013:518; On *Kadi I*, see Juliane Kokott and Christoph Sobotta, 'The Kadi Case – Constitutional core values and international law – finding the balance?' (2013) 23(4) EJIL 1015 - 1024.

a) Practice in the United States

Individual challenges against targeted sanctions in the United States have been mounted in the domestic arena long before similar UN measures have received increased scrutiny. For the purposes of this research, it is interesting to note that most individuals affected by domestic asset freezes are actually not nationals or residents of the United States but rather aliens connected to a primary sanctions target (e.g. Iran). Under US law therefore, the question emerges whether non-resident aliens would have recourse to constitutional protections at all, considering that for non-nationals, protection under the Constitution was only available in a territory-bound manner.[442] Phrased in another way, the issue is whether the US Constitution applied extraterritorially when the underlying coercive measure (targeted economic sanctions) took extraterritorial effects.

The leading precedent on the extraterritorial application of the US Constitution is *United States v Verdugo-Urquidez* concerning the Fourth Amendment's restraints on search and seizure. Mr. Verdugo-Urquidez's home in Mexico was subject to a search by US drug enforcement agencies without a warrant and the evidence found was later introduced into court proceedings in the United States. Verdugo-Urquidez objected, arguing that using the illegally obtained evidence at trial would violate his Fourth Amendment rights. The Supreme Court, however, denied the challenge, stating that '[a]liens receive constitutional protections [only] when they have come within the territory of the United States and developed substantial connections with this country.'[443] This, however, was not the case as Verdugo-Urquidez's only connection with the United States was his imprisonment on US territory. Accordingly, the Fourth Amendment did not apply to the search and seizure of his property in Mexico.

Courts have subsequently used this analysis in cases in which non-resident aliens applied to be removed from targeted economic sanctions programmes: For instance, in *People's Mojahedin Org. of Iran v US Dep't of State*, the Court of Appeals for the District of Columbia Circuit has relied on *Verdugo* to deny the petitioner organization, which has been designated as a foreign terrorist organization, recourse to the Due Process Clause

442 Kal Raustiala, 'The Geography of Justice' (2005) 73 FordhamLR 101, 118.
443 *United States v Verdugo-Urquidez* 494 US 259, 271(1990).

of the Fifth Amendment because petitioner was a foreign entity without property or presence in the United States.[444]

The exact scope of when an alien has 'developed substantial connections' to activate constitutional protection is still inconclusive. The language in the opinion of *People's Mojahedin Org. of Iran* seemed to suggest that the presence of property within the United States would be sufficient to trigger Fifth Amendment rights. This interpretation would of course extend due process rights to a significant number of affected individuals and entities, as mostly those with 'blocked' property in the United States would raise challenges against a sanctions order. However, subsequent court decisions have granted constitutional protection only if another (territorial) connection with the United States existed apart from the presence of property.[445] In the *Kadi* proceedings in the United States, the court explicitly left unanswered the question of whether property could trigger at least the limited application of the Constitution.[446]

### b) Practice in Europe

In the European Union, individual rights protection against targeted sanctions is mainly provided by the CJEU. In fact, challenges against targeted sanctions have resulted in a particularly prolific jurisprudence of the courts

444 *People's Mojahedin Org. of Iran v US Dep't of State* 182 F 3d 17, 22 (DC Cir 1999); To be sure, the inapplicability of the Constitution does not leave the affected individuals and entities completely without protection as they still have access to the statutory mechanisms of administrative and judicial review, albeit with only very limited grounds to reverse an adverse listing decision, see Rachel Barnes, 'United States Sanctions: Delisting Applications, Judicial Review and Secret Evidence' in Matthew Happold and Paul Eden (eds), *Economic Sanctions and International Law* (Studies in international law volume 62. Hart Publishing 2016), 204.

445 See *Al-Aqeel v Paulson*, 568 F Supp 2d 64 (DDC 2008) citing *Nat'l Council of Resistance of Iran v Dep't of State*, 251 F 3d 192, 201 (DC Cir 2001). In this case, plaintiff was the controlling officer of an Oregon corporation and in this role, he travelled to the United States. He also assisted the organization in its acquisition of property in Missouri, among others.

446 *Kadi v Paulson*, Civil Action No. 2009–0108 (DDC 2012); it should also be noted that the 'substantial connections' for Fifth Amendment purposes is not to be equated with the 'minimum contacts' requirement established for the determination of personal jurisdiction; see on this: *In re Terrorist Attacks on September 11*, 2001, 740 F Supp 2d 494, 507–08 (SDNY 2010); See also *In re Terrorist Attacks on September 11*, 2001, 538 F 3d 71 (2d Cir 2008).

unparalleled by other jurisdictions.[447] In the case concerning *Bank Mellat*, the question emerged whether the bank, which the Council claimed was an emanation of the Iranian State and therefore a government entity, could claim EU fundamental rights protection.[448] However, in contrast to the position in the United States, the mere physical location of the affected individual or the presence of territorial ties with the Union has never been a factor in determining the level of protection. This is in line with modern interpretations of the scope of application of the EU Charter of Fundamental Rights, which is explicitly 'addressed to the institutions, bodies, offices and agencies of the Union' without claiming territorial limitations like the ones found in international human rights treaties.[449] Thus, whenever the EU acts, its fundamental rights follow, irrespective of the location of the affected.[450]

At least when it comes to targeted sanctions, this approach seems to be more consistent than the US position, which claims that its regulations apply to situations with only fleeting connection to the United States but is reluctant to extend constitutional rights to non-resident aliens. One possible explanation may be that the US Constitution has a much stronger focus on the status of the individuals under its protection than the EU Charter of Fundamental Rights, which is more concerned with limiting the power of State authority.[451] From the EU perspective, there is no doubt that the Union has acted within its territories and directly caused the violations of fundamental rights, which therefore triggers the application of the charter. In *Boumediene* however, the US Supreme Court has shown its willingness to relax the requirements for the extraterritorial application

447 For a summary of the jurisprudence, see Luca Pantaleo, 'Sanctions Cases in the European Courts' in Matthew Happold and Paul Eden (eds), *Economic Sanctions and International Law* (Studies in international law volume 62. Hart Publishing 2016).

448 CJEU, Case T-496/10, *Bank Mellat v Council* [2013] ECLI:EU:T:2013:39, paras. 35 – 46.

449 Art. 51 (1) of the EU Charter of Fundamental Rights.

450 Violeta Moreno-Lax and Cathryn Costello, 'The Extraterritorial Application of the EU Charter of Fundamental Rights: From Territoriality to Facticity, the Effectiveness Model', *The EU Charter of Fundamental Rights: A Commentary* (Hart Publishing 2014), at 1682; In note 7 of Lorand Bartels, 'The EU's Human Rights Obligations in Relation to Policies with Extraterritorial Effects' (2014) 25(4) EJIL 1071.

451 See Kal Raustiala, *Does the Constitution Follow the Flag?: The Evolution of Territory in American law* (Oxford University Press 2009), at 170.

of constitutional rights and adopted a more functional approach.[452] It remains to be seen whether this approach will also level the playing field in challenges against individual sanctions in the future.[453]

### 6. Conclusion

The analysis above has shown that the phenomenon, which commentators have tried to capture with an expression as simple as 'extraterritorial sanctions', constitutes in fact an immensely complex web of measures engaging very different mechanisms. We have seen that the United States has dominated State practice in the area of extraterritorial economic sanctions while other nations so far have (mostly) restricted themselves to reacting against these assertions of jurisdiction. In particular, legislators, regulators and courts in the United States have tried to stretch the applicable scope of their rules using a variety of different triggers. These include a theory based on parental control over foreign subsidiaries, a territorial hook based on the specific mechanism of US dollar transactions, nearly all of which technically cross US banks and finally, secondary trade boycotts that carry trade restrictions as possible consequences of violation.

Perhaps most surprisingly, this chapter has established that European States have reacted rather inconsistently to US assertions of extraterritorial jurisdiction: It is a myth that US extraterritorial sanctions are universally and continuously condemned, a myth that has its roots in historical incidents such as the *Pipeline*-memorandum and the EC/EU blocking statute against the Helms-Burton Act and the ISA. To be sure, European States still *do* protest certain US sanctions, such as when the Union reactivated said blocking statute against Iran sanctions after the failure of the JCPOA or when Germany and Austria voiced their opposition to the expansion of Russia sanctions targeting the Nord Stream 2 Pipeline. At the same time, however, the EU has remained conspicuously silent on the extension of Iran sanctions in 2010 and 2012 as well as the enactment of extraterritorial sanctions against Russia in 2014 in light of the situation in Eastern Ukraine. Similarly, there is no record that European States have protested US sanctions based on correspondent account jurisdiction. While France did protest the fines levied against BNP Paribas because of their dispropor-

---

452 *Boumediene v Bush*, 553 US 723 (2008).

453 *Ibrahim v Department of Homeland Security*, 669 F 3d 983 (9th Cir 2012) offers a glimpse into the functional approach adapted to sanctions cases.

tionality, it avoided the questions of extraterritoriality. Switzerland even accepted US jurisdiction and instead focused on the reputational damage suffered by its own financial system as a result of the US sanctions breach.

As Beaucillon has correctly pointed out, these inconsistencies do not particularly help in establishing the positive law.[454] This chapter has argued two mutually reinforcing reasons for this development. On the one hand, the inconsistent response by European States is explained by political convenience. US sanctions are protested against on grounds of extraterritoriality when the two blocs differ on the fundamental policy issues addressed by the sanctions. Therefore, because economic sanctions as tools of 'enforcement' in international law serve a host of domestic policy interests, the response necessarily has to differ according to these interests. On the other hand, however, this chapter has concluded that the legal status of most US sanctions measures is far from settled in international law. Assessing the US State practice against the normative background established in part B offers no conclusive answer to the (il-)legality of extraterritorial economic sanctions.

Specifically, this chapter has entertained the idea that the most controversial jurisdictional triggers used by the United States are all arguably only variations of territoriality: First, the assertion of jurisdiction against controlled foreign subsidiaries is materially identical to the (undoubtedly) territorial regulation imposing strict liability on domestically incorporated parent companies for the conduct of their dependent subsidiaries abroad. Second, the usage of the US financial system is arguably an essential constituent element of monetary transfers denominated in US dollars which therefore justifies the exercise of territorial jurisdiction over such transfers. Third, there is a growing number of scholarly opinions that equate secondary trade boycotts such as those of the ISA with 'regular' territorial restrictions to trade. Further to this last point, there is also a body of EU sanctions which may achieve similar 'trade-chilling' effects as US secondary trade boycotts. Thus, it is arguable that the territoriality principle of customary international law actually allows the United States to unilaterally set regulations with a global reach, in stark contrast to the objective of the territoriality-based system of jurisdiction. The uncertain legal status of US extraterritorial sanctions under customary international law principles of jurisdiction renders these principles functionless in regulating the actions of States and in providing order in international relations.

---

454 Beaucillon (n 26), 125.

Finally, this chapter has examined the protection of due process rights of individuals affected by these coercive measures. While this issue is not strictly connected with the scope of State jurisdiction under international law, it does have an extraterritorial dimension. In particular, we have seen that the US jurisprudence restricts constitutional rights to those with a substantial connection to the United States. Foreigners, who are frequently the targets of economic sanctions, are therefore more restricted in exercising their due process rights. This approach of the United States is inconsistent with their own aggressive regulatory extraterritoriality.

Because economic sanctions serve to pursue a wide range of different interests, they often do not stand in isolation. For instance, country-based sanctions programs are often accompanied by general export control regulations. Moreover, the shifted focus of economic sanctions towards financial institutions means that these rules are often enforced alongside more internationally harmonized anti-corruption regimes. Similarly, the above-mentioned case of *Licci v Lebanese Canadian Bank* has shown a clear connection between economic sanctions and human rights litigation under the ATS. Further analysis of these related areas in the following chapters may therefore also benefit the discussion of extraterritorial economic sanctions.

## III. Non-Proliferation and Export Control

### 1. Introduction

Non-proliferation, i.e., the prevention of the spread of certain weapons and other security sensitive goods, materials and technologies, is one of the most pressing international security challenges.[455] Non-proliferation may relate to both weapons of mass destruction (**WMDs**) including nuclear, biological and chemical weapons, and conventional weapons including small arms and light weapons.[456] Additionally and of growing importance for international trade and commerce, non-proliferation also refers to the

455 Certain aspects of international security can be characterized as global public goods, see Krisch (n 10). This concept is discussed in more detail below at D.II.1b) Universality and Community Interests.

456 On limits posed by international law on the trade in SALWs, see Zeray Yihdego, *The Arms Trade and International Law* (Studies in international law vol. 15, Hart Pub 2007).

regulation of dual-use items, i.e. goods that have legitimate civilian applications but may also be used for military purposes, for instance as precursors to WMDs or to facilitate human rights violations such as surveillance equipment. More recently, both the rise of non-State actors[457] as well as the rapid emergence of new technologies pose particular challenges to non-proliferation regulation: On the one hand, in the aftermath of the 9/11 terrorist attacks, States have been increasingly focused on preventing WMDs and related dual-use technologies from falling into the hands of terrorist groups.[458] On the other hand, the rapid emergence of new technologies such as 3D printing, which makes it possible to produce weapons from a distance, exacerbate the need for non-proliferation regulation to adapt quickly.[459]

One of the most central instruments to curb the spread of weapons systems is to control the transfer of sensitive goods and technologies, often termed as export control or strategic trade control.[460] The objective of these regimes is to limit trade in such items to friendly or reliable end users.[461] A particular risk to export control policies is posed by the issue of diversion, i.e., when the first recipient of the controlled items in a reliable country decides to re-export or re-transfer these items to an unwanted end user. Trying to prevent such diversions naturally raises specific problems of extraterritoriality: Once the controlled goods and technologies have been exported, they are no longer within the territory of the original exporting State and the exporting State is no longer able to exercise territorial juris-

457 Non-State actors may be defined as individuals or entities not acting under the lawful authority of any State, see Security Council Resolution 1540 (2004), adopted on 28 April 2004, S/RES/1540 (2004); For Katz Cogan (n 52), 344 – 345, the rise of non-State actors is one of the main reasons for what he describes as the regulatory turn in international law.

458 See for instance, The White House, National Security Strategy 2017, at 8: 'We would face grave danger if terrorists obtained inadequately secured nuclear, radiological, or biological material'.

459 Esmée de Bruin, 'Export Control Regimes—Present-Day Challenges and Opportunities' in Robert Beeres and others (eds), *NL ARMS Netherlands Annual Review of Military Studies 2021* (NL ARMS. T.M.C. Asser Press 2022), 43.

460 For the debate on terminology, see Sibylle Bauer, 'Internationale Entwicklungen in der Exportkontrolle' in Arnold Wallraff, Dirk Ehlers and Hans-Michael Wolffgang (eds), *Recht der Exportkontrolle: Bestandsaufnahme und Perspektiven: Handbuch zum Exportkontrollrecht.* zugleich Festgabe für Dr. Arnold Wallraff zum 65. Geburtstag (Schriften zum Aussenwirtschaftsrecht 2015), 74 – 75.

461 This means that export control regulations are often directed towards States and non-State entities that are in any case subject to wider embargo policies or economic sanctions; See on these, above at C.II. Economic Sanctions.

diction over these items. Still, it may have an interest in ensuring that the exported goods and technologies do not fall into unwanted hands. On the other hand, the receiving party, State or non-State, may want to use the goods to achieve certain economic or military goals, including by granting third parties access to the items. During the Cold War, this conflict has led to deep diplomatic clashes between the United States and its European allies on extraterritoriality, culminating in the *Pipeline* incident. Although such strong confrontations have fortunately not occurred after the end of the Cold War, the underlying issues remain and are more problematic than ever.

This chapter starts out with an overview of various international efforts and instruments to regulate the proliferation of sensitive goods, technologies and materials, highlighting export control as a growing concern of international governance (section 2). It will also be shown that while these instruments may have broad scopes of application, they do not justify the exercise of extraterritorial jurisdiction. The core of this chapter, section 3 and section 4, then analyses two specific techniques used to extend domestic jurisdiction to the importing country with regard to further re-exports or re-transfers. On the one hand, particularly the United States argues with a jurisdictional authority *qua* origin of the exported articles (section 3) while most countries engaging in export control seek to extend their legal capacities by requiring importers to voluntarily submit to domestic export regulation (section 4). Section 5 concludes that while there is legitimate practical need for extraterritorial export control, current international law principles are rather hostile towards these regulatory mechanisms.

## 2. International Instruments

As already discussed, the export control of strategic and security sensitive goods, materials and technologies is one of the most important mechanisms to counter the proliferation of certain weapons and related materials. Thus, although export control has always primarily been a matter of national security and domestic foreign policy,[462] essential parts of these regimes are determined by obligations derived from a host of fragmented international and multilateral instruments. In general, three different types

462 See for instance the findings made by the US Congress in the Export Administration Act of 1979 ('EAA'), Pub. L. 96–72 (93 Stat 503), Sec. 2, 50 U.S.C.app. § 2401.

of measures govern the non-proliferation policies in international law, i.e., binding international treaties, informal multilateral export control regimes and finally, measures imposed by the Security Council.[463]

a) International Treaties

Historically, the most significant international treaties related to non-proliferation all concerned WMDs and the materials to manufacture them, including the Treaty on the Non-Proliferation of Nuclear Weapons (**NPT**),[464] the Convention on the Prohibition of the Development, Production and Stockpiling of Bacteriological (Biological) and Toxin Weapons and on their Destruction (**BTWC**)[465] and the Convention on the Prohibition of the Development, Production, Stockpiling and Use of Chemical Weapons and on their Destruction (**CWC**).[466] While the respective treaties differ in their precise scope and design, they all reflect the common problem underlying technology export controls, i.e., the balance between the security interests of the exporting State and the economic interests of the receiving State to peacefully use the controlled technology.[467] As mentioned above, this balance is also at the heart of many disputes on the extraterritoriality of unilateral measures in this field.

The NPT, the first treaty in this series, is particularly problematic in this respect: Its non-proliferation duties are inherently discriminatory as they

463 Michael Bothe, 'Proliferation of Weapons of Mass Destruction: A Problem of Extra-Territoriality' in Günther Handl, Joachim Zekoll and Peer Zumbansen (eds), *Beyond Territoriality: Transnational Legal Authority in an Age of Globalization* (Queen Mary studies in international law. Martinus Nijhofff Publishers 2012), 491 f.

464 Treaty on the Non-Proliferation of Nuclear Weapons (adopted 1 July 1968, entered into force 5 March 1970) 729 UNTS 161 ('NPT').

465 Convention on the Prohibition of the Development, Production and Stockpiling of Bacteriological (Biological) and Toxin Weapons and on their Destruction (adopted 10 April 1972, entered into force 26 March 1975) 1015 UNTS 163 ('BTWC').

466 Convention on the Prohibition of the Development, Production, Stockpiling and Use of Chemical Weapons and on their Destruction (adopted 13 January 1993, entered into force 29 April 1997) 1974 UNTS 45 ('CWC').

467 See for instance Oliver Meier, 'Dual-Use Technology Transfers and the Legitimacy of Non-Proliferation Regimes' in Oliver Meier (ed), *Technology Transfers and Non-Proliferation: Between Control and Cooperation* (Routledge global security studies. Routledge/ Taylor & Francis Group 2014), 4.

divide State parties into two categories and limit the possession of nuclear weapons to a specific group of States, the nuclear-weapons States. This was thought necessary to stabilise the strategic power balance between the United States and the UK on the one hand and the Soviet Union on the other hand through mutual deterrence. This bipolar construction was later replaced by a multipolar concept of stability after France and China joined the treaty as nuclear-weapons States.[468] With regard to these nuclear-weapons States, Art. I of the NPT establishes an absolute prohibition on the transfer of nuclear weapons and explosive devices as well as the transfer of control of any such weapons and devices to any other recipient. Non-nuclear-weapons States on the other hand may not receive them, manufacture or otherwise acquire them.[469] As a corollary to these unequal obligations, the treaty establishes the inalienable right of all States to develop the research, production and use of nuclear energy for peaceful purposes.[470] Thus, ensuring that nuclear material and technology transferred for peaceful purposes are not diverted into military programs becomes a primary objective of the NPT. However, to achieve this objective, the NPT did not explicitly rely on the establishment of decentralised trade control mechanisms but rather opted for the creation of a specialized international organization, the International Atomic Energy Agency (**IAEA**), which monitors compliance with the NPT through the conclusion of safeguards with non-nuclear-weapons States.[471] Nonetheless, multiple non-nuclear-weapons States were able to divert nuclear materials into military programs,[472] which has sparked the adoption of additional multilateral and domestic export control measures.

In contrast to the NPT, both the BTWC and the CWC are non-discriminatory as they prohibit any State to develop, produce, stockpile or otherwise acquire the respective weapons and related materials. Both instruments also establish prohibitions on the transfer of regulated items for military purposes to any person whatsoever. At the same time, both Conventions grant State parties the right to participate in, the 'fullest possible

468 Bothe (n 463), 492 f.

469 NPT, Art. I, II.

470 NPT, Art. IV (1).

471 NPT, Art. III.

472 For instance, in 1974, India was able to successfully test a nuclear explosive device, Philippe Achilleas, 'Introduction Export Control' in Dai Tamada and Philippe Achilleas (eds), *Theory and Practice of Export Control: Balancing International Security and International Economic Relations* (SpringerBriefs in Economics. Springer 2017), at 6; Bothe (n 463), 496.

exchange' of regulated materials, equipment and technologies for peaceful purposes.[473] In this regard, both Conventions also rely on export control as an (additional) system to balance the objectives of non-proliferation and economic development. Within the BTWC regime, the Sixth and the Seventh Review Conference, interpreting Art. III of the Convention, called for the implementation of effective domestic export controls.[474] The CWC addresses the issue of export controls in the treaty itself and requires State parties to review their existing national legislation in the field of trade in chemicals.[475]

Apart from the treaties concerned with the regulation of the non-proliferation of WMDs, the recently adopted Arms Trade Treaty (**ATT**) deserves special mention as the most far-reaching international instrument dealing with the transfer of conventional weapons. The ATT's scope includes a broad range of different weapons and an extensive definition of regulated activities, covering export, import, transit, trans-shipment and brokering.[476] In particular, prohibited activities include the transfer of conventional arms contrary to Security Council resolutions or other international agreements as well as in situations where a State party has knowledge that the transfer will lead to the commission of violations such as genocide or crimes against humanity.[477] While these provisions mainly reflect existing obligations under international law, the ATT also requires State parties to maintain an export control system under their jurisdiction. It even specifies certain characteristics of the system, as the State must, before the authorization of exports, consider several factors including the potential impacts of the export on international peace and security as well as the risk of serious human rights violations.[478] Of particular interest for our purposes are the ATT's provisions regarding the prevention of the diversion of weapons for illicit purposes. While the treaty does not mention extraterritorial jurisdiction, the ATT provides for the possibility for the original exporting State to adopt a range of preventive measures, which include the requirement to submit end-use certificates or even post-

473 BTWC, Art. X; CWC, Art. II (9).

474 Sixth Review Conference of the States Parties BTWC, 'Final Document of the Sixth Review Conference', (2006) BWC/CONF.VI/6; Seventh Review Conference of the States Parties BTWC, 'Final Document of the Seventh Review Conference', (2012) BWC/CONF.VII/7.

475 CWC, Art. XI (2) (e).

476 Collectively referred to as 'transfer', ATT, Art. 2 (2).

477 Ibid., Art. 6.

478 Ibid., Art. 7 (1).

shipment inspections.[479] This provision is further flanked by an obligation to cooperate and share information with each other to combat possible diversions. The provisions of the ATT regarding export controls are therefore far-reaching and evidence of an evolving international attitude that sees unregulated arms trade as a particular global issue.

### b) Informal Multilateral Regimes

Because the provisions concerned with export control within the above-mentioned international treaties (in particular with regard to dual-use goods) are vague and indeterminate in nature, interested States have concluded a number of informal multilateral regimes to coordinate their policies in this matter. There are now four major multilateral export control regimes. Of those, three are concerned with specific WMDs, related technologies and their means of delivery (the Nuclear Suppliers Group, the Australia Group, and the Missiles Technology Control Regime), while the Wassenaar Arrangement addresses exports of conventional weapons and dual-use goods.[480] These regimes are generally constituted by the major exporting countries, which means that they are exclusively concerned with the supply side of the trade in weapons and other sensitive technology.

Apart from providing a forum for member States to regularly meet and share proliferation relevant information, the main purpose of these networks is the development and coordination of common guidelines as well as control lists, i.e., lists of sensitive items the transfer and re-transfer of which need to be monitored.[481] These lists, often containing detailed technical descriptions of the items, are then to be implemented in domestic regulation.

Some of the guidelines published by these networks contain recommendations for national export control measures, and importantly, at times endorse the assertion of extraterritorial jurisdiction. For instance, the rec-

---

479 Ibid., Art. 11 (1), (2); see also Stuart Casey-Maslen and others, *The Arms Trade Treaty: A commentary* (Oxford commentaries on international law, First edition, Oxford University Press 2016), 11.52 f.

480 Bruin (n 459), 34 – 35.

481 Masahiko Asada, 'The Role of the Security Council in WMD-Related Export Control: Synergy Between Resolution 1540 (2004) and Sanctions Resolutions' in Dai Tamada and Philippe Achilleas (eds), *Theory and Practice of Export Control: Balancing International Security and International Economic Relations* (SpringerBriefs in Economics. Springer 2017), 30.

ommendations on arms brokering legislation mentions the possibility for member States of the Wassenaar Arrangement to establish licensing requirements for nationals engaged in brokering activities regardless of where these activities take place.[482] Similarly, another agreement established under the Wassenaar Arrangement encourages participating States to adopt legislation preventing their nationals and entities registered in their territory from transporting arms in third countries.[483] Both documents thus recommend States to assert extraterritorial jurisdiction based on the nationality principle.

The Participating States of the Wassenaar Arrangement have also addressed the issue of diversion and re-export for both conventional military as well as dual-use items.[484] For instance, the 'Statement Of Understanding On Implementation Of End-use Controls For Dual-use Items'[485] contains guidance for States to adopt effective and flexible end-use controls. Among other things, States are encouraged to require the submission of end-use certificates and may – if appropriate on a case-by-case basis – demand assurance that the final end-user shall not conduct re-exports without approval from the government of the original exporting country.[486]

However, the Wassenaar Arrangement as well as the other informal regimes, due to the sensitive nature of the regulatory area in question, are all designed as legally non-binding political commitments. Therefore, the overall effectiveness of these arrangements is somewhat questionable, in particular, because decision-making in these fora is generally based on consensus,[487] and there are no enforcement mechanisms with regard to partic-

---

482 Participating States of the Wassenaar Arrangement, Best Practices for Effective Legislation on Arms Brokering, 1 (b), https://www.wassenaar.org/app/uploads/2019/consolidated/Best-Practices-for-Effective-Legislation-on-Arms-Brokering.pdf, last accessed on 13 April 2022.

483 Participating States of the Wassenaar Arrangement, Elements for Controlling Transportation of Conventional Arms Between Third Countries, Element 2, https://www.wassenaar.org/app/uploads/2019/consolidated/4-Elements-for-Controlling-Transportation-of-Conventional-Arms.pdf ,last accessed on 13 April 2022.

484 Wassenaar Arrangement, Public Documents Vol. III, Compendium of Best Practice Documents, https://www.wassenaar.org/app/uploads/2019/12/WA-DOC-19-PUB-005-Public-Docs-Vol-III-Comp.-of-Best-Practice-Documents-Dec.-2019.pdf, last accessed on 13 April 2022, pp. 76 – 87.

485 Ibid., p. 80.

486 Ibid., pp. 86 – 87.

487 Bauer (n 460), 78.

ipating States that do not adhere to the common standards.[488] Thus, unless the best practice documents and statements issued by these regimes are adopted by more formal institutions such as the IAEA or the Organization for the Prohibition of Chemical Weapons,[489] these recommendations are not legally binding and can in no way serve as a basis under international law for the exercise of extraterritorial jurisdiction.

### c) Security Council Resolutions

The instruments analysed so far have distinct weaknesses: On the one hand, international treaties contain vague and indeterminate provisions on non-proliferation export controls; on the other hand, informal multilateral regimes lack effective enforcement mechanisms and participation by the majority of (non-exporting) States. At least with regard to WMDs, these weaknesses are partly mitigated by Security Council Resolution 1540. The resolution, which forms part of a sequence of measures reacting to the 9/11 terrorist attacks, seeks to prevent non-State actors form acquiring and developing WMDs, including their means of delivery.

To this end, paragraph 1 of the resolution creates the universal mandate for all UN member States to refrain from supporting non-State actors seeking to develop or otherwise acquire WMDs. Paragraph 2 of the resolution obligates States, in accordance with their national procedures, to adopt and enforce appropriate effective legislations prohibiting such conduct. Finally, paragraph 3 of the resolution calls on all member States to establish domestic measures to prevent the proliferation of WMDs, including by establishing controls over 'related materials'. Specifically, States shall establish and maintain laws and regulations to control proliferation-relevant export, transit, trans-shipment and re-export, including end-user controls.[490] 'Related materials' in Resolution 1540 refers to dual-use goods and are defined as 'materials, equipment and technology covered by relevant mul-

---

488 Cindy Whang, 'The Challenges of Enforcing International Military-Use Technology Export Control Regimes: An Analysis of the United Nations Arms Trade Treaty' (2015) 33(1) Wisconsin international law journal 114, 130 – 131.

489 Thilo Marauhn, 'Global Governance of Dual-Use Trade: The Contribution of International Law' in Oliver Meier (ed), *Technology Transfers and Non-Proliferation: Between Control and Cooperation* (Routledge global security studies. Routledge/ Taylor & Francis Group 2014), at 58.

490 Security Council Resolution 1540 (2004), adopted on 28 April 2004, S/RES/ 1540 (2004).

tilateral treaties and arrangements, or included on national control lists, which could be used for the design, development, production or use of nuclear, chemical and biological weapons and their means of delivery'.[491] While the resolution does not explicitly specify the 'multilateral arrangements', this term is likely referring to the export control regimes discussed above.[492] However, this does not make the control lists adopted by these arrangements mandatory on all UN member States. As paragraph 6 of Resolution 1540 shows, States are rather encouraged to develop their own national control lists.[493]

The universal ambit and binding nature of Resolution 1540 prompt the question whether paragraph 2 and/or paragraph 3 of the resolution legitimizes the establishment of extraterritorial laws, including extraterritorial export control regulation.

Volz, for instance, argues that the obligation under paragraph 2 of the resolution to adopt and enforce appropriate (criminal) laws legitimizes the use of extraterritorial jurisdiction to prohibit non-State actors to manufacture, acquire, possess, develop, transport, transfer or use WMDs. He submits that the *effet utile* of the measures requires that any UN member State has the competence to punish any non-State actor found on domestic territory for having engaged in the prohibited conduct. This includes the case that a foreigner had violated the prohibitions abroad and is only later present on the territory of the member State. The punishment of non-State actors for their conduct abroad, however, would only be possible if Resolution 1540 granted member States the competence to establish *prescriptive* jurisdiction over such foreign conduct.[494] If Volz is correct, then paragraph 2 of the resolution arguably legitimizes extraterritorial export and re-export prohibitions of WMDs as this provision also refers to the 'transport' and 'transfer' of WMDs. This conclusion is not imperative, however, as it could be argued that export and re-export controls are rather subject to paragraph 3 of the resolution as *lex specialis*. In contrast to paragraph 2 of the resolution, paragraph 3 explicitly obligates the establishment of 'domestic' controls (likely meaning 'not extraterritorial').

---

491 See the Definitions in the Footnote to Security Council Resolution 1540 (2004).

492 Asada (n 481), 36.

493 The adoption of national lists concerned with WMD proliferation mirroring these produced by the various multilateral arrangements was only made mandatory in relation to North Korea with Security Council Resolution 1718 (2006), adopted on 14 October 2006, S/RES/1718 (2006); see further: ibid., 36 – 37.

494 Volz (n 24), at 331 – 332.

However, even if we accepted Volz's proposition that paragraph 2 of Resolution 1540 allows States to adopt extraterritorial export control legislation, this provision would still not justify extraterritoriality of most national export control regulations: On the one hand, paragraph 2 of the resolution only applies to the transport and transfer of the 'weapons' themselves, but not to dual-use goods. As mentioned above, dual-use goods are covered in Resolution 1540 through the definition of 'related materials' and while paragraph 3 of the resolution explicitly also controls such related materials, paragraph 2 does not. On the other hand, Resolution 1540 only concerns the proliferation of WMDs to non-State actors, while much of domestic export control measures are (also) concerned with recipients acting under the lawful authority of States. Thus, even a broad interpretation of Resolution 1540 would not serve as a basis for most extraterritorial export control regulations. Therefore, whether such measures comply with international law must be ascertained according to the customary jurisdictional principles.

### 3. Jurisdiction Based on the 'Nationality' of Goods

#### a) Practice in the United States

In the United States, rapid globalization including intensifying trade, technology transfer and investment networks has been historically perceived as a threat to the effectiveness of unilateral strategic export controls.[495] The growing capacity and possibility of foreign nations to divert controlled US goods and technology have been a thorn in the side of US regulators. It is no surprise, therefore, that the United States has pioneered the extensive use of extraterritorial export controls. Apart from extending US regulations to domestic controlled foreign subsidiaries,[496] one of the primary mechanisms employed to achieve this objective is the enforcement of re-export controls.

495 Kenneth W Abbott, 'Defining the Extraterritorial Reach of American Export Controls: Congress as Catalyst' (1984) 17 Cornell International Law Journal 79, 92; Gregory Bowman, 'A Prescription for Curing U.S. Export Controls' (2014) 97(3) Marquette Law Review 599, 628 f.

496 See above at C.II.2. The Extension of Personality-based Jurisdiction to Foreign Subsidiaries.

US re-export controls have existed at least since the end of the Second World War.[497] Today, multiple statutes and regulations administered by different government agencies govern this complex area of law. The Export Administration Regulations (**EAR**)[498] covers a broad range of dual-use goods, the commercially most important category.[499] In addition to the EAR, other notable mechanisms concerned with export and re-export control include the International Traffic in Arms Regulation (**ITAR**),[500] which covers conventional defence articles and the Atomic Energy Act,[501] which establishes the Nuclear Regulatory Commission overseeing nuclear equipment and technologies. Finally, certain country-based economic and trade sanctions programs, which often include extensive export controls beyond the category of goods mentioned above, are administered by OFAC under various legal authorities.[502]

The EAR restricts trade in controlled goods based on an evaluation of five different criteria, namely the specific characteristics of the item or technology, the destination country of the prospective transfer, the ultimate end-user and the ultimate end-use as well as the conduct in question (for instance, the EAR contains specific rules for financing, freight forwarding etc.).[503] For exports not originating within the United States, the EAR defines four different situations in which it nevertheless claims authority: First, the EAR controls the re-export of all US origin items (wherever located) to other countries, i.e., the physical transfer of goods from one foreign country to another without them passing through US territory.[504] Second, the EAR also applies to certain transactions between third countries involving purely foreign-made products if the items in question 'incorporate', are 'bundled' or 'commingled' with controlled US

497 Mestral and Gruchalla-Wesierski (n 152), at 77 f.

498 Export Administration Regulations, 15 C.F.R.§§ 730–774 ('EAR'); The EAR was based on the authority of the EAA. The EAA was supposed to expire, but has been 'kept alive' through Executive Orders, see Wei Luo, 'Research Guide to Export Control and WMD Nonproliferation Law' (2007) 35 International Journal of Legal Information 447, 449 – 450; In 2018, the Export Controls Reform Act of 2018, Pub. L. 115–232 (HR 5040) repealed the EAA and now provides the new authority.

499 Bowman (n 495), 619.

500 International Traffic in Arms Regulation, 22 C.F.R. §§ 120–130 ('ITAR').

501 Atomic Energy Act of 1954, Pub. L. 83–703, 68 Stat. 919 (1954), 42 U.S.C. §§ 2011–2297.

502 See above at C.II.1c) Overview of US Economic Sanctions.

503 EAR, 15 C.F.R. § 736.2 (a).

504 EAR, 15 C.F.R. § 736.2 (b) (1).

origin commodities or technology exceeding a certain *de minimis* level. Generally, foreign-made items are 'contaminated' and thus subject to US export control regulations if they include US content that makes up more than 25 % of the total fair market value of the product. However, for re-exports to certain countries and categories of goods considered particularly problematic, this threshold value may drop to 10 % or there may be no threshold value at all.[505] Third, foreign goods are also subject to the EAR if they do not contain any US components but are produced directly using US origin technology or software.[506] And finally, the EAR claims authority with regard to foreign goods that are not themselves produced using US origin technology but where the facility used for manufacturing them is a direct product of US origin technology or software.[507] In each of these cases, the transactions may either be prohibited or subject to a licence issued by various US government agencies. Violation of these regulations may carry both administrative and criminal sanctions even in cases where the foreign re-exporter had no knowledge of the applicable export control regulations.[508] A particularly sensitive sanction for foreign multinational enterprises is the possibility for US agencies to deny export privileges to these companies including restricting their access in general to US goods and technologies.

While enforcement of extraterritorial export control regulations has received only sparse attention after the highly political Pipeline episode,[509] recent cases regarding Chinese telecommunications companies have risen to unexpected prominence. In one case, US authorities alleged that the Chinese manufacturer ZTE and its affiliates had purchased controlled US origin equipment and subsequently re-exported them to Iran without obtaining necessary licenses. Apart from violating the general comprehensive US economic sanctions against Iran, ZTE also specifically exported telecommunications equipment with certain surveillance components (which were listed pursuant to the Wassenaar Arrangement) and thus violated the EAR.[510] ZTE pleaded guilty and paid fines exceeding USD 1 billion in a massive settlement involving various US agencies. In addition,

505 EAR, 15 C.F.R. § 736.2 (b) (2) and § 734.4.

506 EAR, 15 C.F.R. § 736.2 (b) (3).

507 EAR, 15 C.F.R. § 734.3 (a), § 736.2 (b) (3).

508 *Iran Air v Kugelman*, 996 F 2d 1253, 1257–59 (DC Cir 1993).

509 See above at C.II.2b)bb) Diplomatic Protest against US Assertions of Control-based Jurisdiction.

510 See for instance, Factual Resume, *United States v ZTE Corporation*, 3–17-cr-120k (ND Texas 2017), paras. 22 and 43.

the company agreed to a denial of export privileges for up to seven years which, however, was initially suspended subject to certain probationary conditions.[511]

However, one year after the initial closure of the case, the Bureau of Industry Security (**BIS**) found that the company had made false statements with regard to disciplinary measures that ZTE was required to take against several employees engaged in the original export scheme.[512] It thus revoked the suspension of the denial order, barring the company from importing necessary US goods and technologies. Even though US President Trump later intervened and had the denial order removed as the ZTE measures increasingly evolved into one item of negotiation within the overall trade affair between the United States and China,[513] this case demonstrates that the United States is willing and able to enforce its re-export controls against foreign corporations.

### b) Practice in China

China has continuously opposed US actions against its technology companies. The reactions have been relatively muted in the beginning but significantly escalated after the United States raised the stakes by enacting more intrusive regulations against ZTE and other national champions. The Chinese side argued that it opposed 'unilateral sanctions against Chinese entities by any country according to its domestic law'.[514] While the Chinese government does not explicitly refer to possible violations of international law as a basis for its opposition, the focus on 'unilateral' and 'domestic law' may hint that China views US export control measures as impermissibly extraterritorial. However, given the general preference of

---

511 Department of Commerce, *In the Matter of Zhongxing Telecommunications Equipment et al*, Order of 15 April 2018 Activating Suspended Denial Order relating to Zhongxing Telecommunications Equipment Corporation and ZTE Kangxun Telecommunications Ltd., at 2 f.

512 Ibid., at 4.

513 Department of Commerce, *In the Matter of Zhongxing Telecommunications Equipment et al*, Order of 23 July 2018 Terminating Denial Order Issued on April 15, 2018, Against Zhongxing Telecommunications Equipment Corporation and ZTE Kangxun Telecommunications Ltd., 83 Fed. Reg. 34825.

514 Regular Press Conference of the Ministry of Commerce (16 May 2019), available at http://english.mofcom.gov.cn/article/newsrelease/press/201905/20190502864790.shtml, last accessed on 13 April 2022.

China to resolve conflicts through informal compromise as well as the chaos of the overall tension between the United States and China, of which the recent actions are just one small component, it is hard to tell whether these statements reflect *opinio iuris*.

On the other side, China has most recently adopted its new Export Control Law, which came into force on 1 December 2020.[515] Among other things, the new Chinese Export Control Law includes a provision that allows for retaliatory measures against other nations if they apply their export control regulation in a manner threatening the national security or national interest of China.[516] It does not seem far-fetched to believe that this provision is a reaction to the perceived extraterritorial nature of US export control laws.

The Chinese Export Control Law also introduces re-export controls. In this regard, Article 45 of the new law prohibits the transit, transhipment, through transportation, and re-export of any controlled item.[517] According to this provision, therefore, the Chinese Export Control Law applies to re-exports of controlled Chinese origin goods occurring solely between third countries. Notably however, a percentage test similar to the *de minimis* rule under the EAR, which was included in one of the earlier draft versions of the law,[518] was removed from the final law. Under the percentage test of the draft Chinese Export Control Law, the law would have applied to the transfer of an item from a jurisdiction outside of China to a third country or region if it contained controlled Chinese items exceeding a certain value threshold. This provision of the draft Chinese Export Control Law had caused tremendous international uncertainty and during its public comment phase, no less than 14 US, European and Japanese industry associations submitted a joint statement urging for the reconsideration of this provisions.[519] While the percentage test was eventually not included in

515 Standing Committee of the National People's Congress, Export Control Law of the People's Republic of China (promulgated on 17 October 2020, entered into force 1 December 2020), available at http://www.npc.gov.cn/npc/c30834/202010/cf4e0455f6424a38b5aecf8001712c43.shtml, last accessed on 13 April 2022.

516 Export Control Law of the People's Republic of China, Art. 48.

517 Export Control Law of the People's Republic of China, Art. 45.

518 Draft Chinese Export Control Law, Art. 64, available at http://www.cistec.or.jp/english/export/china_law/02_fuken1.pdf, last accessed on 13 April 2022.

519 The Computing Technology Industry Association et al., 'Joint Comments by Industrial Associations of the United States, Europe and Japan on China's Export Control Law Draft', at 6: 'Reexports have extra-territorial effects, which should be eliminated or highly limited', available at http://www.cistec.or.jp/service/china_law/180309-01-e.pdf, last accessed on 13 April 2022.

the final Export Control Law, it may be possible for the test to be revived through administrative regulations.

c) Practice in Europe

European practice with regard to re-export controls has been inconsistent.[520] The most significant European action has actually been a series of *reactions* in 1982 against the scope of US regulations during the already mentioned *Pipeline* incident. In the same diplomatic note criticizing the US use of control-based jurisdiction,[521] the EC also protested the export prohibitions to the Soviet Union based on the origin of the goods or technologies involved.[522] After the 1982 *Pipeline* incident however, European States have started to either silently acknowledge the existence of US re-export controls without further protest or in exceptional cases even started to collaborate with US authorities in limited areas. The UK for instance has recently concluded a treaty with the United States (the British-US Defence Trade Cooperation Treaty) which allows for the licence-free export and import of certain ITAR listed goods to British firms. In return, however, the treaty stipulates that further re-transfers and re-exports are subject to control and that in particular, the UK government, before granting an authorization, shall require documentation including US approval of the proposed transaction.[523] Although the explicit inclusion of a provision on mutual re-export control may be a novel approach, it seems that British authorities have informally supported US re-export policies already before the conclusion of the Defence Trade Cooperation Treaty.[524]

520 See further Quentin Genard, 'European Union Response to Extraterritorial Claims by the United States: Lessons from Trade Control Cases' [2014] Non-Proliferation Papers 1.

521 See above at C.II.2b)bb) Diplomatic Protest against US Assertions of Control-based Jurisdiction.

522 European Community: Note and Comments on the Amendments of 22 June 1982 to the Export Administration Act, Presented to the United States Department of State on 12 August 1982, 21 ILM (1982) 891.

523 Treaty between the Government of the United Kingdom of Great Britain and Northern Ireland and the Government of the United States of America concerning Defense Trade Cooperation, Treaty Series No. 26 (2013), Art. 9 (1).

524 See the verbal exchange between Mr. Jenkin and Mr. Lincoln, House of Commons, Defence Committee, Third Report of Session 2007–08 on the UK/US Defence Trade Cooperation Treaty, at 18.

While European States have thus backed down from their hostile attitude regarding US re-export controls, their own efforts in preventing the diversion of exported goods are much less intrusive. In particular, European States have not assumed jurisdiction over transactions between third countries based on the origin of the involved goods (or the origin of the components of the goods or the origin of the underlying technology). Rather, the European system of re-export controls generally relies on the use of end-user certifications.[525]

d) Comparative Normative Analysis

States have a legitimate interest that sensitive items and technologies posing potential security threats are not used or disposed in any way contrary to the conditions under which the original export was licenced. This is well recognized and several international documents including Security Council Resolution 1540 refer to the establishment of re-export controls to this end.[526] However, while the State of origin undoubtedly has jurisdiction over the primary export of controlled goods in the moment that these goods are physically removed from its territory, that territorial jurisdiction of the exporting State generally ceases to exist once the goods have reached the dominion of another (the importing) State.[527] The question thus becomes whether re-export regulations are justified by some jurisdictional basis under international law other than territoriality. In this regard, the nationality principle, the protective and the effects principle as well as considerations of anti-evasion all potentially support domestic re-export controls. However, the following analysis confirms that for the majority of cases, none of these principles justify regulating exports between third State parties after the controlled goods have left the territorial jurisdiction of the original exporting State.[528]

525 See below at C.III.4b) Practice in Europe.

526 See above at C.III.2c) Security Council Resolutions.

527 *American President Lines Ltd v China Mutual Trading Co Ltd.*, Supreme Court of Hong Kong, 1953 American Maritime Cases 1510. The facts of the case are summarized in Cynthia D Wallace, *The Multinational Enterprise and Legal Control: Host State Sovereignty in an Era of Economic Globalization* ([2. ed.], Martinus Nijhoff 2002), at 599.

528 Andrea Bianchi, 'Comment to Professor Maier' in Karl M Meessen (ed), *Extraterritorial Jurisdiction in Theory and Practice* (Kluwer Law Internat 1996), 95; Achilleas (n 472), 13; Volz (n 24), at 85 – 86; Christian Forwick, *Extraterritori-*

The United States seems to view the origin of goods and technologies to be something similar to the nationality of natural or legal persons. Goods and technologies that contain at least a *de minimis* level of US origin content are considered as 'items subject to the EAR' which remain under the jurisdiction of the United States even after these goods have been exported abroad.[529] However, outside of the United States, this theory has not been accepted in practice: For instance, during the *Pipeline* incident, the EC argued that US re-export controls could not be based on the nationality principle because '[g]oods and technologies do not have any nationality and there are no known rules under international law for using goods or technology situated abroad as a basis of establishing jurisdiction over the persons controlling them.'[530] This view is also overwhelmingly shared in literature.[531] Nationality is considered to have its basis in the notion of attachment or allegiance to a State as well as in the existence of reciprocal rights and duties. However, unlike ordinary natural persons, goods and technologies can neither develop feelings of affiliation towards a nation nor enjoy the benefits of nationality nor be bearer of rights and obligations.[532] Thus, because goods do not possess any nationality, it is not possible under international law to use their origin as basis for extraterritorial re-export controls.

Because export controls relate to matters of national security and other threats to the domestic territory or economy, it does not seem too far-fetched to consider the protective or the effects principle to justify jurisdiction over persons controlling certain sensitive goods.[533]

The application of the protective principles requires a threat to the State's fundamental interests, such as its security, integrity, sovereignty or important governmental functions.[534] Because there is a tendency for States to quite easily assume a danger to the security and integrity of

*ale US-amerikanische Exportkontrollen: Folgen für die Vertragsgestaltung* (Abhandlungen zum Recht der Internationalen Wirtschaft vol 25, Verlag Recht und Wirtschaft 1992), at 77.

529 EAR, 15 C.F.R. § 734.3.

530 European Community: Note and Comments on the Amendments of 22 June 1982 to the Export Administration Act, Presented to the United States Department of State on 12 August 1982, 21 ILM (1982) 891, 894.

531 See e.g., Bowman (n 495), 654 ff; certain exceptions are accepted, for instance with regard to marine vessels, aircrafts and spacecrafts as well as cultural property.

532 Forwick (n 528), at 77.

533 *United States v Evans*, 667 F Supp 974, 980 – 981 (SDNY 1987).

534 See above B.I.2e) The Protective Principle.

the State,[535] the literature is rightly restricting jurisdiction based on the protective principle to direct threats.[536] Thus, the protective principle is at most applicable for very exceptional cases of re-export, such as when precursors to WMDs or other weapons are diverted to terrorist organisations planning an imminent attack on the State.[537] However, certainly the vast majority of re-exports of controlled items do not meet this requirement. Rather, re-exports in general do not threaten the existence or essential functions of the original exporting State in such a way as to justify application of the protective principle.

Similarly, the effects doctrine cannot generally justify the extension of jurisdiction to re-exports. In this regard, this basis of jurisdiction requires the occurrence of actual effects; the mere potential or threat of negative implications is not a sufficient basis to assert effects-based jurisdiction.[538] Most re-exports certainly do not satisfy this requirement because the mere transfer of goods between two parties located abroad hardly ever creates any tangible effect within the original exporting State. However, if a re-export should, under exceptional circumstances, indeed result in direct and substantial effects to the State's national security, then the protective principle would also likely apply. In this case, considerations with regard to the effects principle would be superfluous. Accordingly, the role of the effects principle in justifying re-export controls is rather limited.

The most convincing argument to allow for (limited) jurisdiction over extraterritorial re-exports seems to stem from considerations of anti-evasion. In fact, even authors in support of origin-based re-export controls implicitly argue with their purpose to contain abuse and to enhance the efficiency of the entire control system.[539] For instance, if a transaction involves exporting controlled goods from the United States to Iran with a short storage transit in Germany, it would be reasonable to assume that US

535 See Ryngaert, *Jurisdiction in International Law* (n 2), 115.

536 See above B.I.2e) The Protective Principle.

537 More restrictive: Mestral and Gruchalla-Wesierski (n 152), at 30.

538 Ryngaert, *Jurisdiction in International Law* (n 2), 114; The court in *United States v Evans*, 667 F. Supp. 974, 980 – 981 (SDNY 1987) applied both the protective and the effects principle.

539 According to Karl M Meessen, 'Extraterritoriality of Export Control: A German Lawyer Analysis of the Pipeline Case' (1985) 27 German Yearbook of International Law 97, 100 f., 'there is a basis for jurisdiction for regulating foreign-state-to-foreign-state exports if the regulations relate to goods exported from the regulating state or are produced under its licence'; See also: Wallace (n 527), 611 f.

jurisdiction extended to the entire transfer. The transit through Germany does not materially change the overall direction of the export from the United States to Iran. Because the entire transfer from the United States to Iran must be regarded as a single export in this specific case, territorial jurisdiction of the State of origin sufficiently justifies regulation of the transit through Germany.[540]

The same should apply if a US company, because it is prohibited to directly export certain controlled items to Iran, arranged with a German company that it would instead export the goods to the German importer, however, under the mutual understanding that the goods should be eventually forwarded to Iran. The purpose of the German company is thus to act as an intermediary, disguising the intended transfer of the goods from the United States to Iran. In this case, it could be argued that the United States should not only be able to assert jurisdiction over the first export from US territory to Germany, but also over the re-export of the items from Germany to Iran. In this regard, both the German intermediary company and the US exporter engaged jointly in an evasive scheme, justifying the exercise of jurisdiction also over the re-export.

It would, however, go too far if one were to consider every re-export to fall under considerations of anti-evasion. Specifically, if an unsuspecting US company exported controlled items to a German importer, and the importer later decides on his own volition to divert the items to a sensitive destination, this re-export cannot be regarded as an act of evasion. The German importer is not bound by US export control regulations (assuming he did not voluntarily subject himself to such regulations[541]). Therefore, because he is not required to follow US export controls, his conduct cannot be considered an evasion of these controls. Unlike the above example, the German importer is also not acting jointly with the US counterpart, which would justify US jurisdiction over the entire evasive scheme. Thus, while anti-evasion may justify some US re-export controls, this principle certainly cannot support the vast majority of EAR controls based on the origin of the controlled goods.

540 In this sense: Abbott (n 495), at 134 – 137 proposes a rule where US authority ceases when the goods have 'come to rest' in another jurisdiction.

541 See below at C.III.4. Jurisdiction Based on Voluntary Submission.

### 4. Jurisdiction Based on Voluntary Submission

#### a) Practice in the United States

As already indicated above, another regulatory technique to prevent the potentially adverse effects of re-exports involves the use of voluntary submissions, such as certificates, contracts and similar instruments in which the purchaser guarantees that he/she will not use or transfer the received goods contrary to the original license. Despite the fact that US law applies *eo ipso* to re-exports of all items and technologies of US origin to third States, US agencies sometimes require foreign importers to additionally submit an end user statement. For instance, 15 C.F.R. § 748.9 (b) and § 748.11 require an application for an export licence to include a 'Statement by Ultimate Consignee and Purchaser' for certain defence equipment as well as for exports to the PRC.[542] In this statement, the end user must declare that he/she will not re-export the items received unless specifically authorized by the EAR or by prior written approval of the BIS.[543]

Moreover, the United States sometimes requires importers of US origin goods to consent to physical on-site visits in the host country in order to inspect that the imported goods are only used according to the license and have not been re-transferred or re-exported. One such program is the Validated End-User (**VEU**) Program in which companies from certain foreign countries (most notably China) can apply for a privileged status resulting in a more streamlined export control licensing procedure to these approved end-users.[544] Among others, one of the considerations for foreign companies to receive VEU authorization is consenting to on-site reviews by US Government officials to verify the end-user's compliance

542 EAR, 15 C.F.R. § 748.9 (b) and § 748.11 (a); See also Mestral and Gruchalla-Wesierski (n 152), 82.

543 Form BIS-711 of the US Department of Commerce: '[E]xcept as specifically authorized by the U.S. Export Administration Regulations (15 C.F.R. parts 730–774), or by prior written approval of the Bureau of Industry and Security, we will not reexport, resell, or otherwise dispose of any items approved on a license supported by this statement (1) to any country not approved for export [...], or (2) to any person if we know that it will result directly or indirectly, in disposition of the items contrary to the representations made in this statement or contrary to Export Administration Regulations.'.

544 EAR, 15 C.F.R. § 748.15.

with the conditions of the authorization.[545] However, even prior to the establishment of the VEU Program in 2007, the United States had assumed the possibility to conduct physical on-site verifications for military items[546] as well as for dual-use items.[547] With regard to dual-use items, the BIS is posting Export Control Officers at various locations around the world to conduct such verifications. If a verification is not possible for instance because of lack of cooperation by the foreign company or interference by the host government, the companies may be included on the Unverified List by the Department of Commerce which will inhibit their ability to receive further exports.[548]

### b) Practice in Europe

During the *Pipeline* incident, the EC not only criticized US re-export controls based on the 'nationality' of goods, it also condemned the use of private submissions to justify US jurisdiction. In the 1982 regulations, the US government relied on prior private submissions to prohibit the export and re-export of direct products of US origin technology: Among others, such re-export was prohibited (1) if the foreign user of the technology had been required to give a written assurance, at the time of the original technology transfer, that it would not transfer the technology or any of its direct products to the Soviet Union; or (2) if the foreign user had agreed to abide by US export control regulations in a license agreement or similar contract with its American supplier.[549] The EC, in its diplomatic memorandum, rejected this assertion of jurisdiction, arguing that the United States attempted to misuse the freedom of contract in order to circumvent rules of international law: Private contractual submissions, the EC argued, could not serve as a valid basis for jurisdiction.[550]

545 EAR, 15 C.F.R. § 748.15 (a) (2).

546 Andrea Edoardo Varisco, Kolja Brockmann and Lucile Robin, 'Post-shipment Control Measures: European Approaches to On-site Inspections of Exported Military Materiel' (2020) https://www.sipri.org/sites/default/files/2020-12/bp_2012_post-shipment_controls.pdf, p. 16.

547 Ibid.

548 EAR, 15 C.F.R. § 744.15 (c).

549 See Abbott (n 495), 87.

550 European Community: Note and Comments on the Amendments of 22 June 1982 to the Export Administration Act, Presented to the United States Department of State on 12 August 1982, 21 ILM (1982) 891, 895 f.

However, despite these differences during the *Pipeline* incident, contemporary administrative practice of most EU member States frequently makes use of end user certificates including private submissions to the jurisdiction of the exporting State. According to Art. 12 (2) of the Council Regulation (EU) 2021/821, which regulates export controls with regard to dual-use goods, member State authorities must require an end-use statement as part of the application documents for any license.[551] While the exact certifications end-users have to give with regard to re-export differ from country to country, Germany, for instance, requires that end-users declare that no re-export will be undertaken without the prior approval of the German government (*Genehmigungsvorbehalt*).[552] In principle therefore, the end-user abroad must abide by German export control regulations, non-compliance with which may have consequences for future licensing decision.[553] This approach, levelling end-use certificates to strengthen re-export controls is also explicitly endorsed by the EU Council in its 'Best practice recommendations for elements of a Community End Use Certificate'.[554] Other member States apart from Germany have thus adopted similar regulations.[555]

Similar to the United States, European nations have recently started to conduct physical on-site verifications within the territory of the importing nation or to require the importing State to consent to such verifications. In Germany for instance, according to § 21 (5) of the Foreign Trade Ordinance, German authorities may condition export licence approval on the submission of a certification issued by the importing country that it agrees to on-site post-shipment verifications.[556] However, during the pilot phase since May 2017, this provision was only applied to exports to governmen-

551 Regulation (EU) 2021/821 of the European Parliament and of the Council of 20 May 2021 setting up a Union regime for the control of exports, brokering, technical assistance, transit and transfer of dual-use items (recast), [2021] OJ L206/1.

552 Federal Office for Economic Affairs and Export Control, 'Manual: Completion of German end-use certificates', p. 9 – 10, available at https://www.bafa.de/SharedDocs/Downloads/DE/Aussenwirtschaft/afk_eve_ausfuellanleitung_eng_sonstige_gueter.pdf?__blob=publicationFile&v=2, last accessed on 13 April 2022.

553 Ibid.

554 Council of the European Union, Best practice recommendations for elements of a Community End Use Certificate, 17135/08, COMER 228, Annex, at 2.

555 For a discussion of other EU member State practice, see Odette Jankowitsch-Prevor and Quentin Michel (eds), *European Dual-Use Trade Controls: Beyond Materiality and Borders* (Peter Lang 2014).

556 § 21 (5) of the German Foreign Trade Ordinance.

tal recipients of small arms and light weapons and other specific types of firearms so that the full potential of the provision has not been tested in practice yet.[557]

c) Comparative Normative Analysis

The practice of end user certificates, in which the purchaser of controlled goods agrees to abide by the export control regulations of the exporting State, raises the question whether submissions by private parties may serve as a basis for the exercise of extraterritorial jurisdiction. Phrased differently, is the exporting State permitted under international law to exercise jurisdiction over a purchaser abroad simply because that purchaser has consented to such jurisdiction. The answer to this question is crucial as re-export controls are ordinarily not justified by any of the traditional jurisdictional principles.[558]

When the importer declares in an end-user certificate that he will not re-export the received items without prior administrative approval of the exporting State, he consents to the power of the exporting State to create rules with regard to his conduct, in particular to allow or to prohibit a further re-export. We can thus interpret this consent as a voluntary submission of the importer to the (extraterritorial) jurisdiction to prescribe of the original exporting State. While the EC argued strongly against the validity of such private consent to US jurisdiction during the *Pipeline* incident,[559] States, in contemporary practice, make widespread use of end-user certificates or contractual clauses to secure their export control strategy.

In light of this development, Ryngaert has argued that there are generally no reasons why a private company should not be able to voluntarily 'bond' to the regulatory standards of another country because the submission to the jurisdiction to prescribe of the exporting State would not diminish the regulatory competence of the home State of the importer.[560] If the home State of the importer indeed disapproved of the possibility of domestic importers to subject themselves to foreign jurisdiction, it

557 Edoardo Varisco, Brockmann and Robin (n 546), p. 15 – 16.

558 See above at C.III.3d) Comparative Normative Analysis on the question that there is ordinarily no basis under international law for re-export controls.

559 Supporting this view also, Volz (n 24), 216 – 217.

560 Ryngaert, 'Extraterritorial Export Controls (Secondary Boycotts)' (n 345), 634 f. who notes that this happens very commonly in the field of international financial regulation.

would always retain the possibility to explicitly prohibit such conduct (for instance by using a blocking statute).[561] Support for Ryngaert's position may further be found in principles of private international law, where the possibility to contractually apply foreign law or to submit disputes to a certain jurisdiction has been long accepted.[562]

However, there are compelling arguments against accepting private submissions to foreign regulations as a valid jurisdictional basis. From a practical perspective, allowing importers to voluntarily subject themselves to the regulation of the exporting State would increase the possibility of conflict if the rules of both States contradicted each other, which may result in unwanted legal limbos.[563] However, the potential of conflict alone would not suffice to dismiss jurisdiction based on private submissions as conflicting prescriptive jurisdiction is a regular occurrence in international law, for instance if regulations prescribed by two States based on nationality and territoriality differ. More fundamentally however, the scope of prescriptive jurisdiction of a State is traditionally determined by the existence of a genuine link between the State and the situation at hand in a form such as territoriality, effects or nationality. It is doubtable whether such a genuine link may be replaced by voluntary private submissions. Rather, under traditional doctrine, private entities cannot alter the sovereign legal position of States, either through contract with or through submission to another government.

This conclusion would necessarily also apply to the submission of the importer to post-shipment verifications including on-site visits. In fact, unlike mere approval requirements for re-exports, such physical controls would amount to an assertion of enforcement jurisdiction by the original exporting State. If the importer cannot alter the scope of its home State's jurisdiction to prescribe, then it is still less able to dispose of its home State's jurisdiction to enforce, which is strictly territorial under international law. An exporting State may not exercise jurisdiction to enforce through on-site verifications based solely on the consent of the importer as doing so would severely encroach on the territorial sovereignty of the importing State. Rather, the consent of the home government, either for

561 Ibid., 635.

562 Mills (n 14), 230 – 233.

563 See for instance Simon Rice, 'Discriminating for World Peace' in Jeremy M Farrall and Kim Rubenstein (eds), *Sanctions, Accountability and Governance in a Globalised World* (Connecting international law with public law. Cambridge University Press 2009), at 367.

individual verifications or in general through an international agreement on the matter, must be additionally present.[564]

In practice, however, this constellation poses less problems than the submission of domestic importers to the exporting State's extraterritorial jurisdiction to prescribe. This is because in general, such on-site verifications are only conducted with the approval or in conjunction with the government of the importing State. With regard to the VEU for instance, the United States had already previously concluded a specific agreement with China on the issue of verification.[565] The recently introduced possibility of physical inspections in German export control regulations also requires the consent not of the individual importer, but its home country.[566]

### 5. Conclusion

The end of the Cold War and the rise of new transnational threats in conjunction with the process of globalization and advancements in communication technology have dramatically changed the international security landscape. The risk that conventional weapons and WMDs, as well as dual-use goods and technologies that have both civil and military application, may land into the wrong hands has grown into a pressing global concern. At the same time however, private companies and developing States have legitimate interests to profit from these goods and technologies economically. Export control has established itself as the standard mechanism to balance these two objectives – limit the possibly devastating effects of proliferation, while allowing trade with non-critical counterparts. However, export control regulation has traditionally suffered from territorial limitations, i.e. that jurisdiction over sensitive goods and technologies generally ends once they are outside domestic borders.

Various international instruments, treaties, non-binding multilateral export control regimes and in particular Security Council Resolution 1540 have thought to address the issue, however, none of them offers a firm basis for the assertion of extraterritorial jurisdiction. States have therefore

564 Ernst Hocke and others, *Außenwirtschaftsrecht* (Bärbel Sachs and Christian Pelz eds. Heidelberger Kommentar, C.F. Müller 2017), § 21 AWV Rn. 37.

565 The confidential 2004 End-Use Visit Understanding, see Hugo Meijer, *Trading with the Enemy: The Making of US Export Control Policy toward the People's Republic of China* (First edition, Oxford University Press 2016), at 309 f.

566 § 21 (5) of the German Foreign Trade Ordinance.

turned to domestic mechanisms and in particular to re-export controls. These are based either on the origin of the goods and technologies or on voluntary consent by the ultimate importer to not further transfer the goods without prior authorization. As we have seen, both of these regulatory approaches have already featured in the 1984 *Pipeline* incident and were then heavily criticized by the EC. Likewise, closer analysis reveals that both mechanisms lack normative support: The exercise of jurisdiction over persons controlling certain goods based on the origin of such goods cannot be sustained under current principles of international law. The nationality principle does not apply to sensitive products or technology and such regulations are also not legitimized by the protective or the effects principle. Only in rare exceptions might there be room for the application of the principle of anti-evasion. Similarly, traditional jurisdictional principles do not envisage the possibility of private companies submitting themselves to the jurisdiction to prescribe of another State as private consent is irrelevant in the face of sovereign rights.

In contrast to the legal position, however, stands the actual contemporary State practice. While States have not explicitly accepted origin-based technology controls, in particular by the United States, they have also not staged major protests and silently acknowledged the existence of such practice. With regard to re-export regulation based on private consent, almost all major exporting countries require end user certificates or similar documents in which the importing party is required to submit itself to the regulatory authority of the exporting State. This State practice indicates that there is an actual need for such regulations. At the current stage of international law however, the principles of jurisdiction do not allow such mechanisms.

While the role of private agreement within the area of security-based export control is only one example, it is indicative of a larger issue, in that the territoriality-based system of jurisdiction is unable to account for interests that are not connected to State sovereignty. However, it is arguable that contemporary forms of regulation are shifting away from a purely sovereignty-centred model to one where private parties are equally taking part in the formulation of rules and may also influence the scope of application of those rules. In this regard, it has already been mentioned that the possibility to confer jurisdiction through private autonomy has long been recognized in private international law.[567] These issues will be examined more closely in the final part of this study.

---

567 See on this: Mills (n 14), 233 – 234.

With regard to export control, the prevention of irregular re-transfers, either through private agreement or other modes, will likely grow in importance in the future. While this development is certainly to be welcomed, it also risks creating conflicting burdens on exporting companies, which may have to comply with different sets of export control regulations for every transaction. In this respect, international harmonization of the lists of controlled goods within multilateral control regimes would go a long way to eliminate double regulation.

## IV. Anti-Corruption

### 1. Introduction

Corruption has become a transnational phenomenon. This is illustrated by no better example than the infamous Ibiza affair when video footage was released showing two senior Austrian politicians together with the supposed niece of a Russian oligarch in a villa on the Spanish holiday island Ibiza, allegedly discussing the trade of public contracts for various political campaign support for the Austrian Freedom Party.[568] While most corrupt practices do not have the potential to cause the collapse of a government within 24 hours, there is a wide international consensus that transnational corruption is an issue that needs to be combatted. However, even though corruption is subject to an international framework of governance, the main thrust of regulation still happens on the domestic level, where more and more States are adopting legislation, often with far-reaching extraterritorial effects.

These laws and related practices form the centre of the following inquiry. Although corruption is an umbrella concept for a wide range of different activities,[569] the primary subject of national and international regulation is bribery, a specific, legally reasonably well-defined offense. Bribery refers to a transaction, in which the bribe-taker (who need not necessarily be a public official) provides the bribe-giver an undue advan-

568 Maik Baumgärtner et. al., 'The Strache Recordings – The Whole Story' *Spiegel International* (17 May 2019), https://www.spiegel.de/international/europe/strache-caught-on-camera-in-ibiza-secret-recordings-a-1267959.html, last accessed on 13 April 2022.

569 The most comprehensive international legal instrument on corruption, the 2003 UNCAC (n 15), prescribes the criminalization of offenses as diverse as bribery, embezzlement, trading in influence, and abuse of functions.

tage by abusing or misusing his or her power in return for a monetary or otherwise valuable benefit.[570] This type of *quid pro quo* bribery is often seen as the most obvious form of corruption and in fact, within common parlance, these two terms are often used interchangeably.

In the previous chapters, we have begun to deconstruct the traditional framework of jurisdiction in customary international law. We have seen that this framework, in contrast to popular assumption, fails to offer a clear doctrinal answer to the (il-)legality of extraterritorial economic sanctions, used in particular by the United States. This is further evidenced by the inconsistent practice of European States, whose reactions to US measures depended highly on political convenience, specifically the alignment between the two blocs on the fundamental policy issues addressed by the sanctions.[571] The following analysis builds upon these findings:

On the one hand, this chapter expands the argument that customary international law principles do not enable clear doctrinal assessments of extraterritorial jurisdiction. To this end, this chapter contrasts the practice in the area of anti-corruption with that in the area of economic sanctions. In fact, regulation in both areas partly rely on similar jurisdictional triggers, namely the control of foreign subsidiaries by domestic companies and, in the US context, the use of the US financial system. Despite these similarities and in contrast to the situation with secondary sanctions, there is no evidence of any State protest against transnational anti-bribery regulation. This finding adds further uncertainty to the normative status of these triggers under international law.

On the other hand, similar to what has been argued in relation to extraterritorial export controls,[572] I will again contend that the customary international law principles provide an only incomplete picture: Here, the traditional doctrine fails to account for the existence of internationally shared community interests, which in practice greatly affect the acceptance of extraterritorial jurisdiction. In fact, modern anti-bribery regulations at times include a jurisdictional mechanism which goes decidedly beyond those used in secondary sanctions. The lack of protest against these measures can hardly be grounded on doctrinal reasoning because they arguably violate traditional jurisdictional principles. However, an important difference between these two areas is that while economic sanctions

570 Simeon Obidairo, *Transnational Corruption and Corporations: Regulating Bribery through Corporate Liability* (Taylor and Francis 2016), 31 – 32.

571 See above at C.II.2c) Comparative Normative Analysis.

572 See above at C.III.4c) Comparative Normative Analysis.

are frequently levied to 'enforce' particular domestic foreign policy preferences, corruption is almost universally perceived by the international community as a global challenge. Part C chapter II has demonstrated that political interests were a significant determinant of whether European States protested secondary US sanctions. The following analysis takes this finding one step further and argues that the existence of a shared international community interest is the dominant explanation for the lack of protest against extraterritorial bribery regulations.

This global recognition that corruption poses a problem for society has been the result of both the availability of contemporary research highlighting the negative effects of corruption as well as a particular historic development, which had its inception in the form of a single domestic law, the US Foreign Corrupt Practices Act (**FCPA**).[573] Section 2 of this chapter contextualizes extraterritorial corruption regulation within this background. Section 3 then goes on to analyse multiple international regulatory instruments, in particular the OECD Convention on Combating Bribery of Foreign Public Officials in International Business Transactions (**OECD Anti-Bribery Convention**)[574] and the United Nations Convention against Corruption (**UNCAC**).[575] Despite their comprehensive ambition, international treaties do not allow for the regulation of corruption beyond the established customary law principles. Sections 4 to 6, the core of this chapter, focus on three domestic anti-bribery legislations, from the United States, the UK and France respectively, as well as the (muted) international response thereto. These sections will explore how each act achieves extraterritorial effects in light of the traditional principles of jurisdiction in international law, in particular by leveraging parent-subsidiary relationships, the mechanism of correspondent account banking as well as jurisdiction based on 'business presence'. Section 7 concludes accordingly.

---

573 Foreign Corrupt Practices Act of 1977, Pub. L. No. 95–213, 91 Stat. 1494, 15 U.S.C. § 78dd-1 (1977).

574 Convention on Combating Bribery of Foreign Public Officials in International Business Transactions (adopted 17 December 1997, entered into force 15 February 1999) (1998) 37 ILM 1.

575 United Nations Convention against Corruption (adopted 11 December 2003, entered into force 14 December 2005) 2349 UNTS 41 ('UNCAC').

## 2. Foundations of Transnational Anti-Corruption Regulation

It is one of the distinct features of anti-corruption regulation – and important for the normative arguments made later in this chapter – that extraterritorial jurisdiction in this area is embedded within a global agenda. The international community is nowadays largely unanimous in that it views corruption as a global concern demanding urgent reaction. This is supported by a growing body of research providing proof of the negative economic, developmental and political consequences of corruption:[576] It distorts economic growth,[577] reduces the level of private investment as well as public spending[578] and erodes trust in public institutions.[579]

However, this international consensus has been long in the making. In fact, up until the 1970s, some research suggested that corruption may serve to overcome excessively burdensome bureaucratic machineries and thus 'grease the wheels' of economic development.[580] This, coupled with

---

576 See more generally on this: Eugen Dimant and Schulte Thorben, 'The Nature of Corruption: An Interdisciplinary Perspective' (2016) 17(1) German Law Journal 53.

577 Nauro F Campos, Ralitza Dimova and Ahmad Saleh, 'Whither Corruption?: A Quantitative Survey of the Literature on Corruption and Growth' (Bonn 2010). IZA Discussion Paper 5334 http://ftp.iza.org/dp5334.pdf, last accessed on 13 April 2022.

578 According to the researched data, if Bangladesh for instance improved the integrity and efficiency of its bureaucracy to the level of that of Uruguay, private investment would rise by almost 5 %, and its yearly GDP growth rate would rise by over 0.5 %, Paolo Mauro, 'Corruption and Growth' (1995) 110(3) The Quarterly Journal of Economics 681, 700 – 704. See further, Susan Rose-Ackerman and Bonnie J Palifka, *Corruption and Government: Causes, Consequences, and Reform* (Second edition, Cambridge University Press 2016), 29 ff.

579 In the classic study on the effects of corruption by Wade, who for years observed the Irrigation Department of a state in Southern India, he documented how officials extracted bribes from farmers for allocation of water. In fact, corruption ran so deeply in the organisation that officials actively withheld information and created uncertainties among farmers in order to solicit larger bribes. As a result, the credibility of the department had deteriorated to a degree that farmers stopped believing government warnings about actually impeding water shortages, see Robert Wade, 'The System of Administrative and Political Corruption: Canal Irrigation in South India' (1982) 18(3) The Journal of Development Studies 287, 314 – 315.

580 Samuel P Huntington, *Political Order in Changing Societies* (11. printing, Yale Univ. Press 1976), 68 -69; see also Nathaniel H Leff, 'Economic Development Through Bureaucratic Corruption' (1964) 8(3) American Behavioral Scientist 8, who argued that corruption should be treated as an additional way for business

the Cold War, in which both blocs were eager to support allies without regard to potential corrupt practices, initially hindered the establishment of anti-corruption governance at an international level.[581]

Rather, as the now often repeated story goes, international and transnational anti-corruption regulation has its beginnings in the Watergate Scandal in the United States.[582] During the investigations into illegal political campaign contributions, the Watergate Special Prosecutor uncovered the widespread use of slush funds by corporations to pay for bribes to foreign officials in international business transactions.[583] By 1977, in a voluntary disclosure programme ran by the Securities Exchange Commission (**SEC**), over 400 US corporations had admitted to paying bribes to foreign public officials in the amounts exceeding USD 300 million.[584] As a response to the suspected damage to American reputation and to restore public confidence, the US Congress, in a pioneering move, passed the FCPA, the first domestic law dealing with transnational bribery. Specifically, the FCPA targeted the supply side of international corporate bribery, i.e., the active offering of bribes by multinational corporations.

From the initial adoption of the FCPA on, it was one of the main concerns of the American business community that the new law would put US companies under a competitive disadvantage against companies from other capital-exporting States that were not bound by similar anti-corruption regulation.[585] In light of this consideration, the lobbying effort concentrated on (1), persuading Congress to repeal or at least amend the FCPA and (2), encouraging the US government to pursue the adoption

---

to influence government, which, assuming that business groups are more likely to promote growth, can in fact help development.

581 Jan Wouters, Cedric Ryngaert and Ann S Cloots, 'The International Legal Framework against Corruption: Achievements and Challenges' (2013) 14 MelbJIntLaw 1-76, 4.

582 Ibid., 3 – 12; William Magnuson, 'International Corporate Bribery and Unilateral Enforcement' (2013) 51(2) Columbia Journal of Transnational Law 360, 379 – 381.

583 Alejandro Posadas, 'Corruption under International Law' (2000) 10 Duke Journal of Comparative and International Law 345, 349 f.

584 H.R. Rep. No. 95–640, at 4 (1977); Sean Coleman, 'Foreign Corrupt Practices Act' (2017) 54 American Criminal Law Review 1381, 1382; Anita Ramasastry, 'Closing the Governance Gap in the Business and Human Rights Arena: Lessons from the Anti-corruption Movement' in Surya Deva and David Bilchitz (eds), *Human Rights Obligations of Business: Beyond the Corporate Responsibility to Respect?* (Cambridge University Press 2013), 174.

585 Magnuson, 'International Corporate Bribery and Unilateral Enforcement' (n 582), 383 f.

of an anti-corruption treaty on the international level. While the first approach proved to be only moderately successful, the second approach, encouraging the conclusion of an international instrument, eventually succeeded.

After efforts at the UN level to negotiate an agreement on anti-corruption initially failed,[586] the United States shifted its focus to a more homogenous and receptive forum, the OECD. 1997 thus saw the adoption of the OECD Anti-Bribery Convention, chiefly due to the immense pressure applied by the United States.[587] The strong US influence is also reflected in the substance of the OECD Anti-Bribery Convention, which closely tracked its intellectual predecessor, the FCPA. Just like the US statute, the OECD Anti-Bribery Convention mainly requires State parties to criminalize one specific type of offense, the active bribery of foreign government officials by corporations. Eventually, the initial vision of a treaty at the UN level was realized with the UNCAC, which was adopted by the General Assembly in October 2003. As of November 2021, there are now 189 parties to the convention, signalling a near universal approval regarding the necessity of anti-corruption measures.[588]

However, the adoption of international instruments against corruption (of which there are now six[589]) mandating legislation did not correspond with immediate action on the domestic level. In fact, until recently, the United States with the FCPA remained by far the most active player in the

586 Cecily Rose, *International Anti-Corruption Norms: Their Creation and Influence on Domestic Legal Systems* (Oxford University Press 2015), 64.

587 See on the history of the OECD Anti-Bribery Convention, Mark Pieth, Lucinda A Low and Nicola Bonucci, *The OECD Convention on Bribery: A Commentary on the Convention on Combating Bribery of Foreign Public Officials in International Business Transactions of 21 November 1997* (2. ed. Cambridge University Press 2014), at 16 – 22.

588 Latest stats available at https://www.unodc.org/unodc/en/corruption/ratification-status.html, last accessed on 13 April 2022.

589 Apart from the two already mentioned, these are: The Inter-American Convention Against Corruption (adopted 29 March 1996, entered into force 6 March 1997) (1996) 35 ILM 724 ('OAS Convention'), The Criminal Law Convention on Corruption (adopted 27 January 1999, entered into force 1 July 2002) ETS No 173 (1999) (the 'COE Criminal Law Convention'), The Convention Drawn Up on the Basis of Article K.3(2)(c) of the Treaty on European Union on the Fight against Corruption Involving Officials of the European Communities or Officials of Member States of the European Union [1997] OJ C 195/2 and The African Union Convention on Preventing and Combating Corruption (adopted 11 July 2003, entered into force 5 August 2006) 43 ILM 5 (2003) ('AU Convention').

enforcement of transnational anti-corruption regulation.[590] The number of FCPA investigations has skyrocketed from about three per year between 1978 and 2000 to around 100 per year today.[591]

Within the OECD framework, the OECD Working Group on Bribery in International Business Transactions (**OECD Working Group**) has developed an elaborate and effective peer review system to encourage action at the domestic level. In particular, the Working Group's growing frustration with the UK's inadequate and delayed implementation of the Convention may have been one of the drivers behind the eventual adoption of the UK Bribery Act.[592] Similarly, the Working Group's dissatisfaction with low enforcement levels of anti-corruption legislation in France[593] may have prompted the adoption of law n° 2016–1691 on transparency, the fight against corruption, and the modernization of the economy (referred to as **Sapin II**).[594] As we shall see, both the UK Bribery Act 2010 and the French Sapin II contain provisions with highly extraterritorial effects that may go well beyond what the OECD Anti-Bribery Convention requires. Thus, these two recent European pieces of legislation as well as the notorious American FCPA form the core of the normative inquiry into extraterritoriality related issues within the field of anti-corruption.

### 3. International Anti-Corruption Instruments

This chapter argues that the jurisdictional principles of customary international law fail to account for the status of anti-corruption as a widely

---

590 Daniel P Ashe, 'The Lengthening Anti-Bribery Lasso of the United States: The Recent Extraterritorial Application of the U.S. Foreign Corrupt Practices Act' (2005) 73(6) FordhamLR 2897, 2915.

591 Annalisa Leibold, 'Extraterritorial Application of the FCPA under International Law' (2015) 51 Willemette Law Review 223, 233.

592 Bribery Act 2010 (UK) c 23 ('Bribery Act'); Working Group on Bribery, 'United Kingdom: Phase 2bis: Report of the Application of the Application of the Convention on Combating Bribery of Foreign Public Officials in International Business Transactions and the 1997 Recommendation on Combating Bribery in International Business Transactions' (16 October 2008), para 79; Peter Alldridge, 'The U.K. Bribery Act: "The Caffeinated Younger Sibling of the FCPA"' (2012) 73 Ohio State Law Journal 1181, 1197; Rose (n 586), 84 – 92.

593 Working Group on Bribery, 'Phase 3 Report on Implementing the OECD Anti-Bribery Convention in France' (October 2012), para 15.

594 Loi n° 2016–1691 du 9 décembre 2016 relative à la transparence, à la lutte contre la corruption et à la modernisation de la vie économique ('Sapin II').

shared community interest, which in practice greatly affects the acceptance of extraterritorial regulation in this area. The previous section has briefly sketched how combatting corruption has developed into an international priority issue. This section serves to ascertain the normative framework of our inquiry, in particular, that despite this international consensus, extraterritorial regulation is still subject to the limitations of customary international law principles of jurisdiction. Specifically, the international treaties mentioned above do not allow for (among parties) a wider regulatory scope overriding the established permissive principles. Rather, although international treaties at times require an extensive interpretation of certain jurisdictional bases, they in fact closely reflect established customary international law doctrine.

#### a) The Jurisdictional Provisions of the OECD Anti-Bribery Convention

At its core, the OECD Anti-Bribery Convention requires the criminalization of active corporate bribery. In addition, State parties have to establish measures regarding the maintenance of books and records and prohibit, among others, the establishment of off-the-books accounts and the making of off-the-books or inadequately identified transactions for the purpose of bribery.[595] The Convention also includes a requirement that State parties have to make the bribery of foreign officials a predicate offense for the purpose of the application of their money laundering legislation.[596] In implementing these measures, States are not required to achieve uniformity or to change the fundamental principles of their domestic law, but rather, the Convention's goal is to assure 'functional equivalence' among its parties.[597] For instance, the Convention recognizes that not all State parties have legal systems that recognize the criminal liability of corporations. In these cases, the Convention allows for civil or administrative sanctions of legal persons, as long as they are effective, proportionate and dissuasive.[598]

---

595 OECD Anti-Bribery Convention, Art. 8 (1).

596 Ibid., Art. 7.

597 Working Group on Bribery, 'Commentaries on the Convention on Combating Bribery of Foreign Public Officials in International Business Transactions' (21 November 1997) in OECD, Convention on Combating Bribery of Foreign Public Officials in International Business Transactions and Related Documents, OECD Doc DAFFE/IME/BR(97)20 (8 April 1998) 12, 12 [2] ('OECD Anti-Bribery Convention Commentaries').

598 OECD Anti-Bribery Convention, Art. 3 (2).

Apart from substantial rules, the Convention provides for rules on mutual legal assistance as well as extradition,[599] and, of particular interest for our purposes, rules regarding the establishment of jurisdiction. According to Arts. 4 (1) and 4 (2), State parties are required to exercise territorial jurisdiction and, if their domestic laws already provide for this basis, active personality jurisdiction. The exercise of territorial jurisdiction extends over the bribery of foreign officials 'when the offence is committed in whole or in part in its territory'. This accurately reflects the territoriality principle as established by the Harvard Draft. However, already signalling an extensive application of this principle in domestic law, the official commentaries to this rule provide that this 'basis for jurisdiction should be interpreted broadly so that an extensive physical connection to the bribery act is not required'.[600]

In contrast to the obligatory exercise of territorial jurisdiction, Art. 4 (2) of the Convention requires the assertion of active personality jurisdiction only for these States that already exercise it for other crimes.[601] This limitation in particular served to accommodate State parties with a common law tradition, which historically did not accept jurisdiction based on nationality. The Convention did not want to burden States with an obligation to exercise active personality jurisdiction beyond what they have already assumed according to domestic law. Similarly, it is acceptable that a State only exercises nationality-based jurisdiction contingent on the availability of dual criminality according to its domestic law.[602]

With the acceptance of both a wide territoriality-based and active personality-based jurisdiction, the drafters of the OECD Anti-Bribery Convention have explicitly advocated for a certain degree of extraterritoriality in the fight against corruption. As such, the OECD Anti-Bribery Convention also contains a brief provision on the issue of concurrent jurisdiction. Within the framework of the Convention, this may be the case if the national of one State party bribed a foreign official within the territory of another State party so that there is an overlap of nationality and territoriality-based jurisdiction. Concurrent jurisdiction may also occur when a complex bribery transaction passes the territory of multiple jurisdictions or includes nationals from multiple State parties. In these cases, State parties shall consult with each other so as to determine the 'most appro-

---

599 Ibid., Art. 9 and 10.

600 OECD Anti-Bribery Convention Commentaries, para. 25.

601 OECD Anti-Bribery Convention, Art. 4.

602 OECD Anti-Bribery Convention Commentaries, para. 26.

priate' jurisdiction for prosecution.[603] However, the OECD Anti-Bribery Convention does not provide guidance on how the 'most appropriate' jurisdiction should be determined nor which factors should flow into the deliberation.[604]

Finally, the commentary to the OECD Anti-Bribery Convention stipulates that an act should not be deemed bribery under Art. 1 of the Convention if the advantage granted to the foreign official was 'permitted or required by the written law or regulation of the foreign public official's country'.[605] This clarification has the potential to mitigate jurisdictional conflicts between the anti-corruption law of a company's home State and the laws of the host State where the corrupt practice took place: A payment that is considered legal in the host State should also not be extraterritorially criminalized by the company's home State. However, it is unlikely that the OECD included this exception based on jurisdictional concerns. Rather, this exception was probably more intended to mitigate concerns of commercial competitiveness in countries where bribery was accepted.[606]

### b) The Jurisdictional Provisions of the UN Convention Against Corruption

Compared to the OECD Anti-Bribery Convention, the UNCAC pursued a diametrically different strategy. The objective of the Ad Hoc Committee negotiating the treaty was to create a broad and comprehensive convention: Thus, while the OECD Anti-Bribery Convention focused on the criminalization of one specific behaviour, the UNCAC addresses a wide range of different offenses considered corrupt including the bribery of domestic as well as foreign officials, embezzlement, trading of influence, abuse

---

603 OECD Anti-Bribery Convention, Art. 4 (3).

604 International Bar Association (n 12), 229.

605 OECD Anti-Bribery Convention Commentaries, para. 8.

606 This affirmative defence is also recognized by the FCPA in § 78dd-1 (c), § 78dd-2 (c) and § 78dd-3 (c); See further, Bartley A Brennan, 'The Foreign Corrupt Practices Act Amendments of 1998: Death of a Law' (1990) 15 North Carolina Journal of International Law and Commercial Regulation 229, 242 – 243; However, it should be noted that the local law exception has only played a marginal role in practice; in the United States, it was raised (but not accepted) in *United States v Kozeny* 582 F Supp 2d 535, 539 (SDNY 2008), see Mike Koehler, 'On The Eve Of Trial, Battle Over The FCPA's "Local Law" Affirmative Defense In U.S. V. Ng Lap Seng', http://fcpaprofessor.com/eve-trial-battle-fcpas-local-law-affirmative-defense-u-s-v-ng-lap-seng/, last accessed on 13 April 2022.

of functions and illicit enrichment.[607] The Convention also applies to corrupt dealings limited to private parties.[608] Apart from criminalization, the UNCAC also contains additional provisions on preventive measures, asset recovery and rules geared towards the effective enforcement of the Convention, such as freezing of proceeds of crime and the protection of whistle-blowers.

Despite the breadth of the UNCAC, particularly in light of the range of conduct it criminalizes in Part III of the Convention, the actual effects on domestic legislation may have been more limited. This is because the UNCAC distinguishes between mandatory and non-mandatory provisions: For instance, while the bribery of national public officials, the active bribery of foreign public officials, embezzlement, money laundering and obstruction of justice carry the language that State parties 'shall adopt' the necessary measures, other offenses come with a significantly weaker mandate for the State parties, in that they only 'shall consider' criminalization.

This distinction between mandatory and non-mandatory rules is further reflected in the Convention's approach towards the establishment of jurisdiction. According to Art. 42 UNCAC, State parties are required to establish jurisdiction when the offence is committed in their territory as well as when the offender is present in their territory and the State does not extradite the offender because he or she is one of its nationals.[609] The first instance concerns traditional territoriality-based jurisdiction. However, compared to the OECD Anti-Bribery Convention, it is notable that the UNCAC does not explicitly mention the case when the offense is only committed 'in part' within the territory of a State party. Whether this omission was intentional or whether it is simply a semantic error that does not carry any difference in interpretation is debated.[610] The second instance of mandatory jurisdiction concerns cases in which a national of a State party has committed an offense abroad and is later found within that State's territory. If the State party refuses extradition because of a prohibition to extradite its nationals, it has to prosecute based on the active personality principle.

The UNCAC also provides for the discretionary exercise of active personality jurisdiction in other cases as well as passive personality jurisdic-

607 UNCAC, Art. 15 -20.

608 UNCAC, Art. 21 -22.

609 UNCAC, Art. 42 (1) and 42 (3).

610 Wouters, Ryngaert and Cloots (n 581), 46; International Bar Association (n 12), 227 – 228.

tion and jurisdiction based on the protective principle.[611] Additionally, Art. 42 (4) of the UNCAC allows States to exercise jurisdiction based on the *aut dedere aut iudicare* principle, that is, if an offender is found within its territory and the State does not extradite him or her based on some other reason than nationality.[612] This basis extends beyond customary international law standards: As neither the offender nor the behaviour in question need to have any other connection to the prosecuting State party apart from the offender's presence, it is functionally a 'quasi-universal' jurisdiction.[613] With these additional bases to assert extraterritorial jurisdiction, the UNCAC, in principle, goes even further than the OECD Anti-Bribery Convention, which makes no mention of these possibilities. However, these principles do not play a major role in practice as only territorial and active personality jurisdiction is frequently asserted by domestic legislation.[614] Nonetheless, as will be discussed below, these two jurisdictional bases allow for near universal prosecution of corruption.

### 4. Regulation through Parent-Subsidiary Relationships

#### a) Practice in the United States

As indicated above, the United States has, for a long time, set the benchmark for anti-corruption legislation and enforcement with the FCPA.

611 UNCAC, Art. 42 (2).

612 Wouters, Ryngaert and Cloots (n 581), 47.

613 See already above at B.I.3. Treaty-based Extensions of Jurisdiction.

614 While no international instrument on corruption mentions the exercise of universal jurisdiction, some authors have considered that particularly heinous forms of corrupt practices may rise to crimes against humanity under Art. 7 (1) of the Rome Statute of the International Criminal Court, see Ilias Bantekas, 'Corruption as an International Crime and Crime against Humanity: An Outline of Supplementary Criminal Justice Policies' (2006) 4(3) JICJ 466, 474 and Ben Bloom, 'Criminalizing Kleptocracy?: The ICC as a Viable Tool in the Fight against Corruption' (2014) 29(3) American University International Law Review 627, 637 – 640. However, others scholars disagree, arguing that corruption, even if 'grand' on scale, is not on par with the other explicitly mentioned crimes of the Rome Statute, see Claudia Letzien, *Internationale Korruption und Jurisdiktionskonflikte: Die Sanktionierung von Unternehmen im Fall der Bestechung ausländischer Amtsträger* (Juridicum – Schriftenreihe zum Strafrecht, Springer Fachmedien Wiesbaden 2018), 272; Jessica A Lordi, 'The U.K. Bribery Act: Endless Jurisdictional Liability on Corporate Violaters' (2012) 44 Case Western Reserve Journal of International Law 955.

Particularly, in recent times, US agencies have advanced multiple expansive jurisdictional theories to regulate or sanction foreign individuals and companies for bribery offenses.[615] When studying FCPA cases and enforcement actions, it is important to remember that, similar to economic sanctions, this area of law generally gets a pass on judicial scrutiny as most of the cases are settled through non-prosecution agreements, deferred prosecution agreements or pleas.[616] Therefore, it is often unclear, on what basis or principle the enforcement agencies are grounding their jurisdictional assertions as their documents often only provide sparse argumentation. That said, many of the enforcement actions targeting essentially extraterritorial conduct concern foreign subsidiaries of 'domestic' corporations. From a normative point of view, these instances are particularly interesting because they have a certain resemblance to the control doctrine, which, in the area of economic sanctions, has at times led to substantial disagreement between nations.[617]

#### aa) The Jurisdictional Scope of the FCPA

The FCPA contains two sets of rules, first, a prohibition of bribery of foreign public officials (*the anti-bribery provisions*) and second, the requirement that corporations 'make and keep books, records, and accounts, which, in reasonable detail, […] reflect the transactions and dispositions of the assets' as well as 'devise and maintain a system of internal accounting controls' (*the accounting provisions*). Both sets of rules have been utilized to target foreign behaviour. However, at first glance, none of the jurisdictional bases of the FCPA directly mention foreign subsidiaries:

The accounting provisions (15 U.S.C. § 78m(b)(2)(A)) apply to 'issuers', which flows from the fact that the FCPA forms part of the Securities Exchange Act of 1934. 'Issuers' include any company with a class of securities listed on a national exchange in the United States or any company with

615 Leibold (n 591), 233 – 235 shows that UK, German, Swiss and French company were among the most heavily targeted by FCPA enforcement actions and that 8 out of the 10 highest monetary penalties resulting from such actions were paid by non-US companies.

616 Mike Koehler, 'The Facade of FCPA Enforcement' (2010) 41 Georgetown Journal of International Law 907, 909.

617 See above at C.II.2. The Extension of Personality-based Jurisdiction to Foreign Subsidiaries.

a class of securities traded in the over-the-counter-market in the United States and required to file reports with the SEC.[618]

The personal scope of the anti-bribery provisions is complex. In principle, the anti-bribery provisions apply to three groups of persons: (1), issuers,[619] as defined above, (2) so-called 'domestic concerns', i.e. individuals who are citizens or residents of the United States as well as any corporation, partnership or other organization that is organized under the laws of the United States, or that has its principle place of business in the United States,[620] and (3), officers, directors, employees, or agents of issuers and domestic concerns, regardless of whether they are nationals or foreigners.[621] However, foreign officers, directors, employees, or agents as well as companies not incorporated in the United States only fall under the scope of the FCPA if they 'make use of the mails or any means or instrumentality of interstate commerce corruptly in furtherance' of bribery.[622] This additional requirement need not to be satisfied if the person concerned is an US issuer or otherwise a 'United States person'.[623]

Interestingly for our purposes, the original 1977 draft of the FCPA by the US House of Representatives asserted jurisdiction also over foreign subsidiaries owned or controlled by citizens or nationals of the United

618 Criminal Division of the U.S. Department of Justice and the Enforcement Division of the U.S. Securities and Exchange Commission, 'A Resource Guide to the U.S. Foreign Corrupt Practices Act: Second Edition' (2020), at 9 and 43.

619 FCPA, § 78dd-1.

620 FCPA, § 78dd-2 (h) (1).

621 FCPA, § 78dd-1 (a); FCPA § 78dd-2 (a); Finally, the anti-bribery provisions also apply to any other person, provided that they conduct any act in furtherance of bribery 'while in the territory of the U.S.' (§ 78dd-3 FCPA) The scope of this territoriality-based jurisdiction is subject to discussion in C.IV.5. Correspondent Account Jurisdiction .

622 FCPA, § 78dd-1 (g) and § 78dd-2 (i). Note however that 'instrumentality of interstate commerce' is defined very broadly so that it rarely limits the application of the FCPA anti-bribery provisions in practice, see Criminal Division of the U.S. Department of Justice and the Enforcement Division of the U.S. Securities and Exchange Commission (n 618), at 10; see also below n 644.

623 Note that according to § 78dd-2 (h) of the FCPA, 'domestic concerns' and 'United States persons' are not synonymous. Legal persons are only qualified as 'United States persons' if they are organized under the laws of the United States while it suffices for the qualification as 'domestic concern' if they have their principal place of business in the United States. Thus, it is possible to be a 'domestic concern' but not a 'United States person'. In this case, the FCPA anti-bribery provisions only apply if an instrumentality of interstate commerce was used.

States as a subcategory of 'domestic concerns'. Surprisingly however, this explicit expansion of the active personality principle has been specifically dismissed by the US Senate because of the 'inherent jurisdictional, enforcement, and diplomatic difficulties raised by the inclusion of foreign subsidiaries of U.S. companies in the direct prohibitions of the bill'.[624] The Senate ultimately decided against such an extraterritorial assertion. This is surprising because the FCPA hails from about the same time as the infamous *Pipeline* incident, in which US regulators confidently resorted to the control doctrine.[625] In the decades following the passage of the statute however, the actual enforcement practice has more and more strayed away from the cautious stance of the Senate, and without regard to any jurisdictional or diplomatic issues, liberally sought to bring foreign subsidiaries under the purview of the FCPA. Technically, this has been possible through two regulatory innovations, by interpreting corrupt payments made by foreign subsidiaries as violations of the accounting provisions and by holding US domestic parents as well as foreign subsidiaries liable through the agency doctrine.

#### bb) Parent and Subsidiary Liability Based on the Accounting Provisions

Since the beginning of the new millennium, the SEC and the DoJ, who are jointly responsible for the enforcement of the FCPA, have started to use an expansive reading of the accounting provisions to pursue alleged briberies by foreign subsidiaries of domestic corporations. In general, violations of these provisions may carry both civil or criminal liability. While criminal liability may only be imposed if the person or corporation 'knowingly' or 'willfully' failed to implement internal control mechanisms or falsified books and records, no such mental requirement exists for civil liability.[626]

Although the accounting provisions only apply to issuers directly, an issuer's books and records also include those of its consolidated subsidiaries and affiliates.[627] Thus, issuers are not only required to follow the rules

624 H.R. Rep. No. 95–831, at 13–14 (1977); See also *Restatement (Third) of the Foreign Relations Law of the United States* (n 5), § 414, Reporter's Notes 5; Magnuson, 'International Corporate Bribery and Unilateral Enforcement' (n 582), 398.

625 See for the control doctrine above at C.II.2. The Extension of Personality-based Jurisdiction to Foreign Subsidiaries.

626 FCPA, § 78m (b) (4) – (5).

627 Criminal Division of the U.S. Department of Justice and the Enforcement Division of the U.S. Securities and Exchange Commission (n 618), 44; However,

themselves, but also to ensure compliance with the accounting provisions throughout their controlled (domestic or foreign) subsidiaries. While the extension of the accounting provisions to controlled (foreign) subsidiaries through consolidated books and records may not be considered unusual in itself, FCPA enforcement agencies have used this mechanism to target extraterritorial conduct by interpreting bribery related offenses of foreign subsidiaries as violations of the accounting provisions.

An early example of this trend can be found in the 2004 case *SEC v Schering-Plough Corporation*.[628] In it, the SEC charged Schering-Plough Corporation with violation of the accounting provisions. Factually however, it alleged that Schering-Plough Poland, a subsidiary of the defendant, had made multiple corrupt payments to a charity, whose founder and president was at the same time the director of a government health authority in Poland. The SEC did not claim that the parent organization, Schering-Plough Corporation, approved these payments or that it even knew of them. However, as the payments were disguised as donations, they were thus falsely reflected in Schering-Plough Poland's books and records and – through consolidation – eventually inaccurately recorded in the books and records of the parent organization. Because of this, Schering-Plough Corporation itself had violated the accounting provisions of the FCPA. In effect, the parent organization was held liable for an FCPA violation because of the bribes paid by its foreign subsidiary.[629] Moreover, as civil liability under the accounting provisions does not require knowledge or wilfulness, this mechanism in fact establishes a parent organization's strict liability for all of its foreign subsidiaries' dealings.[630]

---

the issuer's obligations are explicitly limited to majority-owned subsidiaries and affiliates. In this regard, § 78m(b)(6) of the FCPA stipulates that if an issuer only has minority control (less than 50 % of voting power) with respect to a domestic or foreign firm, it merely has to ensure that it uses its influence in good faith to cause these subsidiaries to maintain an accounting system as required by the FCPA.

628 Complaint, *SEC v Schering-Plough Corp.*, 1:04cv00945 (DDC 2004).

629 Ibid., at 1.

630 Ashe (n 590), 2926; Koehler, 'The Facade of FCPA Enforcement' (n 616), 979; further examples are described by Karen E Woody, 'No Smoke and no Fire: The Rise of internal Controls absent anti-bribery Violations in FCPA Enforcement' (2017) 38 Cardozo Law Review 1727, 1740 – 1743; see also Gwynne Skinner, 'Rethinking Limited Liability of Parent Corporations for Foreign Subsidiaries' Violations of International Human Rights Law' (2015) 72 Washington and Lee Law Review 1769, 1858 who uses this point as an argument to enact a similar

However, FCPA enforcement agencies have used the accounting provisions not only to hold domestic corporate parents liable but also to press criminal charges directly against the foreign subsidiaries. These actions are based on a theory that, by engaging in bribery, the foreign subsidiaries violate the FCPA accounting provisions because they *cause* their corporate parent's books and records to become false. This is due to the fact that the corrupt payments of the foreign subsidiaries are disguised and then inaccurately consolidated into the books and records of the corporate parent.

For instance, using this theory, the DoJ entered into a plea agreement with the Brazilian subsidiary of Walmart Inc. in 2019. The Statement of Facts alleged that Walmart Brazil retained the services of a 'Brazil Intermediary', who used to be a former government official, to obtain licences and permits.[631] As to the violation of the accounting provision, Walmart Brazil 'falsely recorded $527,000 in payments to Brazil Intermediary as payments to certain Brazil construction companies [...] These false records were then consolidated into Walmart's financial records and were used to support Walmart's own financial reporting'.[632] Thus, under this theory, Walmart Brazil caused corrupt payments to be falsely recorded in Walmart's books and records contrary to the accounting provisions. However, because corrupt payments by controlled companies are usually falsely reflected in the consolidated books and records of the corporate parent, this causation-theory effectively means that the accounting provisions directly prohibit briberies of foreign subsidiaries abroad. As demonstrated in the Walmart Brazil case, FCPA enforcement agencies also do not shy away from directly asserting jurisdiction against foreign subsidiaries.[633]

### cc) Parent and Subsidiary Liability Based on the Agency Theory

The re-interpretation of the accounting provision is not the only mechanism with which US authorities regulate the conduct of foreign controlled

---

statute in the field of egregious human rights violations or environmental torts by a parent organization.

631 *United States v WMT Brasilia S.a.r.l.*, Criminal No. 1:19cr192, Plea Agreement of 20 June 2019, at 32 – 33.

632 Ibid., at 31.

633 See for other examples: Criminal Information, *United States v Hewlett-Packard Polska, SP Z O.O.*, No 14-cr-202 EJD (ND Cal 2014) and Criminal Information, *United States v ZAO Hewlett-Packard A.O.*, 5:14-cr-201 DLJ (ND Cal 2014).

subsidiaries. A second strand of argumentation revolves around the expansive use of the agency doctrine. Similar to the first approach, this theory allows for charges against parent organizations based on quasi-strict liability for the conduct of their subsidiaries as well as directly against the foreign subsidiaries. However, resorting to agency law, enforcement agencies may prosecute violations not only of the accounting provisions, but also of the arguably more severe anti-bribery provisions of the FCPA.

Before moving on to the specifics of agency theory under the FCPA, it might be useful to understand some basic concepts: In general, US agency law establishes the vicarious liability of corporations for the acts of their agents.[634] Particularly interesting for our purposes is the fact that under certain circumstances, this theory may establish that a corporate subsidiary was acting as an agent of the parent.[635] In this case, agency law may serve to overcome the principle of limited liability and is in this sense related to the doctrine of piercing the corporate veil.[636] Whether a subsidiary can be deemed an agent of the parent organization is determined on a fact-specific basis with the decisive factor being the degree of control that the parent enjoyed over the subsidiary.[637] However, even though the Resource Guide to the FCPA stipulates that the evaluation of the agency relationship depends on the practical realities of actual parent-subsidiary interaction,[638] in reality, it seems that the simple existence of a parent-subsidiary relationship at all is almost sufficient to assume agency under the doctrine.

*In the Matter of Aloca Inc*, the leading case with regard to the SEC's and the DoJ's interpretation of agency, sheds some light into the logic used

634 Jennifer A Zerk, *Extraterritorial Jurisdiction: Lessons for the Business and Human Rights Sphere from Six Regulatory Areas* (A Report for the Harvard Corporate Social Responsibility Initiative to Help Inform the Mandate of the Unsg's Special Representative on Business and Human Rights. Working paper/ Corporate Social Responsibility Initiative vol 59, Harvard University, John F. Kennedy School of Government 2010), 170 – 171.

635 Justin F Marceau, 'A Little Less Conversation, A Little More Action: Evaluating and Forecasting the Trend of More Frequent and Severe Prosecutions Under the Foreign Corrupt Practices Act' (2007) 12 Fordham Journal of Corporate & Finance Law 285, 298.

636 Marcela E Schaefer, 'Should a Parent Company Be Liable for the Misdeeds of Its Subsidiary?: Agency Theories Under the Foreign Corrupt Practices Act' (2019) 94 New York University Law Review 1654, 1661 – 1666.

637 Vivian Grosswald Curran, 'Harmonizing Multinational Parent Company Liability for Foreign Subsidiary Human Rights Violations' (2016) 17 Chicago Journal of Interanational Law 403, 426.

638 Criminal Division of the U.S. Department of Justice and the Enforcement Division of the U.S. Securities and Exchange Commission (n 618), 28.

by US authorities.[639] The case concerned two of Alcoa's subsidiaries and the use of an intermediary to bribe officials in Bahrain in relation to long-term supply agreements with the State-owned Aluminium Bahrain B.S.C. (**Alba**). According to the SEC's Order, no 'officer, director or employee of Alcoa knowingly engaged in the bribe scheme'.[640] Nevertheless, the SEC found Alcoa liable for violation of the FCPA's anti-bribery provision because the subsidiaries carrying out the scheme were deemed to be agents of the parent corporation. The factors that led to this determination include among others, that (1), Alcoa appointed the majority of seats on a Strategic Council to the subsidiaries, (2), the entities transferred personnel between them, (3), Alcoa set the business and financial goals for the subsidiaries, (4), the subsidiaries' employees reported functionally to Alcoa and (5), that Alba was a significant customer of Alcoa. Additionally, (6), members of the Alcoa management had met with Alba officials and the intermediary and (7), they had approved the terms of related contracts with Alba and the intermediary.[641] It is obvious that all of the above criteria, perhaps apart from the last two, are often fulfilled in any parent-subsidiary relationship unless the subsidiaries are acting completely independently. Thus, agency relationships between parent and subsidiary are easily constructed according to the SEC and the DoJ.

With agency relationships between parent and subsidiary corporations established, US authorities now have the tools to target foreign subsidiaries directly. This is because both § 78dd-1 FCPA regarding issuers and § 78dd-2 FCPA regarding domestic concerns also claim direct jurisdiction over any (foreign) agent acting on their behalf.[642] We can see this mechanism at work in the case against Diagnostic Products Corporation (**DPC**), where it seems that the presence of an (unsubstantiated) agency relationship between parent and subsidiary was considered not only as an appropriate basis for liability of the parent corporation but also for direct prosecution of the foreign subsidiary.

---

639 Another important decision clarifying the agency doctrine in relation to the FCPA has been rendered most recently in *US v Hoskins*, Ruling on Defendant's Rule 29(C) and Rule 33 Motions, 3:12-cr-00238 (D Conn 2020); however, the ruling did not discuss the circumstances under which foreign subsidiaries may be considered agents of their domestic parents.

640 SEC, *In the Matter of Aloca Inc.*, Order of 9 January 2014, Administrative Proceeding File No. 3–15673, at 10.

641 Ibid.

642 Leibold (n 591), 229; Wilson (n 378), 1081.

Factually, DPC's subsidiary in China was found to have bribed physicians and laboratory personnel employed in government-owned hospitals in China in exchange for agreements that the hospitals would purchase the company's products. Similar to the Alcoa case, the SEC's order established DPC's violation of the FCPA anti-bribery provision without claiming that the parent organization had any knowledge of the subsidiary's conduct.[643] In addition, the DoJ criminally charged the Chinese subsidiary, DPC Tianjin. The criminal information does not provide any thorough analysis on what grounds the DoJ is asserting its jurisdiction over the Chinese entity, though it does mention that DPC Tianjin was acting as an agent to its parent organization.[644]

Concluding, we can observe that while the US legislator has originally rejected applying the FCPA to foreign subsidiaries of domestic concerns, enforcement agencies have allowed this practice to return through the backdoor. If any subsidiary may be considered an agent of the parent corporation and the FCPA is, without further qualification, applicable to any agent of a domestic concern, then *de facto*, the FCPA applies directly to foreign subsidiaries owned or controlled by domestic concerns.[645]

### b) Practice in Europe

#### aa) The UK Bribery Act 2010

Before the Bribery Act 2010, the UK anti-corruption framework consisted of a medley of laws from the nineteenth and early twentieth century along

643 SEC, *In the Matter of Diagnostics Products Corporation*, Order of 20 May 2005, Administrative Proceeding File No 3–11933, at 2.

644 Criminal Information, *United States v DPC (Tianjin) Co. Ltd.*, 05-cr-482 (CD Cal 2005), at 2; As for the requirement that DPC Tianjin has to 'make use of the mails or any means or instrumentality of interstate commerce corruptly in furtherance' of bribery, the Information mentions that DPC Tianjin sent emails from Tianjin to Los Angeles containing monthly reports. These monthly reports reflected the corrupt payments as 'selling expenses', see p. 5 – 7; However, if regular monthly reports fulfil the requirement of making use of the mails or any means or instrumentality of interstate commerce, than foreign subsidiaries of US companies will almost always fulfil this requirement.

645 See for the same conclusion, Michael S Diamant, Christopher W Sullivan and Smith Jason H. 'FCPA Enforcement Against U.S. and Non-U.S. Companies' (2019) 8 Michigan Business & Entrepreneurial Law Review 353, 363 and Wilson (n 378), 1081.

with a bribery prohibition stemming from UK common law. Thus, the overhaul of UK bribery regulation with the adoption of the Bribery Act 2010 was followed with widespread attention even outside the UK. One of the particularly thorny issues concerned its extensive extraterritorial effects and the resulting potential to disrupt international business.[646] As such, one author has referred to the Act as the 'The Caffeinated Younger Sibling of the FCPA'.[647]

The Act criminalizes four offenses: Sec. 1 and 2 of the Act are concerned generally with the offering and receiving of bribes while Sec. 6 addresses the bribing of foreign public officials specifically. However, the focus of much discussion has been on Sec. 7 of the Bribery Act: This novel corporate offense establishes the liability of a 'relevant commercial organisation' if an 'associated person' bribes another person intending to obtain or retain business or an advantage related to the conduct of business. For the purposes of Sec. 7, it is not necessary that the associated person as such must have been prosecuted for violation of the Bribery Act as long as there is sufficient evidence concerning his or her acts as to satisfy the standard burden of proof in criminal proceedings.[648] If an associated person has been found guilty of bribery according to this standard, Sec. 7 establishes the liability of the commercial organisation even if there was no knowledge, intention or even recklessness on behalf of the commercial organisation.[649] Instead, a defence is given if the accused organisation can show that it had adequate procedures in place designed to prevent associated persons from undertaking bribery.[650]

The particularly wide scope of Sec. 7 of the Bribery Act stems from the extensive definition of the terms 'relevant commercial organisations' and 'associated person'. Broadly speaking, 'relevant commercial organisations' include any corporation or partnership that is incorporated or formed

646 See for German commentaries: Jan Kappel and Otto Lagodny, 'Der UK Bribery Act – Ein Strafgesetz erobert die Welt: Ein kritischer Diskussionsanstoß' [2012] StV 695, 696; Marc Engelhart, 'Der britische Bribery Act 2010' (2016) 128(3) Zeitschrift für die gesamte Strafrechtswissenschaft, 882; Robert Schalber, *Der UK Bribery Act und seine Bedeutung im Rahmen von Criminal Compliance* (Schriften zu Compliance v.13, 1st ed. Nomos Verlagsgesellschaft 2018).

647 Alldridge (n 592).

648 Ibid., 1202; Additionally, with regard to the associated person, the UK Bribery Act contains an affirmative defence in line with the OECD Convention, in that a payment, which is permitted or required under local law, does not trigger liability, UK Bribery Act, Sec. 6 (3) (b).

649 Ibid., 1202.

650 UK Bribery Act, Sec. 7 (2).

under the laws of the UK or that carries on a business, or part of a business in the UK.[651] Importantly for our purposes, examining the jurisdictional reach of Sec. 7 of the Bribery Act along corporate affiliations, the definition of 'relevant commercial organisations' excludes foreign subsidiaries. Therefore, unless the subsidiary of a UK company conducts business on the territory of the UK itself, Sec. 7 does not directly apply to them. This is consistent with the UK's longstanding rejection of the control doctrine, which has also been noted during the review by the OECD Working Group.[652]

However, while foreign subsidiaries may not be subject to Sec. 7 of the Bribery Act directly, their corrupt conduct may entail the liability of their parent corporation. This is because the definition of 'associated persons' includes any person who performs any kind of service on behalf of the commercial organization. The Bribery Act explicitly mentions employees, agents and subsidiaries. The exact scope is largely up to a fact specific determination on a case-by-case basis.[653] In practice, the Serious Fraud Office (**SFO**), the UK agency tasked with enforcing the Bribery Act, has brought a substantial number of proceedings based on the liability of domestic companies for the acts of their foreign subsidiaries. Recently for instance, Sweett Group plc, a construction and professional service company, was convicted and sentenced for failure to prevent one of its subsidiaries from making corrupt payments to secure a contract in the United Arab Emirates.[654] In certain circumstances, the government has indicated that the definition of 'associated persons' may also extend to other affiliates such as suppliers, contractors and (minority-controlled) joint ventures.[655]

---

651 UK Bribery Act, Sec. 7 (5).

652 Working Group on Bribery, 'United Kingdom: Phase 2bis: Report of the Application of the Convention on Combating Bribery of Foreign Public Officials in International Business Transactions and the 1997 Recommendation on Combating Bribery in International Business Transactions' (16 October 2008), para 26.

653 UK Bribery Act, Sec. 8 (5).

654 News Release, 'Sweett Group PLC sentenced and ordered to pay £2.25 million after Bribery Act conviction', https://www.sfo.gov.uk/2016/02/19/sweett-group-plc-sentenced-and-ordered-to-pay-2-3-million-after-bribery-act-conviction/, last accessed on 13 April 2022; see also *Director of the Serious Fraud Office (SFO) v Eurasian Natural Resources Corporation Ltd* [2017] EWHC 1017 (QB) (8 May 2017) concerning alleged bribery by the Kazakh subsidiary of a UK company.

655 Ministry of Justice, 'The Bribery Act 2010: Guidance about Procedures which Relevant Commercial Organisations Can Put into Place to Prevent Persons Associated with them from Bribing (Section 9 of the Bribery Act 2010)' (2011), paras. 37 – 43; In 2015, the SFO concluded proceedings against Standard Bank

### bb) The French Law Regarding Transparency, the Fight against Corruption and the Modernization of Economic Life

The most recent addition to the current trend of tightening domestic anti-bribery regulation is the French Law Regarding Transparency, the Fight against Corruption and the Modernization of Economic Life (also referred to as Sapin II), which was adopted in December 2016. The law was born out of the continuous critique of the OECD Working Group on the insufficient enforcement of existing anti-bribery regulations in France as well as growing frustration with unilateral US actions, which resulted in the payment of massive fines from French companies to the US treasury.[656] In fact, Sapin II was preceded by a 2016 report prepared for the French National Assembly's Commission of Foreign Affairs and Commission of Finance studying the extraterritoriality of US legislation. In particular, although the report did not expressly condemn the FCPA as violating principles of international law,[657] it lamented in strong words the United States' use of the FCPA to advance its own economic and geopolitical objectives by specifically targeting French companies.[658] It recommended that France should strive to level the playing field with the SEC and the DoJ by strengthening the enforcement capacities of French authorities against domestic as well as foreign firms. This way, US authorities may be more readily persuaded into cooperation instead of resorting to unilateral action.[659] Finally, the new French legislation has also taken account of

plc for bribes paid by its sister company Stanbic Bank Tanzania Limited, both of which were then subsidiaries of the South African Standard Bank Group. The SFO based its enforcement on the fact that both companies had acted jointly on a contract by the Government of Tanzania, which made Stanbic Tanzania an associated person of Standard Bank plc, see *Serious Fraud Office v Standard Bank plc* [2014] Case No U20150854 paras 6 – 11.

656 Margot Sève, 'Sapin II: Is the Era of Compliance and Criminal Settlements upon France?' [2017] RTDF 2, 1.

657 Karine Berger 'Rapport d'information déposé en application de l'article 145 du règlement en conclusion des travaux de la mission d'information commune sur l'extraterritorialité de la législation américaine' n° 4082 (5 October 2016), pp. 77 – 78; it should be noted that the report took specific notice of the FCPA's application to conduct of foreign issuers without any territorial ties to the United States, see also below C.IV.4a)aa) The Jurisdictional Scope of the FCPA.

658 Ibid., 16 – 20.

659 Ibid., 84 – 87.

other developments across Europe, particularly the above discussed UK Bribery Act.[660]

Apart from the creation of a new anti-corruption agency[661] and the institutionalisation of a French-style Deferred Prosecution Agreement termed the '*convention judiciaire d'intérêt public*',[662] the most significant legislative changes for our purpose concern the extension of the jurisdictional scope of the French prohibition on bribery and the establishment of mandatory corporate compliance obligations.[663] Under Art. 17 of the law, the management of companies falling under the scope of the law[664] is required to establish comprehensive internal measures and procedures, including a code of conduct with regard to corruption, whistleblowing procedures, accounting controls, risk assessment and training programs.[665] The obligations are explicitly also applicable to foreign subsidiaries of French companies if the latter publishes consolidated financial statements. However, foreign subsidiaries are deemed to satisfy the requirements of Art. 17 if their French corporate parent has implemented the mandatory obligations throughout its corporate enterprise.[666] Failure to adopt the necessary measures may carry a penalty of up to EUR 200,000 for individuals and EUR 1 million for companies, pronounced by the new French anti-corruption agency.[667] Presumably, these fines may also apply to foreign subsidiaries of French companies directly (though this should be rather unlikely as the French parent itself is in any case subject to the law and is thus likely to be responsible for group-wide procedures).

---

660 Étude d'Impact – Projet de Loi relative à la transparence, à la lute contre la corruption, et à la modernisation de la vie économique, at 30.

661 Sapin II, Art. 1.

662 Ibid., Art. 22.

663 Ibid., Art. 21.

664 These are companies with revenues exceeding EUR 100 million that (a) have 500 or more employees or (b) are part of a group of companies with 500 or more employees, provided that the corporate parent is incorporated in France, ibid., Art. 17 I.

665 Ibid., Art. 17 II.

666 Ibid., Art. 17 I.

667 Ibid., Art. 17 V.

c) Comparative Normative Analysis

In the previous chapters, we have seen that the EU and European States have at times, though not consistently, protested US assertions of control-based jurisdiction. In this regard, we have argued that first, reactions to US sanctions are grounded in political expediency and remain in the realm of inter-subjectivity and second, there is no conclusive doctrinal position that jurisdiction over controlled foreign subsidiaries is contrary to customary international law principles. The following analysis deepens these arguments: In particular, FCPA enforcement practice by US authorities closely resemble the exercise of control-based jurisdiction. Nonetheless, there is no evidence of any State protest against the regulation of transnational bribery through parent-subsidiary relationships. This finding adds further uncertainty to the doctrinal status of control-based jurisdiction under international law. However, before turning to the more problematic control-based jurisdiction (below **bb**)), it should be noted that most of the mechanisms used in domestic anti-bribery legislation to influence foreign subsidiaries do not raise questions under customary international law principles of jurisdiction (below **aa**)).

aa) The Assertion of Jurisdiction in respect of Corporate Group Policies

First, public international law accepts the adoption of regulations that require the domestic parent organization to establish group-wide corporate policies intended to prevent and detect corruption. This is a mechanism employed by both the US FCPA and the French law Sapin II. With regard to the FCPA, these procedures include the obligation to make and keep accurate and reasonably detailed books and records as well as to maintain a system of internal accounting controls. With regard to Sapin II, more sophisticated compliance measures are also required, such as the establishment of a code of conduct with regard to corruption, whistleblowing procedures, risk assessment and training programs.

Even though these regulations indirectly affect controlled foreign subsidiaries, they have generally proved uncontroversial in international relations. That certain, in a wider sense 'fiscal' corporate policies, standards and obligations have to be applied uniformly across an entire corporate group is well-recognized in business practice as well as domestic legislation. Such policies may be necessary for an enterprise's parent organization to provide consistent and consolidated information, for instance to investors and regulatory authorities.[668] This sentiment is also reflected by the principles set out in the Restatement (Third), one of the most sophisticated accounts on jurisdiction based on parent-subsidiary relationships.[669] Indeed, § 414 (2) (b) of the Restatement recognizes that the regulation of foreign affiliated entities in matters such as 'uniform accounting, disclosure to investors, or preparation of consolidated tax returns of multinational enterprises' should generally be presumed reasonable under customary international law.[670]

Both the accounting provisions of the FCPA as well as the more comprehensive compliance measures mandated by Art. 17 of the Sapin II fall into this category of corporate policies addressed by § 414 (2) (b) of the Restatement.[671] This is obvious in relation to the FCPA, which requires the enterprise-wide establishment of certain standards regarding books and records as well as internal controls. These are prime examples of the 'uniform accounting' measures envisioned by the Restatement.[672] However, the same logic also applies to the more extensive requirements of Sapin II. The rationale behind § 414 (2) (b) of the Restatement is that certain corporate matters are typically subject to group policies and that with regard to these matters, home State jurisdiction over corporate parents should also extend to foreign subsidiaries. While the drafters of the Restatement Third in the 1970s and 1980s explicitly only had accounting measures in mind, today, corporate compliance measures are also frequently regulated through single, group-wide frameworks. Thus, both the FCPA accounting provisions as well as Art. 17 of the Sapin II are well permitted under public international law.

Second, public international law also accepts the criminalization of the failure of a domestic parent organization to prevent its subsidiaries from engaging in bribery. This is the mechanism chiefly employed by

668 Stanley Marcuss, 'Jurisdiction with Respect to Foreign Branches and Subsidiaries: Judicial Power in the Foreign Affairs Context under Section 414 of the Foreign Relations Restatement' (1992) 26 The International Lawyer 1, 7.

669 Although there is quite some dispute regarding whether the Restatement (Third) actually represents customary international law, see David B Massey, 'How the American Law Institute Influences Customary Law: The Reasonableness Requirement of the Restatement of Foreign Relations Law' (1997) 22 YaleJIntLaw 419.

670 *Restatement (Third) of the Foreign Relations Law of the United States* (n 5), § 414 (2) (b).

671 In relation to the FCPA, see Marcuss (n 668), 18.

672 Ibid., 18.

Sec. 7 of the UK Bribery Act. Sec. 7 establishes the liability of relevant commercial organisation for the conduct of their associated persons – including subsidiaries – if these engaged in bribery with the intention to 'obtain or retain business or an advantage in the conduct of business' for the commercial organisation.[673] Even though the liability of the parent organization is independent of whether it had knowledge of the actions of the subsidiary, a defence is given if it had in place adequate (compliance) procedures designed to prevent its subsidiaries from undertaking such conduct. Therefore, the focus of Sec. 7 of the UK Bribery Act in fact lies in the actions, or rather omissions of the corporate parent to establish compliance measures, while also *taking into account foreign subsidiary conduct*.[674] The UK Bribery Act (as applied to domestic companies) is therefore closely related to the French Sapin II. In fact, both acts essentially require, under the threat of penalties, domestic corporate parents to introduce compliance measures that also affect controlled foreign subsidiaries. Therefore, it seems logical to evaluate the UK Bribery Act under the same standards as Sapin II. Therefore, applying § 414 (2) (b) of the Restatement (Third) by analogy, such measures generally comport with established principles of jurisdiction under international law.[675]

#### bb) The Assertion of Control-based Jurisdiction under the FCPA

However, the application of the FCPA by US enforcement agencies in practice involves jurisdictional claims that are more dubious under public international law:

First, it was shown above that briberies by foreign subsidiaries automatically trigger the liability of the parent organization for violation of the FCPA.[676] US enforcement authorities rely on two grounds to justify this type of strict liability. For one, the corporate parent may be liable for the conduct of its foreign subsidiaries because of the consolidation of

---

673 Ministry of Justice (n 655), paras. 37 – 42.

674 See for a more thorough doctrinal discussion of Sec. 7 of the UK Bribery Act, Schalber (n 646), p. 80 – 90.

675 This argumentation only considers the case where the parent organization is a UK corporate national. As discussed below in C.IV.6.b)aa) The UK Bribery Act 2010, Sec. 7 of the UK Bribery Act may also apply to parent organizations that are not UK corporate nationals. In this case, the doctrinal evaluation will be different.

676 See also Skinner (n 630), 1858.

books and records within corporate groups. This consolidation means that corrupt payment of foreign subsidiaries, if they are falsely recorded, also distort the books and records of the domestic corporate parent. And because the books and records of the corporate parent are now false, the parent organisation itself violates the accounting provisions. For the other, general agency theory stipulates that a parent organization may be liable for the acts of its subsidiaries if they can be considered its agents. As we have seen above, however, agency relationships are assumed rather freely by the SEC and the DoJ, leading to broad liability of corporate parents for their foreign subsidiaries.

Second, the United States has also directly enforced the FCPA against foreign subsidiaries. For one, US authorities claim jurisdiction over foreign subsidiaries by way of a causation theory. They argue that if foreign subsidiaries falsely record corrupt payments in their books and records, through consolidation, they cause the books and records of the corporate parent to become false. This not only entails a violation of the accounting provisions by the corporate parents, it also brings the foreign subsidiaries themselves under US jurisdiction. For the other, according to 15 U.S.C. § 78dd-1 (a) and § 78dd-2 (a), the FCPA applies to (foreign) agents. Therefore, the establishment of an agency relationship between corporate parent and subsidiary also allows for the direct prosecution of the foreign subsidiary.

Notwithstanding the different doctrinal underpinnings, these practices involve the exercise of control-based jurisdiction similar to what we have seen in relation to the Cuban sanctions under the CACR and the Iran sanctions according to 31 C.F.R. § 560.215. This is because the above mechanisms in fact allow US authorities to directly exercise jurisdiction *vis-à-vis* any foreign company as long as it is owned or controlled by a US corporate parent. This is evidenced by the causation theory: Because majority-owned subsidiaries generally consolidate their books and records with those of the corporate parent, any bribery by any subsidiary constitutes a violation of the accounting provisions subject to the reach of US enforcement agencies. However, a similar effect is also achieved through the application of the agency doctrine: Because the SEC and the DoJ seemingly equate the agency relationship to the mere existence of a parent-subsidiary structure, any foreign subsidiary can be considered an agent and therefore, also falls under the scope of the FCPA.[677]

677 As noted above, technically, the FCPA's anti-bribery provisions cover foreign subsidiaries only if they 'make use of the mails or any means or instrumentality

The US practice under the FCPA lends further credence to the argument that the normative status of control-based assertions of jurisdiction remains unresolved under customary international law principles. First of all, despite the fact that the FCPA, under the interpretation of US authorities, engages jurisdiction structurally similar to the control theory as applied in the area of economic sanctions, no State has apparently protested the enforcement of the FCPA. Second, the application of the FCPA provides an example for a point that I have made earlier, namely that the direct assertion of jurisdiction over a foreign subsidiary can also be interpreted as a territorial regulation addressing the domestic parent corporation.[678] As the practice shows, US authorities have used territorial triggers – the consolidation of books and record and the agency doctrine – to hold parent organizations strictly liable for the conduct of subsidiaries abroad. However, they have also used the same triggers to directly prosecute the foreign subsidiaries. It is not entirely clear when enforcement agencies choose one option instead of the other. They have sometimes also used both options concurrently.[679] From the perspective of the regulator therefore, it seems that these different methods are largely interchangeable. However, if there is no difference, then the formal distinction under customary international law between jurisdictional claims directly addressing foreign subsidiaries and jurisdictional claims only addressing the territorial parents does not seem to be particularly useful.

### 5. Correspondent Account Jurisdiction under the FCPA

While enforcement practice has endowed the FCPA with an expansive reach based on personal affiliation with a US company,[680] its territorial scope may be no less problematic. As with the extension of FCPA jurisdiction to foreign subsidiaries, the plain text of the Act appears innocuous. According to § 78dd-3 of the FCPA, persons other than issuers or domestic

of interstate commerce'. However, this requirement is interpreted so broadly that virtually every foreign subsidiary fulfils it, see above at n 644.

678 See above at C.II.2c) Comparative Normative Analysis.

679 See Complaint, *SEC v ENI S.p.A and Snamprogetti Netherlands B.V.*, 4:10-cv-2414 (SD Tex 2010): In this case, the SEC charged the issuer ENI with violating the accounting provisions and the Dutch subsidiary Snamprogetti with violating the anti-bribery provisions as agent of ENI as well as with violating the accounting provisions.

680 See C.IV.4a) Practice in the United States.

concerns are prohibited from corruptly using 'the mails or any means or instrumentality of interstate commerce or to do any other act in furtherance of' bribing a foreign official 'while in the territory of the United States'. This prohibition applies to agents and other affiliates of that person as well.[681]

Unsurprisingly, the DoJ and the SEC adhere to an expansive interpretation of territorial jurisdiction under the FCPA. Most notably, just as OFAC in the area of economic sanctions, these two agencies have at times relied on electronic monetary transfers clearing through US banks as a possible basis for jurisdiction. This is illustrated by the enforcement action against JGC Corporation, a Japanese engineering company, which was part of a joint venture with American, French and Dutch counterparts involved in the bribery of Nigerian officials. The criminal information in this case did not allege that JGC undertook any conduct within the United States. Still the DoJ found two grounds according to which it could exercise jurisdiction over the Japanese company. First, the DoJ argued that jurisdiction could be based on allegations that JGC Corporation conspired as well as aided and abetted issuers and domestic concerns. Second and more importantly, the DoJ also asserted territorial jurisdiction because the Japanese company caused a number of wire transfers that passed through US correspondent accounts.[682]

While US jurisprudence in relation to economic sanctions has explicitly endorsed correspondent account jurisdiction in the *Zarrab* case,[683] this basis remains untested in court in relation to the FCPA. It should be noted, however, that other aggressive theories of territorial jurisdiction advanced by FCPA enforcement agencies have had only mixed success under judicial intervention.[684] In relation to correspondent account jurisdiction specifi-

---

681 FCPA, § 78dd-3.

682 Criminal Information, *United States v JGC Corporation*, No. 11-cr-260 (SD Texas 2011), paras. 21 – 22; It is typical for the DoJ and the SEC to rely on multiple theories of jurisdiction. In fact, up to now, the DoJ and the SEC have yet not enforced the FCPA in a case based solely on correspondent account jurisdiction, see Wilson (n 378), 1072.

683 See above at C.II.3a) Practice in the United States.

684 See for instance *SEC v Sharef et al.*, No. 1:2011cv09073 at 15 (SDNY 2013): The prosecution alleged that the defendant, a senior executive at Siemens, had pressured another Siemens executive, Regendantz, into paying bribes to Argentine government officers. Regendantz later made falsified filings to the SEC in connection with the corrupt payments. The prosecution argued that these falsified financial statements, because they were made to the SEC, formed a viable jurisdictional basis for FCPA liability of the defendant. However, the court was

cally, a recent decision of the Second Circuit indicates that this theory may not be accepted by the US judiciary with regard to the FCPA.

The case concerns a UK citizen, Lawrence Hoskins, who was working for a French multinational enterprise and who was allegedly involved in a bribery scheme in Indonesia. For the relevant time, he had never set foot in the United States. The DoJ primarily grounded its jurisdiction over Hoskins on the theory that Hoskins conspired with US-based companies and employees. The court dismissed this argument based on conspiracy. Relying heavily on the legislative history of the FCPA as well as the presumption against extraterritoriality, the court concluded that the US legislator consciously and clearly defined the classes of persons subject to the jurisdictional scope of the law. Essentially, foreign nationals and foreign companies could only fall under the jurisdiction of the FCPA if they were either agents, employees, officers, directors, and shareholders of US citizens or US companies, or if they violated the FCPA while 'present' in the United States.[685] Mere conspiracy or complicity was not enough to trigger jurisdiction under the FCPA.

Applying this holding, *Hoskins* seems to put a bar to correspondent account jurisdiction in relation to the FCPA. Specifically, for persons that are not agents, employees, officers, directors, or shareholders of US citizens or US companies, *Hoskins* explicitly requires foreign companies to be present in the United States while violating the FCPA.[686] The mere

---

not convinced that defendant's actions, even if they eventually 'touched' the United States because of the SEC filings, were sufficiently connected to the US territory to base jurisdiction on. It consequently dismissed the case. However, the US government prevailed on similar allegations in *SEC v Straub*, 921 F Supp 2d 244, 262 – 264 (SDNY 2013); *SEC v Straub*, No. 11 Civ. 9645 (RJS) at 16 (SDNY 2016).

685 See *United States v Hoskins*, 902 F 3d 69, 85 (2d Cir 2018).

686 See also *United States v Goncalves et al.*, No 1:09-cr-00335-RJL (DDC 2009): In this case, the court dismissed the US government's argument that it had jurisdiction over the defendant *Patel* based on the allegation that *Patel* had mailed a package from the UK to the United States containing an original copy of the agreement of a corrupt transaction. The judge's decision and reasoning were not reduced to writing. However, commentators note that the judge required that the relevant act, mailing of the package, must have been performed while the defendant was physically present in the United States, see Mike Koehler, 'The Foreign Corrupt Practices Act under the Microscope' (2012) 15 University of Pennsylvania Journal of Business Law 1, 50 and Leibold (n 591), 246 – 247.

causation of wire transfers that pass through US based bank accounts as alleged in *JGC* may not satisfy this threshold of presence.[687]

Despite *Hoskins*, it is too early to tell how correspondent account jurisdiction would fare under judicial intervention. Thus, until that time, this basis remains part of the US State practice. The technical mechanism and normative implications of jurisdiction based on correspondent accounts have been discussed *en detail* with regard to the enforcement of economic sanctions.[688] To sum up, as a consequence of the unique design of the US monetary system, virtually all wire transfers denominated in US dollars technically pass through US-based banking institutions, even if they are sent from one non-US account to another. Thus, for corrupt payment denominated in US dollars, a good argument can be made that a constituent element of the act (the corrupt payment) passed through US territory. Therefore, it is arguable that the United States may assume jurisdiction based on subjective territoriality. Thus, this kind of correspondent account jurisdiction does seem to comport with the doctrinal framework of jurisdiction under international law even though it would lead to almost unlimited jurisdiction of the United States in relation to corruption worldwide (similar to what we have seen in relation to extraterritorial economic sanctions).[689]

### 6. Jurisdiction based on 'business presence'

In contrast to correspondent account jurisdiction, which has remained a distinctly US American feature, all three pieces of legislation examined above achieve extraterritorial reach by including jurisdiction based on 'business presence'. I use this term to describe the assertion of jurisdiction

687 Moreover, *Hoskins* also defeats the other jurisdictional theory of the DoJ in the JGC case. Applying *Hoskins*, JGC Corporation could not be held liable for conspiring or aiding and abetting issuers and domestic concerns. Rather, a foreign company that did not violate the FCPA while present in the United States could only be liable as an agent, employee, officer, director, or shareholders of US citizens or US companies. In *JGC* however, there was no indication that the Japanese company was an agent or shareholder of the involved issuers and domestic concerns.

688 See C. II.3 c) Comparative Normative Analysis.

689 See however also Wilson (n 378), 1080; Leibold (n 591), 254; de la Torre, Mateo J. 'The Foreign Corrupt Practices Act: Imposing an American Definition of Corruption on Global Markets' (2016) 49 Cornell International Law Journal 469.

premised on the fact that a foreign natural person or company is economically active on domestic territory. Even though already the FCPA included a variation of this practice through its issuer-based regulation, 'business presence' as a jurisdictional trigger has been rediscovered by newer European legislation. Although rarely discussed in literature, this jurisdictional basis is significant as it seems to fall neither under the territoriality nor under the nationality principle.

#### a) Practice in the United States

As mentioned above, the FCPA employs jurisdiction based on 'business presence' through its application to issuers. Issuers, in a nutshell, include all companies whose stocks can be traded on a national exchange in the United States. Therefore, issuers need not to be US nationals in the sense of international law. Rather, foreign companies, i.e., companies that are neither incorporated nor have their seat of management in the United States, can list their stocks on US exchanges as well. Thus, the reach of the issuer-based jurisdiction of the FCPA is irrespective of corporate nationality, but only dependent on the 'presence' of the companies at domestic stock exchanges.

#### b) Practice in Europe

##### aa) The UK Bribery Act 2010

As mentioned above, the UK Bribery Act 2010 saw, in its Sec. 7, the introduction of a new corporate criminal offense for failure to prevent bribery on an organisation's behalf. Sec. 7 applies to 'relevant commercial organisations', defined as a body or partnership incorporated or formed in the UK, or any other incorporated body or partnership which carries on a business or *part of a business* anywhere in the UK.[690] While the first part of this definition encompasses UK corporate nationals according to the traditional active personality principle, the second part is based on 'business presence' as it covers all (foreign) companies if they only carry on 'part of a business' in any part of the UK irrespective of corporate nationality.

---

690 UK Bribery Act, Sec. 7 (5).

According to the official guidance to the UK Bribery Act, the interpretation of the term 'part of a business' will be done 'by applying a common sense approach':[691] Thus, companies would only fall under the scope of the Act if they have a 'demonstrable business presence' in the UK. For instance, the government notes that it would not expect a corporation to qualify as a relevant commercial organisation merely because its stocks are being traded on the London Stock Exchange. Moreover, the guidance states that having a UK subsidiary would not, in itself, fulfil the requirement of carrying on 'part of a business' in the UK as a subsidiary may act completely independently of its corporate parent.[692] Despite this 'common sense approach', the Ministry of Justice itself notes that 'the section 7 offence is endowed with extraordinary scope'.[693]

This extraordinary scope of Sec. 7 of the Bribery Act is demonstrated by the recent Deferred Prosecution Agreement entered between UK authorities and Airbus SE. Airbus SE is not a UK corporate national as the company is incorporated in the Netherlands and has its seat of management in France. The conduct alleged took place across Sri Lanka, Malaysia, Indonesia, Taiwan and Ghana. Nonetheless, the judge approving the Deferred Prosecution Agreement found jurisdiction under Sec. 7 of the Bribery Act as Airbus SE carried on part of its business in the UK. As relevant businesses, the judge notes that Airbus SE operates in the UK through two of its subsidiaries, Airbus Operations Limited as well as Airbus Military UK Limited.[694] In effect therefore, any foreign company, as long as it entertains a 'demonstrable business presence' within the UK, may be subject to prosecution under Sec. 7 of the Bribery Act for failure to prevent bribery committed by any of its associated persons on its behalf in any other third country.[695]

---

691 Ministry of Justice (n 655), para. 36.
692 Ibid.
693 Ministry of Justice, 'Bribery Act 2010: Post Legislative Scrutiny Memorandum', para. 58.
694 *Director of the Serious Fraud Office v Airbus SE* [2020] Case No U20200108, paras. 14 – 21.
695 Lordi (n 614), 956.

### bb) The French Law Regarding Transparency, the Fight Against Corruption and the Modernization of Economic Life

The UK Bribery Act's venture into new jurisdictional territories (and presumably the lack of international protest against these assertions) has inspired other countries to follow the lead. In fact, the newest addition to the increasing number of domestic anti-bribery legislation with strong extraterritorial implications, the French Sapin II, has adopted very similar language.[696] According to its Art. 21, which amends the jurisdictional scope for bribery offenses, the law applies to French nationals, regular residents as well as persons that exercise all or part of their economic activity on French territory.[697] This jurisdictional provision applies equally to individuals and legal persons. According to a recent *Circulaire* published by the French Ministry of Justice, 'all or part of their economic activity' is supposed to be interpreted broadly and specifically to include at least foreign companies having a subsidiary, branches, commercial offices, or other establishments in France.[698]

### c) Comparative Normative Analysis

Comparing the three different legislations, we have seen that all of them advance jurisdictional assertions based on a loosely defined 'business presence' of a company on the domestic territory. In the United States, the FCPA covers stock issuers generally, which includes non-US companies that list their stocks on domestic exchanges. The UK Bribery Act creates a corporate criminal offense for failure to prevent bribery that applies to organisations that only carry on part of a business within domestic territory. Similarly, Sapin II prohibits bribery by natural and legal persons as long as that person exercises part of its economic activity in France.

I will argue here that this kind of jurisdiction – based on the 'business presence' of the company within domestic territory – is not clearly

696 Sève (n 656), 5; Étude d'Impact – Projet de Loi relative à la transparence, à la lute contre la corruption, et à la modernisation de la vie économique, at 40.

697 Loi n° 20161691 du 9 décembre 2016 relative à la transparence, à la lutte contre la corruption et à la modernisation de la vie économique, Art. 21: 'personne résidant habituellement ou exerçant tout ou partie de son activité économique sur le territoire français'.

698 Ministry of Justice, Circulaire de politique pénale en matière de lutte contre la corruption international, p. 9.

supported by traditional doctrine of jurisdiction and may thus violate international law under certain circumstances. This finding is in stark contrast to actual State practice, which has not seen any significant protest against these legislations. The acceptance of extraterritorial jurisdiction in this area is likely explained by the wide international consensus on the need for combatting corruption as a globally shared community interest. Ultimately, this points to a larger deficiency of the customary international law principles of jurisdiction which relies on formal connections between the State and the object of the assertion of jurisdiction without regard to the substantial content of the regulation.

Jurisdiction based on 'business presence' has received only sparse attention in literature to date and it is sometimes seen as an expression of the territoriality principle. This argument seems straightforward: For instance, the FCPA applies to issuers which list on a domestic exchange. Thus, jurisdiction is derived from the territorial location of the stock exchange.[699] Sec. 7 of the UK Bribery Act applies to all commercial organisations as long as they carry on part of their business within the UK. Sapin II prohibits bribery by natural and legal persons as long as that person exercises part of its economic activity in France. Thus, jurisdiction in these two cases is premised on the existence of some sort of territorial business activity in a specific location.

However, despite this territorial connection, jurisdiction based on 'business presence' cannot be subsumed under the territoriality principle in customary international law. To simplify things, let us apply the jurisdictional basis of 'business presence' to a natural person. Assume that someone owns real estate in France which she rents out commercially, has a bank account in France and maybe even employs someone in France to take care of day-to-day matters. Undoubtedly, this person would exercise an 'economic activity' within France. However, as long as this person does not set foot within French borders, she would certainly not fall under French territorial jurisdiction. France would have no authority to prescribe whether she should rest on a Saturday or Sunday (outside of France), whether she is allowed to smoke marijuana (outside of France), or, for our purposes, whether she is allowed to bribe public officials in third countries.

The same applies to companies as well. Carrying on part of a business within domestic territory does not vest the territorial State with the power to regulate all other conduct without any territorial connection. In reality,

699 Wouters, Ryngaert and Cloots (n 581), 48.

provisions such as Sec. 7 of the UK Bribery Act are not so much an expression of the territoriality principle, but can be rather regarded as a disguised extension of active personality. Once a company conducts part of its business in the UK, it is subject to the Bribery Act for any act of bribery anywhere in the world. Therefore, under the Bribery Act, the actual act of bribery need not have a nexus to UK territory but rather to a specific company, namely any company that conducts part of a business in the UK.[700] Put differently, while active personality with regard to corporations requires that the corporation is either incorporated under domestic laws or has its seat of management in a certain country, the UK Bribery Act can be interpreted as to extend active personality jurisdiction to those companies that merely conduct part of a business in the country. There is no basis in international law for such an extension.

Thus, because jurisdiction based on 'business presence' – as it is asserted by Sec. 7 of the UK Bribery Act as well as Sapin II – is justifiable neither according to the territoriality nor according to the active personality principle, it is in fact not recognized under customary international law principles.[701]

This jurisdictional basis is also significant in practical terms: Since it is likely that most multinationals would have at least sporadic business dealings within the UK or France, jurisdiction based on 'business presence' may in effect have quasi-universal reach.[702] To cite the UK Ministry of Justice, Section 7 'would catch, for example, a bribe paid in Sweden, by a Philippine national on behalf of a Brazilian engineering company, that

---

700 Kappel and Lagodny (n 646), 699; Nathalie I Thorhauer, *Jurisdiktionskonflikte im Rahmen transnationaler Kriminalität* (Nomos Verlagsgesellschaft mbH & Co. KG 2019), 280.

701 To a somewhat limited extent, the same argument applies to issuer-based jurisdiction as well. It is arguable that subjecting issuers to certain domestic rules, regardless of where they are incorporated or acting, is in reality the inclusion of a new class of corporations into the active personality principle. However, it is arguable that the territorial jurisdiction over the listing of stocks also entails jurisdiction over ancillary conduct in preparation of or otherwise necessary for the listing itself. Thus, the State in which the stock exchange is located has territorial authority to prescribe rules regarding required reporting, accounting and disclosure obligation in relation to the listing itself. However, whether this includes FCPA accounting provisions or even the anti-bribery provisions is certainly debatable.

702 Lordi (n 614), 976; She then goes on to examine whether bribery may be considered a crime under international law for which universal jurisdiction is warranted, which she denies.

carries on a lift maintenance business in the UK, in respect of a contract relating to an infrastructure project in New Zealand'.[703] It is noteworthy, however, that not only have these legislations not received significant backlash from other States, but rather, they have prompted other OECD parties to draft legislation mirroring these provisions. Thus, State practice indicates approval for using this sort of jurisdictional hook at least in the area of anti-bribery.[704]

The acceptance of jurisdiction based on 'business presence' as practiced in more recent legislation such as the UK Bribery Act and Sapin II is significant. In the area of economic sanctions, States have at times reacted furiously over any purported infringement of their sovereignty through extraterritorial jurisdiction even if such assertions had a possible basis under international law. The complete lack of protest against at least highly dubious legislation in the area of anti-bribery suggests that there is fundamental difference in the assessment of jurisdiction in the area of secondary sanctions than in the area of anti-bribery. The most probable explanation of this diverging State practice is the underlying objective of the respective regulation. While economic sanctions are frequently levied to 'enforce' particular domestic foreign policy preferences, corruption is almost universally perceived by the international community as a global challenge. And even though this may seem obvious to us now, the doctrinal consequences of these findings are far from trivial: As has been discussed above at length, customary international law on jurisdiction is largely a formal regime looking for a nexus between the regulating State and the object of regulation. This analysis shows that this regime is inadequate because it fails to account for the growing importance of community interests possibly underlying exercises of extraterritorial jurisdiction.

### 7. Conclusion

The international anti-corruption regime has undoubtedly been a success story in the last few decades. Public perception of corruption has evolved

703 Ministry of Justice, 'Bribery Act 2010: Post Legislative Scrutiny Memorandum', para. 58.

704 Australia has, for instance, proposed legislation targeting corporate and financial crime. The Crimes Legislation Amendment (Combatting Corporate Crime) Bill 2019 introduces a new offense mirroring section 7 of the UK Bribery Act; the bill is available at https://www.aph.gov.au/Parliamentary_Business/Bills_Legislation/Bills_Search_Results/Result?bId=s1246, last accessed on 13 April 2022.

and while it was originally viewed as an issue that was best tacitly tolerated, it is now acknowledged as one of the most pressing problems of the globalized society. Within this bigger picture, extraterritorial regulation has primarily focused on one specific behaviour, that of transnational bribery: The analysis in this chapter has shown how the United States, acting in the aftermath of the domestic Watergate Scandal, has set an influential precedent in this respect with the FCPA and later successfully pressured other OECD partners to join its lead. Today, the international framework consists of six major international conventions on anti-corruption as well as numerous pieces of domestic legislation, many of which contain provisions with sweeping extraterritoriality.

Examining legislation in the United States, in the UK and in France, the analysis in this chapter has made two arguments with regard to the customary international law principles of jurisdiction. First, this chapter has expanded on the thesis that these principles do not allow for a clear distinction between permissibly territorial and impermissibly extraterritorial jurisdiction, which diminishes the functionality of these principles in regulating international relations. Second, this chapter has demonstrated that the customary international law principles of jurisdiction are also incomplete, in particular because – outside of universal jurisdiction – they generally do not allow for considerations in relation to the substance of the regulation. This stands in contrast to State practice, in which the regulatory object – anti-corruption – may greatly affect the acceptance of any assertion of jurisdiction.

In relation to the first argument, the analysis in this chapter further demonstrates that traditional jurisdictional principles offer no conclusive answer as to the (il-)legality of control-based assertions of jurisdiction. In the area of anti-corruption, the United States, the UK and France all regulate the behaviour of foreign subsidiaries (and other associates) of domestic corporations to ensure that such measures are not frustrated by shrewd corporate organization. Technically, this is accomplished (1), by mandating group-wide accounting and compliance measures to prevent and detect bribery, (2), by attaching liability to the parent organisation of the enterprise for the behaviour of its subsidiaries, and (3), by directly criminalizing the conduct of the foreign subsidiary. Specifically, US enforcement authorities employ all three modalities, including directly asserting jurisdiction over foreign subsidiaries.

We have previously seen that control-based economic sanctions have at times drawn strong negative responses from affected States. However, the examined practice of anti-corruption regulation supports the argument that the doctrinal status of control-based jurisdiction is far from settled under traditional international law principles: First, despite the fact that FCPA enforcement against foreign subsidiaries essentially engages control-based jurisdiction, no State has apparently protested such actions in contrast to the widespread rejection of this jurisdictional basis in the area of economic sanctions. Second, we have argued that control-based jurisdiction essentially constitutes a disguised variation of territoriality. This is because the direct assertion of jurisdiction over a foreign subsidiary and the territorial regulation addressing the domestic parent corporation are identical in substance. This view is again confirmed by actual FCPA practice. The analysis in this chapter has shown that US enforcement authorities directly pursue foreign subsidiaries using the same jurisdictional theories they are using to target domestic corporate parents, lending credence to the argument that both methods are in fact interchangeable.

In relation to the second argument, this chapter has demonstrated that the status of anti-corruption as a universally shared objective greatly influences the acceptance of assertions of extraterritorial jurisdiction in practice. In particular, both the UK Bribery Act and the French Sapin II contain a novel jurisdictional trigger, which allows for the criminal prosecution of companies that merely conduct a limited portion of their economic activity within the respective domestic territory. Even though this type of jurisdiction based on 'business presence' may ostensibly rely on a territorial nexus, it is actually not covered by the territoriality principle. Rather, jurisdiction based on 'business presence' is to be seen as an extension of the active personality principle, for which there is no basis under prevailing international law.

Despite the possible doctrinal issues under international law, such extraterritorial anti-bribery regulation is not known to have caused discord between States in a way that similar measures in the area of economic sanctions have done.[705] In fact, inspired by the successes of the FCPA and the UK Bribery Act, even more States are currently pondering to strengthen their domestic anti-bribery regulation with extraterritorial effects.[706] It seems therefore arguable that in the regulatory area of anti-bribery, States

705 Zerk (n 634), 36 – 37.

706 Australia and Ireland have introduced or passed new legislations amending existing anti-bribery legislation; For Australia, see the Crimes Legislation Amendment (Combatting Corporate Crime) Bill 2019; For Ireland, see Criminal Justice (Corruption Offences) Bill 2018, available at http://www.irishstatutebook.ie/eli/2018/act/9/enacted/en/html, last accessed on 13 April 2022.

are willing to accept a greater degree of extraterritoriality even though traditional jurisdictional principles may not support certain assertions. This is most likely the result of the fact that corruption is deemed harmful almost everywhere in the world and in particular, that the fight against transnational bribery is acknowledged not only as a domestic priority, but as a global objective.[707]

The development and acceptance of the transnational anti-bribery regime may be significant for similar regulatory challenges. The success of the FCPA to catalyse (near) universal change is seen as a prime example of how unilateral, extraterritorial regulation can affect the international community for the better.[708] It proves, so the argument goes, that the provision of global public goods need not, and maybe should not wait for cooperative action when multilateral consensus is elusive. Rather, unilateral measures by a powerful player may fill the regulatory void immediately, pressing other nations to join in.[709]

Still, caution is warranted: Despite the positive overall development of the global anti-bribery regime, the unilateral, extraterritorial enforcement of the FCPA by the United States has not been without its challenges. While it is without doubt, that precisely the aggressive extraterritorial action against foreign companies have prompted other States to reconsider their stance on transnational bribery, suspicion of an unfair bias of the SEC and the DoJ towards domestic corporations have been growing. This claim is bolstered by recent numbers, which find that fines against non-US companies amount for 67 % of total fines and that these companies pay, on average, five times the penalty of domestic companies.[710] Extraterritoriality of the FCPA may therefore not really be a tool to 'level the playing field' but rather to protect domestic economic interests. As shown above, this was one of the main points of criticism levied by the report studying US extraterritoriality presented to the French National Assembly. Whether there is merit to this claim or not, it shows that unilateral extraterritoriality, left unchecked, always contains the risk of abuse.[711]

---

707 See, however, for a more critical account: Steven R Salbu, 'Extraterritorial Restriction of Bribery: A Premature Evocation of the Normative Global Village' (1999) 24(1) YaleJIntLaw 223.

708 Magnuson, 'International Corporate Bribery and Unilateral Enforcement' (n 582), 404; Ryngaert, *Unilateral Jurisdiction and Global Values* (n 10), 68.

709 Magnuson, 'Unilateral Corporate Regulation' (n 10), 540 – 541.

710 Leibold (n 591), 236.

711 Magnuson, 'International Corporate Bribery and Unilateral Enforcement' (n 582), 411 – 413.

However, even if States enforce their own legislation in an impartial way, issues may arise. There is a risk of burdening companies with multiple and even conflicting regulatory standards with regard to compliance measures. Worse, without coordination among States, individuals and companies possibly face double prosecution, which may greatly diminish the legitimacy of the discussed regulations. That this is not a hypothetical is proven by existing case material.[712] Going into the future, these issues have to be dealt with seriously to not jeopardize an international achievement in the regulation of anti-bribery that was not easy to come by.[713]

## V. Business and Human Rights

### 1. Introduction

It is no longer a secret that business enterprises have a profound impact on the enjoyment of human rights. Corporations have engaged in or facilitated human rights abuses such as child labour, forced expropriation, environmental harms, suppression of civil unrest, violation of rights of indigenous people and other forms of reprehensible behaviour.[714] Against this backdrop, the question of how to increase the accountability of business enterprises for their negative human rights impact has emerged as a pressing issue worldwide in both political and academic debate.

In the last two decades, the growing discipline of business and human rights has provided the most promising venue for the task to develop a response. To this end, States, international organizations, business enterprises and other non-governmental actors have devised a staggering amount of public and private initiatives to tame the behaviour of corporations

---

712 Letzien (n 614), 15 – 18; International Bar Association (n 12), 211 – 216.

713 One way to tackle this challenge would be to contemplate harmonization within a single international instrument that, among others, sets out the details with regard to compliance/due diligence measures and mandates cooperation between jurisdictions. See for some suggestions of how such legislations could look like: Lindsey Hills, 'Universal Anti-Bribery Legislation Can Save International Business: A Comparison of the FCPA and the UKBA in an Attempt to Create Universal Legislation to Combat Bribery around the Globe' (2014) 13 Richmond Journal of Global Law and Business 469, 490 – 492.

714 See documentation at https://business-humanrights.org/en, last accessed on 13 April 2022 and the analysis by John G Ruggie, *Just business: Multinational corporations and human rights* (Amnesty international global ethics series, First edition, W.W. Norton & Company 2013), 19.

with respect to their human rights impact. The number of different measures reflects the complexity of the regulatory task at hand. A particular challenge is posed by transnational corporations, which operate worldwide and are therefore able to evade any particular State's jurisdiction.[715] Moreover, these global economic enterprises wield tremendous political power: For instance, comparing annual governmental revenue and corporate revenue, a study by NGO *Global Justice Now* finds that 69 of the 100 largest economies in the world are today multinational corporations (**MNC**s).[716] As such, developing host States, in which these companies operate, may not be willing or even able to regulate these powerful private entities.[717] In recent years therefore, seeking regulation and remedies for corporate human rights abuses in the home States (the State of incorporation or the State in which a corporation is headquartered) of those MNCs has become increasingly *en vogue*.[718] This particular mode to enhance corporate accountability inevitably raises new and old questions of extraterritorial jurisdiction.

This current shift has been long in the making and section 2 of this chapter seeks to, briefly, trace the different historic antecedents that laid the foundation for the current dominance of extraterritorial home State regulation. Despite progress at the UN level on a binding treaty establishing international legal obligations on businesses,[719] the arguably less ambitions 'Protect, Respect and Remedy' Framework (the **Framework**)

715 Larry C Backer, 'Multinational Corporations, Transnational Law: The United Nation's Norms on the Responsibilities of Transnational Corporations as a Harbinger of Corporate Social Responsibility in International Law' (2006) 37(2) Columbia Human Rights Law Review 287, 309.

716 Global Justice Now compared the annual revenue of corporations and the annual revenue of countries taken from the CIA World Factbook 2017 and the Fortune Global 500, https://www.globaljustice.org.uk/news/69-richest-100-entities-planet-are-corporations-not-governments-figures-show/, last accessed on 13 April 2022.

717 Beth Stephens, 'The Amorality of Profit: Transnational Corporations and Human Rights' (2002) 20 Berkeley Journal of International Law 45, 82 - 83.

718 See for instance the Maastricht Principles on Extraterritorial Obligations of States in the area of Economic, Social and Cultural Rights (Maastricht Principles), available at http://www.etoconsortium.org/nc/en/main-navigation/library/maastricht-principles/?tx_drblob_pi1%5BdownloadUid%5D=23, last accessed on 13 April 2022.

719 In 2014, the UN Human Rights Council established the 'Open-ended intergovernmental working group on transnational corporations and other business enterprises with respect to human rights', see UN Human Rights Council, Resolution 26/9,'Elaboration of an international legally binding instrument on

and the UN Guiding Principles (the **Guiding Principles**) implementing this Framework[720] are still the primary reference in the business and human rights discourse. They serve as the starting point for a closer look at extraterritoriality in business and human rights, which follows in section 3.[721] Sections 4 and 5, the core of this chapter, turn to domestic measures in the United States and Europe that affect corporate behaviour in extraterritorial settings. Section 4 focuses on human rights legislation and administrative regulations that address business conduct abroad through parent-subsidiary or lead-supplier relationships. A strong argument can be made that these regulations have not caused protest by other States as on the one hand, these measures do not clearly violate established jurisdictional principles, and, on the other hand, the objectives of these regulations – respecting and protecting human rights – are universally endorsed. In contrast, section 5 turns to transnational litigations, which have drawn more international attention, as a means of remedy for victims of abuses. In fact – as will be shown – exercises of jurisdiction over third-State defendants are not permitted by traditional jurisdictional principles. However, this finding is lamentable given the interests of the victims of grave human rights abuses and points towards a larger need for reform. Section 6 concludes.

---

transnational corporations and other business enterprises with respect to human rights', A/HRC/RES/26/9.

720 UN Human Rights Council, 'Guiding Principles on Business and Human Rights: Implementing the United Nations "Protect, Respect and Remedy" Framework: Report of the Special Representative of the Secretary-General on the Issue of Human Rights and Transnational Corporations and Other Business Enterprises', A/HRC/17/31 (UN Guiding Principles); The UN Guiding Principles operationalize the 2008 'Protect, Respect and Remedy Framework for Business and Human Rights' also developed by the Special Representative: UN Human Rights Council, 'Protect, Respect and Remedy: A Framework for Business and Human Rights: Report of the Special Representative of the Secretary-General on the Issue of Human Rights and Transnational Corporations and Other Business Enterprises', A/HRC/8/5.

721 For a critique of the UN Guiding Principle's approach to extraterritoriality, see Daniel Augenstein and David Kinley, 'When Human Rights "Responsibilities" become "Duties": the Extra-Territorial Obligations of States that Bind Corporations' in Surya Deva and David Bilchitz (eds), *Human Rights Obligations of Business: Beyond the Corporate Responsibility to Respect?* (Cambridge University Press 2013).

## 2. Foundations of Business and Human Rights

The term 'Business and human rights' suggests that this area of regulation can be approached from two very distinct perspectives, namely 'business' and 'human rights'. Indeed, for quite some time, negative human rights impacts by corporations were primarily associated not with legal obligations, but with the corporate social responsibility (**CSR**) of businesses themselves. This has shifted markedly in the past decades and the modern concept of business and human rights has primarily turned towards the establishment of binding regulation (below **a**)). However, despite multiple serious efforts, the prospects of a legally binding instrument at the international level remain uncertain (below **b**)). In place of such an obligatory instrument, the international community adopted the UN Guiding Principles, which provide the primary reference also for business and human rights regulations at the domestic level (below **c**)).

### a) Corporate Social Responsibility and Business and Human Rights

Business and human rights as an area of regulation is connected to the concept of CSR: Historically, few legal obligations existed for corporations in relation to their negative impact on the enjoyment of human rights. Rather, this issue has been addressed, if at all, by businesses themselves as part of their CSR policies.[722] Even today, business leaders sometimes regard business and human rights as a branch or the newest development within the area of CSR.[723] This view was also partly shared in academic commentary which at times described business and human rights as the 'latest lens through which to view the social responsibility of corpora-

722 Justine Nolan, 'From Principles to Practice: Implementing Corporate Responsibility for Human Rights' in Jena Martin and Karen E Bravo (eds), *The Business and Human Rights Landscape: Moving Forward, Looking Back* (Cambridge University Press 2015), 396 ff.

723 See for instance Worth Loomis, 'The Responsibility of Parent Corporations for the Human Rights Violations of their Subsidiaries' in Michael K Addo (ed), *Human rights standards and the responsibility of transnational corporations* (Kluwer 1999): 'I define human rights broadly to include environmental rights, anti-bribery rights, and the right of every individual to benefit from ethical behavior in general, both from corporations and from governments.' See further Robert McCorquodale, 'Corporate Social Responsibility and International Human Rights Law' (2009) 87 (2009) JOBE 385, 391.

tions',[724] a 'new layer of debate on corporate social responsibility',[725] or a new expectation for businesses as a condition for giving them a 'social license to operate'.[726]

Although a single universally accepted definition of CSR does not exist and its understanding depends heavily on one's own academic or professional background, the notion has overwhelmingly been associated with voluntary mechanisms.[727] For instance, in its CSR strategies of 2001 and 2011, the European Commission defined CSR as 'a concept whereby companies integrate social and environmental concerns in their business operations and in their interaction with other stakeholders on a voluntary basis'.[728] From a business point of view, the argument in favour of CSR policies is therefore often found in the 'business case' for CSR, which means that investing in social causes can in the end lead to greater profits.[729] It also means that CSR remains an essentially management-driven add-on, which companies will engage in if it is beneficial, that is profitable, for business operations.[730]

Because the focus of CSR is placed on the creation of value for corporations, it has always been a somewhat imperfect solution in relation to negative human rights impacts. The notion that human rights would be subject to considerations of profitability does not seat well with the peremptory nature of these rights. Therefore, when legal scholars, NGOs and international organizations, already having a certain set of identified human rights norms in mind, entered this area, their energy naturally

---

724 Michael K Addo and Jena Martin, 'The Evolving Business and Society Landscape: Can Human Rights Make a Difference?' in Jena Martin and Karen E Bravo (eds), *The Business and Human Rights Landscape: Moving Forward, Looking Back* (Cambridge University Press 2015), 349.

725 Backer (n 715), 311.

726 Patricia Illingworth, 'Global Need: Rethinking Business Norms' in Jena Martin and Karen E Bravo (eds), *The Business and Human Rights Landscape: Moving Forward, Looking Back* (Cambridge University Press 2015), 192.

727 Ibid., 180.

728 European Commission, 'Promoting a European framework for Corporate Social Responsibility' (COM(2001) 366), para. 8; European Commission, 'A renewed EU strategy 2011–14 for Corporate Social Responsibility' (COM(2011) 681), para. 1.

729 Archie B Carroll and Kareem M Shabana, 'The Business Case for Corporate Social Responsibility: A Review of Concepts, Research and Practice' (2010) 12(1) IJMR 85; for an application of the 'business case' to business and human rights, see Addo and Martin (n 724), 376.

730 McCorquodale, 'Corporate Social Responsibility and International Human Rights Law' (n 723), 391.

turned onto the creation of binding legal obligations, which they deemed more effective than mere social pressure.[731]

### b) Historic Development of Business and Human Rights at the International Level

Arguably, efforts by international organizations to place business and human rights on their policy agenda started in the 1970s.[732] In 1976, the OECD created its OECD Guidelines on Multinational Enterprises, which provided non-binding principles and standards for responsible business conduct in a global context.[733] One year later, the International Labour Organization (**ILO**) adopted the Tripartite Declaration of Principles Concerning Multinational Enterprises and Social Policy, urging companies to follow the ILO conventions and other labour practices as well as to respect the Universal Declaration of Human Rights and the corresponding international Covenants.[734] Since their creation, both documents have been revised multiple times and they still constitute some of the most important standards in business and human rights.

A first substantial attempt at establishing legally binding international corporate human rights obligations was undertaken by the United Nations Sub-Commission on the Promotion and Protection of Human Rights in 2003 when it adopted the 'Norms on the Responsibilities of Transnational Corporations and Other Business Enterprises with Regard to Human Rights' (the **Draft Norms**).[735] Although one of the authors of the Draft Norms praised the outcome as a 'restatement of the international legal

731 Ibid., 385.

732 Tagi Sagafi-nejad and John H Dunning, *The UN and Transnational Corporations: From Code of Conduct to Global Compact* (United Nations Intellectual History Project, Indiana University Press 2008), 41 ff.

733 OECD, 'Guidelines for Multinational Enterprises', 21 June 1976,15 ILM 969, the latest version can be found here: http://mneguidelines.oecd.org/guidelines/, last accessed on 13 April 2022.

734 General Policy 8 of the International Labour Organization, 'Tripartite Declaration of Principles Concerning Multinational Enterprises and Social Policy', 16 November 1977, 17 ILM 422, the latest version can be found here: http://www.ilo.org/empent/Publications/WCMS_094386/lang--en/index.htm, last accessed on 13 April 2022.

735 Sub-Commission on the Promotion and Protection of Human Rights, 'Norms on the responsibilities of transnational corporations and other business enterprises with regard to human rights', UN Doc E/CN.4/Sub.2/2003/12/Rev.2.

principles applicable to businesses with regard to human rights',[736] and while they were strongly welcomed by NGOs and some academics, they were met with resistance by virtually anyone else.[737] Corporations, which still enjoyed the benefit of being allowed to largely self-regulate their human rights impacts through CSR policies, were particularly opposed to the Draft Norms. Because of the widespread resistance, the UN Commission on Human Rights ultimately adopted a decision stating that the Draft Norms had 'no legal standing'.[738]

The demise of the Draft Norms served as the catalysing point for the appointment of the Special Representative of the Secretary-General on human rights and transnational corporations and other business enterprises (the **SRSG**), John Ruggie.[739] Over the course of six years, the SRSG conducted nearly fifty international consultations and drafted or commissioned various research reports. The process eventually culminated in the 'Protect, Respect and Remedy' Framework and the implementing Guiding Principles.[740] These documents, perhaps because they were much less ambitious than the Draft Norms, have received widespread support. They were unanimously endorsed by the Human Rights Council in 2011 and since then, have become the primary reference for the business and human rights debate.[741]

However, far from ending the decade-long debate, they have prompted various domestic, regional and international actions and responses. Specifically, the endorsement of the Guiding Principles has triggered renewed interest of the international community in a legally binding instrument on business and human rights. In 2014, the Human Rights Council established an intergovernmental working group to further explore such

736 David S Weissbrodt and Muria Kruger, 'Norms on the Responsibilities of Transnational Corporations and Other Business Enterprises with Regard to Human Rights' (2003) 97 AJIL 901 - 922, 901.

737 D. Kinley and R. Chambers, 'The UN Human Rights Norms for Corporations: The Private Implications of Public International Law' (2006) 6(3) HRLRev 447, 458.

738 UN Commission on Human Rights, Decision 2004/116, 'Responsibilities of transnational corporations and related business enterprises with regard to human rights'.

739 Nadia Bernaz, *Business and human rights: History, Law and Policy – Bridging the Accountability Gap* (Human rights and international law, Routledge 2017), 188 f.

740 Ruggie (n 714), Introduction xx.

741 UN Human Rights Council, Resolution 17/4, 'Human rights and transnational corporations and other business enterprises', A/HRC/RES/17/4.

prospects.[742] The working group has recently released the second revised draft instrument focused on domestic due diligence obligations as well as access to remedy for victims of corporate abuses.[743] Despite progress, the mandate is facing considerable hurdles including the lack of participation of a number of key States.[744] Thus, the future of the still ongoing mandate remains uncertain.

### c) The UN Guiding Principles

Until such time when a binding treaty comes into force, the Guiding Principles with their near universal endorsement offer the most established restatement of substantive and procedural standards within the area of business and human rights. Ruggie himself admitted that the Guiding Principle's normative contribution was not so much to elaborate new legal obligations, but rather to define and link existing standards and practices of States and business within a single and coherent template.[745] This template consists of three pillars: the State's duty to protect against human rights abuses by corporations; the corporate responsibility to respect human rights; and the need for effective access to remedy.[746]

Rather uncontroversial and consistent with existing international human rights law is the first pillar, the State duty to protect. It rests on the established doctrine that States not only have the obligation to refrain from violating human rights themselves, but also to protect against violations stemming from private third parties such as corporations. A landmark case in this regard is *López Ostra v Spain*, decided by the ECtHR in 1994, in which the court held that a State may violate the victim's right under

742 UN Human Rights Council, Resolution 26/9, 'Elaboration of an international legally binding instrument on transnational corporations and other business enterprises with respect to human rights', A/HRC/RES/26/9.

743 See Second Revised Draft of legally binding instrument to regulate, in international human rights law, the activities of transnational corporations and other business enterprises, available at: https://www.ohchr.org/Documents/HRBodies/HRCouncil/WGTransCorp/Session6/OEIGWG_Chair-Rapporteur_second_revised_draft_LBI_on_TNCs_and_OBEs_with_respect_to_Human_Rights.pdf, last accessed on 13 April 2022.

744 Ryan Turner, 'Transnational Supply Chain Regulation: Extraterritorial Regulation as Corporate Law's new Frontier' (2016) 17 MelbJIntLaw 1, 14 – 16; O'brien 151.

745 Ruggie (n 714), 83.

746 UN Guiding Principles, General Principles.

Art. 8 of the Convention if it allows a privately owned waste plant to emit harmful pollution.[747] Similarly, in the case concerning the Ogoni people in Nigeria, the African Commission on Human and People's Rights found that the State had failed to protect the local population's rights against the damaging acts of oil companies.[748] Comparable decisions have also been rendered by the Inter-American Commission on Human Rights[749] and the Human Rights Committee.[750] In line with this jurisprudence, the Guiding Principles restate that the State's duty regarding business and human rights includes the taking of 'appropriate steps to prevent, investigate, punish and redress private actors' abuse'.[751]

The second pillar – and maybe the cornerstone of Ruggie's work – contrasts the comprehensive legal obligations of the State with the social responsibility of corporations to respect. By distinguishing between the different nature of the two pillars, one being legal and the other social, Ruggie may have overcome one of the most vicious challenges against the Draft Norms. Respect in this sense may be translated into a simple 'do no harm', that is, do not violate, facilitate or otherwise get involved in human rights violations.[752] This includes actual or potential human rights violations arising not only from a company's own activities along the entire enterprise but also through its relationship with third parties. However, mere passivity would not be enough to discharge this responsibility; rather, companies would have to develop institutional capacities for human rights due diligence.[753] The concept of due diligence is further developed throughout the second pillar and Ruggie dedicates five entire principles to elaborate the practical steps necessary.[754]

Human rights due diligence is defined as 'an ongoing management process that a reasonable and prudent enterprise needs to undertake' to meet its responsibility to respect human rights and which may differ 'in

747 ECtHR, *López Ostra v Spain*, App No 16798/90, Judgment of 9 December 1994.

748 African Commission on Human and People's Rights, *Social and Economic Rights Action Center (SERAC) and Center for Economic and Social Rights (CESR) v Nigeria* [2001] No 155/96, para. 61.

749 Inter-Am. Commission on Human Rights, *Maya indigenous community of the Toledo District v Belize* [2004] Case 12.053, Report No 40/04, para. 152.

750 Human Rights Committee, *Länsmann v Finland* [1994] Communication No 511/1992, U.N. Doc. CCPR/C/52/D/511/1992.

751 Principle 1, UN Guiding Principles.

752 Ruggie (n 714), 95.

753 Principle 11 to 15, UN Guiding Principles.

754 Principle 17 to 21, UN Guiding Principles.

light of its circumstances (including sector, operating context, size and similar factors)'.[755] This notion of human rights due diligence has been particularly influential, with both States and international organizations referring to it in the design of regulations and policies. While Ruggie has not been the first to connect business and human rights with due diligence, he was arguably the one who saw the potential of the concept to bridge the intellectual gap between human rights practitioners and business leaders. In fact, the terminology of due diligence existed both in international human rights law as well as business practice and the SRSG indeed drew from both traditions when constructing his concept of human rights due diligence:[756]

On the one hand, due diligence is well established under international human rights law: For instance, in its seminal *Velasquez-Rodriguez* case, the Inter-American Court held that

> '[a]n illegal act which violates human rights and which is initially not directly imputable to a State (for example, because it is the act of a private person or because the person responsible has not been identified) can lead to international responsibility of the State, not because of the act itself, but because of the lack of due diligence to prevent the violation or to respond to it as required by the Convention'.[757]

On the other hand, however, companies have long engaged in their own kind of due diligence measures, which are understood as risk-mitigating internal control mechanisms, for instance to prevent criminal misconduct by employees or to comply with anti-bribery regulations.[758] Thus, framing human rights as another operational risk that companies needed to control appealed to businesses as well.

Finally, because the framework is lacking in a specific monitoring mandate itself, the SRSG made access to remedies his third and final pillar to provide the Guiding Principles with coercive teeth. According to Ruggie, remedies include a broad range of measures not limited to State-based

---

755 Office of the United Nations High Commissioner for Human Rights, 'The Corporate Responsibility to Respect Human Rights: An Interpretive Guide', 4.

756 Robert McCorquodale, 'International Human Rights Law Perspectives on the UN Framework and Guiding Principles on Business and Human Rights' in Lara Blecher, Nancy K Stafford and Gretchen C Bellamy (eds), *Corporate Responsibility for Human Rights Impacts: New Expectations and Paradigms* (American Bar Association 2014), 68.

757 IACtHR, *Velásquez Rodríguez v Honduras* [1988] Series C No 4, para. 172.

758 Ruggie (n 714), 99; Nolan (n 722), 407.

judicial measures, but also non-judicial grievance mechanisms as well as corporate and other non-State based redress mechanisms.[759] Among State-based judicial measures, high-profile litigations against alleged corporate human rights abusers, such as those brought under the American ATS, are of particular practical relevance as well as symbolic value.

Despite the near universal acknowledgement of the Guiding Principles, Ruggie himself has described them as only the beginning of the journey towards corporate accountability for human rights abuses.[760] In particular, because the Guiding Principles explicitly eschewed the creation of binding obligations on businesses and the prospects of an international instrument are still uncertain, it is up to domestic law to fill the regulatory vacuum based on the concepts delivered by the SRSG. However, since host countries may not be willing or even able to exercise authority over powerful multinational corporations, the potential of extraterritorial home State regulation has garnered special interest.

### 3. Extraterritoriality in Business and Human Rights

#### a) Extraterritorial Jurisdiction as a Matter of Permission

During the drafting of the Guiding Principles, extraterritoriality has featured as a focal point at various stages of the project and multiple expert consultations and extended reports to study extraterritorial jurisdiction in the area of business and human rights were commissioned.[761] Despite that, the SRSG ultimately had to admit that the topic remained highly contentious.[762] While he conceded that '[t]here are strong policy reasons for home States to set out clearly the expectation that businesses respect human rights abroad', he remained indecisive on the legal aspects: Accordingly, the Guiding Principles concludes that

> 'States are not generally required under international human rights law to regulate the extraterritorial activities of businesses domiciled in

759 Principle 25 to 31, UN Guiding Principles.

760 Ruggie (n 714), 170.

761 See Zerk (n 634); Olivier De Schutter, 'Extraterritorial Jurisdiction as a Tool for Improving the Human Rights Accountability of Transnational Corporations' (2006).

762 Ruggie (n 714) 139 f.

their territory and/or jurisdiction. Nor are they generally prohibited from doing so, provided there is a recognized jurisdictional basis'.[763]

This conclusion touches on the specific, dual nature of extraterritoriality in the context of business and human rights as it integrates both the concept of jurisdiction under *international human rights law* and jurisdiction proper under *general international law*. While the last sentence of the above-quoted paragraph refers to the permissive jurisdictional principles under general international law which are at the heart of this study, the first part of the conclusion addresses the concept of jurisdiction in international human rights law and the question whether an extraterritorial *obligation* of States exists to regulate foreign business conduct of 'their' home companies in relation to human rights.[764]

With regard to the question of permission, Ruggie's reference to the recognized jurisdictional basis to prescribe in international law means that he did not have to resolve the many contentious issues within this body of law. However, Ruggie offered some concretisation in the commentaries to the Guiding Principles where he endorsed a distinction between direct extraterritorial jurisdiction and domestic measures with extraterritorial implications. This distinction is also followed by Zerk in her more in-depth study on extraterritorial jurisdiction prepared to assist the SRSG: She reserves the concept of extraterritorial jurisdiction only for 'direct assertions of jurisdiction over the foreign conduct of individuals and companies', whereas other measures that 'try to influence conditions, standards and behaviour in other countries' are referred to as domestic measures with extraterritorial implications.[765] The idea is that while some measures may (purposefully) target foreign conduct, they may also be addressing a domestic situation or using a domestic trigger and that these measures form a category different from 'direct extraterritorial jurisdiction'. Therefore, an import restriction on goods produced abroad that do not adhere to certain human rights standards would constitute a 'domestic measure with extraterritorial implications'.[766] Another example would be a regulation

763 Commentary to Principle 2, UN Guiding Principles.

764 Augenstein and Kinley (n 721); McCorquodale, 'International Human Rights Law Perspectives on the UN Framework and Guiding Principles on Business and Human Rights' (n 756).

765 See Zerk (n 634), 15.

766 Ibid., 15: 'An import ban on products produced using environmental standards unacceptable to the regulating state is one example [of a domestic measure with extraterritorial implications].'; Scott (n 10), 109: 'in the vast majority of cases,

that requires parent companies to report on their overall human rights policy and impacts, including those of their overseas subsidiaries, because this measure would rely 'entirely on territory as the jurisdictional basis'.[767]

Even though this distinction has been rather influential with academic commentators,[768] Ruggie himself ultimately avoided associating clear normative consequences with it. While the context does suggest that in his opinion, the category of 'domestic measures with extraterritorial implications' would normally raise no issues under international law, the SRSG merely noted that the different ways to influence extraterritorially the human rights behaviour of companies are not 'equally likely to trigger objections under all circumstances'.[769] Ruggie's reluctance to offer a clear position reflects the complexity of the issue at hand. In fact, at least some of the 'domestic measures with extraterritorial implications' include trade and procurement regulations structurally similar to secondary trade boycotts, which have caused tremendous international uproar. The discussion below will return to this issue and attempt to connect the considerations from different areas of regulation.

### b) Extraterritorial Jurisdiction as a Matter of Obligation

In the area of business and human rights, academic debate exists not only with regard to the scope of permitted extraterritorial jurisdiction; rather, progressive scholars have also created a vast body of writing on the issue of extraterritorial obligations. Their starting point is mostly rooted in the jurisprudence of human rights courts and treaty body decisions interpreting the scope of application of human rights treaties. For instance, while the European Convention on Human Rights (**ECHR**), the American Convention on Human Rights (**ACHR**) and the International Covenant on Civil and Political Rights (**ICCPR**) all contain clauses that generally

---

territorial extension is used to condition access to the EU market for imported goods or services'.

767 Human Rights Council, 'Business and Human Rights: Further Steps towards the Operationalization of the "Protect, Respect and Remedy" Framework', A/HRC/14/27 (9 April 2010), para. 49.

768 Nadia Bernaz, 'Enhancing Corporate Accountability for Human Rights Violations: Is Extraterritoriality the Magic Potion?' (2013) 117(3) JOBE 493, 496 – 497; Augenstein and Kinley (n 721), 277 – 279; see already above at A.III.2. Extraterritoriality and Extraterritorial Jurisdiction.

769 Ibid., para. 49.

limit the human rights obligation of States to natural or legal persons within their jurisdictions, the competent treaty organs have extended the protection of the treaties to situations outside the State's territory.[770] Apart from a State's territory, jurisdiction has generally been interpreted to cover extraterritorial situations in which the State is exercising 'effective control', 'authority' or 'power' over certain persons or territory.[771] The conclusion drawn from this jurisprudence is that the triggering moment for the establishment of extraterritorial application of human rights treaties is the existence of a situation in which the affected foreigner is under the *de facto* power of the State. This line of decision is well accepted among modern human rights scholars.[772]

The actual innovation, however, is the argument that such situations of *de facto* power also arise when a foreigner is the victim of corporate human rights abuses and when the perpetrating business enterprise is subject to the factual power of the home State. Thus, because the home State is in a position to 'control' the enterprise, it is also able to indirectly exercise authority over the victim. This wide definition of 'control' is engaged for instance if the enterprise is a recipient of home State support such as export credits and more radically, if the corporate parent of the business enterprise is incorporated in the home State, which thus places the entire corporate group under the regulatory influence of the home State.[773]

770 ECtHR, *Loizidou v Turkey*, Preliminary Objections, App No 15318/89, Judgment of 23 March 1995, para. 62; Inter-Am. Commission on Human Rights, *Victor Saldano v Argentina* [1999] Report No 38/99, para. 19.

771 See for instance: Human Rights Committee, 'General Comment No. 31: The Nature of the General Legal Obligation Imposed on States Parties to the Covenant', CCPR/C/21/Rev.1/Add.13, para. 10.

772 Milanovic (n 27), 417; See further the conclusions reached by Fons Coomans and Menno T Kamminga, 'Comparative Introductory Comments on the Extraterritorial Application of Human Rights Treaties' in Fons Coomans and Menno T Kamminga (eds), *Extraterritorial Application of Human Rights Treaties* (Intersentia 2004), 3 – 4.

773 McCorquodale, 'Corporate Social Responsibility and International Human Rights Law' (n 723), 399 – 389; Augenstein and Kinley (n 721) for instance write at 285 – 286: 'A state's de jure authority to exercise extra-territorial jurisdiction under public international law not only delimits the state's lawful competence to regulate and control business entities as perpetrators of extra-territorial human rights violations, but also constitutes a de facto relationship of power of the state over the individual that brings the individual under the state's human rights jurisdiction and triggers corresponding extra-territorial obligations.'

A regularly cited example in this regard is *Kovačič*, in which the ECtHR accepted jurisdiction in a case concerning a Slovenian law, which prohibited the Croatian applicants from withdrawing funds from their accounts in the Croatian branch of a Slovenian bank.[774] The Slovenian government had argued that the requirements of Art. 1 ECHR were not fulfilled as the State had no effective control over the applicants: Because the applicants' deposits were situated on Croatian territory, they were thus subject to Croatian and not to Slovenian jurisdiction. The court, however, was not swayed by this argument as the Slovenian law at issue explicitly related to the accounts opened with the Slovenian bank's branches situated outside Slovenian territory.

Several UN treaty bodies have also adopted decisions suggesting that a State's human rights obligations might extend to extraterritorial conduct and effects that are under domestic control.[775] Recently, the Committee on Economic, Social and Cultural Rights, in its Concluding Observations regarding the United Kingdom, held that the country should 'adopt appropriate legislative and administrative measures to ensure the legal liability of companies domiciled under the State party's jurisdiction for violations [...] abroad committed directly by these companies or resulting from the activities of their subsidiaries'.[776] The Committee on the Rights of Child has taken a similar approach: While emphasizing that, in the case of transnational corporations, the primary regulatory responsibility lies within the host State, the '[h]ome States also have obligations [...] to respect, protect and fulfil children's rights in the context of businesses' extraterritorial activities and operations'.[777]

On a scholarly level, a notable development has been the establishment of the Maastricht Principles on Extraterritorial Obligations, which seek

---

774 ECtHR, *Kovačić and Others v Slovenia*, App No 44574/98, 45133/98 and 48316/99, Decision of 1 April 2004, the case was later struck out because full payments were made in the interim.

775 Committee on Economic, Social and Cultural Rights (CESCR), 'General Comment No. 14: The Right to the Highest Attainable Standard of Health', E/C.12/2000/4, para. 39; CESCR, 'General Comment No. 15: The Right to Water', E/C.12/2002/11, para. 31; CESCR, 'General comment No. 24 on State obligations under the International Covenant on Economic, Social and Cultural Rights in the context of business activities', E/C.12/GC/24, para. 33.

776 CECSR, 'Concluding observations on the sixth periodic report of the United Kingdom of Great Britain and Northern Ireland', E/C.12/GBR/CO/6, para. 12.

777 Committee on the Rights of the Child, 'General comment No. 16 (2013) on State obligations regarding the impact of the business sector on children's rights, CRC/C/GC/16', paras. 42 – 46.

to restate extraterritorial obligations of States with regard to economic, social and cultural rights on the basis of standing international law.[778] Despite this, the existence of such a hard 'duty to regulate' MNCs in an extraterritorial context remains contentious.[779] Accordingly, the following analysis shows that while States are engaging in a wide range of different regulations and policies to protect human rights extraterritorially, the design and scope of these measures are at times quite flexible and do not indicate an acceptance of an extraterritorial duty to regulate.

### 4. Regulation through Parent-Subsidiary or Lead-Supplier Relationships

#### a) Trade, Procurement and Investment Measures

Long before Ruggie identified the State duty to protect human rights as the first pillar of the Framework and the Guiding Principles, States were already engaging in policies that would squarely fall into the business and human rights context today. Many of these leverage trade, public procurement or investments/divestments to achieve extraterritorial human rights objectives.

##### aa) Practice in the United States

In the United States, market access restrictions in relation to human rights performance were introduced as early as 1930. Specifically, Sec. 307 of the Smoot-Hawley Tariff Act of 1930 prohibited the import of all goods 'mined, produced, or manufactured wholly or in part in any foreign country by convict labor or forced labor'.[780] However, for the most time since its enactment, the law had little impact because of a 'consumptive demand' clause, which exempted from Sec. 307 of the Smoot-Hawley Tariff Act of 1930 all products for which the domestic production did not satisfy the domestic consumptive need. However, this consumptive demand exception was repealed in a 2016 amendment and enforcement was significantly strengthened. Since the entry into force of the amendment,

---

778 See Maastricht Principles (n 769).

779 Claire M O'Brien, 'The Home State Duty to Regulate TNCs Abroad' (2016), 27 – 35.

780 Sec. 307 Smoot-Hawley Tariff Act of 1930, Pub. L. 71–361, 19 U.S.C. § 1307.

the US Customs & Border Protection (**CBP**) has already taken more than 30 enforcement actions as contrasted to only 39 actions in the previous 86 years, indicating a significant policy shift.[781]

CBP enforces the provision though the issuing of 'withhold release' orders if there are reasonable indications that imported goods have been mined, produced or manufactured in a foreign country by forced or indentured child labour. To gather the necessary information, CBP allows any person who believes that certain goods fall under the scope of the act to submit complaints to the agency. To release shipments subject to enforcement actions, the importer has to submit certifications of origin as well as detailed statements showing that the product was manufactured without forced labour. The Smoot-Hawley Tariff Act of 1930 may have strong extraterritorial implications because in practice, importers have to conduct extensive due diligence in relation to their foreign suppliers and may require them to adhere to strict forced labour standards themselves if they want to continue engaging in exports to the United States. If CBP continues this line of thorough enforcement, the Tariff Act of 1930 has the potential to become a potent tool to combat forced labour, in particular because NGOs may file formal complaints about labour practices around the world.[782]

Human rights considerations are also reflected, albeit in weaker form, in US public procurement regulations. The primary document governing procurement by US federal agencies is the Federal Acquisition Regulation (**FAR**), which consolidates legislation, executive orders and treaties.[783] Subpart 22.15 of the FAR prohibits the acquisition of goods produced by forced or indentured child labour. To implement this provision, the US Department of Labor maintains a 'List of Products Requiring Contractor Certification as to Forced or Indentured Child Labor', which includes goods suspected of being produced by forced child labour. Entries on the list are framed broadly and for instance encompass bricks from

781 See Forced Labor section on the CBP website: https://www.cbp.gov/trade/forced-labor/withhold-release-orders-and-findings, last accessed on 13 April 2022.

782 See for instance: Press Release, 'ILRF Files Complaint to Halt Imports of Forced Labor-made Goods from Turkmenistan', http://www.laborrights.org/releases/ilrf-files-complaint-halt-imports-forced-labor-made-goods-turkmenistan, last accessed on 13 April 2022.

783 Federal Acquisition Regulation, 48 C.F.R. Chapter 1.

Afghanistan and toys from China.[784] To receive an offer from a procuring agency, a bidder must certify that either, (a) he will not sell a product on the list, or (b), he has made a good-faith effort to determine whether forced child labour was used.[785]

Furthermore, government contractors are prohibited from engaging in human trafficking related activities and are required to pass these prohibitions, including disclosure obligations, down their supply chains.[786] Additionally, if the procurement relates to services exceeding USD 500,000 and is to be performed outside the United States, the contractor has to prepare a compliance plan, which has to be posted on the company website, and annually certify that it has implemented this compliance plan. The compliance plan has to fulfil a number of minimum requirements, including an awareness programme, a whistleblowing scheme, a recruitment and wage plan as well as procedures to prevent any prohibited human trafficking down the supply chain and to monitor, detect, and terminate contracts with subcontractors or agents engaging in prohibited activities.[787]

#### bb) Practice in Europe

The EU is increasingly willing to use its strength in international trade to achieve social and ecological objectives. This is for instance evidenced in the field of public procurement. Under the European system, the award of public contracts exceeding certain monetary values is harmonized across the Single Market through EU directives. In 2014, these directives have received a major overhaul and may now provide State authorities additional opportunities to take human rights into account during the procurement process. As a general principle, under Art. 18 (2) of the Public

---

784 US Department of Labor, List of Products Produced by Forced or Indentured Child Labor, https://www.dol.gov/agencies/ilab/reports/child-labor/list-of-products, last accessed on 13 April 2022.

785 48 C.F.R. § 22.1503.

786 48 C.F.R. § 52.222 – 50.

787 Ibid.; even though these procurement regulations exist on the books, their actual enforcement record is less stellar. An international study conducted by the International Learning Lab on Public Procurement and Human Rights concluded that the United States maintains only weak monitoring measures operationalizing those procurement policies, see Claire M O'Brien, Nicole Vander Meulen and Amol Mehra, 'Public Procurement and Human Rights: A Survey of Twenty Jurisdictions' (2016), 38 – 47.

Procurement Directive,[788] member States shall take appropriate measures to ensure that contractors comply with applicable obligations in the fields of environmental, social and labour law. Notably, these obligations refer to the ILO Core Conventions as well as several international environmental treaties. Bidders violating these obligations may be excluded from the procurement process.[789] Further, in cases of an 'abnormally low' tender, authorities are required to reject the offer if they can establish that the 'abnormally low' offer is the result of violations against said obligations.[790] Another rule having a human rights dimension is Art. 57 (1) (f) of the Directive, which requires the exclusion of contractors who (including a member of its administrative, managing or supervising body) have been convicted of child labour or other forms of human trafficking.[791] Furthermore, at the stage of awarding the contract, the new Directive allows for the incorporation of social and environmental criteria alongside more traditional economic considerations, subject to the conditions of proportionality, non-discrimination, and link to the subject matter of the contract.[792]

While these new procurement provisions are to be welcomed from a human rights perspective, they still seem to be 'weaker' than what comparable US regulations provide for. For instance, US regulations mandatorily prohibit the procurement of goods produced using forced or child labour as well as transactions with bidders engaged in human trafficking. Under the EU Public Procurement Directive, a mandatory exclusion only exists with regard to convicted offenders, even though a conviction may rarely happen if the violations occurred down the supply chain in an extraterritorial setting. In almost all other cases, exclusion will be in the discretion of State authorities based on a violation of Art. 18 (2) of the Directive.

b) Mandatory Supply Chain Regulation

As seen above, the UN Guiding Principles establish the corporate responsibility to protect not only with respect to a company's own activities but also with respect to its relationships with third parties, in particular

788 Directive 2014/24/EU of the European Parliament and of the Council of 26 February 2014 on public procurement and repealing Directive 2004/18/EC [2014] OJ L 94/65.

789 Ibid., Art. 57 (4) (a).

790 Ibid., Art. 69 (4).

791 Ibid., Art. 57 (1) (f).

792 Ibid., Art. 67 (2).

its affiliates and suppliers.[793] Confronted with the technical difficulties of regulating the complex web of multinational and transnational corporations, States are increasingly establishing requirements with regard to the transparency of supply chains. This modus of regulation incentivizes or obliges corporations to identify, prevent, mitigate and account for human rights risks in their supply chains, which includes conducting sufficient human rights due diligence. In contrast to the above identified public procurement and trade measures, which at times require supply chain due diligence as well, these regulations are often rooted in national corporate or securities legislation. The specific mechanisms of regulation differ in coercing force. The arguably strongest rules impose mandatory requirements, which are sometimes backed by severe penalties, in contrast to mere disclosure requirements, which depend on conscious consumers and activist investors to act upon the information made available. The most severe forms of regulation often come with significant extraterritorial effects, as subjected companies may have to impose human rights standards along the supply chain or terminate contractual relationships with individual suppliers, many of which are located abroad.

aa) Practice in the United States

The most well-known example of a mandatory supply chain regulation in the United States is the heavily contested rule regarding conflict minerals in the Democratic Republic of Congo (the **DRC**) and neighbouring countries, introduced through Sec. 1502 of the Dodd-Frank Wall Street Reform and Consumer Exchange Act.[794] The provision requires stock issuing companies that manufacture or contract to manufacture certain conflict minerals, defined as tin, tantalum, tungsten and gold, to investigate and disclose certain information regarding the sources of those minerals. These conflict minerals form integral parts of many consumer electronics but are at the same time linked to the financing of armed groups in the DRC.[795]

---

793 See above C.V.2c) The UN Guiding Principles.

794 Dodd-Frank Wall Street Reform and Consumer Exchange Act, Pub.L. 111–203, H.R. 4173.

795 Erika George, 'Influencing the Impact of Business on Human Rights: Corporate Social Responsibility through Transparency and Reporting' in Lara Blecher, Nancy K Stafford and Gretchen C Bellamy (eds), *Corporate Responsibility for Human Rights Impacts: New Expectations and Paradigms* (American Bar Association 2014), 258 – 260.

The Final Rule promulgated by the SEC to implement Sec. 1502 establishes a three-step process: First, the companies have to determine whether they are subject to the conflict minerals disclosure obligation. If affirmed, the affected business enterprises have to conduct a reasonable country of origin inquiry to determine whether the minerals were sourced from the DRC or one of its neighbouring countries. This requirement is satisfied if the company is able to obtain reliable representations from the facilities at which its conflict minerals were processed.[796] If the inquiry determines that minerals used did not originate from the DRC or neighbouring countries, the company has to take no further steps apart from disclosing this finding with the SEC. If, after the reasonable-country-of-origin inquiry, the company knows or at least cannot rule out the possibility that minerals originated from the DRC or neighbouring countries, it is obliged to perform due diligence on the source and the supply chain of the minerals. In this case, the company has to submit a Conflict Minerals Report (**CMR**) as an attachment to the filing for the SEC.[797] The CMR has to detail the due diligence measures taken to determine whether products of the company contain minerals that directly or indirectly finance or benefit armed groups. The due diligence process has to conform with a nationally or internationally recognized due diligence framework such as the OECD Due Diligence Guidance for Responsible Supply Chains of Minerals from Conflict-Affected and High-Risk Areas (the **OECD Due Diligence Guidance**).[798] Additionally, the CMR has to undergo an independent private sector audit, which is to be conducted in accordance with standards established by the Comptroller General of the United States and the result of this audit has to be filed with the SEC as well.[799]

These provisions are strengthened through a number of transparency requirements and enforcement possibilities. Because the reasonable-country-of-origin inquiry and, if applicable, the CMR have to be filed with

796 Conflict Minerals Final Rule, 77 Fed. Reg. 56.311 -313.

797 Ibid., 56.320. There is no obligation to submit the CMR if the due diligence leads to the positive determination that its conflict minerals in fact did not originate in the DRC or a neighbouring country.

798 Ibid., 56.326; See OECD, OECD Due Diligence Guidance for Responsible Supply Chains of Minerals from Conflict-Affected and High-Risk Areas (2011), available at http://www.oecd.org/corporate/mne/mining.htm, last accessed on 13 April 2022.

799 Ibid., 56.328.

the SEC,[800] failure to comply with these provisions, for instance through false or unreliable statements, are subject to injunctive, civil, or criminal sanctions. In particular, if such statements lead to injuries on the part of shareholders in a stock transaction, these shareholders can use a private right of action to hold the company liable.[801] Furthermore, companies have to disclose their reasonable-country-of-origin inquiry and their CMR not only to the SEC, but also make them public on their internet websites. Originally, companies were required to label their products as either 'DRC conflict free' or 'have not been found to be "DRC conflict free"'. However, this last requirement has been partially struck down as unconstitutional compelled speech.[802]

Sec. 1502 has extraterritorial implications in multiple ways. For one, just like the FCPA[803] it applies to companies that issue stocks on US exchanges and that are required to file reports with the SEC regardless of whether they are domestic or foreign.[804] For the other, the provision may have had significant effects on the conduct of the upstream supply chain of US companies, particularly smelters and refiners, which have to disclose the sources of their minerals and which in turn requires them to conduct thorough due diligence. An EU communication estimated the number of companies in Europe indirectly affected by the rule to be between 150.000 and 200.000.[805] On the intergovernmental level, the International Conference on the Great Lakes Region (the **ICGLR** or the **Conference**), an international organization comprising the DRC and its neighbouring countries, has introduced a Regional Certification Mechanism to help mineral producers in the region to comply with Sec. 1502.

Despite its strong extraterritorial implications, Sec. 1502 has not been the subject of vehement State protest. In fact, while the ICGLR lamented the *de facto* embargo on the mineral sector of the region and the ensuing

---

800 See Sections 13(p)(1)(A)(ii) and 13(p)(1)(D) of the Securities Exchange Act of 1934, 17 C.F.R. § 240.13p-1.

801 Karen E Woody, 'Conflict Minerals Legislation: The SEC's New Role as Diplomatic and Humanitarian Watchdog' (2013) 81 FordhamLR 1315, 1336 – 1338.

802 *National Ass'n of Manufacturers v SEC*, 800 F 3d 518 (DC Cir 2015).

803 See above: C.IV.4a)aa) The Jurisdictional Scope of the FCPA.

804 See on this the letter by Taiwan Semiconductors Manufacturing Company Ltd. to the SEC, https://www.sec.gov/comments/s7-40-10/s74010-46.pdf, last accessed on 13 April 2022.

805 High Representative of the Union for Foreign Affairs and Security Policy, Joint Communication to the European Parliament and the Council, Responsible sourcing of minerals originating in conflict-affected and high-risk areas: Towards an integrated EU approach, JOIN(2014) 8 final, at 7.

disruption of the local economy, the Conference opposed a US domestic proposal to repeal Sec. 1502, arguing that such action might lead to a resurgence of armed groups.[806] Moreover, the Conference as well as individual States did not suggest that the act at issue violated international law principles because of its extraterritorial implications.

### bb) Practice in Europe

After years of discussion between the Commission, the Parliament and the Council, the EU, partly inspired by the US model, adopted its own version of conflict minerals regulations in 2017.[807] Aimed at the same minerals, tin, tantalum, tungsten and gold, the EU regulation imposes due diligence obligations directly onto the importers, in contrast to Sec. 1502, which addressed all stock issuing companies. The due diligence measures adopted have to be consistent with the OECD Due Diligence Guidance.[808] As with Sec. 1502, importers must have their activities and processes certified via independent third-party audits and disclose their supply-chain policies and related information to authorities and the public. To ease the burden on importers, they are exempted from the private audit requirement if they can provide evidence that they only sourced from smelters and refiners which themselves comply with the conflict minerals regulation and are included in a list of global responsible smelters and refiners.[809]

Comparable to Sec. 1502, the EU Conflict Minerals Regulation has extraterritorial implications. However, because the EU regulation targets the direct importers at the beginning of the downstream supply chain, it does not affect an end-purchaser's entire supplier base. Accordingly, the EU estimates that only about 500 smelters and refiners globally will be in-

806 See International Conference on the Great Lakes Region, Declaration on Section 1502 of the US Dodd Frank Act, http://www.icglr.org/index.php/en/homepage/135-laast-news/763-icglr-declaration-section-of-the-us-dodd-frank-act, last accessed on 13 April 2022.

807 Regulation (EU) 2017/821 of the European Parliament and of the Council of 17 May 2017 laying down supply chain due diligence obligations for Union importers of tin, tantalum and tungsten, their ores, and gold originating from conflict-affected and high-risk areas (hereinafter: EU Conflict Minerals Regulation).

808 See Art. 4 and 5 of the EU Conflict Minerals Regulation.

809 See Art. 6, 7 and 9 of the EU Conflict Minerals Regulation.

directly subjected to the regulation.[810] It seems plausible that, as importers move towards companies included in the list of global responsible smelters and refiners to avoid the obligation to conduct third-party audits, domestic as well as foreign companies will pursue compliance with the EU Conflict Minerals Regulation to not lose business.[811]

On the national level, after a similarly tedious legislative process, France in 2017 adopted its law regarding the *devoir de vigilance*, or duty of care of parent companies and subcontracting companies. Despite its limited scope of addressees – the law applies only to companies incorporated or registered in France that employ more than 5,000 employees themselves or through their French subsidiaries or more than 10,000 employees globally – it introduced, at that time, unprecedented obligations in business and human rights. Companies subject to the regulation are required to elaborate, disclose and implement an effective *plan de vigilance* of reasonable measures to identify and prevent any serious violations of human rights, fundamental freedoms, and the health and safety of persons and the environment. This duty of care includes among others risk-mapping, preventive and mitigating measures and more importantly, a mechanism

810 European Commission, The regulation explained, http://ec.europa.eu/trade/policy/in-focus/conflict-minerals-regulation/regulation-explained/, last accessed on 13 April 2022.

811 The legislative process shows that the final regulation has been a carefully crafted compromise, after discarding both 'softer' and 'harder' regulatory options. The Commission had initially pushed for a voluntary self-certification system, which meant that meeting the due diligence requirements would be voluntary for importers who wanted to be certified as a responsible importer. In contrast, the European Parliament opted for mandatory due diligence by importers in addition to a disclosure requirement for stock issuing companies mirroring that of Sec. 1502. The original impact assessment also considered an import ban on conflict minerals if importers could not demonstrate compliance with OECD due diligence guidelines. For more details, see Anita Thoms, 'Offenlegungspflichten für Konfliktmineralien in den USA und der EU' in Arnold Wallraff, Dirk Ehlers and Hans-Michael Wolffgang (eds), *Recht der Exportkontrolle: Bestandsaufnahme und Perspektiven: Handbuch zum Exportkontrollrecht.* zugleich Festgabe für Dr. Arnold Wallraff zum 65. Geburtstag (Schriften zum Aussenwirtschaftsrecht 2015), 135 – 138; European Parliament, Press Release of June 16 2016, http://www.europarl.europa.eu/pdfs/news/expert/infopress/20160615IPR32320/20160615IPR32320_en.pdf, last accessed on 13 April 2022; European Commission, Impact Assessment, SWD(2014) 53 final, at 39.

to regularly assess the situation of subsidiaries and suppliers with the objective to prevent serious violations.[812]

To enforce the regulation, the company may be subjected to injunctive measures in case of breach and may be held liable for civil damages resulting from a negligence in implementing the 'plan de vigilance'. A third sanctions mechanism, which provided for a fine of up to 10 million Euros, was struck down for violating the constitutional principle of criminal legality as the particular conditions under which the fine could be levied were defined too broadly in the opinion of the Conseil Constitutionnel.[813] Therefore, the mechanism that provides coercive teeth to the new regulation is the possibility of civil liability, which gives foreign nationals in third countries access to a tort-based remedy in France against the corporate parent. In effect, therefore, the parent/subcontracting company may have to account for violations by its subsidiaries or suppliers along its global supply chain. This last point has also been raised in the constitutional challenge as it supposedly violated the principle of personal responsibility, that is, the principle that one cannot be held liable for actions and omissions of third parties. However, the Conseil Constitutionnel rejected this argument, because the company incurs liability only if there is a direct causality between the failure to exercise its duty of care and the violation sustained by the victim, even if the damage occurred abroad.[814] However, the effectiveness of this tort regime is severely curtailed as the burden of proof to substantiate the relationship between negligence on behalf of the parent/lead company and the violation lies with the victims, for whom it may be difficult to obtain information about the internal control structures of a multinational enterprise.[815]

The French law on *devoir de vigilance* has sparked multiple legislative initiatives on mandatory corporate due diligence across Europe. Most notably, Germany adopted its Corporate Due Diligence in Supply Chains Act on 22 July 2021.[816] While the law imposes similar due diligence

812 Loi relative au devoir de vigilance des sociétés mères et des entreprises donneuses d'ordre, texte adopté n° 924.

813 Conseil constitutionnel, 23 March 2017, Decision no. 2017–750 DC, paras. 9 – 14.

814 Ibid., para. 27.

815 Sandra Cossart, Jérôme Chaplier and Tiphaine Beau de Lomenie, 'The French Law on Duty of Care: A Historic Step Towards Making Globalization Work for All' (2017) 2(2) Business and Human Rights Journal 317, 321.

816 Gesetz über die unternehmerischen Sorgfaltspflichten in Lieferketten, BGBl. 2021 Part I p. 2959.

obligations, it has a significantly larger scope of application compared to the French law on *devoir de vigilance*: Beginning from 1 January 2024, German and foreign companies with a registered branch in Germany that employ more than 1,000 employees in Germany are subject to the law.[817] However, unlike the French law, the Corporate Due Diligence in Supply Chains Act does not provide for direct civil liabilities of German companies for failure to comply with their obligations; rather, the law is exclusively to be enforced by the Federal Office for Economic Affairs and Export Control.[818]

#### c) Disclosure and Transparency Requirements

Moving away from mandatory human rights due diligence obligations, States may choose to require companies to disclose – to the government, shareholders, consumers or the public – the measures they have undertaken with regard to CSR or a specific business and human rights situation, including when they have not taken any action. Disclosure requirements have a long tradition in US securities legislation: They were first introduced in the aftermath of the 1929 stock market crash to prevent fraud and give shareholders the access to necessary information to make prudent investment decisions.[819] Social disclosure requirements follow a similar idea to empower consumers and other activist stakeholders to receive information and base decisions on the social performance of companies, thus eventually pressuring corporations to act in a more accountable way.[820]

##### aa) Practice in the United States

One of the most significant pieces of legislation on the state level is the California Transparency in Supply Chains Act of 2010 (the **CTSCA**), with which California has spearheaded the supply chain due diligence

817 Gesetz über die unternehmerischen Sorgfaltspflichten in Lieferketten, § 1.
818 Gesetz über die unternehmerischen Sorgfaltspflichten in Lieferketten, § 3 and 19.
819 Woody, 'Conflict Minerals Legislation' (n 801), 1320 – 1322; George (n 795), 256.
820 Julia Planitzer, 'Trafficking in Human Beings for the Purpose of Labour Exploitation: Can Obligatory Reporting by Corporations Prevent Trafficking?' (2016) 34(4) Netherlands Quarterly of Human Rights 318, 329 – 331.

movement with regard to forced labour.[821] The CTSCA requires retailers and manufacturers doing business in California with annual gross receipts exceeding 100 million to disclose their efforts in combatting corporate forced labour and human trafficking. The term 'doing business' is understood broadly and includes any company actively engaged in any transaction for the purpose of financial or pecuniary gain or profit.[822] As such, the regulation potentially targets foreign corporations that are neither organized nor domiciled in the State of California. The companies have to make the disclosure public on their internet presence and describe activities undertaken with regard to five different topics, including the verification and audit of supply chains by the company itself or by third parties, whether the company requires certification of suppliers, international accountability as well as training measures. The disclosure requirements apply even if the company has not taken any measures with regard to forced labour and human trafficking.[823]

The statute is enforceable through injunctions filed by the State Attorney General, though enforcement activity up to now seems to have been rather low.[824] To provide further teeth for the legislation, private citizens have started proceedings related to the CTSCA under various statutes, including the California Unfair Competition Law, False Advertising Law, and Consumer Legal Remedies Act. In the most prominent of these cases, *Sud v Costco Wholesale Corp.*, the plaintiffs alleged that Costco was misleading consumers by disclosing on its website that it engaged in supply chain monitoring to prevent modern slavery when in fact prawns from Southeast Asia that Costco sold to consumers were farmed using forced labour. The case was eventually dismissed for lack of standing as the plaintiffs failed to prove that they purchased prawns from Costco specifically because of Costco's disclosure.[825] However, if the case would have succeeded, it could have forced Costco to address these issues within their foreign supply chain, which in the end could have led to a change of behaviour of persons and companies abroad.

---

821 California Transparency in Supply Chains Act of 2010, ch. 556, 2010 Cal. Stat. 2641 (2010), Cal. Civ. Code § 1714.43.

822 Kamala D Harris, 'The California Transparency in Supply Chains Act: A Resource Guide' CTSCA Resource Guide, at 3.

823 Ibid., at 4.

824 Cal. Civ. Code, § 1714.43, subd. (d); See also Planitzer (n 820), 329.

825 *Sud v Costco Wholesale Corp. et al*, No. 15-cv-03783-JSW (ND Cal. 2017), at 8.

bb) Practice in Europe

The CTSCA has acted as a catalyser for similar legislation around the world and in particular, led to the adoption of the UK Modern Slavery Act of 2015.[826] Sec. 54 of the Act requires commercial organizations, i.e. corporations and partnerships that supply goods or services with a global enterprise turnover above a certain threshold, to disclose the steps they have taken to ensure that slavery and human trafficking are not taking place in their business as well as their supply chains.[827] Companies subject to the regulation are encouraged to disclose information about their organization and supply chains, their policies related to human trafficking and slavery, their due diligence, risk management and performance monitoring measures as well as employee training.[828] Importantly, just like the CTSCA and the UK Bribery Act, the regulation applies not only to companies incorporated or domiciled in the UK, but also to any commercial organization that carries out at least part of its business in the UK.[829] Therefore, the Act will equally apply to foreign companies active in the UK that meet the turnover threshold.

Some commentators have lamented that the Act does not cover foreign subsidiaries of UK based companies that are not integrated into the parent company's supply chain and do not conduct business in the territory of the UK: Because these subsidiaries are not themselves acting in the UK, the Modern Slavery Act does not directly apply to them, and because they are not part of the supply chain of the parent company, technically the parent company is exempt from disclosing information about them. Thus, a UK company may still employ forced labour abroad by utilizing subsidiary corporations that are separated from the parent company's sup-

826 In the United States, on the federal level, the proposed federal Business Transparency on Trafficking and Slavery Act was initially rejected; see on this proposal Sophia Eckert, 'The Business Transparency on Trafficking and Slavery Act: Fighting Forced Labor in Complex Global Supply Chains' (2013) 12(2) Journal of International Business and Law. The UK Modern Slavery Act in turn has been the main inspiration for Australia, which has most recently adopted the Modern Slavery Act 2018, https://www.legislation.gov.au/Details/C2018A00153, last accessed on 13 April 2022.

827 Sec. 54 UK Modern Slavery Act 2015.

828 Sec. 54 (5) UK Modern Slavery Act 2015.

829 Sec. 54 (12) UK Modern Slavery Act 2015.

plier base.[830] The government seems to have acknowledged the existence of this loophole, as the official guidance points out that 'seeking to cover non-UK subsidiaries in a parent company statement, or asking those non-UK subsidiaries to produce a statement themselves, would represent good practice and […] is highly recommended'.[831] However, as this part of the guidance is non-binding in nature, it need not be discussed whether directly subjecting foreign subsidiaries to the Modern Slavery Act would have amounted to exercising control-based jurisdiction, which has been heavily contested within the context of economic sanctions.

#### d) Comparative Normative Analysis

Partly prompted by the UN Guiding Principles, States have begun to adopt a number of domestic measures seeking to address the extraterritorial human rights impact of corporations. Apart from long-standing trade and procurement measures, new regulatory patterns such as mandating supply chain due diligence or requiring social disclosure have emerged. Several techniques are used to equip these measures with extraterritorial reach: On the one hand, trade restrictions, public procurement selection criteria and similar measures influence foreign corporations by granting or withdrawing economic benefits based on their behaviour abroad. On the other hand, mandatory supply chain due diligence and disclosure obligations require companies at the top of the supply chain, which are the direct subjects of regulation, to ensure the transparency and integrity of the individual links with regard to their human rights performance. To fulfil this duty, the regulated companies in turn have to impose obligations on their foreign subsidiaries and suppliers and require them to mitigate human rights related risks, using their corporate control (in case of subsidiaries) or business relationships (in case of subcontractors) as leverage.[832]

---

830 International Trade Union Confederation, Closing the loopholes – How legislators can build on the UK Modern Slavery Act, at 11 – 12, https://www.ituc-csi.org/closing-the-loopholes-how, last accessed on 13 April 2022.

831 Transparency in Supply Chains etc. A practical guide, paras. 3.11 – 3.13, https://www.gov.uk/government/uploads/system/uploads/attachment_data/file/471996/Transparency_in_Supply_Chains_etc__A_practical_guide__final_.pdf, last accessed on 13 April 2022.

832 See more about this new mode of regulation: Galit A Sarfaty, 'Shining Light on Global Supply Chains' (2015) 56 HarvIntlLJ 419, 434.

These recent initiatives in the area of business and human rights have not drawn strong criticism from affected countries, let alone faced challenges that they are contrary to international law. Three reasons might be brought up for this: First, the actual extraterritorial effects of some these measures for commercial organisations abroad are often not excessively intrusive. Second, even where the extraterritorial effects of the regulations are more intense, such as in the case of Sec. 1502 of the Dodd-Frank Act, these measures do not clearly violate international law as it could be argued that they are justified by established jurisdictional principles. Third, I will argue that the general acceptance of extraterritorial business and human rights regulations is connected to the substantive content of these measures as respecting and protecting human rights are universally endorsed objectives.

First, certain business and human rights regulations may not cause strong reactions simply because their effects are rather weak. For instance, disclosure obligations such as those contained in the CTSCA or the UK Modern Slavery Act actually allow companies to not take any action with regard to forced labour and similar employment practice within their supply chain. While doing so may reflect badly on the company in the eyes of the consumer, there is no legal obligation to conduct due diligence or to terminate business relationships with suppliers engaged in egregious labour practices. Therefore, both acts should be viewed in line with provisions such as the EU Non-Financial Reporting Directive,[833] the French Grenelle II legislation[834] and amendments to the Danish Financial Statements Act.[835] Less than hard regulations, the primary purpose of these acts is to raise awareness about corporate social responsibility and the impact of corporate conduct within senior management and to induce a gradual change in corporate culture over time.[836]

---

833 Directive 2014/95/EU of the European Parliament and of the Council of 22 October 2014 amending Directive 2013/34/EU as regards disclosure of non-financial and diversity information by certain large undertakings and groups [2014] OJ 330/1.

834 Art. 225 of the Loi n° 2010–788 du 12 juillet 2010 portant engagement national pour l'environnement (Grenelle II).

835 Act amending the Danish Financial Statement Act (Accounting for CSR in large businesses).

836 See also Rachel Chambers, 'An Evaluation of Two Key Extraterritorial Techniques to Bring Human Rights Standards to Bear on Corporate Misconduct: Jurisdictional Dilemma Raised/Created by the Use of the Extraterritorial Techniques' (2018) 14(2) ULR 22, 24.

Second, in relation to measures with more intensive extraterritorial effects such as Sec. 1502 of the Dodd-Frank Act, the EU Conflict Minerals Regulation or certain trade and procurement policies, the rather muted response to these regulations may be explained by doctrinal considerations: Indeed, there are persuasive arguments that the measures examined above do not clearly violate principles of international law as it could be argued that they are justified by traditional jurisdictional principles.

Specifically, Sec. 1502 of the Dodd-Frank Act as well as similar due diligence legislations can be readily subsumed under the territoriality or active personality principle. To be sure, these measures have extraterritorial implications: For instance, the lead company may – compelled by due diligence and/or disclosure rules – only retain those suppliers which fulfil certain compliance requirements. Thus, suppliers abroad have to *de facto* subject themselves to these compliance requirements if they are to continue business with the lead company. Still, these measures are justified by the territoriality or active personality principle because only the lead company, which is domestically incorporated or has its seat of management within domestic territory, is responsible for performing the obligations under the due diligence regulations. The lead company may choose whether and how it enforces these obligations along its global supply chain. Finally, it is only the conduct of the lead company which gives rise to liability for failure to comply with these regulations.

The situation is slightly more complicated in relation to trade and procurement measures, which deny the access to domestic market or domestic economic benefits if certain human rights obligations are not fulfilled abroad. For instance, as discussed above, the Smoot-Hawley Tariff Act of 1930 prohibits the importation of goods if they were manufactured using forced labour. These measures are somewhat similar to secondary trade boycotts such as Sec. 5 (a) of the ISA: There as well, the access to domestic market is conditioned on conduct abroad, specifically, the requirement not to undertake certain business dealings with Iran. Secondary trade boycotts have historically caused international outrage and sometimes been regarded as illegal under international law because they purportedly prescribe obligations onto foreigners regarding their conduct abroad.[837] However, this opinion has come under attack in more recent literature: Some commentators argue that secondary trade boycotts do not involve extraterritorial jurisdiction because in fact, access to domestic market or the granting of domestic economic benefits is nothing more than a terri-

837 See above at C.II.4. Secondary Trade Boycotts.

torial matter. In the terminology of the SRSG Ruggie, these regulations fall into the category of measures described as having mere extraterritorial implications in contrast to 'direct extraterritoriality'.[838] As explained in detail above, it is at least contentious whether market access measures conditioned on human rights behaviour abroad violate jurisdictional principles of international law.[839]

Third, the reluctant reaction of foreign governments against business and human rights measures may be at least partly connected to the substantive content of the regulations.[840] Because they arguably address universally recognized human rights standards, voicing open opposition may reflect negatively on the critics. The dynamics at work here are thus similar to those in the case of the FCPA and other anti-corruption measures with strong extraterritorial reach, where, as we have seen, the (near) universal character of corruption as a pressing global issue strengthened the acceptance of unilateral extraterritorial regulation.[841] However, because of the wide and at times uncertain scope of the discussed human rights legislations, future case law and administrative interpretation might change that cautious attitude, especially considering that normative conflicts with local regulations are well possible. In this respect, the State practice regarding transnational human rights litigations might foreshadow the future development for extraterritoriality in domestic regulations.

### 5. Transnational Human Rights Litigation

As already mentioned, both the ongoing discussion in relation to the establishment of a binding international instrument for business and human rights as well as the third pillar of the UN Guiding Principles emphasise the importance of facilitating access to remedies for victims of abuses. However, there may be a lack of effective redress mechanisms for victims within the host State in which MNCs are operating, either because the local legal system lacks resources or because the locally incorporated sub-

838 Commentary to Principle 2, UN Guiding Principles; see also above at C.V.3. Extraterritoriality in Business and Human Rights.
839 See above at C.II.4c) Comparative Normative Analysis.
840 See also Commentary to Principle 2, UN Guiding Principles.
841 See for this comparison: Ramasastry (n 584); for more on the FCPA and other anti-bribery legislation, see above at C.IV. Anti-Corruption.

sidiary is underfunded or defunct.[842] In these cases, a need arises for the victims to state their claim for compensation in some other forum, often in the home State where the parent company of the MNC is incorporated. In the last decades, this has spurred the development of a whole range of transnational tort litigations with grave human rights abuses as the underlying cause. In US courts, litigation based on the ATS has become the 'lynchpin' of transnational human rights litigation and received enormous practical and academic attention.[843] In several more recent decisions however, the US Supreme Court has significantly curtailed its jurisdictional reach (below **a**)). Even though the rather expansive interpretation of the ATS has received mixed reaction in Europe, several doctrinal developments are making European courts increasingly attractive to human rights litigation (below **b**)). From a doctrinal perspective, the exercise of jurisdiction over third-State defendants is not permitted by traditional jurisdictional principles. However, given the interests of the victims of grave human rights abuses, this fact is lamentable and point towards a larger need for reform (below **c**)).

### a) Practice in the United States

Neither the history nor the plain text of the ATS suggest that it would one day become the central mechanism for victims of human rights abuses worldwide to remedy their wrongs in US courts. Enacted by the first Congress in 1789, the statute provides federal district courts with jurisdiction over 'any civil action by an alien for a tort only, committed in violation of the law of nations or a treaty of the United States'.[844] The 'law of nations' in this provision refers to customary international law. In effect therefore, the statute allowed foreigners to claim compensation for a tort in a US federal court, when that tort at the same time constituted a violation of customary international law or of an international treaty to which the United States is a party.[845]

---

842 Anil Yilmaz Vastardis and Rachel Chambers, 'Overcoming the Corporate Veil Challenge: Could Investment Law Inspire the Proposed Business and Human Rights Treaty?' (2018) 67(02) ICLQ 389, 389.

843 Note, 'Developments in the Law – Extraterritoriality' (n 343), 1233.

844 28 U.S.C. § 1350 (2012).

845 See Bernaz, *Business and human rights* (n 739), 260.

After a relatively uneventful 200 years, the statute was rediscovered by the Second Circuit in 1980, when in *Filartiga v Pena-Irala*, the court held that the ATS could apply to a claim for damages in a case involving the torture of two Paraguayan citizens by a Paraguayan government officer. In the court's opinion, customary international law recognized the torturer as *hostis humani generis*, an enemy of all mankind, so that the requirements of the statute, a civil claim relating to a tort that violates the law of nations, were fulfilled.[846] In subsequent jurisprudence, courts gradually expanded the scope of the ATS to other violations of international human rights law. For the purposes of our discussion of extraterritoriality in the context of business and human rights, *Kadic v Karadžić* constituted the first milestone, in which the ATS was applied to non-State individual actors,[847] while in *Doe I v Unocal Corp*, the act was invoked for the first time against a corporate defendant for its alleged complicity in human rights abuses.[848] The partly successful claim in *Unocal* has sparked an increasing number of actions against both US and non-US companies for involvement in human rights abuses abroad.

The Supreme Court, in subsequent decisions, mostly reigned in this development. In *Sosa v Alvarez-Machain*, the court considered a case of unlawful abduction and detention, the relevant parts of which took part in Mexico. While the court did allow suits in the fashion of *Filartiga* to move forward, it held that jurisdiction under the ATS was only available for causes of action that were as specific and universally accepted as the international norms the first Congress had in mind in 1789. According to the Supreme Court, such torts included piracy, violations of safe conduct, such as injury to a wartime enemy who was granted a specific guarantee of safety, and offenses against ambassadors.[849] However, even after *Sosa*, ATS litigation flourished and according to research conducted by Jonathan Drimmer, until 2012 alone, about 180 ATS lawsuits in US courts against corporate defendants have been filed.[850] Unsurprisingly, this practice has

846 *Filartiga v Pena-Irala*, 630 F 2d 876, 887 (2d Cir 1980).

847 *Kadic v Karadžić* 70 F 3d 232, 239 (2d Cir 1995).

848 *Doe I v Unocal Corp* 963 F Supp 880, 891 – 892 (CD Cal 1997).

849 *Sosa v Alvarez-Machain* 542 US 692, 724 (2004).

850 Table of cases annexed in Michael D Goldhaber, 'Corporate Human Rights Litigation in Non-U.S. Courts: A Comparative Scorecard (Human Rights Litigation in State Courts and Under State Laws)' (2013) 3 University of California Irvine Law Review 127, 137 – 149, see also Note, 'Developments in the Law – Extraterritoriality' (n 343), 1237.

increasingly caught the attention and at times triggered hostile responses by affected businesses and States abroad.

The development culminated in the controversial Supreme Court decision in *Kiobel v Royal Dutch Petroleum*. In *Kiobel*, the plaintiffs, Ogoni people in Nigeria, claimed that Royal Dutch Shell and its Nigerian subsidiary aided and abetted government human rights violations by providing material assistance and payment to violent police forces that raided Ogoni villages and massacred and raped in the region.[851] Two distinct questions were controversial going into the Supreme Court decision. The first concerned whether the ATS applied to causes of action based on corporate liability, given that while international law recognized individual responsibility for certain egregious crimes, its status on corporations is ambiguous at best. The second question asked whether and to what extent the ATS is applicable to conduct occurring almost entirely abroad, that is, the question of extraterritoriality.

In effect, the court majority opinion decided the case only on the second issue and held that the plaintiffs' claims under the ATS were barred because of the presumption against extraterritoriality.[852] As mentioned above, this presumption restricts the application of laws to 'within the territorial jurisdiction of the United States', unless an express legislative intent to the contrary can be demonstrated.[853] This was not the case with the ATS however, where, according to the Supreme Court, nothing in the text nor the historical background served to rebut this presumption. As a result, the ATS was restricted to only cover claims that 'touch and concern the territory of the United States with "sufficient force"'.[854] Following the decision, a jurisprudential split emerged among different lower courts in relation to the issue of extraterritoriality. While some courts interpreted the 'touch and concern' criterion to require a flexible case-by-case analysis considering all circumstances, others read the Supreme Court opinion

---

851 *Kiobel v Royal Dutch Petroleum Co.*, 569 US 108, 113 (2013).

852 Ibid., at 1664.

853 *Morrison v National Australia Bank Ltd.*, 561 US 247, 255 (2010) (quoting *EEOC v Arabian Am. Oil Co. (Aramco)*, 499 U.S. 244, 248 (1991)); see above at B.I.2.a)bb) The US Presumption against Extraterritoriality.

854 *Kiobel v Royal Dutch Petroleum Co.*, 569 US 108, 125 (2013); For commentaries on this decision, see e.g. Vivian Grosswald Curran and David Sloss, 'Reviving Human Rights Litigation After Kiobel' (2013) 107 AJIL 858; Paul L Hoffman, 'Kiobel v. Royal Dutch Petroleum Co: First Impressions' [2013] Columbia Journal of Transnational Law 28, 44; Caroline Kaeb and David J Scheffer, 'The Paradox of "Kiobel" in Europe' (2013) 107 AJIL 852, 857.

more restrictively and required the violation of international law to have taken place on US territory.[855]

While *Jesner v Arab Bank, PLC*, the next significant case to reach Supreme Court, provided the court with a prime opportunity to clarify on the 'touch and concern' criterion, the court ultimately decided the case on other grounds. The allegation in *Jesner* concerned conduct similar to what we have already seen above when analysing OFAC's enforcement actions, namely, the financing of terrorists via the American banking system.[856] The claimants, victims of terrorist attacks abroad, sought redress from Arab Bank, PLC, which allegedly facilitated these attacks through monetary transactions passing through Arab Bank's branch in New York. Thus, one of the main issues of the case concerned the question whether this conduct alone did touch and concern US territory with sufficient force to displace the presumption against extraterritoriality.[857] The Supreme Court however, did not clarify on the issue of extraterritoriality, but rather affirmed the Second Circuit's dismissal of the case based on the question unresolved in *Kiobel*, namely, whether the ATS provides a cause of action against corporate defendants at all.[858] Contrary to the views of several *amici curiae*,[859] the Supreme Court held that at least foreign corporations, such as Arab Bank, PLC, could not be subjected to ATS suits.[860]

In its most recent decision in an ATS case, *Nestlé USA, Inc. v Doe*, the Supreme Court revisited the issue of extraterritoriality. In this case, claimants from Mali alleged that they were trafficked into Côte d'Ivoire as children and enslaved to produce cocoa. While the corporate defendants, including *Nestlé USA*, did not own or operate farms in Côte d'Ivoire, they did buy cocoa from farms there and provided the farms with resources including training, fertilizer, tools and cash, in exchange for the exclusive rights to purchase their cocoa. The Supreme Court barred the suit from

855 See Note, 'Clarifying Kiobel's "Touch and Concern" Test' (2017) 130 HarvLRev 1902, 1910.

856 See above at C.II.3. Territoriality and US Dollar Transactions by non-US Financial Institutions.

857 *Jesner v Arab Bank, PLC*, 138 S Ct 1386 (2018), Brief for the United States as *amicus curiae* in support of neither party, 27 – 29.

858 *Jesner v Arab Bank, PLC*, 138 S Ct 1386, 1399 (2018); see also *In re Arab Bank, PLC Alien Tort Statute Litigation*, 808 F 3d 144 (2d Cir 2015).

859 *Jesner v Arab Bank*, Brief for the United States as *amicus curiae* in support of neither party, 17 – 24; Brief of International Law Scholars in support of petitioners, 4 – 5.

860 *Jesner v Arab Bank, PLC*, 138 S Ct 1386, 1408 (2018).

going forward. It held that the alleged conduct amounted only to 'general corporate activity',[861] which, just like 'mere corporate presence', did not serve to displace the presumption against extraterritoriality. In essence, the only marginal US-based conduct of defendants was not sufficient for a US court to exercise ATS jurisdiction over the case.[862]

Although the series of decisions since *Kiobel* have significantly limited the categories of possible litigations under the ATS, the door may not have been completely closed. Since it is yet unclear whether the holding in *Jesner* is restricted to foreign corporations, ATS suits may still be brought successfully against domestic corporations. If that is the case, it is not inconceivable that future litigations may involve corporate actions with a connection to US territory firm enough to overcome the requirements set by the Supreme Court in both *Kiobel* and *Nestlé*.

### b) Practice in Europe

Considering the potentially global scope of ATS litigation in the United States, it is unsurprising that the EU as well as European States have followed the series of cases with great interest. Particularly during the *Kiobel*-saga, they have voiced their opinions in *amicus curiae* briefs, which therefore provide a unique window into the interpretation of international law by these States (below **aa**)). However, even before *Kiobel*, human rights lawyers have already been looking for alternative venues to remedy gross human rights violations. Even though litigants in European courts cannot base their claims on an ATS-like mechanism, which specifically concerns the violation of a norm of public international law, human rights violations may be alleged as tort claims.[863] Compared to the ATS, filing suits essentially alleging personal injury, in which international human rights law *per se* might only play a marginal role, may seem much less empowering for the claimants.[864] However, with a number of recent legal and doctrinal innovations, the case for seeking remedies in Europe is getting increasingly stronger (below **bb**)).

---

861 See on this already: *Kiobel v Royal Dutch Petroleum Co.*, 569 US 108, 125 (2013).

862 *Nestlé United States, Inc. v. Doe.* 141 S Ct 1931 (2021).

863 Bernaz, *Business and human rights* (n 739), 275.

864 Ibid., 275; Richard Meeran, 'Access to Remedy: the United Kingdom Experience of MNC Tort Litigation for Human Rights Violations' in Surya Deva and David Bilchitz (eds), *Human Rights Obligations of Business: Beyond the Corporate Responsibility to Respect?* (Cambridge University Press 2013), 379.

### aa) Amicus Curiae Briefs in the Kiobel Proceedings

The most positive position towards ATS litigation in the fashion of *Kiobel* was expressed in the *amicus curiae* brief of the European Commission on behalf of the European Union. In the opinion of the Commission, the scope of the ATS should be interpreted with reference to the jurisdictional framework of international law. Of the traditional jurisdictional bases, special focus is dedicated to universal jurisdiction, which the Commission argues may support civil litigation under the ATS in certain circumstances.[865] Restating that universal jurisdiction is a well-established concept in the criminal context, the Commission endorses the application of the same principles to the civil context. The need for an effective remedy for particularly heinous crimes also includes civil reparations. The brief specifically pointed out to the already existing practice of bringing *actions civiles* to seek monetary compensation within a criminal universal jurisdiction proceeding.[866] However, according to the Commission, universal civil jurisdiction has to be restricted by similar requirements as its criminal counterpart, meaning that it should only be exercised for the most heinous of crimes and only after exhaustion of local remedies.[867]

While the Commission has thus embraced a progressive stance, European States that filed briefs in the *Kiobel* case disagreed with the assessment. The UK and the Netherlands (the home States of the respondent Royal Dutch Shell) for instance, argued in their respective brief that universal civil jurisdiction was entirely unknown to international law.[868] The German brief, while not explicitly discussing the issue of universal civil jurisdiction, similarly set out that US courts should surrender jurisdiction to more appropriate forums with a greater connection to the case and that proceeding otherwise may interfere with a third country's sovereignty.[869]

---

865 See generally, Donald F Donovan and Anthea Roberts, 'The Emerging Recognition of Universal Civil Jurisdiction' (2006) 100 AJIL 142.

866 *Kiobel v Royal Dutch Petroleum Co.,* 569 US 108 (2013), Brief of the European Commission on behalf of the European Union as *amicus curiae* in support of neither party, 13 – 18 and 25.

867 Ibid., 26 – 33.

868 *Kiobel v Royal Dutch Petroleum Co.,* 569 US 108 (2013), Brief of the governments of the Kingdom of the Netherlands and the United Kingdom of Great Britain and Northern Ireland as *amici curiae* in support of neither party, 12 – 13.

869 *Kiobel v Royal Dutch Petroleum Co.,* 569 US 108 (2013), Brief of The Federal Republic of Germany as *amicus curiae* in support of respondents, 10.

### bb) Transnational Human Rights Litigation in Europe

Even though governments across Europe have yet to take up the Commission's stance regarding universal civil jurisdiction, several legal developments have made courts in Europe, and specifically in the UK, increasingly more attractive as venues to redress human rights violations. These include, first, the restriction of the discretionary doctrine of *forum non conveniens*, second, the assumption of a duty of care of parent corporations in relation to subsidiary conduct, third, the possibility of suing foreign subsidiaries as necessary or proper parties in proceedings against European-based parent companies and fourth, the growing acceptance of *forum necessitatis* for defendants not subject to Art. 4(1) of the Brussels I Regulation.

First, the application of *forum non conveniens*, a common law doctrine which has presented a hurdle for litigation in jurisdictions such as Canada, Australia and the United States,[870] has been largely restricted in Europe. Essentially, *forum non conveniens* allows a domestic court to decline exercising jurisdiction when it determines that another forum is more suitable for the action.[871] Within the EU, however, human rights suits against corporate defendants are cast as tort based litigation, the allocation of jurisdiction for which is governed by the Brussels I Regulation.[872] According to Art. 4(1) of the Brussels I Regulation, courts are required to assert jurisdiction over all persons domiciled in their respective EU member State. Thus, member State courts have adjudicatory jurisdiction over European-based parent companies of MNCs even if the alleged conduct has primarily occurred abroad. Moreover, according to the CJEU, courts are not allowed to decline jurisdiction based on *forum non conveniens*.[873] This development has especially benefitted the UK as a forum for human rights litigation.[874] Following Brexit, the Brussels I Regulation no longer applies in the UK as of 31 December 2020. Thus, *forum non conveniens* currently poses a risk to

---

870 Richard Meeran, 'Multinational Human Rights Litigation in the UK: A Retrospective' (2021) 6(2) Business and Human Rights Journal 255, 259.

871 CJEU, C-281/02, *Owusu v Jackson* [2005] ECR I-01383, para. 8.

872 Regulation (EU) No. 1215/2012 of the European Parliament and of the Council 12 December 2012 on jurisdiction and the recognition and enforcement of judgments in civil and commercial matters (recast) (hereinafter: Brussels I), OJ 2012 L 351/1.

873 CJEU, C-281/02, *Owusu v Jackson* [2005] ECR I-01383.

874 Meeran, 'Access to Remedy: the United Kingdom Experience of MNC Tort Litigation for Human Rights Violations' (n 864), at 380 lists 9 cases in recent years.

UK-based actions again. However, the UK is in the process of joining the Lugano Convention,[875] which, once successful, would essentially restore the situation under Brussels I.[876]

Second, British and Dutch courts, among others, have imposed material liability on parent companies – when their (foreign) subsidiaries were the direct perpetrators of tort-based violations – based on the doctrine of duty of care. This doctrine has been applied in a series of asbestos related cases, including *Chandler v Cape Plc*, in which UK courts have held that a parent company, under certain circumstances, may owe a duty of care to employees of its subsidiaries.[877] Because the parent companies are held liable for their direct negligence in their own acts or omissions, the concept of duty of care does not run counter to the principle of legal separateness of corporate entities.[878] Subsequent decisions after *Chandler* have considerably widened the scope for assuming duty of care:[879] Even though the Court of Appeal in two cases in 2018 still required a rather high level of control of the domestic parent company over the foreign subsidiary to establish a duty of care in relation to the activities of the subsidiary,[880] the UK Supreme Court opted for a more flexible interpretation in *Vedanta*, arguing that it came down to a case-by-case analysis.[881] Specifically, the UK Supreme Court held in *Vedanta* and most recently in *Okpabi*[882] that defective group-wide policies may be sufficient to impose a duty of care on the parent company.

Third, another feature of human rights litigation in Europe is that domestic parent corporations and their foreign subsidiaries themselves are

875 Convention on jurisdiction and the recognition and enforcement of judgments in civil and commercial matters, OJ 2007 L 339/3.

876 Meeran, 'Multinational Human Rights Litigation in the UK: A Retrospective' (n 870), 260.

877 *Chandler v Cape Plc*, [2012] EWCA Civ 525, at 80; see also *Lubbe v Cape Plc* [2000] UKHL 4.

878 Meeran, 'Multinational Human Rights Litigation in the UK: A Retrospective' (n 870), 260.

879 Though the process has been far from linear: for instance, duty of care was rejected in a factually similar case shortly after, *Thompson v The Renwick Group plc* [2014] EWCA Civ 635.

880 *Okpabi and others v Royal Dutch Shell Plc and another* [2018] EWCA Civ 191; *AAA & Others v Unilever PLC and Unilever Tea Kenya Limited* [2018] EWCA Civ 1532.

881 *Vedanta Resources Plc and Konkola Copper Mines Plc v Lungowe and Others* [2019] UKSC 20.

882 *Okpabi & Others v Royal Dutch Shell plc & Anor* [2021] UKSC 3.

often sued together. While no adjudicatory jurisdiction would ordinarily exist with regard to the foreign subsidiary as they are incorporated in third States and thus outside the scope of Art. 4 of the Brussels I regulation, it is possible to join the subsidiaries in the litigation against the parent corporation as co-defendants. Under English law for instance, this requires the foreign subsidiary to be a necessary or proper party in the case against the parent company.[883] This litigation strategy has also been used in the Netherlands version of the *Kiobel* litigation, *Akpan*, where plaintiffs sought damages for oil spills against Royal Dutch Shell Plc and its Nigerian subsidiary at the same time. The Dutch courts deciding this case assumed jurisdiction over the Nigerian subsidiary as a third State defendant because the claim was intertwined with that against Royal Dutch Shell and maintaining the cases in the same court would thus promote efficiency.[884]

Fourth, with regard to defendants not domiciled within the EU, which consequently are not regulated under Brussels I, the concept of *forum necessitatis* has been developed next to the above-mentioned strategy of joining defendants. *Forum necessitatis* refers to the establishment of adjudicative jurisdiction *vis-à-vis* situations for which no ordinary jurisdictional basis exists, but in which the right to a fair trial or the right to access to justice requires hearing the case, i.e., if doing otherwise would amount to a denial of justice because the plaintiffs cannot reasonably bring a claim in any other forum.[885]

Two forms of *forum necessitatis* are distinguished: a pure form, where the imminent denial of justice alone is sufficient to trigger jurisdiction and a mixed form, in which apart from an imminent denial of justice, at least some sort of connection with the State must exist.[886] Most prominently,

---

883 See on this option more generally: Daniel Augenstein and Nicola Jägers, 'Judicial Remedies: The Issue of Jurisdiction' in Juan J Álvarez Rubio and Katerina Yiannibas (eds), *Human Rights in Business: Removal of Barriers to Access to Justice in the European Union* (Routledge 2017), 17; Arnauld Nuyts, 'Study on Residual Jurisdiction: Review of the Member States' Rules concerning the "Residual Jurisdiction" of their Courts in Civil and Commercial Matters pursuant to the Brussels I and II Regulations' (2007).

884 *Akpan v Shell*, ECLI:NL:GHDHA:2015:3587; The decision is part of a series of cases against Royal Dutch Shell in the Netherlands, see also *Oguru-Efanga v Shell*, ECLI:NL:GHDHA:2015:3588.

885 See Art. 26 of the Proposal for a Regulation of the European Parliament and of the Council on Jurisdiction and the Regulation and Enforcement of Judgments in Civil and Commercial Matters, COM (2010) 748 final.

886 Mills (n 14), 224 – 225.

the Netherlands contemplates a form of pure necessity jurisdiction.[887] For instance, in the Dutch case *El-Hojouj v Unnamed Libyan Officials*, The Hague District Court accepted jurisdiction over a Palestinian doctor who was allegedly imprisoned in Libya, which at the time of the litigation provided no adequate forum for dispute resolution.[888]

In contrast, French courts exercise a mixed form of *forum necessitatis*. Relying on this basis, the Paris Court of Appeal has accepted jurisdiction over a Gabonese company, COMILOG.[889] The case concerns the dismissal of almost 900 workers in Congo by COMILOG in 1991 without due notice or any compensation. The workers sued in Congo; however, their efforts were stymied as the Congolese courts failed to deliver an interim decision on a jurisdictional challenge raised by COMILOG in 1994. In this procedural delay for over 20 years without further prospects, the Paris Court of Appeal saw an objective denial of justice. Additionally, the workers could also present a sufficient connection of the case to France, as COMILOG was subsequently acquired by a French multinational corporation. Thus, in the view of the court, both requirements of the mixed form of *forum necessitatis* under French law were satisfied.[890]

### c) Comparative Normative Analysis

Notwithstanding the variety of legal doctrines discussed, from a normative point of view, it seems only necessary to distinguish between two different categories, on the one hand cases against corporations domiciled in the forum State and on the other hand, cases against entities domiciled in third States. While the first scenario occurs in numerous countries, claims

887 Cedric Ryngaert and Lucas Roorda, 'Business and Human Rights Litigation in Europe and Canada: The Promises of Forum of Necessity Jurisdiction' (2016) 80(4) RabelsZ 783 2016, 783, 786.

888 *El-Hojouj v Unnamed Libyan Officials*, The Hague District Court (21 March 2012) LJN: BV9748; also mentioned in *Kiobel v Royal Dutch Petroleum Co.*, 569 US 108 (2013), Brief of the governments of the Kingdom of the Netherlands and the United Kingdom of Great Britain and Northern Ireland as Amici Curiae in support of neither party, 23.

889 Cour d'appel de Paris (pole 6, ch 2), 20 June 2013, n° 12/08935; Cour de Cassation, civile, Chambre Sociale, 28 January 2015, 13–22.994, 13–22.995, 13–23.003, 13–23.004, 13–23.005, 13–23.006.

890 However, this decision was later overturned by the French Cour de cassation, Arrêt n°2024 du 14 septembre 2017 (15–26.737; 15–26.738), ECLI:FR:CCASS:2017:SO02024.

against entities from third States have almost exclusively been litigated under the ATS. While recent decisions in *Kiobel*, *Jesner* and *Nestlé* have tremendously curtailed the extensive jurisdiction of US courts, litigation against corporations not domiciled in the forum State may find another home in the nascent doctrine of *forum necessitatis*.

I will argue here that while the first category, claims against corporations domiciled in the forum State, raises no issues under jurisdictional principles of international law, the same cannot be said about the second category, claims against corporations domiciled in third States. In fact, both doctrines advanced to justify these human rights litigations, universal civil jurisdiction and *forum necessitatis* are not generally accepted under customary international law. This is lamentable in particular with regard to *forum necessitatis*, where the State exercising jurisdiction is arguably subject to two conflicting international norms, on the one hand the rules concerning prescriptive jurisdiction and on the other hand, international human rights norms regarding access to justice. Ultimately, this points to a larger deficiency of the customary international law principles of jurisdiction, which almost exclusively recognizes formal connections to States as bases for assertions of jurisdiction without regard to the interests of potentially affected individuals.

#### aa) Jurisdiction over Corporations Domiciled in the Forum State

In principle, commentators view the first situation, litigation against corporations domiciled in the forum State, more sympathetically from the perspective of international law. The exercise of jurisdiction is arguably justified either by the territoriality principle or by the active personality principle. Territoriality is engaged if at least part of the relevant conduct falls onto domestic territory, for instance if the corporate parent directed or facilitated human rights abuses by its subsidiaries from its headquarters, even though the actual violation is felt abroad.[891] It is arguably also a case of territoriality if the corporate parent, in its home State, failed to undertake adequate human rights due diligence, subsequently resulting in harm abroad. Additionally, jurisdiction over corporations domiciled in the forum State may also be based on the active personality principle. This is because these corporations will likely possess the nationality of the forum

891 See also *Al Shimari v CACI Premier Tech., Inc.*, 758 F 3d 516, 530 (4th Cir 2014); *Mujica v AirScan Inc.*, 771 F 3d 580, 594 (9th Cir 2014).

State, as they will be either incorporated in the forum State or at least have their principal place of business there.

It is true that asserting jurisdiction against a domestic parent corporation based on human rights violations of its affiliates/subsidiaries abroad raises certain questions of extraterritoriality. However, as the litigations frequently concern the conduct, facilitation or omission of the domestic parent, these cases are better compared to prescriptive regulation addressing group wide due diligence or disclosure requirements with regard to foreign subsidiaries and affiliates such as the UK Bribery Act. Thus, as long as the focus of the litigation is clearly on the domestic conduct of the parent corporation, assuming jurisdiction will most likely not run counter to international law despite the possible extraterritorial implications.[892]

State practice seems to support this conclusion: Even after *Kiobel*, *Jesner* and *Nestlé*, the United States still accepts jurisdiction under the ATS for claims against US corporations for sufficiently US-based conduct. A similar situation presents itself in the UK as well as the Netherlands where a transnational (human-rights) tort claim has a possibility of succeeding if the defendant corporation is domiciled in the EU and substantially, if the corporation has acted against or neglected a duty of care *vis-à-vis* a third State victim.[893] So far, there has also been no State protesting these kinds of jurisdictional assertions (quite unlike in ATS cases against foreign defendants). In sum therefore, asserting adjudicatory jurisdiction over corporations domiciled in the forum State arguably raises few issues of international law.[894]

#### bb) Jurisdiction over Corporations Domiciled in Third States

The second situation concerns litigations against corporations not domiciled in the forum, such as in the case of *Kiobel*. As these cases cannot rely on the active personality principle and rarely satisfy territoriality, traditional jurisdictional principles as set out in part B of this study would suppose a violation of international law. However, progressive scholars

892 For the same conclusion see Sofia Massoud, *Menschenrechtsverletzungen im Zusammenhang mit wirtschaftlichen Aktivitäten von transnationalen Unternehmen* (Interdisziplinäre Studien zu Menschenrechten vol 2, 1. Auflage 2018, Springer Berlin; Springer 2018), 117 – 119.

893 Augenstein and Jägers (n 883), 27.

894 See for this conclusion also Bernaz, 'Enhancing Corporate Accountability for Human Rights Violations' (n 768), 496.

have called this result into question. They argue that in relation to business and human rights claims, rules of prescriptive jurisdiction are modified or superseded by the nature of these cases, because jurisdiction is exercised to remedy grave human rights violations, i.e., to vindicate the community interest of upholding human rights.[895]

This argument is in particular embodied in the notion of universal civil jurisdiction. Conceptions of universal civil jurisdiction seem to be the logical extension of the more established principle of universality in criminal matters: If a certain conduct may give rise to procedures under international criminal law, it should likewise be remedied using tort-based civil litigation.[896] Moreover, the possibility for victims to bring *actions civiles* to claim monetary compensation within criminal prosecution based on universality may be seen as support for this doctrine.[897] In 2015 therefore, the *Institut de Droit International* formulated a resolution that not only allowed the exercise of universal civil jurisdiction, but also *de lege ferenda*, rendered it obligatory with regard to reparation for international crimes.[898]

However, State practice does not offer much support for this progressive concept. After the US Supreme Court's decisions following *Kiobel*, no State exists that exercises freestanding universal civil jurisdiction. Within the *Kiobel* proceedings, numerous States protested this doctrine in *amicus curiae* briefs while Argentina was the only nation accepting an unrestricted

895 August Reinisch, 'Human Rights Extraterritoriality: Controlling Companies Abroad' in Eyal Benvenisti and Georg Nolte (eds), *Community Interests Across International Law* (First edition. Oxford University Press 2018), 408 – 409; another argument is advanced by Kohl who asserts that business and human rights claims are not even subject to rules of prescriptive jurisdiction, because such claims are civil and not regulatory or criminal in nature, see Uta Kohl, 'Corporate Human Rights Accountability: The Objections Of Western Governments To The Alien Tort Statute' (2014) 63(03) ICLQ 665, 677. This argument does not persuade: human rights litigation not only concerns the compensation for personal injuries suffered between ordinary citizens, but it also sets standards of (human rights) conduct, violations of which may give rise to sanctions; see in general above at A.III.5. Regulation, Public Law and Jurisdiction.

896 See on this comparison between criminal law and tort law with regard to universality: Donovan and Roberts (n 865), 154.

897 *Kiobel v Royal Dutch Petroleum Co.*, 569 US 108 (2013), Brief of the European Commission on behalf of the European Union as *amicus curiae* in support of neither party, 13 – 18.

898 Institut de Droit International, Universal Civil Jurisdiction with Regard to Reparation for International Crimes, Resolution of 30 August 2015.

version of universal civil jurisdiction.[899] Given this record, it is hard to argue that this doctrine has found acceptance in customary international law *de lege lata*.[900] Besides, even if we accept universal civil jurisdiction in general, the usefulness of this doctrine to hold corporations accountable for human rights abuses is still doubtable: Because universal civil jurisdiction would be grounded in its criminal counterpart, any legal deficiency of universal criminal jurisdiction would arguably also be reflected in civil litigation. For instance, it is highly unclear what standards have to be fulfilled for secondary liability – aiding and abetting – or whether corporate liability is at all possible.[901]

Because of the unsettled status of universal civil jurisdiction and ultimately because of its lack of practical relevance, scholarly attention has turned to *forum necessitatis* as another variant of the argument that rules regarding prescriptive jurisdiction are modified when it comes to violations of human rights. In principle, the doctrine of *forum necessitatis* provides for jurisdiction in cases in which failure to do so would amount to a denial of justice because it is impossible, unacceptable or unreasonable for claimants to bring proceedings in any other forum with a closer factual connection to the case.[902] Unlike universal civil jurisdiction, *forum necessitatis* has enjoyed modest endorsement and a number of European as well as non-European States recognize or exercise this kind of jurisdiction.[903]

---

899 *Kiobel v Royal Dutch Petroleum Co.*, 569 US 108 (2013), Brief for the Government of Argentine Republic as *amicus curiae* in Support of Petitioners.

900 See *Arrest Warrant of 11 April 2000 (Democratic Republic of the Congo v Belgium)* (n 69), Joint Separate Opinion of Judges Higgins, Kooijmans and Buergenthal; See also Cedric Ryngaert, 'From Universal Civil Jurisdiction To Forum Of Necessity: Reflections On The Judgment Of The European Court Of Human Rights In Nait-Liman' [2017] Rivista di Diritto Internazionale 782, 795 – 796; Paul D Mora, 'The Alien Tort Statute After Kiobel: The Possibility For Unlawful Assertions Of Universal Civil Jurisdiction Still Remains' (2014) 63(03) ICLQ 699, 709 – 719.

901 For instance regarding secondary liability, the subjective (that is mental) standard required to establish aiding and abetting is unclear in international criminal law, see Bernaz, *Business and human rights* (n 739), 272 – 273 referring to, among others, the *Akayesu Case* (Judgement), No ICTR-96–4-T, Trial Chamber (2 September 1998), para. 545 and the *Furundzija Case* (Judgment), No IT-95–15/1-T, Trial Chamber (10 December 1998), para. 249.

902 Augenstein and Jägers (n 883), 28.

903 See Nuyts (n 883), 66; Chilenye Nwapi, 'A Necessary Look at Necessity Jurisdiction' (2014) 47 UBC Law Review 211, 225 – 226; *Nait-Liman v Switzerland* App No 51357/07, Judgment of 15 March 2018, paras. 84 – 86.

Despite this, the ECtHR, which recently examined the issue in the non-business-related case *Nait-Liman v Switzerland*, concluded that necessity jurisdiction is not accepted in customary international law *de lege lata*. The applicant in this case, before coming to Switzerland, has allegedly suffered torture at the hands of Tunisian government agents in his home country. Because a claim in Tunisia would have been unreasonable, he filed for civil damages in Switzerland based on *forum necessitates.* On appeal, the Swiss Federal Court dismissed the claims for lack of jurisdiction. Swiss law provided for a mixed form of *forum necessitatis*, which, in addition to the imminent denial of justice, required 'sufficient connections' to Switzerland in order to establish a case of *forum necessitatis*. The Swiss court opined that this requirement was not satisfied, as, *at the time of tortious conduct*, no relationship between the alleged tortious acts to Switzerland existed and the subsequent residence of the victim in Switzerland was immaterial.[904]

The ECtHR examined whether denying jurisdiction in the present case because of insufficient factual connections to Switzerland violated the applicant's rights of access to court under Art. 6 of the Convention. Essentially, the court asked whether under human rights law, there was a duty to establish a pure form of necessity jurisdiction. However, it held that the dismissal by the Swiss Federal Court both pursued a legitimate aim and was proportionate to achieve these aims.[905] To arrive at this conclusion, the court examined both universal civil jurisdiction and pure *forum necessitatis* to determine that customary international law enshrined neither of the two. Thus, by applying a mixed form of *forum necessitatis* and declining jurisdiction on the basis of an insufficient connection between the case and Switzerland, the Swiss Federal Court had acted within its wide margin of appreciation under Art. 6 of the Convention.[906]

However, not only is pure *forum necessitatis* not supported under customary international law, the same is also true in relation to mixed forms of *forum necessitates* in certain instances. As the imminent denial of justice is not recognized in traditional jurisdictional doctrine as a valid basis for the exercise of jurisdiction, the legality of mixed forms of *forum necessitatis* depends on the other connections between the case in question and the forum State. Jurisdiction is permitted only if the factual connections between the claimant or conduct in question and the forum State are such

---

904 *Nait-Liman v Switzerland* App No 51357/07, Judgment of 15 March 2018, para. 30.

905 Ibid., para. 217.

906 Ibid., paras. 176 – 216.

that these connections amount to one of the recognized jurisdictional principles. In the COMILOG case for instance, notwithstanding the fact that the Congolese workers had no access to reasonable judicial recourse in Congo, traditional doctrine would ask whether the factual circumstances satisfy one of the permissive principles. This may prove problematic here: The only connection relied upon by the Court of Appeal was that COMILOG later became a foreign subsidiary of a French corporation. Thus, this exercise could be tantamount to asserting regulatory jurisdiction based on the control doctrine, which as discussed above, is at least disputed in international law doctrine.[907]

Of course, if necessity jurisdiction may only be exercised when one of the traditional principles is fulfilled, then the doctrine of *forum necessitatis* would clearly be obsolete, as in these cases, jurisdiction would be permitted even if no imminent denial of justice on part of the victims was in question. In this regard, a more flexible approach to *forum necessitatis* would seem desirable as the State deciding on whether to act is arguably subject to two conflicting international norms, on the one hand the customary rules concerning prescriptive jurisdiction and on the other hand, international human rights norms regarding access to justice. Thus, the graver the alleged human rights violation, the more legitimate it would seem to permit States to exercise jurisdiction based on even less substantial factual connections. In extreme cases, the mere presence of the claimant or some of the defendant's assets within the forum State should possibly suffice.

Therefore, while we have concluded for the area of economic sanctions that the formalistic nature of the traditional bases of jurisdiction paved the way for abuses by powerful States, the opposite occurs here, where the recognized principles limit the possibility to expand jurisdiction in cases even though doing so may be considered legitimate in order to provide private individuals with access to justice.

### 6. Conclusion

The UN Guiding Principles as a high-level policy document are but the starting point of the discussion which seeks to create mechanisms to prevent, mitigate and account for the negative human rights impacts of

907 See above C.II.2c) Comparative Normative Analysis.

businesses.[908] As a binding international treaty on business and human rights still has little prospect, home States of MNCs are increasingly resorting to domestic mechanisms to mitigate extraterritorial threats to human rights. So far, States have employed two mostly independent regulatory techniques to control corporate behaviour with regard to human rights, through the adoption of regulation establishing human rights obligations for companies along parent-subsidiary or lead-supplier relationships and by creating redress mechanisms for affected individuals. In both strands, the normative issue of extraterritoriality adds further complexity to an already delicate political process.

In the first strand, States are increasingly employing trade measures such as import restrictions or due diligence regulations to combat forced and child labour. Most commentators view these measures as unproblematic from the perspective of extraterritorial jurisdiction and there have been no sustained State protests against these measures. Of the reasons we have discussed above, two shall be highlighted in these concluding remarks. First, such measures are often permitted by international law principles as they can frequently rely on a domestic nexus, be it access to a territorially circumscribed market or the domicile of the parent/lead company.[909] Second, the lack of opposition may also be indicative of more substantial considerations, namely that these measures are justified through their objective of upholding internationally agreed human rights.[910] For the doctrine of jurisdiction under international law, this seemingly means that the determination of the legality of a particular exercise of extraterritorial jurisdiction may not be able to rely on formal criteria only, but may well have to look into the substantive content of each regulation.

With respect to transnational human rights litigation, the redress mechanisms may be divided into two categories for the purpose of analysing jurisdictional issues, litigation against home State companies in connection with violations by subsidiaries/suppliers abroad and stand-alone litigation against third State companies. In the first scenario, it may be argued that a territorial link exists between the forum State and the alleged tortious conduct of the subsidiaries/suppliers. In this case, while there are extrater-

---

908 Ruggie (n 714), 170 – 172.

909 Meng, *Extraterritoriale Jurisdiktion im öffentlichen Wirtschaftsrecht* (n 43), discussing the ISA at 292 – 293; Cleveland (n 272), on human rights motivated selective purchasing laws at 61 – 62; Bernaz, 'Enhancing Corporate Accountability for Human Rights Violations' (n 768), 498.

910 Vázquez (n 431), 816; Bartels, 'Article XX of GATT and the Problem of Extraterritorial Jurisdiction' (n 427), 374.

ritorial effects, the parent/subcontracting company in the home State is generally asked to remedy a foreign harm caused by its own actions or inactions so that issues of jurisdiction should not arise.

Finally, proceedings may be brought against third State defendants. While the ATS has traditionally provided the most promising venue, recent jurisprudence in *Kiobel*, *Jesner* and *Nestlé* may shift attention to another doctrine, *forum necessitatis*. These concepts raise difficult normative issues. Even though the European Commission has expressed sympathy towards such concepts,[911] it is submitted that both ATS-style litigation under universal civil jurisdiction as well as necessity jurisdiction have not found general acceptance yet. This is lamentable in particular with regard to *forum necessitatis*, which essentially deals with balancing two competing values of international law and where an exercise of jurisdiction may be legitimate even without a 'sufficient connection'. Currently, however, there is no evidence that the territoriality-based system of jurisdiction may reflect this particular situation.

The future of business and human rights, in particular with regard to the issue of extraterritoriality, is highly uncertain. Developments at the domestic level will remain essential. In this regard, the anti-corruption movement has shown that the definition of narrow and specific conducts may raise the international acceptability of extraterritorial jurisdiction.[912] For the business and human rights agenda, this means there is a need for the creation of international consensus about specific obligations of corporations to respect human rights, even in their foreign operations. In this respect, further elaboration on and harmonization of the notion of human rights due diligence may play a vital role. In France, the law regarding 'devoirs de vigilance' already sketches possible contours of such duties. Finally, apart from due diligence obligations, which are more of a procedural nature, the identification of substantive prohibitions on certain conduct within the area of business and human rights would possibly allow for further extraterritorial action. As we have seen both with regard to certain egregious labour practices and with regard to the suppression of conflict minerals, exercises of jurisdiction with extraterritorial implications

---

911 *Kiobel v Royal Dutch Petroleum Co.*, 569 US 108 (2013), Brief of the European Commission on behalf of the European Union as *amicus curiae* in support of neither party, 13 – 18.

912 See more generally on the possible learnings from the anti-corruption movement for the development of business and human rights: Ramasastry (n 584), 174.

have met little resistance, presumably because there is widespread consensus on an international level to outlaw the specific conducts in question.

## VI. Synthesis: The Deficient Territoriality-based System

In a process, which may be described as the globalization of regulation, powerful States are increasingly trying to project their own policy and governance preferences extraterritorially. This occurs in relation to requirements on the ethical conduct of business, for instance through the regulation of both foreign bribery and corporate human rights standards. However, States may also seek to extend their domestic foreign policy considerations, such as through economic sanctions and export control regulations, where the objective is often less to mitigate immediate national security threats but rather to prompt longer-term change in the target's behaviour. All of these issue areas pose salient questions, as extraterritoriality is not employed in these regulations to protect the domestic populace or market from immediate adverse effects. To achieve these regulatory goals, States have resorted to a host of complex regulatory mechanisms. Some of these have recurred among different subject areas and will thus be analysed in a cross-sectorial manner, including

1) conditioning market access and other territorial economic benefits on conduct or circumstances abroad,
2) using parent-subsidiary relationships to extend jurisdiction to foreign subsidiaries of domestic multinational corporations,
3) leveraging territoriality to regulate conduct based on only fleeting territorial connections or to regulate companies based on territorial 'presence' and
4) securing regulatory authority through consent of the affected individual/company.

For instance, we have seen that States are willing to condition access to their market or economic benefits on a corporation's human rights records abroad, thus incentivizing foreign companies to uphold these standards.[913] However, even before this mechanism has found its way into human rights regulations, similar (and more severe) measures have been used by the United States to ensure compliance with its economic sanctions.[914] Moreover, crosscutting different regulatory fields, the United States and

913 C.V.4a) Trade, Procurement and Investment Measures.
914 C.II.4a) Practice in the United States.

European States are leveraging the fact that they often serve as home States to multinational corporations to induce change abroad by resorting to so-called parent-based regulation. This mode of regulation typically either attributes liability to the parent company of a multinational corporation if its subsidiaries violate domestic regulations abroad or directs the parent company to implement domestic regulatory measures throughout the corporate group. We have seen this mechanism most prominently in recent anti-corruption legislation[915] and the administration of economic sanctions,[916] but it has also served as a basis for transnational human rights litigation.[917]

The following synthesis demonstrates how these regulatory mechanisms have challenged the traditional, territoriality-based system of jurisdiction in international law. These challenges are twofold: On the one hand, the functionality of the system is severely curtailed because several of these regulatory mechanisms cannot be clearly categorized within the formal territoriality *versus* extraterritoriality dichotomy (below **1.**). On the other hand, the system restricts extraterritorial jurisdiction to a fixed set of sovereignty-based principles, even though other considerations should also influence the legitimacy of jurisdictional assertions (below **2.**).

## 1. The Normative Inconsistency of Territoriality

### a) Market Access Regulation Conditioned on Extraterritorial Circumstances

Using access to a State's territory, its (ultimately territorial) domestic market or other economic benefits as leverage is one of the most widely used but also most controversial regulatory techniques to affect behaviour abroad. We have examined this type of regulation more closely referring to Sec. 5 (a) of the ISA and subsequent legislation. Sec. 5 (a) of the ISA and similar regulation stipulated a number of sanctions, such as a prohibition on US banks to grant loans or a domestic procurement prohibition, which were levied against companies worldwide that were heavily invested or investing in the Iranian petroleum sector. Comparable measures are also found in the area of business and human rights. The United States for

915 C.IV.4. Regulation through Parent-Subsidiary Relationships.
916 C.II.2. The Extension of Personality-based Jurisdiction to Foreign Subsidiaries.
917 C.V.5. Transnational Human Rights Litigation.

instance conditions market entry of certain products and the eligibility for public procurement on the human rights performance of the foreign economic operator, for instance on the absence of human trafficking and other degrading labour practices within its supply chain.

The reactions of affected States to these measures have been inconsistent and guided by political factors: While the EC has strongly criticized the original ISA, the EU has later accepted strong expansions of the same sanctions in 2012 and similar measures against Russia in 2014. More recently, however, Germany and Austria have again voiced strong opposition to renewed Russia sanctions that indirectly affected domestic industrial interests.[918] Within the area of business and human rights, using domestic market access and other economic benefits to condition foreign conduct has generally fared better and drawn less international criticism. The inconsistent response to formally very similar measures suggests that the reactions of States are less driven by doctrinal considerations of territoriality and extraterritoriality rather than by political motivations.

It has already been discussed that one reason for the inconsistent practice is that such measures are situated in a legal grey area under international law.[919] It suffices here to point out to some concluding observations regarding the debate. Measures based on market access are characterized by their dual nature: On the one hand, they seek to influence foreign behaviour; On the other hand, domestic privileges, such as the eligibility for public procurement or the ability to receive loans from domestic banks, are being affected. Even though academic commentary has advanced numerous proposals to analyse market access conditions under international law, the result of the legal analysis particularly depends on whether one focuses on the domestic condition or on the foreign implications thus triggered. This is the reason why Bartels and Scott, for instance, while they both rely on essentially the same factual understanding, come to normatively opposite results:

According to Bartels, the essence of measures based on market access is that their application is defined by something located or occurring abroad. Therefore, such measures should be considered extraterritorial and consequently need to satisfy principles of extraterritorial jurisdiction under international law.[920] Scott, on the contrary, analyses such measures from

---

918 C.II.4b) Practice in Europe.

919 See above at C.II.2c) Comparative Normative Analysis.

920 Bartels, 'Article XX of GATT and the Problem of Extraterritorial Jurisdiction' (n 427), 381: even according to Bartels however, not all exercises of jurisdiction

the opposite angle: While it may be true that regulators in these cases are required to take into account conduct or circumstances abroad, the essential part of the regulation is that its actual application is triggered by the territorial connection. This kind of 'territorial extension' is to be distinguished from actual 'extraterritoriality', where the regulatory measure is precisely not dependent on any territorial trigger.[921] Therefore, Bartels would consider Sec. 5 (a) of the ISA, where application of sanctions is determined by a foreign company's investment into Iran, to be extraterritorial. Scott, consequently, would regard such measures as mere 'territorial extensions'.[922]

Other attempts to conceptualize market access conditions within the international law framework have been undertaken by Meng and Vazquéz. For Meng, the pertinent question in determining the extraterritoriality of a regulation is whether such regulation carries with it (intended) coercive effects or mere factual effects.[923] For instance, the prohibition of the importation of goods produced abroad under subpar environmental standards would not be considered extraterritorial – even though the effects on foreign exporters may be significant – because these effects are merely the result of growing economic interconnectedness and not intended.[924] However, it may be difficult in practice to distinguish between intended coercive effects and mere factual effects and Meng himself seems not to have been always consistent in his approach.[925] Vazquéz, on the other hand, asks whether the market access condition seeks to compel conduct regulated by internationally recognized norms, in which case its extraterri-

---

that affect foreign interests are 'extraterritorial'; generic tariffs and subsidies, for instance, would not be defined by something located or occurring abroad.

921 Scott (n 10), 90; Other authors have developed similar categorizations with slightly different terminology. For instance, the above-mentioned report conducted by Zerk during the elaboration of the UN Guiding Principles on Business and Human Rights follows a comparable approach by distinguishes between 'direct assertions of extraterritorial jurisdiction' and 'domestic measures with extraterritorial implications', see above C.V.3a) Extraterritorial Jurisdiction as a Matter of Permission; see also Cooreman (n 38), at 84, who distinguishes between extraterritoriality '*strictu sensu*' and 'measures with an extraterritorial effect'.

922 Scott (n 10), 96 – 98.

923 Meng, *Extraterritoriale Jurisdiktion im öffentlichen Wirtschaftsrecht* (n 43), 86.

924 Ibid., 76 – 77.

925 For instance, he views Sec. 5 (a) of the ISA as unproblematic under principles of jurisdiction, even though he acknowledges the strong and intended coercive effects of the legislation, see also above at C.II.4c) Comparative Normative Analysis.

toriality would be justified.[926] The wide spectrum of academic opinion is testament to the controversial nature of market access conditions under international law.

On a final note, as measures based on market access are very versatile, it should be noted that this discussion is by no means limited to the subject areas examined in this study. For instance, Directive 2008/101/EC, which subjects also foreign airlines to the EU Emissions Trading System (**ETS**),[927] has led to very similar controversies and intensive State protest. The directive provides that for all flights departing or arriving within EU territory, all airlines must monitor, report and verify their emissions, and to surrender allowances against those emissions including for *emissions generated throughout the part of the flight taking place outside the EU airspace*.

This provision led to intense State protest including a joint statement by 23 EU partners, calling on to the EU to cease the application of Directive 2008/101/EC to third State airline operators.[928] The United States went even one step further and prohibited compliance with the ETS for US companies.[929]

The CJEU, however, seized to provide clarity on this provision, considered the approach of Directive 2008/101/EC to be compatible with international law. It argued that the territorial connection, i.e., flights arriving or departing within the EU, was a sufficient basis for application of the ETS also to the emissions generated throughout the part of the flight taking place outside EU airspace. In this regard, the court argued that foreign airlines voluntarily accessed the European market as they had a choice to structure their commercial flights in a way to not touch EU airports if they did not want to be subjected to the ETS.[930] However, despite the CJEU judgment, the EU has limited the application of Directive 2008/101/EC to

---

926 Vázquez (n 431), 817.

927 Directive 2008/101/EC of the European Parliament and of the Council of 19 November 2008 amending Directive 2003/87/EC so as to include aviation activities in the scheme for greenhouse gas emission allowance trading within the Community, OJ L 8/3 (2009).

928 Joint Declaration of the Moscow Meeting on Inclusion of International Civil Aviation in the EU ETS of 22 February 2012.

929 European Union Emissions Trading Scheme Prohibition Act of 2011, Pub. L. No. 112–200.

930 CJEU, C-366/10, *Air Transport Association of America and Others v Secretary of State for Energy and Climate* Change [2011] ECR I-13755, paras. 127 ff.

flights *within* the EU to soothe the critics and to support the development of measures at the international level.[931]

This example confirms that market access conditions remain a thorny issue in the subject areas examined in this study and beyond. In relation to such measures, the traditional international law framework offers no bright-line rules to distinguish territoriality from extraterritoriality.

### b) Parent-based Regulation of Multinational Corporations

For the nation State, the seemingly unstoppable rise of multinational corporations has been generally regarded as a curse to effective regulations.[932] This is related to naked power politics as many of the world's largest multinational corporations dwarf the economic strength of States,[933] but also to the legal structure of these enterprises, which utilise a complex web of direct investments to avoid regulation.[934] In theory, establishing foreign incorporated subsidiaries all over the world allows multinational corporations to act anywhere through ownership and control while at the same time, the legal doctrine of corporate separateness – in principle – shields the foreign subsidiaries from regulatory measures enacted by the home State of the parent company.[935] However, we have seen that in multiple regulatory areas, States have advanced different regulatory techniques to bind foreign subsidiaries to domestic standards of conduct.

---

931 European Commission, 'Reducing emissions from aviation', https://ec.europa.eu/clima/eu-action/transport-emissions/reducing-emissions-aviation_en, last accessed 18 March 2022.

932 The number of multinational corporations has risen from barely 7,000 in 1970 to 82,000 in 2009 and it is safe to assume that by now, it has already exceeded the 100,000, see UN Conference on Trade and Development, World Investment Report 2009: Transnational Corporations, Agricultural Development and Production xxi, UNCTAD/WIR/2009.

933 Comparing annual governmental revenue and corporate revenue, a study by NGO *Global Justice Now* has shown that already in September 2016, 63 of the 100 largest economies in the world were multinational corporations, Global Justice Now, http://www.globaljustice.org.uk/controlling-corporations, last accessed on 13 April 2022.

934 Liesbeth F H Enneking, *Foreign Direct Liability and Beyond: Exploring the Role of Tort Law in Promoting International Corporate Social Responsibility and Accountability* (Zugl.: Utrecht, Univ. Diss. 2012, Eleven Internat. Publ 2012), 14.

935 Grosswald Curran (n 637), 406.

In very rare instances, domestic regulators have tried to address the foreign incorporated subsidiary directly. This has been most clearly articulated in the United States' use of economic sanctions, which has generally drawn strong opposition. An exception hereto are the 2012 amendments to the Iran sanctions, which were equally addressing foreign incorporated subsidiaries, but which have been tacitly tolerated by the EU.[936] Similarly however, the United States has employed an extensive agency doctrine in conjunction with the anti-bribery provisions of the FCPA to directly prosecute foreign subsidiaries for criminal violations.[937] Here as well, no State protests have apparently ensued.

More often, measures of home States of multinational corporations target the domestic parent company of the corporate group to indirectly control the conduct of foreign subsidiaries. This is achieved either by regulating the parent companies in relation to their foreign subsidiaries or by attaching liability to the parent companies for the conduct of their subsidiaries. In the *Fruehauf* case for instance, the US treasury instructed the domestic parent company to direct its French subsidiary to refrain from the fulfilment of a transaction contrary to US economic sanctions.[938] In relation to the FCPA, US enforcement agencies have held parent companies strictly liable for regulatory violations of their overseas subsidiaries.[939] In the area of business and human rights, parent-based regulation is mostly discussed in the form of a *duty of care*, or *devoir de vigilance*, on the part of the parent company for the conduct of the foreign subsidiary, but not in the form of strict liability.[940] Such measures have generally not been met with protest in the area of business and human rights as well as anti-corruption. However, with regard to the *Fruehauf* case, a French court denied giving effect to the direction of the parent company *vis-à-vis* its French subsidiary.[941]

Academic commentators have generally judged this sort of jurisdictional assertions unfavourably in cases, in which the home State regulator has directly addressed the foreign controlled subsidiary (such as in the

936 C.II.2b)bb) Diplomatic Protest against US Assertions of Control-based Jurisdiction.
937 C.IV.4a)cc) Parent and Subsidiary Liability Based on the Agency Theory.
938 C.II.2b)cc) Jurisprudence with regard to US Assertions of Control-based Jurisdiction.
939 C.IV.4a) Practice in the United States.
940 C.V.5b) Practice in Europe.
941 See above at C.II.2b)cc) Jurisprudence with regard to US Assertions of Control-based Jurisdiction.

*Pipeline* incident). They argue that such measures can be based neither on territoriality, as the foreign subsidiary is located outside domestic territory, nor on the nationality principle, as the foreign subsidiary is not a corporate national of the home State. In this regard, it is settled opinion in international law that corporate nationality is determined by either the place of incorporation or the seat of management, but not by the nationality of the shareholder/s.[942] In contrast, regulations aimed at the domestic parent company, either requiring it to direct the conduct of its foreign subsidiaries or holding it (strictly) liable for the conduct of these subsidiaries, have been regarded more favourably under the territoriality principle.

However, as argued above, this purely formal distinction between regulations addressing the domestic corporate parent and regulations addressing the foreign subsidiary is not entirely convincing. This is because every direct assertion of jurisdiction over a foreign subsidiary could be rephrased as a territorial regulation addressing the domestic parent company and holding it strictly liable for the conduct of its foreign subsidiaries abroad. Both regulations would achieve the same substantial result; in both cases, it is solely the conduct of the subsidiary that forms the subject of the regulation. Under such circumstances, it seems inconsistent to deem one instance a prohibited exercise of extraterritorial jurisdiction and the other one a permitted assertion of territorial jurisdiction.

In this regard, we are faced with a debate which is very similar to what we have just seen with regard to market access measures, which condition the import of certain goods on production processes or other circumstances abroad. There as well, it was questionable whether these measures should properly be characterised as territorial or extraterritorial. Just as in the case of market access conditionality, the traditional approach to jurisdiction provides no clear answers to the issue of jurisdiction over foreign controlled subsidiaries.

Therefore, as mentioned above, the Restatement Third convincingly takes a different approach and argues that this kind of jurisdictional assertion cannot solely be assessed based on whether the regulation formally addresses the domestic parent company or the foreign subsidiary. Rather, the Restatement suggests that the legality of such assertions of jurisdiction can only be judged by considering several circumstances, with the formal addressee being only one relevant factor. Accordingly, not all assertions of jurisdiction targeting foreign subsidiaries should be regarded as illegal, and

942 *Barcelona Traction Light and Power Co, Ltd. (Belgium v Spain)* (n 126), 36.

not all assertions of jurisdiction targeting domestic parent companies as legal, under customary international law.

c) Regulation of Conduct Based on Only Fleeting Territorial Connections or Based on Territorial 'Presence'

As mentioned, States overwhelmingly still nominally rely on territorial connections as the dominating basis for the exercise of jurisdiction addressing foreign individuals and companies. However, because of the growing territorial scope of economic operators and their business conduct, establishing territorial connections is not necessarily difficult for domestic regulators. This study has more closely examined two regulatory mechanisms which leverage territorial connections to significantly expand the jurisdictional reach of the regulating State.

First, States are exercising jurisdiction over conduct with only very limited territorial 'touchpoints'. This has been most clearly shown with regard to US prosecutions of foreign individuals and companies for violations of US economic sanctions or the FCPA based on the controversial theory related to monetary transfers through correspondent bank accounts.[943] Put simply, wire transfers denominated in US dollars are regularly settled through electronic systems linked to the US Federal Reserve Banks so that technically, such transactions all pass through US territory. According to this theory, monetary transfers between two parties with no relation to the United States whatsoever would fall under US jurisdiction as long as the transfer was made in US dollars. Despite the potentially unlimited scope of US jurisdiction based on this theory, these prosecutions have led to protest by the defendant's home State only in two instances and even then, the issue of extraterritorial jurisdiction was never explicitly mentioned.[944]

Second, the UK Bribery Act 2010 introduced a new mechanism for the regulation of foreign conduct based on the 'presence' of a company on domestic territory. According to Sec. 7 of the Act, any commercial organisation 'which carries on a business, or part of a business, in any part of the United Kingdom' may be held liable if a person associated to the organisation commits bribery and if the organisation cannot show adequate procedures designed to prevent such associated persons from bribery. As

943 See for instance the prosecution of Reza Zarrab at C.II.3a) Practice in the United States.

944 C.II.3b) Practice in Europe.

already mentioned, this provision is problematic because the actual act of bribery as well as the implementation of adequate procedures may well take place outside the UK, so that there is no territorial connection to the conduct to be regulated, but only a connection to the subject of regulation itself.

The UK Bribery Act can be seen as the latest development in a trend to subject companies that are not incorporated nor have their seat of management within domestic territory, but that are merely commercially present, to a growing number of regulations. Other examples include US security regulations, which also apply to non-US companies that issue stocks in the United States or that otherwise register their securities for sale. We have examined this type of issuer-based jurisdiction more closely referring to Sec. 1502 of the Dodd-Frank Act[945] as well as the FCPA. This mechanism was also used in the Sarbanes-Oxley Act of 2002, which sought to improve the corporate governance of US companies. However, with the exception of the Sarbanes-Oxley Act, this mode of regulation, which subjects foreign companies to a host of organisational rules based merely on their presence within domestic territory, has generally not led to international reactions.

In the literature, these regulations have yet to be considered jointly in a comprehensive manner. While the above-mentioned laws and regulations have at times been criticized as too far reaching, academic commentators have not yet undertaken a systematic assessment as to whether or when mere commercial presence – as opposed to being domestically incorporated or having a domestic principal place of business – suffices to prescribe rules abroad for foreign companies. It seems arguable that these regulations may rely on this presence as an evident territorial connection. However, this conclusion is by no means imperative. Analysing the UK Bribery Act, it has been argued that, in fact, the assertion of jurisdiction in relation to commercial organisations that merely carry on part of a business in the UK for failure to prevent bribery abroad amounts to an illegal extension of the corporate nationality principle as the relevant conduct occurs entirely outside the UK.[946] Again, the jurisdictional analysis seems largely to depend on whether such analysis focuses on the existing territorial connection such as the commercial presence of the addressee or on the foreign conduct being regulated. There is thus a parallel issue to regulation based on market-access conditionality, where it was equally

945 See above at C.V.4b)aa) Practice in the United States.

946 Kappel and Lagodny (n 646), 699; see also C.IV6c) Comparative Normative Analysis.

unclear under traditional jurisdictional principles whether the relevant part of the measure was the domestic restriction or the command to a foreign addressee.

## 2. The Restriction to Considerations of State Sovereignty

Finally, individual consent has emerged as a recurring issue in this research. In its most obvious form, US administration of export control relies (in part) on the consent of the foreign purchaser to be bound by certain regulatory standards. To be eligible to receive sensitive US goods and technology, the purchaser frequently has to guarantee the observance of US rules in relation to re-export and end-use even outside of US territory. However, consent has also emerged as an argument to justify the assertion of jurisdiction over foreign economic operators in a number of other cases. For instance, claims of jurisdiction over non-US issuers in securities matters, such as the above-mentioned Sarbanes-Oxley Act or Sec. 1502 of the Dodd-Frank Act, are sometimes justified based on the notion that, with the registration of securities with the SEC, the non-US issuer has voluntarily subjected itself to all related US regulation.[947] A variation of this argument has also found its way into the CJEU judgement on the extraterritoriality of the EU ETS, where the court stated that it was possible for airline operators, who did not want to be subject to the regulation, to avoid flying into or out of the Union.[948]

Especially in relation to export control cases, the clearest example of using consent to establish prescriptive authority, actual practice has proven to be inconsistent. While the EC has strongly protested this mechanism in the controversial *Pipeline* incident, where previous written submission to US regulations was utilised as one of the bases for jurisdiction over foreign companies,[949] modern export controls seem to largely rely on such consent. Academic commentary has equally been divided: The majority, in line with the EC's arguments in the *Pipeline* incident, seems to support the view that private parties could not dispose of what is essentially State sovereignty, the deciding aspect when it comes to the allocation

947 Detlev F Vagts, 'Extraterritoriality and the Corporate Governance Law' (2003) 97(2) AJIL 289, 293 raises this argument in relation to the Sarbanes-Oxley-Act.

948 See above at C.VI.1a) Market Access Regulation Conditioned on Extraterritorial Circumstances.

949 See above at C.III.4b) Practice in Europe.

of regulatory competences.[950] In this regard, it is argued that the scope of prescriptive jurisdiction of a State is exclusively determined by the existence of a genuine link between the State and the object of regulation such as territoriality, effects, nationality or universality. Thus, unless one of these principles of jurisdiction under the traditional approach is given, assertions based on the individual consent of the affected are contrary to international law.

This is lamentable though as this approach to jurisdictional principles does not reflect actual contemporary practice. The State practice in the area of export control, where almost all major exporting countries use end-user certifications or similar documents requiring the importing party to submit themselves to the approval of the exporting State, indicates that there is an actual need for this regulatory mechanism. In this case therefore, the issue with the territoriality-based system of jurisdiction is not its *flexibility*, that its principles are too malleable to provide normative consistency, but rather its *rigidity*, in that it is unable to account for interests that are not connected to State sovereignty.

This rigidity of the traditional approach to jurisdiction leads to particularly acute issues in relation to the interests of individual natural or juridical persons.[951] Apart from the above-mentioned limitations placed on consent-based jurisdiction, it also restricts the concept of *forum necessitates* in the area of business and human rights. As elaborated, *forum necessitatis* refers to the establishment of adjudicative jurisdiction in situations in which the individual rights of the plaintiff require the assertion of jurisdiction as otherwise, the plaintiff would face a denial of justice. Despite this imminent denial of justice, establishing such necessity jurisdiction without cumulatively satisfying one of the traditional jurisdictional bases is not accepted in customary international law *de lege lata*. Here as well, a more flexible approach would seem desirable, as the State deciding on whether to act may legitimately have to consider the individual right of fair trial and access to justice.[952]

---

950 Volz (n 24), 216 – 217; Forwick (n 528), 82.

951 Ryngaert, 'Extraterritorial Export Controls (Secondary Boycotts)' (n 345), 634 f.; Mills (n 14), 230 – 233.

952 C.V.5c) Comparative Normative Analysis.

### 3. Conclusion

The above synthesis has demonstrated that modern regulatory mechanisms have challenged the traditional, territoriality-based system of jurisdiction in international law in two ways. First, this system is not capable of providing order in international relations because there are no normatively consistent boundaries of territoriality: Under traditional doctrine, the answer to the question whether certain forms of regulation should be regarded as territorial or extraterritorial would demand identifying the territorial part of the conduct or situation and assess, whether this part is 'relevant' in a normative sense so that it triggers the legitimate exercise of jurisdiction. However, the answers to these determinations mostly depend on who you ask. In practice therefore, States are able to exploit these legal uncertainties and may nominally rely on territorial connections while setting regulations with a global reach. Contrary to its objective, the territoriality-based system of jurisdiction is thus not able to limit the regulatory competences of States.

Second, the system does not allow for considerations not rooted in State sovereignty, even when these should influence the legitimacy of jurisdictional assertions. On the one hand, we have observed that the acceptance or rejection of exercises of jurisdiction by other States also depend on the material political or legal interests involved. Thus, States are less inclined to protest certain forms of extraterritorial regulations if these regulations are intended to serve the interests of the international community. On the other hand, with regard to exercises of jurisdiction on the basis of private submissions and the principle of *forum necessitatis*, there is a real need for States to be able to account for the rights and the autonomy of individual natural and juridical persons.

## D. The Way Forward

The previous parts of the study have been in large part guided by the research question, whether the territoriality-based system of jurisdiction is still capable of providing order in international relations by delimiting regulatory competences between States. The answer to this question depends on whether it is possible to define normatively consistent boundaries of territoriality to be respected by States. Through a multitude of examples, however, this study has demonstrated that indeed, ever more intricate and sophisticated legal arguments have proved futile in providing such consistent boundaries. As several commentators have noted, globalization and in particular the advent of internet have made it increasingly difficult to pinpoint the exact location of a certain conduct and to answer the question whether such conduct is territorial or extraterritorial.[953] In addition, however, this study has shown that modern transnational regulation itself has become more complex in that the measures often seek to compel conduct by someone else than the formal (territorial) addressee of the regulation. These measures often rely on the dense personal and commercial ties between the regulatory subjects to impact behaviour beyond territorial boundaries, aiming to export domestic norms and standards. In these cases, the question is not only where the conducts to be regulated are exactly located, but also, with regard to regulations involving multiple elements, which of these elements are relevant for the normative inquiry of territoriality versus extraterritoriality.

At the same time, the interests of transnational regulation have become much more complex than the architects of Westphalian sovereignty could have ever imagined. Considerations of State sovereignty are complemented by international community interests as well as the rights and the autonomy of individuals. However, the traditional approach to jurisdiction offers only limited possibility to balance these considerations. Because the territoriality-based system is thus deficient on multiple accounts, this part of the study offers an alternative conception of extraterritorial jurisdiction. This research proposes that functionally, extraterritorial jurisdiction as a regulatory technique resembles domestic exercises of public authority *vis-à-vis* individuals. Therefore, States exercising extraterritorial jurisdiction

953 See already Lowe and Staker (n 50), 308 – 309; Svantesson (n 64), at 42 – 43.

under international law should not only consider the sovereignty of States, but also respect other aspects of both legitimation and limits, in particular, the relationship between the regulating State and the addressee and the international community at large.

To this end, this part proceeds in three steps. Chapter I argues why this particular new conception for extraterritorial jurisdiction in international law was chosen. It explains why it is necessary, possible and reasonable to abandon the territoriality-based system in favour of an approach highlighting the function of extraterritorial jurisdiction also as an exercise of public authority. Chapter II of this part further develops the two concepts of legitimation and limits. While this chapter discusses different possible theoretical approaches to legitimize (extra-)territorial jurisdiction, it also serves to rebut the notion that the allocation of interstate jurisdiction is solely a matter of sovereignty. In particular, it will be shown how, already today, individuals have a role possibly both legitimizing and limiting extraterritorial jurisdiction contrary to what critics would consider an impermissible enmeshment of strictly separate spheres.[954] Chapter III will then seek to translate these theoretical considerations into a framework for the lawful exercise of extraterritorial jurisdiction, which seeks to be both doctrinally coherent and practical in its application.

## I. Arguing for a New Approach to Jurisdiction in International Law

The first two parts of this study have identified serious shortcomings of the traditional, territoriality-based system of jurisdiction. However, the mere identification of a problem says relatively little about if, and how, these issues should be dealt with. First, while contentious exercises of extraterritorial jurisdiction have caused discord and instability in international relations in the present, one might argue that future developments, in particular further harmonization of law across and cooperation between States may render the study of new approaches to extraterritorial jurisdiction obsolete. Second, even if the progressive development of extraterritorial jurisdiction were necessary, it might not be possible to simply abandon

954 Modern international law acknowledges a strengthened role for individuals, transforming them from mere objects to bearers of rights and duties alongside States, see Anne Peters, *Jenseits der Menschenrechte: Die Rechtsstellung des Individuums im Völkerrecht* (Jus Internationale et Europaeum vol 88, Mohr Siebeck 2014).

territoriality. After all, territorial sovereignty has been such a fixture in international law that it might be actually inevitable. Thirdly, before moving to a radical new conception of extraterritorial jurisdiction that may also have repercussions for international law in general, it may be worth considering whether the principles available today, and in particular the principle of non-intervention, may achieve the desired results. The next sections address these considerations in this order. The fourth and last section of this chapter introduces some preliminary consideration on the reasons behind the approach advocated for in this study.

### 1. Alternative Approaches to Solve Concurrent Jurisdiction

#### a) Substantive Harmonization

Although the process of globalization rendered the territoriality-based system incapable of establishing jurisdictional order between sovereign States, the further development of globalization in the future may instead offer a cure to these problems. In particular, harmonization of the underlying substantive rules may mitigate potential State conflicts. With regard to jurisdiction, it operates on the assumption that with harmonized laws in different countries, States have less incentive to regulate extraterritorially because it would not change the normative result of the situation. And even if a State chooses to prescribe rules extraterritorially, legal certainty for affected individuals will increase as they will only have to deal with one set of substantive rules instead of potentially multiple conflicting commands. However, while appealing in principle, harmonization suffers from some well-known problems.

From a more theoretical perspective, several authors have noted that substantive harmonization and multilateral agreements are not negotiated in a power and interest free vacuum. On the one hand, the attitude of States towards international negotiations in any particular subject area is often dependent on domestic political factors. Harmonization may be pursued if the domestic constituency perceives that the benefits accrued will outweigh the potential costs.[955] As one author notes, such multilateral negotiations are in reality 'two-level games', where the State is not only bargaining with other parties to the agreement, but also with domestic

955 Tonya L Putnam, *Courts without Borders: Law, Politics, and U.S. Extraterritoriality* (Cambridge University Press 2016), 78 – 80.

groups at home.[956] On the other hand, relative power differences between the negotiating States may result in agreements that substantially favour the preferences of the stronger parties, despite the fact that all States are nominally equal in such processes. This is because more powerful States will generally have better access to critical information and possess the necessary clout to coerce, cajole or entice their less well-equipped counterparts to adopt their positions.[957] Thus, conflicts between States may arise and the legitimacy of substantive harmonization may be undercut because of doubts surrounding the fairness of the negotiation process. At this point of course, it should be noted that unilateral exercises of extraterritorial jurisdiction are also manifestations of power and that to date, only the world's largest economies, including the EU and the United States, have successfully pursued this avenue. Moreover, affected individuals still have more legal certainty under unfairly harmonized rules than under conflicting rules imposed through different States, even if one of the States exercising extraterritorial jurisdiction happens to be much more powerful than other States.

From a more practical perspective however, given the divergent policy spectrum around the world, substantive harmonization is difficult or even elusive in many regulatory areas. The requirement of consent by all parties to reach an international agreement means that, more often than not, harmonization happens around the lowest common denominator.[958] Moreover, even if an agreement is eventually reached, it does not guarantee effective national implementation as monitoring of international treaties can be difficult or (politically and financially) costly.[959] Therefore, even with agreed harmonized standards, extraterritorial regulation may still be used to supplement a perceived lack of national implementation measures. Thus, despite a general trend towards greater convergence in many regulatory areas, extraterritorial jurisdiction will remain a feature of international law for many years to come. In addition, international harmonization efforts seem to have hit a bump in the road lately because multiple States are currently retreating from multilateralism.

956 Magnuson, 'Unilateral Corporate Regulation' (n 10), 534.
957 Ryngaert, *Jurisdiction in International Law* (n 2), 203 – 208.
958 Magnuson, 'Unilateral Corporate Regulation' (n 10), 533 – 534.
959 See for an example for successful monitoring within the OECD, above at C.IV.4b)aa) The UK Bribery Act 2010.

### b) Cooperation

Sometimes, when substantive harmonization has less prospect for success, enhanced cooperation, including requirements of notice or even mutual recognition, constitutes the politically more viable option. A prime example in this regard is the area of global antitrust enforcement. While the adoption of an international agreement on competition and anticompetitive practices had been on the agenda of the WTO for some time, resistance in particular by developing nations has stopped such lofty ambitions, which will likely remain elusive in the future.[960] Even between the industrialised bloc of the EU and the United States, stark substantive divergences exist in relation to their municipal competition policies.[961]

Nonetheless, the EU and the United States, the two most dedicated promoters of extraterritorial antitrust enforcement, have entered into an agreement on mutual cooperation, which, among other things, mandates each party to notify the other whenever it becomes aware that its enforcement activities may affect important interests of the other party.[962] Moreover, the agreement contains a mechanism of positive comity, according to which each party may request the other party to initiate proceedings on its own territory if anti-competitive behaviour there affects the interests of the requesting party. However, despite the conclusion of a supplemental agreement on positive comity, use of this mechanism in practice remains scarce.[963] More recently, the International Competition Network has provided the most promising forum for informal enforcement cooperation and possibly substantial convergence. The increased cooperation through these venues seems to have yielded at least some benefit in relation to managing concurrent extraterritorial jurisdiction as evidenced by the successful multilateral enforcement action in the *Marine Hose* case. Perhaps most significantly in this example, the UK and the United States managed to negotiate a 'split-jurisdiction' deal, where the prison sentences imposed

---

960 Zerk (n 634), 92 – 93; Ryngaert, *Jurisdiction in International Law* (n 2), 202.

961 Avi-Yonah (n 237), 29.

962 Agreement Regarding the Application of Competition Laws between the Government of the United States and the Commission of the European Communities, (1991) 4 CMLR 823; (1995) 30 ILM 1487, [1995] OJ L 132, Art. II 1.

963 Putnam (n 955), 142; for another treaty, which contains a provision on comity in transnational environmental regulation, see: North American Agreement on Environmental Cooperation, (1993) 32 ILM 1480, Art. 22.

upon the executives of the cartel members were coordinated to avoid possibly two separate sentences in both the UK and the United States.[964]

Inspired by this and similar examples, most studies on extraterritorial jurisdiction agree that increased international cooperation is a helpful and desirable solution to avoid conflicts between States and to enhance the effectiveness of extraterritorial law regimes.[965] This is likely to be true with regard to some issues associated with the exercise of unilateral extraterritorial jurisdiction. However, cooperation is by no means a panacea as will be illustrated by two exemplary arguments: For one, while cooperation on the enforcement level might concentrate eventual proceedings in one State, it does not avoid the issue that it is impossible for the affected individual to know beforehand, which State will take the lead and which laws will be applied.[966] Thus, in the event of diverging or even conflicting legal standards by different States, individuals may still be faced with a difficult of even impossible compliance task. For the other, even solely administrative or procedural cooperation is subject to the restraints of domestic political preferences and may be more or less available depending on the concrete area of regulation, the agencies and regulators involved and the perceived costs and benefits.[967]

## 2. The History of the Territoriality Principle

The continued (almost slavish) reliance of States on territoriality even in an age of de-territorialisation may create the impression that there are no viable alternatives to this principle as the primary concept for the allocation of regulatory competences.[968] In order to propose a different conception of jurisdiction, this mystery should be debunked already now. It is essential to recall that, in fact, territoriality has been a rather recent historical development.[969] As several authors have pointed out, territoriality was unknown in the ancient world and allegiances then were based

964 Zerk (n 634), 103.
965 Ibid., 216 – 217; International Bar Association (n 12), 26.
966 International Bar Association (n 12), 28.
967 Pierre-Hugues Verdier, 'Transnational Regulatory Networks and their Limits' (2009) 34(1) YaleJIntLaw 113, 126 – 128.
968 Svantesson (n 13), at 13 has termed it the 'Tyranny of Territoriality'.
969 For an impressive overview of the development of territoriality, see Ryngaert, *Jurisdiction in International Law* (n 2), 50 – 62.

on connections such as personality, race or nationality.[970] Well up into Medieval Europe, sovereignty was not associated with geographical coordinates but rather with dominion over a tribe. For instance, the sovereign of the Capetian dynasty in France was originally called *King of the French* before it acquired a territorial title, *King of France*.[971] The idea of congruence between legal authority and territory fully gained traction in Europe only during the rise of the modern nation-State after the Westphalian Peace of 1648.[972] Since then, political, ideological and philosophical factors as well as technological innovations in cartography contributed to the development of the territoriality principle as it is still applied today. But it was only by the end of the eighteenth century, that territoriality had been enshrined as the primary jurisdictional basis in multiple criminal codes in continental Europe.[973]

It is equally worth noting that even in the heyday of territoriality, the principle has been riddled with exceptions. For instance, States have enjoyed jurisdiction over pirates on the high seas based on universality for centuries.[974] Equally, nationality based jurisdiction remained accepted and essential as a complement to territoriality in continental Europe.[975] On the other hand, European States frequently sought to exempt their own nationals from local territorial jurisdiction in non-Western States, such as Turkey, Morocco and China, through the maintenance of consular courts. These courts had jurisdiction over disputes involving their own nationals as well as for disputes between nationals and locals abroad and applied their home-State law instead of the local territorial law, which was seen as strange and barbaric.[976] Thus, for instance, an American living in Shanghai could be subject to the jurisdiction of the US District Court for China and US law instead of Chinese law.[977] It is clear that this practice constituted a significant breach with traditional ideals of Westphalian sovereignty

---

970 Ford (n 119), 868 – 872; Shalom Kassan, 'Extraterritorial Jurisdiction in the Ancient World' (1935) 29 AJIL 237, 240.

971 Henry S Maine, *Ancient Law: Its Connection with the Early History of Society, and its Relation to Modern Ideas* (3rd American, from 5th London ed. H. Holt 1873), 103 – 104; Ford (n 119), 873.

972 Raustiala, 'The Geography of Justice' (n 442), 107.

973 See for instance for Germany, § 3 of the Reichsstrafgesetzbuch of 15 May 1871; for more examples, see Ryngaert, *Jurisdiction in International Law* (n 2), 54 – 61.

974 See above at B.I.2f) The Universality Principle.

975 See for instance for Germany, § 4 of the Reichsstrafgesetzbuch of 15 May 1871.

976 Kassan (n 970), 238 – 239.

977 Scully (n 30), 6.

and was often only possible through the conclusion of coercive, unequal treaties between the Western and the affected non-Western States in a way not possible nor desirable today.[978] However, this example, and the other historical anecdotes related upon above, plainly contradict the narrative that strict territoriality is necessarily the only possible alternative for the allocation of jurisdictional authority between States.

### 3. Extraterritorial Jurisdiction regulated by the Principle of Non-Intervention

Not only was the development of territoriality as the cardinal normative principle of the jurisdictional order in international law a relatively recent phenomenon. It was also the result of one specific interpretation of Westphalian sovereignty, which emphasised aspects of internal and external independence and in particular, viewed territory as the natural physical corollary to State sovereignty. However, State sovereignty as a principle may have meaning and application beyond territorial sovereignty. Therefore, while territoriality has arguably failed in providing the normative backbone for allocating jurisdictional competences between States, this need not necessarily mean that State sovereignty may not still serve as the guiding principle to a progressive approach. Indeed, it is argued here that sovereignty and the principle of non-intervention, interpreted through a modern lens, are in fact capable of mitigating some of the issues found with the formalistic inquiry of territoriality versus extraterritoriality. Still, a reconfiguration of sovereignty alone is not sufficient to account for other bases of legitimation, in particular, the rights and interests of individuals.

In the introduction to this research, it was already explored that the principle of non-intervention, as a manifestation of State sovereignty, formed one of the outer limits of jurisdiction in international law.[979] Violation of the principle of non-intervention has two requirements, it must occur within a subject area that constitutes a domestic affair of the affected State and it must be conducted using methods of coercion.[980] This two part definition offers a rather wide margin for interpretation and

978 Ryngaert, *Jurisdiction in International Law* (n 2), 61.

979 A.III.1. State Jurisdiction and State Sovereignty.

980 *Case concerning military and paramilitary activities in and against Nicaragua (Nicaragua v United States of America)* (n 273), 108; Ronzitti (n 270), 3 – 6.

development compared to the formal distinction between territoriality and extraterritoriality.

So far, it has been argued that the traditional bases of jurisdiction, territoriality, nationality and the protective principle all establish a genuine link to the subject matter of regulation so that the specific matter is drawn out of the domestic affairs of the affected State. However, what constitutes domestic affairs is not fixed and may change over time. Formerly domestic affairs may suddenly also be in the interest of other States.[981] This issue is particularly debated with regard to grave violations of basic human rights.[982] However, the same idea may also be transposed to other situations, where it could be said that how one State regulates a certain subject matter is not an exclusively domestic issue, but also concerns other States or the international community at large. Simply by redefining the boundaries of domestic affairs thus opens up the possibility to break away from the supremacy of territoriality.

In addition, however, the rigidity of the territoriality-based system of jurisdiction may also be mitigated by focusing on the second requirement for a violation of the principle of non-intervention, which is the existence of coercion. The relevance of the existence of coercion is reflected in the different treatment of enforcement and prescriptive jurisdiction. Traditional doctrine poses stricter requirements on the exercise of jurisdiction when it involves the performance of physical acts on the territory of another State than the mere extension of legislation to cases involving a foreign element.[983] Within prescriptive jurisdiction however, once one of the

981 An Hertogen, 'Sovereignty as Decisional Independence over Domestic Affairs: The Dispute over Aviation in the EU Emissions Trading System' (2012) 1(02) TEL 281, 292.

982 Compare also Kofi Annan's speech to the General Assembly, SG/SM/7136 GA/9596: 'State sovereignty, in its most basic sense, is being redefined by the forces of globalization and international cooperation. The State is now widely understood to be the servant of its people, and not vice versa. At the same time, individual sovereignty -- and by this I mean the human rights and fundamental freedoms of each and every individual as enshrined in our Charter -- has been enhanced by a renewed consciousness of the right of every individual to control his or her own destiny. These parallel developments [...] do not lend themselves to easy interpretations or simple conclusions. They do, however, demand of us a willingness to think anew'.

983 Katharina Meyer, *Grenzen und Entwicklungsmöglichkeiten des Souveränitätsprinzips in transnationalen Handelsbeziehungen: Zur Legitimation grenzüberschreitender Verwaltungszusammenarbeit am Beispiel des Lebensmittelhandels zwischen der Europäischen Union und Drittstaaten* (Jus Internationale et Europaeum, 1. Auflage, Mohr Siebeck 2018), 202 – 203.

formally recognized bases is satisfied, it is irrelevant how intrusive the measure in question is on the affected State. Thus, by focusing on the element of coercion, the principle of non-intervention may be susceptible to a more nuanced approach to jurisdiction in international law, which looks beyond formal categories and assesses the actual intent and content of exercises of jurisdiction.

Despite this flexibility, a mere recourse to modern interpretations of State sovereignty and the principle of non-intervention may not be sufficient. After all, the reconfiguration of the relationship between States would, in essence, still put the interests of States front and centre. Fundamentally however, the exercise of extraterritorial jurisdiction does not only concern other States. Rather, as will be argued in the next section, it is of a truly hybrid functionality, in that it also directly touches upon the rights and interests of individuals. To properly account for this particular nature of extraterritorial jurisdiction requires that we complement considerations of State sovereignty with an equally strong element in relation to the protection of individuals.

### 4. Extraterritorial Jurisdiction as an Exercise of Public Authority

The exercise of extraterritorial jurisdiction occupies a regulatory space between clearly defined domestic law and international law.[984] For instance, the domestic regulation of foreign transnational bribery is a clearly different phenomenon than both the criminalization of bribery within the territorial State as well as the conclusion of an international treaty such as the UNCAC mandating its State parties to criminalize bribery. The domestic criminalization of bribery and the conclusion of the UNCAC also have wholly different legal requirements. The former is of course subject to domestic constitutional constraints, such as the non-retroactivity of criminal law, whereas the latter has to fulfil the requirements of traditional international law, such as the Vienna Convention on the Law of Treaties.[985] One would therefore expect that the domestic regulation of for-

984 Ireland-Piper, *Accountability in Extraterritoriality* (n 113), 4 – 5.

985 Vienna Convention on the Law of Treaties (adopted 22 May 1969, entered into force 27 January 1980) 1155 UNTS 331; unlike domestic constitutional law, the Vienna Convention on the Law of Treaties contains only few material requirements for treaties, the most significant one being that treaties must not conflict with a peremptory norm of general international law (*ius cogens*), see Art. 53 of the Vienna Convention on the Law of Treaties.

eign transnational bribery, as a fundamentally different form of regulation, also has different bases of legality. However, this is not the case: rather its legitimacy is assessed according to the same parameters as the conclusion of the UNCAC, namely the respect for the sovereignty of other States.

As a general principle, it is bad law to subject factually different circumstances to the same legal analysis. Therefore, the hybrid nature of extraterritorial jurisdiction requires that such exercises are not only considered along State sovereignty, but also respect the requirements drawn from its other function. What then, is the other function of extraterritorial jurisdiction? The purpose of exercising extraterritorial jurisdiction is to 'regulate', directly and without mediation through the home State, the conduct of the affected person. Thus, it is argued here that, when a State asserts extraterritorial jurisdiction over a certain case, this act should be regarded as an exercise of public authority over an individual just as if the domestic police arrests someone to uphold public order. In domestic systems, such 'regulation' is associated with the public law of that State. This body of law is tasked with both legitimizing, i.e., defining the situations, in which State coercion is proper, and limiting the exercise of public authority.[986] It is the contention of this study that the correct way of thinking about jurisdiction in international law should, in acknowledging its function as an exercise of public authority, consider aspects of legitimation and limitation inspired by domestic public law, alongside the still prominent category of State sovereignty.

Vigilant readers may already now argue that the above-described approach would impermissibly enmesh two wholly separate spheres, one concerning State sovereignty and the other concerning the protection of individuals. This is fair criticism. However, the proposal is far less ambitious than it may seem at first sight. In fact, it is not an entirely

986 Meyer (n 983), 351; Christian Walter, 'Grundlagen und Rahmenbedingungen für die Steuerungskraft des Völkerrechts' (2016) 76(2) ZaöRV 363, 387; Armin von Bogdandy, Philipp Dann and Matthias Goldmann, 'Völkerrecht als öffentliches Recht: Konturen eines rechtlichen Rahmens für Global Governance' (2010) 49(1) Der Staat 23, 29; Armin von Bogdandy, Matthias Goldmann and Ingo Venzke, 'From Public International to International Public Law: Translating World Public Opinion into International Public Authority' (2017) 28(1) EJIL 115, 123: 'The public law approach […] avails itself of the dual function of modern public law. Accordingly, public authority may only be exercised if it is based on an authorizing act (constitutive or enabling function), and its exercise controlled and limited by substantive and procedural standards (limiting function)'.

new phenomenon to assess acts, which were traditionally only associated with international law, also through the lens of 'regulation'. UN Security Council targeted sanctions are the most prominent example in this regard. It makes sense to consider individual rights in these instances because the sanctions concerned, although they emanate from an international body, directly assert public authority over an individual in a possibly more severe way than domestic police actions. These measures do not stand in isolation; rather, they are part of a larger trend of transnational efforts to assert direct control over individuals to solve global challenges through the means of regulation, a development, which has been aptly characterized as the regulatory turn in international law.[987] In this debate, it has become fashionable to assess the acts adopted in this manner through the lens of individual protection, too.[988] The situation of extraterritorial jurisdiction is somewhat similar and is indeed merely one of the facets of this larger trend. In fact, the hybrid nature of unilateral extraterritoriality makes it even more accessible to an assessment revolving around both State sovereignty and the protection of individuals, than truly international acts such as UN Security Council resolutions.

## II. Theoretical Considerations

### 1. Legitimacy: Democracy and Community Interests

Because extraterritorial jurisdiction occupies a hybrid space between purely domestic and purely international law, its function is also the direct exercise of public authority, albeit with regard to persons or situations in another State. As such, it has been argued that extraterritorial jurisdiction faces similar issues of legitimacy and limitation as domestic public law regulation. Connecting extraterritorial jurisdiction with legitimacy is not exactly a novel approach. In fact, it is widely assumed that the unchecked exercise of extraterritorial jurisdiction, in particular in relation to somewhat contested bases such as the effects principle, poses difficult challenges to the principle of *democratic legitimacy*.

987 Katz Cogan (n 52).

988 Nico Krisch and Benedict Kingsbury, 'Introduction: Global Governance and Global Administrative Law in the International Legal Order' (2006) 17(1) EJIL 1, 5.

Gibney, for instance, in his impassionate critique, claims that extraterritorial jurisdiction diametrically breaks with this principle, because it imposes a rule on foreigners without them being able to participate in the democratic process of norm creation or otherwise influence the content of the rule.[989] According to Ryngaert, these regulations represent mere commands, without the communicative texture that makes laws legitimate.[990] Benvenisti similarly argues that governing foreigners targets the very essence of individual and collective self-determination.[991] Meyer sees a legitimacy deficit even in the particular case, in which the home State has explicitly consented to the application of the foreign regulations to domestic individuals.[992] Parrish, finally, draws the conclusion that these considerations warrant a return to stricter territoriality.[993]

The last author in particular views democracy as the paramount principle for legitimacy in general, which is natural coming out of a domestic context. However, this view may unduly restrict considerations of suitable alternatives. It should already be noted here that with regard to extraterritorial jurisdiction, the attainment of a similar level of democratic legitimacy as in national fora is not realistically feasible. Democracy is of course a concept even more difficult to grasp than jurisdiction, but for the present purpose, it may suffice to recur to the archetypal notion of ruling through the consent of 'the people' governed, typically through elections and other participatory procedures.[994] However, it is not difficult to see that States are not willing or do not even have the organisational means to open up

989 Mark P Gibney, 'The Extraterritorial Application of U.S. Law: The Perversion of Democratic Governance, the Reversal of Institutional Roles, and the Imperative of Establishing Normative Principles' (1996) 19(2) Boston College International and Comparative Law Review 297, at 305.

990 Ryngaert, *Jurisdiction in International Law* (n 2), 193.

991 Benvenisti (n 23), at 302.

992 Meyer (n 1083), 340 – 343; This is because such consent not only affected the home State competence with regard to this specific subject area, but also generally undermined the State sovereignty to freely determine its own mechanisms to legitimize public authority.

993 Parrish, 'Reclaiming International Law from Extraterritoriality' (n 10), 1483 – 1489; However, as we have discussed at length above, such a return does not seem to be possible because it is impossible to define consistent normative boundaries of territoriality.

994 Ibid., 859; For a more precise definition, see Eva Erman, 'Global Political Legitimacy beyond Justice and Democracy?' (2016) 8(1) Int Theory 29, 41, who views democracy as 'as a political organization or decision-making body that is considered legitimate if the rules that govern it are taken by those to whom the rules apply'.

their electoral community to foreigners even though domestic decisions may increasingly affect these people extraterritorially. This may also not be normatively desirable because foreigners are typically only affected in certain specific areas of regulation and unconcerned by the vast amount of general domestic issues.

However, because international democratic legitimation will probably remain an elusive ideal for some time to come, it may be worthwhile to ponder over alternative sources of legitimacy. To this end, it may be particularly enlightening to examine whether and why academic commentators consider the exercise of (extra-)territorial jurisdiction relying on the traditional bases as legitimate. In a next step, this examination may facilitate some general conclusions regarding the legitimacy for the exercise of jurisdiction, which may in turn prove useful for the construction of a new jurisdictional framework.

### a) Territoriality, Nationality and Democracy

#### aa) Territoriality

There is no shortage of contemporary literature, which criticizes the primacy of territoriality within the existing system of jurisdiction, based on practical or normative considerations. However, surprisingly few international law scholars have bothered with examining the question, whether the exercise of public authority on domestic territory itself may be in need of justification in the first place. Admittedly, this is an inquiry that has proved difficult for even the most eminent political philosophers and this study does not pretend to be able to contribute to that debate. Nonetheless, certain insights of that debate may be helpful in identifying mechanisms to enhance the legitimacy of the exercise of extraterritorial jurisdiction.

The first important insight is that, unlike what critiques of extraterritorial jurisdiction implicitly presume, the application of territoriality does not guarantee democratic legitimacy. This claim becomes quite intuitive when one considers the vast number of people subject to territorial rule without having an equal say in participating in the normative formation of that rule. Foreign residents are usually not granted voting rights even if they have lived in a State for decades; Foreign owners of domestic companies or properties may be subject to all kinds of business and planning regulations that they are not able to influence; Finally, visiting travellers have to abide by the same criminal laws as their domestic counterparts.

Thus, if ever territoriality could be equated with democracy, in the modern age of mobility, territorial jurisdiction is at best a rather imprecise proxy.[995] A more promising solution to the legitimacy problem may be found in the already mentioned idea of consent. John Locke most famously argued that when someone travelled or resided upon the territory of a State, that person tacitly consented to the exercise of public authority.[996] While this argument appears appealing in the first place, it suffers from a number of theoretical inconsistencies. For one, 'tacit' consent is a normative fiction and lacks evidence in most practical instances.[997] For the other, for this theory to work, it has to presuppose that State authority is territorially bounded, as otherwise, it cannot explain why someone would 'tacitly' consent to jurisdiction *only* when that person enters the territory of the State, making this a somewhat circular construction.[998]

There are many more conceptions of legitimacy and territoriality, but one last example should suffice to conclude the argument that territoriality is a much weaker mediator for legitimacy than generally assumed by international law scholars. According to Chehtman, the right of the territorial State to punish crimes is not grounded in democracy or consent, but rather in the collective interest of individuals within the State of having a system of criminal laws – a public good – in force, which enhances everyone's sense of dignity and security.[999] This conception is appealing, because interest sets a lower bar then consent: Arguably, even if someone entered the territory of a State with the sole purpose of murdering another person, that perpetrator shares the collective interest of having criminal laws in force because he would not want to be murdered or have his weapons stolen before he can commit his crime. But even this account is somewhat circular in the end. It cannot explain why the individuals in a State would have an interest in the criminal law of precisely the territorial State to be in force. The explanation can only be that the criminal laws

---

995 Ford (n 119), 848 – 849.

996 John Locke, 'Second Treatise of Government', § 119 – 121; A similar argument has been more recently made by Volz (n 24), 216 – 217.

997 See on this Anna Stilz, 'Why do States have Territorial Rights?' (2009) 1(2) Int Theory 185, 193 – 194.

998 See for a more detailed consideration of the concept of consent, Lea Brilmayer, 'Rights, Fairness, and Choice of Law' (1989) 98 YaleLJ 1277, at 1303 – 1306.

999 Alejandro Chehtman, 'The Extraterritorial Scope of the Right to Punish' (2010) 29(2) Law and Philos 127, 133 – 134.

of another State are likely to be unenforceable in the territorial State and thus, the effectiveness of these laws would not add to the sense of dignity and security of the domestic community. However, the unenforceability of foreign laws on domestic territory is again nothing but a highly territorial assumption in itself.

### bb) Nationality

Quite similar to the analysis regarding territoriality in the section above, the most intuitive answer for legitimizing extraterritorial jurisdiction based on the nationality of the regulatory addressee would be the principle of democracy. After all, it is primarily citizens who bear the right to participate in the political process through elections and other procedures and thus, to influence the normative content of the rules governing them.[1000] However, just like the analysis of territoriality, equating the nationality principle with democracy is at best an incomplete view. It at least misses the fact that not all States grant voting rights to all their overseas citizens and that practically, not all nationals living abroad may feel a connection to their home State strong enough to prompt them to participate in the political process.[1001]

Because of these difficulties with the principle of democracy, nationality jurisdiction is sometimes seen as justified based on the special relationship that links citizens to their home State, a notion commonly termed 'allegiance'. According to this conception, the regulatory power of States over their own nationals even abroad stems from the fact that they also offer protection, in particular diplomatic protection, to the same individuals. Thus, the situation resembles somewhat of a *quid pro quo*, where the accep-

---

1000 Brilmayer (n 998), 1298; Following this line of argument, Ireland-Piper sees a potential deficit in legitimacy when extraterritorial jurisdiction is extended beyond nationals to residents who have no right to vote, Ireland-Piper, *Accountability in Extraterritoriality* (n 113), at 26.

1001 See in this regard, Peter J Spiro, 'Perfecting Political Diaspora' (2006) 81(1) New York University Law Review 207, 211: 'Although many states restrict the franchise of nonresidents, the clear trend is toward allowing and facilitating greater electoral participation by external citizens. A few states provide external citizens with discrete legislative representation, while most assimilate external voters into existing internal territorial subdivisions (usually according to place of last residence). Although turnout among external voters has historically been low, there is evidence that such participation is becoming more consequential.'.

tance of nationality jurisdiction is the compensation in exchange for home State protection.[1002] However, this justification equally may not apply to all States, as some may not be willing or able to offer protection, for instance with regard to nationals who had to flee because of persecution.[1003]

### cc) Conclusion

The point of this admittedly rather cursory exercise is to argue that even when it comes to the (almost) universally accepted jurisdictional principles of territoriality and nationality, the search for legitimacy is far from an undisputed matter. In fact, the legitimacy of territorial jurisdiction may have no easy theoretical answer without presupposing territoriality as the foundational ordering principle in international relations. From an empirical perspective, territorial jurisdiction may thus be perceived as legitimate because of a combination of factors, which include ideals of democracy as well as the concept of (tacit) consent, but also the collective interest of individuals found in a certain territory in the provision of a public good. Similar conditions apply to jurisdiction based on the nationality of the addressee, the legitimacy of which is also found in somewhat incomplete justifications based on principles of democracy and an exchange of mutual benefits.

Concepts such as consent, interest in the protection of the law and *quid pro quo* all contribute to the search for legitimacy in the exercise of jurisdiction, but none of them can claim to be conclusive. This may be an unsatisfactory result but it also takes away the pressure of having to find the one mechanism of legitimacy to justify all hard cases of extraterritorial jurisdiction. Rather, it shows that legitimacy is an issue of perception and nuance. What these concepts have in common, however, and what may arguably lie at the heart of territoriality and nationality based jurisdiction in international law, is the idea that the closer and more purposeful someone associates him- or herself with a certain State, the more that State is legitimized to coerce that person through an exercise of public authority. However, this purposeful association may only be indicated by factors such as territoriality or nationality and may certainly be rebutted. For instance, overseas British citizens are only entitled to vote in UK parliamentary

---

1002 Ryngaert, *Jurisdiction in International Law* (n 2), at 106.
1003 Chehtman (n 999), 140.

elections for up to 15 years after leaving the UK.[1004] Given that, it may be questionable whether extending nationality jurisdiction to citizens, who have never lived on UK soil and thus never had any voting rights, is justifiable. Thus, the issue is not one of territoriality or nationality, but rather one of proximity, in the sense of a purposeful association, between the regulator and the addressee or his/her conduct in question.

An opposite example may further clarify the argument: Suppose that a French national is working as a long-time spy exclusively for the German government on Russian territory, and that person commits or is the victim of a serious crime in Russia. In this case, few would consider it unreasonable if the German government initiated action against him, in case he is the perpetrator, or against the perpetrators, in case he is the victim. This would be so even if nominally, Germany can neither rely on territoriality nor nationality as a basis for jurisdiction. Rather, it is the activity as a spy for the German government that creates a specific connection between the regulator and the addressee, which possibly legitimizes the exercise of German public authority.

#### b) Universality and Community Interests

Whether it is interpreted as (democratic) consent or as part of a *quid pro quo* scheme, the legitimacy of the two most acknowledged bases of jurisdiction hinges on the existence of some sort of proximity, traditionally mediated through territory or nationality, between the regulating State and the addressee. However, the existence of some kind of connection is not the only criteria relied upon to construct the legitimacy of exercises of jurisdiction. Universal jurisdiction in particular, though somewhat controversial, seems to cover certain conduct that lacks any physical connection to the regulating State. True enough, at least with regard to core crimes under international law, universal jurisdiction can boast its legitimacy through the positive consent of States, either through treaty or custom.[1005] However, it is far less clear whether this consent of the home State also extends, without restrictions, to the individuals as norm addressees and

1004 See on the British effort to repeal the 15-year rule: Neil Johnston, House of Commons Briefing Paper on Overseas Voters, Number 5923, 25 March 2019, available at https://commonslibrary.parliament.uk/research-briefings/sn05923/, last accessed on 13 April 2022.

1005 See Ryngaert, *Jurisdiction in International Law* (n 2), 193 – 194.

whether it is sufficient to subject them to possibly harsh consequences. In addition, there exists some dispute over the precise catalogue of crimes subject to universal jurisdiction and States have asserted this kind of jurisdiction also outside of the well-recognized core crimes under international law.[1006]

Rather, the justification for universal jurisdictions is often argued based on an overarching community interest in criminalizing certain internationally reprehensible conduct.[1007] Indeed, when the Second Circuit claims that its authority over individuals in Paraguay stems from the fact that, just like pirates, torturers are to be treated as *hostis humani generis*, an enemy of all mankind, it is alluding its legitimacy to the existence and interests of such a common community.[1008]

While the universality principle is the most obvious form of jurisdiction, which relies on community interests as a legitimising factor, it is by no means the only example. This study has discussed at length that the approval of extraterritorial jurisdiction in the areas of anti-corruption and business and human rights stem, at least partly, from the notion that regulations in these matters are supported by a global recognition in fighting certain conduct. Within academic debate, several authors have further explored the possibility to adopt unilateral, extraterritorial action legitimised through the pursuit of a global common good. For instance, Ryngaert, in his seminal work on jurisdiction in international law, posits as his core thesis, that the interests of the international community should take centre stage in any jurisdictional analysis. In particular, when the State with the closest physical connection to a situation fails to adequately remedy the harm, a bystander State may assert extraterritorial jurisdiction in a subsidiary manner, if doing so benefits the global community as a whole. This does not only apply to the pursuit of international justice in the context of core crimes subject to universal jurisdiction. With regard to antitrust regulation for example, global welfare becomes the yardstick. Thus, third States may legitimately intervene, if the home State of an export cartel is not willing to take action against the anticompetitive behaviour and if the economic damage suffered overall is negative on global welfare.[1009]

---

1006 See above at, B.I.2f) The Universality Principle.

1007 Ryngaert, *Jurisdiction in International Law* (n 2), 126 – 128.

1008 *Filartiga v Pena-Irala*, 630 F 2d 876, 887 (2d Cir 1980); see also Devika Hovell, 'The Authority of Universal Jurisdiction' (2018) 29(2) EJIL 427, 444.

1009 Ryngaert, *Jurisdiction in International Law* (n 2), for instance at 230.

There is, of course, debate over whether such an international community with a common purpose exists and whether it is possible to determine its interests without parochial subjective interpretation.[1010] To rephrase this argument in the words of President Guillaume, exercising universal jurisdiction would 'risk creating total judicial chaos. It would also be to encourage the arbitrary, for the benefit of the powerful, purportedly acting as agent for an ill-defined "international community"'.[1011] In response to this well-founded criticism, some commentators have switched from moral considerations based on shared humanity to more functional, and supposedly more objective, arguments.[1012] Particularly, the idea that unilateral extraterritorial action may receive its legitimacy by solving the dilemma of providing global public goods has gained noticeable traction. Public goods are characterized by the notion that they are both non-excludable, meaning that no one can be excluded from their benefits, and non-rivalrous in their consumption, i.e. the goods do not deteriorate if more people use them.[1013] Prime examples of global public goods may be the world climate or the non-proliferation of nuclear weapons. Theoretically, the provision of global public goods constitutes a particularly salient problem, because cooperative international efforts in these areas are often elusive.[1014] Thus, to the extent that in certain areas the efforts of single, powerful States may suffice to mitigate this issue, unilateral extraterritorial action may be legitimate.[1015]

It should be pointed out however that while the concept of global public goods allows for a more fact-based determination than the elusive international community interests, it is still fraught with risk of subjective abuse. Because what a particular State may regard as global public goods and whether or not unilateral or international action is warranted is as

1010 See generally on this concept, Bruno Simma, 'From Bilateralism to Community Interest in International Law' (1994) 250 Recueil des Cours 217, 233.

1011 *Arrest Warrant of 11 April 2000 (Democratic Republic of the Congo v Belgium)* (n 69), 43 (Judge Guillaume).

1012 Martti Koskenniemi, 'What Use for Sovereignty Today?' (2011) 1(1) Asian Journal of International Law 61.

1013 Krisch (n 10), 3.

1014 Ibid., 4.

1015 Some commentators claim that not only may extraterritorial action be legitimate, but also required, particularly in cases involving a human rights dimension, see above at C.V.3b) Extraterritorial Jurisdiction as a Matter of Obligation.

much a scientific as a political question.[1016] Concluding therefore, to the extent that universality may act as a factor legitimizing exercises of unilateral extraterritorial jurisdiction, extra attention has to be paid as to the determination of these international community interests or global public goods.

### c) Proximity, Community Interests and the Rule of Law

The lack of a global demos and the improbability of extending domestic electoral processes to foreigners means that legitimacy in extraterritorial jurisdiction will have to be negotiated in fundamentally different ways.[1017] The sections above have identified two potential criteria, the proximity, i.e. the purposeful association between the regulating State and the addressee or the conduct in question, and the realization of community interests or values, notwithstanding the question whether they are grounded in (quasi)-universal moral considerations or the desire to maintain certain public goods. While these two strands of arguments bear certain resemblance with the often proposed dichotomy of 'input-' and 'output legitimacy', it is important to point out that they are in fact not exactly identical. In particular, proximity between the State and the regulatory subject in itself provides no input legitimacy, which is often equated to being included in participatory processes and which is precisely not granted only because of proximity.[1018] Rather, the more a State can boast significant connections to an individual and the more an individual purposefully associates him- or herself with a State, the more an individual has to expect to be burdened by regulations of that State in a certain way and the more likely it is that the acts of the State respect overall considerations of fairness.

In fact, several authors point out that apart from democratic (input-) legitimacy and effectiveness based (output-) legitimacy, a third mechanism may legitimise the exercise of public authority, the upholding of the rule

---

1016 Finally, even if it is proven that the exercise of extraterritorial jurisdiction to uphold a global public good would result in net positive effects for justice or welfare, it would still create distributional effects that another State may not want to suffer.

1017 Simon Chesterman, 'Globalisation and Public law: A Global Administrative Law' in Jeremy M Farrall and Kim Rubenstein (eds), *Sanctions, Accountability and Governance in a Globalised World* (Connecting international law with public law. Cambridge University Press 2009), 88.

1018 Krisch (n 10), 6 – 7.

of law itself.[1019] The content of this principle is of course just as vague as the content of the other mechanisms of legitimacy and there is great debate in this regard beyond the well-accepted but trite requirement that public authority should be bound by law.[1020] While there may be formal and substantive components to the rule of law,[1021] Meyer correctly points out the commonality between all the different conceptions, which is to provide the individual, to a certain extent, protection against the State.[1022] In this regard therefore, legitimisation through the rule of law may overlap with the other function of public law, the limitation of exercises of public authority. Therefore, protecting the individual against State overreach and, more generally, upholding individual interest, form a third crucial component of a system of jurisdiction in international law based on the function of jurisdiction, i.e. the exercise of public authority in relation to individuals.

While the first two components, the proximity between the regulating State and the addressee or the conduct in question and the realization of community interests or values, feature prominently in academic debate, this last component may need some further elaboration. Therefore, the next chapter serves to appreciate the fact that already now, individual interests play a growing role when it comes to determining the reach of State jurisdiction. The considerations above concerning legitimacy through the protection of individuals and the upholding of individual interests are thus only continuations of a larger trend.

### 2. Individual Interests and State Jurisdiction

In a development parallel to the rise of shared global values and international community interests, State sovereignty has been increasingly curtailed by private rights and interests, a process beginning with the rise

1019 Armin von Bogdandy, 'Supranationale Union als neuer Herrschaftstypus: Entstaatlichung und Vergemeinschaftung in staatstheoretischer Perspektive' (1993) 16 Integration: Vierteljahreszeitschrift des Instituts für Europäische Politik in Zusammenarbeit mit dem Arbeitskreis Europäische Integration 210, 219 – 222; Meyer (n 983), 349.

1020 Tom Bingham, 'The Rule Of Law' (2007) 66 CLJ 67, 69.

1021 Formal components may include procedural safeguards such as participation, transparency and the possibility for judicial review, see below at D.II.4. Procedural Safeguards, Reasoning and Participation.

1022 Meyer (n 983), 352.

of international human rights and traveling to other areas of law from there.[1023] This development has been captured most passionately by Peters, who argues in favour of a paradigm shift, in which individuals bear *primary* international legal personality, possibly even independent from States.[1024] Whether or not one agrees with that proposition, the unquestionable strengthening of the position of individuals has been consequential in relation to the issue of State jurisdiction. The following sections explore the different ways in which individual interests are already now, within the traditional doctrine, shaping the reach of State jurisdiction. The focus is on three different but interrelated aspects, (1), how private party autonomy may possibly be engaged to shape State jurisdiction, (2), how individual fairness may serve as a principle restraining the exercise of jurisdiction and (3), how individual rights may lead to a duty for States to exercise jurisdiction. These already existing interactions between individual interests and the exercise of State competence call into question the belief that jurisdiction is strictly a matter of interstate relations and emphasise the argument in favour of a functional approach to jurisdiction.

#### a) The Potential for Individuals to Shape State Jurisdiction

The possibility for individuals to shape jurisdictional rules manifests itself across different subject areas. While it is most developed in relation to choice-of-law and choice-of-court agreements in private disputes, there are also examples in public regulatory law. Finally, individual consent may not only serve to extend the jurisdictional competence of a State to situations where it would have no regular basis, but in international investment law, it may carry the opposite effect and restrict the ordinary regulatory ambit of the State.

In matters of private international law, the decision whether a court will seize adjudicative jurisdiction and which law it will apply to a civil matter is generally grounded in considerations similar to those in public

1023 See *Prosecutor v Tadic* (Jurisdiction), No IT-94–1-AR72, (2 October 1995), 35 ILM (1996), para. 97: '[…] the impetuous development and propagation in the international community of human rights doctrines, particularly after the adoption of the Universal Declaration of Human Rights in 1948, has brought about significant changes in international law, notably in the approach to problems besetting the world community. A State-sovereignty-oriented approach has been gradually supplanted by a human-being-oriented approach'.

1024 Peters, *Jenseits der Menschenrechte* (n 954), at 364.

international law, namely, territorial or personal connections of the litigants to the forum.[1025] However, unlike in public international law, courts in private disputes are increasingly willing to disregard sovereign connections and instead to enforce private choice-of-law[1026] or choice-of-court agreements[1027] even in the absence of other significant connections to the forum.[1028]

However, what this development means for the issue of jurisdiction under public international law is less settled. Fundamentally, one might question whether the possibility to choose the applicable law and forum in private international law says anything at all about public international law positions. It has been argued that these two bodies are distinct in that private international law is primarily concerned with issues of private fairness and not with the allocation of regulatory authority between States. Thus, choice-of-law and choice-of-court agreements are possible because private international law rules are not constrained by traditional principles of jurisdiction in public international law.[1029] It has already been elaborated above that this strict division between the two areas of jurisdictional law is artificial as private law also reflects considerations of public policy.[1030] It is submitted that this (increasingly recognized) confluence of private and public international law does not mean that civil prescriptive and adjudicative jurisdiction necessarily need to follow the same rules as criminal or regulatory jurisdiction.[1031] However, this is not an issue reserved to the difference between civil and criminal or regulatory jurisdiction. In fact, as this study has demonstrated, even between particular regulatory subject areas, application of jurisdictional rules may be inconsistent.

Mills, therefore, attributes great significance to the fact that increasingly, State authorities defer to individual choice-of-law or choice-of-court agree-

1025 Mills (n 14), 203 – 207.

1026 See e.g., for torts, Art. 14 of the Rome II Regulation (2007).

1027 See e.g., Art. 5 of the Convention of 30 June 2005 on Choice of Court Agreements (adopted 30 June 2015, entered into force 1 October 2015).

1028 See on this more generally, Mills (n 14), 230 – 233.

1029 Akehurst (n 42), at 177: 'It is hard to resist the conclusion that [...] customary international law imposes no limits on the jurisdiction of municipal courts in civil trials'.

1030 *Restatement (Fourth) of the Foreign Relations Law of the United States* (n 42), § 407, reporters' notes 5; Svantesson (n 13), 84 – 85; see above at A.III.5. Regulation, Public Law and Jurisdiction.

1031 For civil prescriptive jurisdiction, Crawford and Brownlie (n 18), at 472; *Restatement (Fourth) of the Foreign Relations Law of the United States* (n 42), § 407, reporters' notes 5.

ments in private international law. He claims that instead of arguing that private international law requires a distinct set of rules, the more consistent solution would be to accept that public international law recognizes, to a certain extent, individuals' power to shape the regulatory authority of States.[1032] One could also argue that a private party's choice of applicable law or forum would at least constitute a significant connection to the chosen State that is ordinarily to be respected also by public authorities.[1033]

These ideas have some merit, not least because similar examples can also be found in areas traditionally having a much stronger public law dimension. For instance, in the area of securities regulation, several US courts have acknowledged the possibility for private parties to contract out of US provisions, including the (strict) security fraud rules of the Securities Act, the Securities Exchange Act and RICO, despite the fact that these acts contained anti-waiver provisions.[1034] This jurisprudence has prompted Choi and Guzman to go one-step further and propose that issuers and investors to security transactions should be able to choose the particular securities regulation applicable to their transaction.[1035] In a similar vein, the previous chapter has already explored how in the area of export control regulations, US authorities have sought to extend their jurisdiction extraterritorially through consent by the purchaser abroad and this sort of agreement has been used to assert both prescriptive and enforcement jurisdiction.[1036] State practice and academic commentary on the validity of private submissions and agreements are contested but they unquestionably carry practical and possibly legal consequences.

---

1032 Mills (n 14), 233 – 234.

1033 Svantesson (n 13), 70.

1034 *Roby v Corporation of Lloyd's*, 996 F 2d 1353, 1366 (2d Cir 1993); to be fair, the court did not blindly follow the private agreement but examined the 'serious question whether United States public policy has been subverted by the Lloyd's clauses', namely the protection of American investors and deterring injuries. In the end, it concluded that because English law provided "adequate remedies", the contractual stipulations should be enforced. Other, similar cases include *Allen v Lloyd's of London*, 94 F 3d 923, 930 – 932 (4th Cir 1996); *Riley v Kingsley Underwriting Agencies*, Ltd, 969 F 2d 953, 957 – 958 (10th Cir 1992).

1035 Stephen J Choi and Andrew T Guzman, 'Portable Reciprocity – Rethinking the International Reach of Securities Regulation' 1997 Southern California Law Review 903.

1036 See above at C.III.4. Jurisdiction Based on Voluntary Submission; the inclusion of enforcement jurisdiction is especially problematic; see also Akehurst (n 42), 147: 'the consent of the individuals […] is irrelevant; the act is a usurpation of the sovereign powers of the local State, which cannot be cured by the consent of the private individuals'.

Finally, international investment law, an area with great significance to economic globalization, may provide the clearest example to just how much issues of State jurisdiction may be 'privatised'. The regulation of foreign direct investment is usually operated through two distinct but connected set of rules, a (typically bilateral) investment treaty between States and, in relation to any specific investment, a contract between investor and host State.[1037] This second type of State contracts has drawn significant attention because of the inclusion of 'stabilization' and 'choice-of-law' clauses that seek to ensure the protection of the investor against the host State.[1038] The possibility for private parties to agree on the application of a certain law without any territorial connection has already been treated above. What makes the present context more interesting, however, is that it is possible for a sovereign State, through a choice-of-law clause included in a contract with a private investor, to partly renounce its regulatory authority. This is significant because unlike choice-of-law agreements in private contracts or private submissions in export control cases, party autonomy here does not serve to expand State jurisdiction, but to curtail it. A similar effect is also achieved by stabilization clauses, in which the host State sometimes agrees to exempt foreign investors to changes to their legislative framework. Here again, the sovereign State, through private contract, is renouncing its power to assert regulatory jurisdiction *vis-à-vis* a private party in its territory.[1039]

### b) Individual Fairness as a Principle Restraining the Exercise of Jurisdiction

Despite the fact that individuals or private entities often bear the cost for extensive jurisdictional assertions leading to concurrent or conflicting regulations, their interests have often been treated as secondary next to ordinary State interests. So far, the principles developed by jurisprudence and literature to restrain the exercise of State jurisdiction, such as comity

---

1037 Karsten Nowrot, 'Steuerungssubjekt und -mechanismen im Internationalen Wirtschaftsrecht (einschließlich regionale Wirtschaftsintegration)' in Christian Tietje (ed), *Internationales Wirtschaftsrecht* (2. Aufl. De Gruyter 2015), 109 – 110.

1038 See on this Crawford and Brownlie (n 18), 629 – 633.

1039 Alessandra Arcuri and Federica Violi, 'Reconfiguring Territoriality in International Economic Law' in Martin Kuijer and Wouter Werner (eds), *Netherlands Yearbook of International Law 2016* (T.M.C. Asser Press 2017), 198 – 200.

and reasonableness, overwhelmingly rely on the balancing of sovereign interests and deference to other States.[1040] Sure enough, the famous § 403 of the Restatement Third does include private considerations into its multifactor balancing test, but as discussed above, this approach should be rejected for other reasons.[1041] Under these circumstances, it is certainly surprising that in the revival of Council Regulation (EC) No 2271/96, the EU blocking statute, the safeguarding of individual interests takes centre-stage.[1042] According to the Explanatory Memorandum, the EU views the US sanctions against Iran as violating international law, 'in so far as they unduly affect the interests of natural and legal persons established in the Union'.[1043] The significance of this statement is that it makes individual interests the yardstick for gauging whether certain measures are normatively prohibited under *international* law.

To be sure, one might question whether such a change in focus makes any difference in practice since ordinarily, the individual interest of not being subjected to exorbitant or conflicting jurisdiction may largely be mediated through the interests of their respective nation State. For instance, if certain conduct that is required by a State's extraterritorial regulation is prohibited by the territorial State (e.g. through a blocking statute), it may raise issues under the principle of non-intervention. At the same time, these situations, sometimes referred to as foreign sovereign compulsion or true conflict, compromise individual rights since it is *de facto* impossible for the affected person to comply with both sets of rules at the same time.[1044] However, this alignment between individual and State interest may not always be the case. This point is illustrated by a number of US extraterritorial drug enforcement cases. In *United States v Cardales* for in-

1040 B.II. Principles Restraining the Exercise of Jurisdiction.

1041 See above at B.II.3. Reasonableness; According to *Restatement (Third) of the Foreign Relations Law of the United States* (n 5), § 403 (2), the reasonableness of an exercise of jurisdiction depends *inter alia* on 'the connections […] between the regulating state and the person principally responsible for the activity […]' and on 'the existence of justified expectations that might be protected or hurt by the regulation'.

1042 On the background of this regulation, see above at C.II.1c)bb) US Sanctions against Iran.

1043 Explanatory Memorandum to Commission Delegated Regulation (EU) …/… amending the Annex to Council Regulation (EC) No 2271/96 of 22 November 1996 protecting against the effects of extra-territorial application of legislation adopted by a third country, and actions based thereon or resulting therefrom, C(2018) 3572 final.

1044 *Hartford Fire Ins. Co. v California* 509 US 764, 798 (1993).

stance, the defendants were seized on board of a Venezuelan flagged vessel some 150 miles south of Puerto Rico and charged with drug trafficking related offenses. They protested that the US constitutional Due Process Clause required that there be a nexus between their conduct and the United States. However, the First Circuit held that it was enough if the exercise of extraterritorial jurisdiction comported with international law principles, which was the case since Venezuela, the flag State, had explicitly consented to the search, seizure, and subsequent prosecution under US law.[1045] Equally, divergence between individual and State interest may occur in the opposite case, when an individual or private entity voluntarily submits itself to the application of foreign law without the consent of the home State, as was noticed in the examples on export control.[1046]

The increasing recognition by States, that individual fairness may diverge from home State interests of non-intervention and may thus constitute a factor restraining extraterritorial jurisdiction in its own rights is to be welcomed. This is particularly true in light of the considerations above, where upholding the rule of law has been identified as a factor legitimizing the exercise of public authority in general. However, this shift may not only be normatively warranted, given that individual and State interests may diverge, but it may also be more applicable in practice as in particular, courts are more used to interpreting issues of individual interests and rights than to balancing sovereign considerations. It may also make more nuanced decisions possible, as it may be easier to determine the intrusiveness or impact of a measure on an individual or private entity than in relation to a State, where a range of diplomatic and other political considerations might come into play.

In practice, given the wide assertions and inconsistent application of jurisdictional rules of extraterritoriality, the individual's interest to be able to know what the law is and foresee which laws might apply to his or her conduct in any given situation may provide a useful yardstick in this matter. Bingham views the principle that 'the law must be accessible and so far as possible, be intelligible, clear and predictable', as one of the core principles of the rule of law.[1047] Thus, if an individual could not have reasonably expected that certain extraterritorial regulations would apply under a particular foreign circumstance, this may raise issues under due process aspects. Several authors have examined this issue and proposed that

---

1045 *United States v Cardales*, 168 F 3d 548, 553 (1st Cir 1999).

1046 See above at C.III.4. Jurisdiction Based on Voluntary Submission.

1047 Bingham (n 1020), 69.

domestic and international law principles mirror these considerations to limit such unfair assertions of jurisdiction and possibly allow individuals to challenge such regulations.[1048] In conclusion therefore, the increasing recognition by States of individual rights and interests as equal to interstate sovereignty for the purpose of restraining the exercise of extraterritorial jurisdiction may not only be normatively more appealing, but also be better-suited for practical application.

### c) Individual Rights Catalysing the Exercise of Jurisdiction

Individual interests may not only shape the jurisdictional reach of States through party autonomy or function as a principle restraining the exercise of (possibly exorbitant) jurisdiction, but also, in a third dimension, compel or obligate States to exercise extraterritorial jurisdiction in the first place. Such jurisdictional duties owed towards individuals may arise out of the international law concept of denial of justice or, more commonly, international human rights.[1049] A prominent example of this is the abovementioned *forum necessitatis*, which allows courts to exercise adjudicative jurisdiction absent any other connecting factor between the case and the forum, if doing otherwise would risk infringing the claimant's right to access to justice. *Forum necessitatis* has found modest acceptance in a number of cases in courts around Europe, the most high profile of which concerned a suit brought in France by ex-employees of a Gabonese mining company in relation to unjust employment termination and failure to provide compensation.[1050]

A comparable obligation to regulate extraterritorially, which stems from a duty to protect individual rights, seems to exist in the area of data protection.[1051] Article 8 of the ECHR not only requires States to refrain from arbitrary interference with individuals' private lives, but also establishes a positive obligation including 'the adoption of measures designed to secure respect for private life even in the sphere of the relations of individuals between themselves'.[1052] In relation to data protection as part

1048 This idea is expanded in Colangelo, 'Spatial Legality' (n 48), at 77; Danielle Ireland-Piper, 'Prosecutions of Extraterritorial Criminal Conduct and the Abuse of Rights Doctrine' (2013) 9(4) ULR 68, 84.

1049 For a detailed account of both notions, see Mills (n 14), 213 – 226.

1050 See above C.V.5b) Practice in Europe.

1051 Uecker (n 140), 162.

1052 ECtHR, *K.U. v. Finland*, App No 2872/02, Judgment of 2 December 2008.

of the substantive content of Article 8 ECHR, this means that States not only need to justify their own data processing activities, but they have to establish an appropriate level of data protection *vis-à-vis* private companies engaged in the processing of individuals' data. For the maximum effective protection of individual rights, it should not make a difference whether the processor is domiciled within domestic territory or abroad. In other words, international human rights law may require States to regulate companies extraterritorially that are interfering with the enjoyment of data protection of individuals under their jurisdiction.[1053]

It is submitted here that such a duty to exercise extraterritorial jurisdiction to vindicate individual rights has not been conclusively established *de lege lata*. However, similar to the recognition of individual interests as a principle restraining the exercise of jurisdiction, the emergence and growing importance of fundamental rights should factor into the process of interest balancing.[1054] Under this conception, a State's possibility to regulate extraterritorially may have to be balanced against individual interests in a dual way, through a positive obligation with regard to the protection of fundamental rights and through a negative duty to refrain from undue interference. Such settings are not unknown in domestic situations and it comes as no surprise that they may play out in similar terms in transnational arenas. After all, increasing international personal and legal connections also mean that a multitude of foreign actors, in addition to domestic ones, may affect individuals' enjoyment of their rights.

### 3. Conclusion

This chapter has argued that it is possible to base the doctrine of jurisdiction in international law, which has traditionally found legitimation in State sovereignty, on a somewhat different theoretical foundation centred around the function of extraterritorial jurisdiction as an exercise of public authority, and in particular, the protection of individual rights and interests.

To this end, this chapter has examined the different grounds of legitimacy put forward by commentators to justify the exercise of public authority

---

1053 Uecker (n 140), 162; the regulation of foreign private companies with regard to data protection is discussed by Walter (n 986), 384 as an example of a modern concept of 'Steuerung' or 'steering' in public international law.

1054 Uecker (n 140), 200 – 204.

based on traditional principles of jurisdiction, such as territoriality, nationality and universality. It has demonstrated, that, far from being grounded in democracy, even these widely accepted principles of jurisdiction have to rely on a host of explanations. Rather, three cardinal considerations legitimizing and limiting exercises of (extra-)territorial jurisdiction emerge from the analysis, the proximity between the regulating State and the addressee or the conduct in question, the realization of community interests or the maintenance of global public goods and the upholding of individual interests as part of the rule of law.

This chapter has then dedicated closer attention to this last aspect: It has argued that already now, individual interests play a growing role in shaping the reach of State jurisdiction, either through the possibility of determining the proper jurisdiction through party autonomy, as a principle restraining the exercise of (possibly exorbitant) jurisdiction, or as a right compelling or obligating States to exercise extraterritorial jurisdiction.

## III. A more Desirable Framework

As noted above, the territoriality based system of jurisdiction in international law leaves much to be desired both because it does not allow for the consideration of important interests apart from State sovereignty and because of its inefficacy of providing order in international relations. In particular, because there are no normatively consistent boundaries of territoriality, States have been able to nominally rely on territoriality while actually setting regulations with a global reach. It is clear that this situation in practice contradicts the purpose of the territoriality-based system of jurisdiction.[1055] However, because this study has particularly lamented the deficiency of the traditional approach in practice, it is the objective of this chapter to lay down the foundations for an applicable jurisdictional framework. Thus, this chapter proves that the considerations above, proximity, community interest and the protection of individual rights and interests, not only provide a good theoretical footing, but that they may be translated into practical variables and tests as well.

To this end, section 1 briefly describes which practical challenges such a new framework must meet in order to be successful in an increasingly

1055 See above at C.VI. Synthesis: The Deficient Territoriality-based System.

complex global order.[1056] It then proposes a number of concrete variables based on the three cardinal considerations legitimizing and limiting exercises of extraterritorial jurisdiction explored above (section 2) before explaining the relationship between these (section 3). Section 4 then goes on to examine certain procedural mechanisms to operationalize the framework. Section 5 puts the framework into practice by applying its principles to the complex regulatory mechanisms identified in part C of this study, which have proven to be particularly challenging for the territoriality-based system of jurisdiction. Section 6 finally anticipates and discusses potential objections to the proposed framework.

### 1. Practical Requirements and Objectives of the New Framework

The theoretical premise so far has been that, *de lege ferenda*, an exercise of extraterritorial jurisdiction should acknowledge the hybrid nature of extraterritorial jurisdiction, in that it also functions as an exercise of public authority. Therefore, the new framework should consider aspects of legitimation and limits inspired by domestic public law, alongside the still prominent category of State sovereignty. Practitioners, that is legislators, administrative agencies and courts, pondering the adoption of legal acts with extraterritorial implications, need to know whether these requirements are satisfied in any given case. While the theoretical considerations always lurk behind any exercise of extraterritorial jurisdiction, they contain principles that few people outside the academic sphere are familiar with. The following is therefore an attempt to flesh out terms and variables that have seen more action in practice. It is equally important to work out how these variables relate to each other in their application. In fact, this has been an issue for which § 403 of the Restatement Third was particularly criticized on, that its free multifactor balancing tests contained no reference whatsoever on how to prioritize or organize the different relevant aspects.[1057]

It is submitted here that, today, issues of extraterritorial jurisdiction are frequently solved through political and diplomatic channels. Nonetheless, the proposed framework relies exclusively on legal factors. Two reasons

1056 A similar approach is taken by Coughlan and others (n 158) at 300 though in addition, they also deal with the question when it is advisable for a State to exercise extraterritorial jurisdiction.

1057 See above at B.II.3. Reasonableness.

suggest this approach. On the one hand, it is important that any framework should be of some use to all three – the legislative, executive and judicial – branches of government involved in the exercise of extraterritorial jurisdiction. In this regard, it should be recalled that particularly in Europe, courts historically have had an uneasy relationship with discretionary balancing of sovereign interests and are more comfortable with rule-based principles.[1058] Moreover, if the framework is to potentially protect the interests of individuals, than the inclusion of political factors would contradict this goal. It is already hard enough to predict how rather open legal variables will be interpreted in practice; however, it would be near impossible for individuals to foresee political aspects in the exercise of extraterritorial jurisdiction.

In this regard, it should already be noted that a certain openness of the jurisdictional framework may be necessary. In fact, in a rapidly changing world shaped by economic globalization technological advances and new threats such as climate change, flexibility may be the most important requirement to any future-proof jurisdictional framework. It would be quite utopian to try to suggest legal principles that can capture every eventuality of complex regulatory mechanisms, today or in the future. Flexibility may be one of the reasons that jurisdiction based on territoriality survived such considerable time. It is arguable that without the recognition of the effects doctrine in the 1950s as an answer to the rise of the modern corporation, the current jurisdictional framework would have been abandoned much earlier. Today, long-settled rules are again in flux.[1059] Thus, a successful framework needs to accept that connections and interests, which legitimize a State to regulate, may change and hitherto unknown connections and interests may develop. How this framework is therefore applied and interpreted *in concreto* may be best found out through case-law and future academic discourse.[1060] In particular, it is expected that on a more granular level, the precise contours of the overarching principles proposed below may differ according to the specific subject matter and interests in question.

---

1058 Ryngaert, *Jurisdiction in International Law* (n 2), 172 – 173; advocating for greater reliance on rules, also Jeffrey A Meyer, 'Dual Illegality and Geoambiguous Law: A New Rule for Extraterritorial Application of U.S. Law' (2010) 95 Minnesota Law Review 110, 120.

1059 See on this: Paul S Berman, 'Legal Jurisdiction and the Deterritorialization of Data' (2018) 71 Vanderbilt Law Review 11, 16.

1060 This approach is also advocated by Svantesson (n 13), 59 – 62.

It is equally clear that there is not one perfect solution to the balance between stability, based on fixed criteria and rules, and individual justice, which may require additional discretion and flexibility. Nonetheless, having considered some preliminary issues on what such a new framework might set out to achieve, the next section tries to fulfil, at least partly, these ambitions by looking at possible variables and tests for this purpose before analysing how these may interoperate in practice.

## 2. The Variables Determining the Legitimacy of Extraterritorial Jurisdiction

### a) Proximity and Substantial Connection

This study has shown above that proximity, as one of the aspects legitimizing extraterritorial jurisdiction, is frequently mediated through factual connections between the regulating State and the addressee or the subject matter. Thus, the more substantial and more purposeful the connections between the two, the more likely extraterritorial jurisdiction will be perceived as justified. This is not surprising and in fact, most would argue that the existence of a connection between the regulating State and the subject of the regulation provides one, if not the most important variable for the normative assessment of exercises of jurisdiction.[1061] After all, it could be argued that the traditional bases of jurisdiction, territoriality, active and passive personality, the protective principle and even the effects doctrine are nothing more than mere applications of this core idea.[1062] According to Crawford therefore, the 'genuine connection between the subject-matter of jurisdiction and the territorial base or reasonable interests of the state in question' can even be summarised as the cardinal principle in this area.[1063]

The dominance of the concept of connection in relation to exercises of jurisdiction is also mirrored in practice, and, as shown above, there are only very few examples of 'extraterritorial' regulations that boast no connecting factor of any kind to the regulating State. Even extraordinary exercises of jurisdiction, such as economic sanctions based on the use

1061 *Restatement (Fourth) of the Foreign Relations Law of the United States* (n 42), § 407; Lowe and Staker (n 50), 295.

1062 Svantesson (n 13), 58.

1063 Crawford and Brownlie (n 18), 457.

of correspondent account banking can at least nominally advance some connection.[1064] An exception to this general finding may be assertions of jurisdiction based on private submission or consent of the affected. However, even in these scenarios it could be argued that the consent itself creates a purposeful connection between the State and the addressee to be regulated.[1065]

Thus, one might question whether falling back to the general variable of proximity would, in practice, make any difference compared to the traditional reliance on one of the enumerated jurisdictional bases. Several aspects indeed suggest that this approach would provide additional value to the doctrinal framework.

First and as already hinted at above, it allows for a more holistic analysis of the ties between an entire situation and the regulating State. Traditionally, the territoriality assessment has focused on (1) whether at least part of the conduct or the situation in question has occurred within domestic territory and (2) whether that territorial part of the conduct or situation is 'relevant' in a normative sense that it triggers the legitimate exercise of jurisdiction. This line of argumentation is for instance frequently used in relation to secondary boycotts levied against foreign companies. In these instances, the foreign companies are prohibited from trading with another third country, the primary target of the boycott, where non-compliance with this obligation may carry sensitive sanctions.[1066] Here, the territorial connection lies in the threatened sanctions themselves, which frequently include the withdrawal of domestic economic benefits or even a cut-off from the domestic market. In this example, the traditional line of argumentation generally leads to a piecemeal all-or-nothing solution: Either, one considers the territorial quality of the sanctions to be 'irrelevant' as it only relates to the enforcement of an otherwise extraterritorial prohibition, or, one considers it 'relevant', in which case all secondary boycotts would be permitted under the territoriality principle.[1067] This binary inquiry should give way for a more holistic approach, which allows the focus

1064 See above at C.II.3. Territoriality and US Dollar Transactions by non-US Financial Institutions.

1065 This is also argued by Svantesson (n 13), 70.

1066 On secondary boycotts, see above at C.II.4. Secondary Trade Boycotts.

1067 Colangelo, 'A Unified Approach to Extraterritoriality' (n 83), at 1044 offers a similar critique to the US presumption against extraterritoriality, which, according to him, localizes an entire multijurisdictional claim based on a single element. For some elaboration on the presumption against extraterritoriality, see above at B.I.2a)bb) The US Presumption against Extraterritoriality.

to shift to the more pertinent questions, more precisely, *what kind* of connection exists between the regulating State and the situation and *how strong and purposeful* this connection is.

Second, the reliance on an enumerated list of jurisdictional bases obscures the fact that there might be other types of connections creating proximity, but which do not neatly fit into one of the existing principles. For instance, Sec. 7 of the UK Bribery Act contains organizational duties applicable to all foreign companies in their global operations as long as they conduct at least part of their business in the UK. However, despite the indisputable existence of proximity between the foreign company and the UK through the 'business presence' of the company, Sec. 7 of the UK Bribery Act may not satisfy the requirements of neither territoriality nor nationality.[1068] Rather, the jurisdictional trigger of 'business presence' seems to be a hybrid combining elements of the two more traditional principles.[1069] To give another example, the application of the new EU GDPR to foreign data processors similarly seems to rely on a combination of acknowledged principles, in this case that of effects and personality.[1070] This aspect also differentiates the concept of proximity used here from the doctrine of 'genuine connection'. As elaborated above, genuine connection has been discussed as a principle possibly limiting exorbitant exercises of jurisdiction, which may otherwise rely on one of the enumerated bases. Proximity as used in this framework also serves the opposite: it expands extraterritorial jurisdiction to cases, in which traditional permissive principles would not apply.

Most importantly, one should not forget that the question, whether a connection exists (or how strong that connection is) between a State and the subject of regulation, is rarely a purely physical matter but that it is also a normative exercise. This is most clearly exemplified in jurisdictional assertions based on the use of correspondent account banking. As discussed above, most monetary transactions denominated in US dollar technically pass through US domestic banks because of the specific way the financial system was set up. This territorial connection is physically important, as any US bank involved in such a transaction has the possibil-

1068 The territoriality principle is not satisfied as the organizational duties prescribed by Section 7 of the UK Bribery Act would likely have to be implemented outside the UK.

1069 See above at C.VI.1c) Regulation of Conduct Based on Only Fleeting Territorial Connections or Based on Territorial 'Presence'.

1070 See Uecker (n 140), 177.

ity to halt the process and thus stop the US dollar transfer.[1071] On the other hand, however, if both the sender and the receiver of the transfer are located in third countries and both parties did not know about the specificities of the US banking system, then the (territorial) passage of financial data through the United States would seem rather random from the perspective of both parties. From a normative perspective therefore, proximity between the subject matter and the United States may not exist, because neither of the two private parties involved purposefully used the US banking system.[1072] A binary test that simply searches for the existence or not of certain connections obscures these nuances and may fail to recognize that a physically significant territorial connection, the location of financial data, may not be particularly important in relation to the entire situation after a normative analysis.

### b) Legitimate Interest and the Subject Matter of Regulation

It has already been argued above that apart from proximity, extraterritorial jurisdiction may also be legitimised through the interest (or purpose) of the regulatory subject matter.[1073] Within the territoriality-centred doctrine on jurisdiction in international law, the regulatory subject matter and the underlying interest only play a marginal role. They are, in theory at least, irrelevant. To achieve this doctrinal purity, considerations of interests are sometimes disguised as arguments about the existence or not of territorial or non-territorial connections. Indeed, this tactic works well with regard to situations, in which the regulatory interest pursued overlaps with the underlying facts creating a relationship of proximity between the regulating State and the addressee. This is evidenced for instance in the case of the effects doctrine, where the negative externalities on domestic competition create a connection between the regulating State and the conduct while at the same time, the restriction of those externalities is the primary regula-

1071 See above at C.II.3. Territoriality and US Dollar Transactions by non-US Financial Institutions.

1072 Berman argues in a similar manner and terms this normative exercise the search for community affiliations, Berman, 'Legal Jurisdiction and the Deterritorialization of Data' (n 1059), 24 – 25.

1073 See also Meng, *Extraterritoriale Jurisdiktion im öffentlichen Wirtschaftsrecht* (n 43), 459.

tory interest for such jurisdictional assertions.[1074] In these scenarios, there is not much gained through a separate analysis of regulatory interests.

However, the limits of this doctrinal purity is found especially with regard to the pursuit of certain, widely shared or internationally recognized interests. Here, the traditional approach can barely explain why certain regulatory objectives may justify broader assertions of jurisdiction over addressees or conduct, which lack a connection to the regulating State. For instance, with regard to universal jurisdiction, it is sometimes argued that the heinousness of the crimes subject to universal jurisdiction not only creates a legitimate interest, but also an actual connection, albeit a normative one, between the matter and any State willing to regulate.[1075] This is not an outrageous claim, because, as we argued, the notion of proximity and connection is as much subject to physical as it is to normative considerations. However, it is contended here that this argument still seems to be somewhat artificial. In particular, the recognition of universal jurisdiction over the crime of piracy, the defining feature of which is that it lacks physical connections to any State, advises against going down the road of normative interpretation. To argue that precisely this lack of physical connections leads to the development of normative proximity seems quite unpersuasive. Thus, as already discussed above, it would be more convincing to justify universal jurisdictions based on an overarching interest in criminalizing certain internationally reprehensible conduct rather than in the existence of a normative connection between the regulating State and the subject matter.[1076]

While the pursuit of certain interests may justify broader assertions of jurisdiction, it should be noted that just because a certain law, executive action or judgment is not meant to realize an international interest, does not automatically make it illegitimate. In fact, States in reality exercise jurisdiction in pursuit of a whole range of interests, only few of which are also 'international' in nature. These interests include not only aspects related to the traditional principles of sovereignty and self-determination such as national security and the interest to determine freely the political, economic, social and cultural structure but also the protection of the rights of individuals under the jurisdiction of the State.[1077] Thus, at the outset, as long as an activity may affect the State exercising jurisdiction, this State

---

1074 Ibid., Meng terms this Ordnungshoheit.
1075 This is the approach taken by Svantesson (n 13), 60.
1076 See above at B.I.2f) The Universality Principle.
1077 Ziegenhain (n 59), 246 – 427.

may have an interest in regulating that subject matter and it would be untenable to regard all these measures as generally illegitimate.[1078]

Instead, the following distinctions may prove to be useful:

First, if a State enacts regulation that pursues no legitimate interest of any kind and is only meant to produce mischief in a third country, this regulation may violate the principle of abuse of rights even if it can nominally advance a significant connection between the State and the situation in question.[1079]

Second, if a State pursues any interest at all, these may be categorized according to the physical location of the concern or the focus of the interest. On the one hand, there are extraterritorial regulations, the primary objective of which is to protect certain domestic interests from harm originating abroad, and on the other hand, there are those measures employed to remedy a genuinely foreign or global situation. We may term these two different types of regulation as inward-looking and outward-looking respectively.[1080] It is especially with regard to outward-looking regulations, in which the international recognition of the interest pursued may influence the legitimacy of these measures, as, by their nature, these interests do not have a domestic focus or a concern located within domestic territory. For these cases, it is often presumed that an otherwise questionable exercise of jurisdiction may be less contentious if it is designed to remedy a particularly weighty shared interest.[1081] This is the argument at the heart of the analysis of extraterritorial anti-corruption legislation, where this research has found that despite the often very intrusive measures, States have only very rarely offered protest in return.[1082] Thus, when the regulation of a particular subject matter is recognized as a global instead of a purely parochial interest, broader jurisdictional claims may be sustained.

---

1078 Ryngaert, *Jurisdiction in International Law* (n 2), 39.

1079 See above at B.II.1b) Abuse of Rights.

1080 See already above at C.I. Focus and Structure.

1081 See for instance Zerk (n 634), 213; Cedric Ryngaert and Marieke Koekkoek, 'Extraterritorial Regulation of Natural Resources: a Functional Approach' in Jan Wouters and others (eds), *Global Governance through Trade: EU Policies and Approaches* (Leuven Global Governance. Edward Elgar Publishing 2015), 265 – 268; Cooreman (n 38), at 138: '[…] jurisdictional boundaries can be more elastic when common norms are concerned'.

1082 See also Avi-Yonah (n 237), 17 – 20 who emphasizes that extraterritoriality is justified because the regulation of corruption requires extraterritoriality and the underlying norms are shared across jurisdictions.

The issue remains as to how one may determine how regionally or globally shared the regulation of a particular subject matter is. In the first place, States might refer to treaties that contain shared norms prescribing certain conduct, such as the UNCAC in the case of anti-corruption regulation.[1083] Where no specific treaties exist, States may also fall back onto other documents proclaiming a shared interest in the matter as well as soft law commitments, which for instance play a significant role in the area of environmental protection.[1084] Finally and as already mentioned above, recognized interests should not be limited to genuine *State* interests, but also extend to private and individual concerns. Thus, a jurisdictional exercise aimed at redressing human rights violations in a third country should not only look to the shared community interest of upholding human rights but also evaluate the position of the individual victim in an equal manner.[1085]

### c) The Intrusiveness of the Measure

Lastly, the normative validity of extraterritorial jurisdiction cannot be reasonably assessed without some reference to the content of the measure at issue and to the question, whether and how it restrains the rights of other States and individuals or harms their legitimate interests.[1086] These considerations reflect possible limitations to jurisdiction as exercises of public authority and as already argued above, individual interests should feature in equal importance next to arguments of State sovereignty.

The essential variable to accomplish meaningful limitations may be that of 'intrusiveness', which already now has featured in some arguments about exercises of extraterritorial jurisdiction. The Sarbanes-Oxley Act provides an apt example in this regard. The Act prescribed rather strict organizational and transparency obligations on non-US issuers as well as foreign audit firms with US-listed clients. The EU strongly criticized these provi-

---

1083 This is the central element of Meyer's approach to extraterritoriality who argues that courts should exercise extraterritorial jurisdiction only if the requirement of dual criminality is satisfied. With regard to corruption, see Meyer, 'Dual Illegality and Geoambiguous Law: A New Rule for Extraterritorial Application of U.S. Law' (n 1058), 170.

1084 Cooreman (n 38), 140 – 148.

1085 See above in particular the concept of *forum necessitatis* at C.V.5. Transnational Human Rights Litigation.

1086 Compare also the central role intrusiveness takes up in the conception of Svantesson (n 13), 165; see also Ziegenhain (n 59), 246.

sions on a number of occasions. However, their main thrust of arguments was not focused on a lack of US territorial connection or a misguided domestic interest, but rather on the fact that the measures contained in the Sarbanes-Oxley Act were deemed to be ineffective, disproportionate and unnecessary.[1087]

Because measures with extraterritorial implications come in all kinds of shapes and designs, it is hard to give precise guidelines for the determination of their intrusiveness. With regard to (in a broad sense) economic regulation, a starting point would be that the more a measure requires its addressees to change their conduct and the more costs the measure causes, the more intrusive the measure is. This is true with regard to the individual or the company affected but also the home State, as measures that are more intrusive generally also lead to a stronger intervention with domestic regulatory frameworks.

Apart from the already mentioned Sarbanes-Oxley Act, an example illustrating this aspect is provided by different human rights related supply chain regulations discussed above. While the CTSCA and the UK Modern Slavery Act only require corporate disclosure as regards to whether certain efforts have been made to combat forced labour and human trafficking along the supply chain, the French law on 'devoir de vigilance' actually requires companies to implement oversight over the supply chain through concrete measures.[1088] Thus, it is rather straightforward to see that the compliance burden on companies (notwithstanding individual differences) is greater in the latter case.[1089]

In relation to this point, it is also important to note that States have certain tools at their disposal to limit the intrusiveness of their extraterritorial measures, in particular by injecting them with flexibility through the granting of exceptions or waivers. With regard to the interests of other States, the principle of mutual recognition may also go a long way. This principle allows another State, when the underlying conditions and standards are largely shared, to make its own determinations with regard to the precise content of its rules. In addition, by recognizing the regulatory

1087 See Comment by the EU Commission Internal Market Director-General Alexander Schaub to the Secretary of the SEC, https://www.sec.gov/rules/proposed/s74902/aschaub1.htm, last accessed on 13 April 2022; Zerk (n 634), 63.

1088 See above at C.V.4b) Mandatory Supply Chain Regulation and C.V.4c) Disclosure and Transparency Requirements.

1089 A similar analysis is undertaken by Dobson and Ryngaert (n 118), 331, with regard to EU regulations on maritime emissions.

framework of another State as essentially equal, mutual recognition shows a certain degree of deference and respect.[1090]

While the above holds largely true also with regard to domestic law, extraterritorial regulation includes another rather unique aspect that may have some bearing on its degree of intrusiveness. Because enforcement jurisdiction is in principle territorially circumscribed, extraterritorial prescriptions of conduct need to recourse to different means to lend them effect. Sometimes, extraterritorial regulations carry no rules of 'enforcement' of any kind while at other times, they may rely on private contractual mechanisms while again at other times, violations may be sanctioned with the withdrawal of domestic benefits, restriction of market access and other harsh territorial measures.[1091] Thus, exercises of extraterritorial jurisdiction differ in their strength of the disincentives provided to discourage their addresses to break the regulation, or in other words, in their degree of persuasiveness.[1092] Because of that, it could be argued that extraterritorial regulations with stronger persuasive force are more intrusive. This makes sense considering that the regulatory subjects are more likely to comply with the foreign prescription under the threat of more coercive sanctions and thus, that these regulations also lead to a stronger degree of interference with domestic affairs from a sovereignty perspective.

### 3. The Relationship between the Variables

The three criteria identified above and their more precise conceptualization reflect considerations of legitimacy and limits to exercises of public authority *vis-à-vis* affected individuals and of State sovereignty in international relations. However, these criteria are not applied on a cumulative basis, but rather, their relationship with each other resembles a sliding

1090 This aspect of flexibility was one of the key factors in the WTO Appellate Body's decision with regard to the United States in Turtle/Shrimp. After striking down the initial measures, which required other countries to adopt 'essentially the same' regulations as the United States, for violation of the chapeau, the Appellate Body accepted subsequent changes that only required foreign regulatory programs to be 'comparable in effectiveness', see *United States – Import Prohibition of Certain Shrimp and Shrimp Products* – Recourse to Article 21.5 of the DSU by Malaysia, WT/DS58/AB/RW, 43–50.

1091 Svantesson (n 13), at 133 terms this bark and bite jurisdiction.

1092 See on this term: Meng, *Extraterritoriale Jurisdiktion im öffentlichen Wirtschaftsrecht* (n 43), 82 – 87; Meyer (n 983), 203 – 208.

scale: The more proximity exists between the State and the subject matter of regulation, the more particular the pursued interests may be. Conversely, the more the regulation is based on a universally shared norm, the weaker the connection may be. Similar considerations apply in relation to the intrusiveness of the measure: Greater underlying proximity and overwhelmingly shared interest allow for regulations more intrusive to the rights and interests of the affected while regulations relying on fleeting connections or pursuing particular interests may need to tread lightly with regard to their intrusiveness. I have termed the first test, which assesses the relationship between the connection and the underlying interest of the regulation the 'abuse of rights' test and the second test, which asks whether in light of the connection and the objective, the regulation should be deemed too intrusive, the 'proportionality' test. In sum, the model can therefore be pictured as a triangle like this:

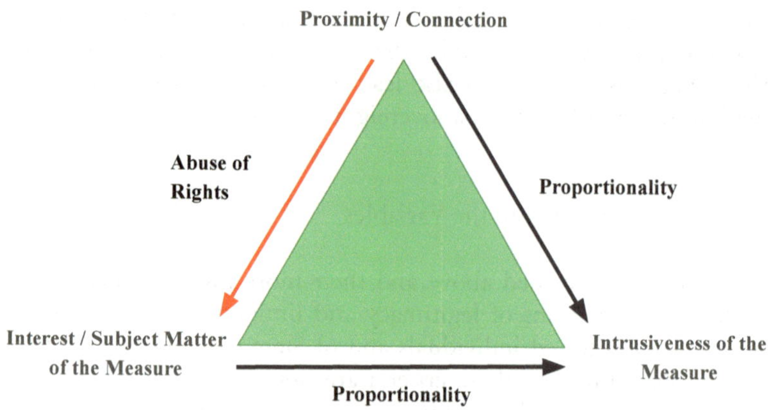


### a) The Abuse of Rights Test

With regard to the 'abuse of rights' test, the pertinent question is whether the proximity or connection relied upon justifies the exercise of extraterritorial jurisdiction to pursue the specific objective at issue. This test lies at the heart of two extreme examples already discussed above: On the one hand, jurisdictional assertions that are not able to show a legitimate interest of any kind and are solely meant to disturb another State should be regarded as such an abuse of rights.[1093] On the other hand, when the pursued interest is universally recognized through a shared and well defined norm, even the absence of any connection would not automatically lead to a dismissal of the jurisdictional claim as abusive.[1094] Between these two extremes of course lie the actually challenging cases that prompted this study in the first place. In this regard, it is important to remember that the abuse of rights test is just one of two steps to evaluate the legitimacy of extraterritorial jurisdiction to restrict its possible negative implications. Thus, as the name suggests, the bar to satisfy this test should not be set too high. In particular, with regard to outward-looking measures, according to the sliding scale principle, there should be no abuse of rights if these measures seek to 'enforce' a norm of universal recognition or otherwise a widely shared community interest.

The most problematic are those instances, in which States use rather questionable connections to pursue a unilateral interest. To strike the (necessarily) delicate balance here, it may be appropriate to seek inspiration in the US jurisprudence on personal jurisdiction, which concerns the very similar question, namely, what kind of contact justifies maintenance of litigation against an out-of-state defendant. In *International Shoe* and subsequent cases, the principle of due process has provided the bar to this question. It requires that an out-of-state person be subject to suit only if he or she enjoys 'certain minimum contacts with [the state] such that the maintenance of the suit does not offend "traditional notions of fair play and substantial justice"'.[1095]

How then, do US courts decide whether the exercise of long-arm jurisdiction is justified or not? *International Shoe* and subsequent cases distinguish between two categories, general or all-purpose jurisdiction and specific or case-linked jurisdiction, depending on the degree of contact, or

---

1093 See on this already at B.II.1b) Abuse of Rights.

1094 In these cases, it could be argued that the regulating State is a 'decentralized enforcer of an international law that covers the globe', see Colangelo, 'Spatial Legality' (n 48), 120 – 121; A similar conclusion is drawn by Cedric Ryngaert, *Selfless intervention: Exercising jurisdiction in the common interest* (Oxford scholarship online, First edition, Oxford University Press 2020), at 213: '[…] one of the main arguments in this monograph is that the legality of jurisdictional assertions resting on weak territorial links may be boosted by these assertions' very contribution to the common interest, and preferably by their embeddedness in, or relationship with international regulatory instruments'.

1095 *International Shoe Co. v Washington*, 326 US 310, 316 (1945).

proximity, between the defendant and the forum.[1096] The exercise of general jurisdiction is limited to 'instances in which the continuous corporate operations within a state [are] so substantial and of such a nature as to justify suit against it on causes of action arising from dealings entirely distinct from those activities'.[1097] In other cases, only specific jurisdiction may be maintained in relation to the adjudication of 'issues deriving from, or connected with, the very controversy that establishes jurisdiction', which has its basis in the 'activity or an occurrence that takes place in the forum State'.[1098] Put differently, unless general jurisdiction exists, a court may exercise personal jurisdiction only if the subject matter in question is in some way connected to the activity or the presence of the defendant in the forum.

While the 'minimum contacts' analysis concerns personal jurisdiction in US jurisprudence, it may be possible to transpose its underlying idea to our abuse of rights test. That is, unless the proximity between the State and the addressee of regulation is so close as to justify all-purpose jurisdiction, extraterritorial jurisdiction may only be exercised if the regulated subject matter and hence the regulatory interest is somewhat related to the specific connection relied upon. Otherwise, if the connection is completely detached from the regulatory interest, it would seem arbitrary to burden the addressee with normative commands that do not arise out of the purposeful association of the private person with the State. Meng similarly argues that the link or connection between a State and the subject matter of regulation is not mechanic, but rather entails a functional dimension. For instance, exercise of jurisdiction under the personality principle may permissibly only regulate such interests that are related to the special allegiance citizens owe to their nation State, but not beyond.[1099] Thus, it is arguably legitimate to extend domestic criminal laws to nationals abroad based on allegiance or to address nationals extraterritorially to uphold re-export restrictions for the sake of national security but not to regulate

1096 *International Shoe Co. v Washington*, 326 US 310 (1945); *Goodyear Dunlop Tires Operations, S. A. v Brown*, 564 US 915 (2011); *J. McIntyre Mach., Ltd. v Nicastro*, 564 US 873 (2011) see also John Drobak, 'Personal Jurisdiction in a Global World: The Impact of the Supreme Court's Decisions in Goodyear Dunlop Tires and Nicastro' (2013) 90 Washington University Law Review 1707.

1097 *International Shoe Co. v Washington*, 326 US 310, 316 (1945).

1098 *Goodyear Dunlop Tires Operations, S. A. v Brown*, 564 US 915, 919 (2011).

1099 This concept of allegiance is problematic, as mentioned above at D.I.1a)bb) Nationality.

general commercial activity under this principle.[1100] The requirement of an inner relationship between the specific connection relied upon and the regulatory interest is particularly useful in analysing extraterritorial economic regulation. Thus, issuing stocks on a domestic exchange may provide the necessary connection to prescribe rules on corporate transparency disclosure obligations in order to pursue the interest of protecting domestic investors. However, while this finding arguably supports the extraterritorial application of the Sarbanes-Oxley Act, it may be an abuse of rights to use listing on stock exchanges as a connection to regulate unrelated contractual matters of the same corporation.

### b) The Proportionality Test

The 'proportionality' test asks whether in light of the proximity between the regulating State and the addressee as well as the regulatory interest at issue, the regulation should be deemed disproportional because it is substantially too intrusive. Svantesson offers an example of how such a balancing test may be operationalized in practice with regard to the area of data protection. As a starting point, he distinguishes between different types of regulatory measures according to three different categories, the abuse prevention layer, the rights layer and the administrative layer.[1101] While the abuse prevention layer contains prohibitions on the unauthorized abuse of personal data, the rights layer guarantees individual positions such as the right of access and the administrative layer prescribes certain organizational obligations on the addressed enterprises, such as the designation of a data protection officer.[1102] While the underlying interest remains the same within all three layers, the protection of residents' individual data in the regulating State, the intrusiveness of the measures in the various layers differ. For a data processing company, creating the mechanisms to guarantee users a right of access or designating and training a data protection officer are arguably more burdensome than simply refraining from unauthorized sharing of data. As a result, Svantesson suggests that for the rights layer or the administrative layer to apply extraterritorially, the

1100 See Meng, *Extraterritoriale Jurisdiktion im öffentlichen Wirtschaftsrecht* (n 43), 601 – 602.

1101 Svantesson (n 13), 193.

1102 Ibid., 192 – 193.

regulated operator must be especially close with the regulating State.[1103] Certain aspects of this approach, such as the particular scope of the layers, may be criticized.[1104] However, the general idea that there is a proportionality relationship between the intrusiveness of the measures on the one hand and the underlying connections as well as the regulatory interest on the other hand holds potential.

The preceding sections have already offered some indication with regard to how the strength of a connection, the weight of an interest as well as the intrusiveness of a measure may be assessed.[1105] As discussed above, determining the proximity between the State and the subject matter of regulation involves a normative assessment of the entire circumstances instead of a fragmented approach relying on specific bases. The weight of an interest (which includes the protection of certain individual interests as well) may be indicated in particular by how widely it is recognized to be a subject matter of importance among affected States. The intrusiveness of a measure significantly depends on its unique design and on how much the regulation requires the addressees to change their behaviour or displaces the affected State of its regulatory authority.

In addition, it is submitted that the legality of any jurisdictional assertion also depends at least partly on the regulatory framework within the affected State. State practice and academic commentators indicate that exercises of extraterritorial jurisdiction may be more contentious if the content of the measure is in conflict with existing forum State regulations.[1106] *Vice versa*, such measures should cause less protest if both States employ largely similar policies on the subject matter. One might justifiably wonder how this notion is consistent with the proportionality test just outlined above which primarily looks at characteristics of the extraterritorial measure itself without reference to external factors. In truth however, the proportionality test is well equipped to capture these differences through the intrusiveness prong. While the intrusiveness of a measure is determined by the specific design of the extraterritorial regulation, it is not possible to fully appreci-

1103 Ibid., 194 – 197.
1104 Uecker (n 140), 198 – 200.
1105 See above at D.II.2. The Variables Determining the Legitimacy of Extraterritorial Jurisdiction.
1106 See for instance *Restatement (Third) of the Foreign Relations Law of the United States* (n 5), § 403(2)(h) lists as one consideration for analysing the reasonableness of exercises of jurisdiction 'the likelihood of conflict with regulation by another State'; Zerk (n 634), at 214 equally views the potential for 'regulatory conflicts' as a possible red light.

ate its effects on the rights or interests of other individuals (and States) without at least some considerations of their respective positions.[1107] Two commonly discussed situations shall exemplify this proposition.

### aa) True Conflicts

'True conflicts' of law or 'foreign sovereign compulsion' describe a situation where one State extraterritorially prohibits certain conduct that another (the territorial) State compels.[1108] In this case, the addressee of the simultaneous regulations is caught between the proverbial rock and a hard place as it is logically impossible for him to fulfil both obligations at once. It comes as no surprise therefore that the affected individuals would perceive such measures as particularly intrusive to their interests as it seems inevitable to face sanctions in one place or the other. At the same time, these measures would usually present a strong intervention into the interests of the affected State as the State has specifically opted for domestic policies contradicting the extraterritorial regulation.[1109] Thus, extraterritorial regulations that cause such a true conflict without any possible exemption may regularly fail the proportionality test because they are overly intrusive to the interests of affected individuals and States. And indeed, States seem to have recognized the delicacy of this issue and the intrusiveness of asserting extraterritorial jurisdiction in these situations and frequently waive compliance obligations or sanctions for affected individuals caught in such a 'true conflict'.[1110]

---

1107 This aspect is also acknowledged by Uecker (n 140), 194.

1108 The terminology is not precise. Colangelo, 'Spatial Legality' (n 48), at 112 terms these situations 'absolute conflicts'; Ziegenhain (n 59), at 42 uses the expression 'true conflict' to describe a situation in which the interests of two States balance each other, so that both States may legitimately exercise jurisdiction over a certain subject matter.

1109 See Colangelo, 'Spatial Legality' (n 48), at 113, 'if foreign law compels the foreign activity, then overriding the application of foreign law would be tantamount to U.S. courts invalidating the public act of another sovereign in its own territory.'.

1110 See for instance, FCPA, § 78dd-1(c); *Hartford Fire Insurance v California* 509 US 764, 798 – 799 (1993).

### bb) False Conflicts

However, the proposition that the intrusiveness analysis has to consider the positions of the affected individuals and States also runs in the other direction. Thus, the proportionality test should be commonly satisfied when the State exercising extraterritorial jurisdiction and the affected State have adopted essentially the same regulation with regard to the specific subject matter. From the individuals' perspective, the extraterritorial regulation in these cases proves less burdensome as in any event, they are bound by a norm of the same substance, the content of which they should know. The affront on the sovereignty of another State is equally mitigated as both States not only follow similar interests but have even adopted comparable norms. One could even claim that the State exercising extraterritorial jurisdiction is in fact administering 'vicarious' justice.[1111] For Meyer, these aspects are so important that he makes this concept, which he terms 'dual illegality', the cornerstone of his doctrine of US judicial application of extraterritoriality.[1112]

This approach convincingly explains why universal jurisdiction, which may be interpreted as a more advanced form of dual illegality, generally should not fail the proportionality test despite occasional protests in practice. Since all States and individuals are bound by the prohibition of certain core international law crimes, being subjected to the jurisdiction of another State should prove to be no additional interference with their rights and interests. On the other hand, exercises of universal jurisdiction to pursue perpetrators of such crimes are in the interest of the entire international community and thus carry a weighty interest. Another example in this regard can be found in the transnational regulation of foreign bribery where the UNCAC and the OECD Anti-Bribery Convention provide for reasonably clear norms that have been adopted in the majority of nations. In these matters again, exercises of extraterritorial jurisdiction do not offend the positions of affected individuals, and, since they also serve to uphold a largely converging global interest, should generally pass the proportionality test even if the connection relied on is rather weak. Also in practice, affected States have not protested FCPA enforcement actions even when they resulted in harsh sanctions for individuals and companies under their jurisdiction or when they were based on most tenuous connec-

1111 Ryngaert, *Unilateral Jurisdiction and Global Values* (n 10), 78.
1112 Meyer, 'Dual Illegality and Geoambiguous Law: A New Rule for Extraterritorial Application of U.S. Law' (n 1058).

tions. Exceptions to this principle of 'false conflicts' certainly exist, such as if the procedural rules of the State exercising extraterritorial jurisdiction are particularly intrusive *vis-à-vis* the affected States and individuals.

However, false conflicts create another problem: While it may be relatively easy in practice to determine whether a true conflict exists, it may be much harder to ascertain whether the regulations of two States are similar enough to affect the proportionality analysis. Although this is a weighty consideration, it does not present an unsurmountable obstacle. In fact, much of the operation of dual illegality in practice may be aligned to the well-known criteria of double criminality in the law of extradition.[1113] For instance, the Ninth Circuit has held in this respect: 'When the laws of both the requesting and the requested party appear to be directed to the same basic evil, the statutes are substantially analogous, and [they] can form the basis of dual criminality.'[1114] If law enforcement agencies and courts have been able for generations to determine whether a pair of domestic and foreign law satisfies the requirement of double criminality, the adaptation of this principle to situations of extraterritorial jurisdiction should equally be in their capabilities.

### 4. Procedural Safeguards, Reasoning and Participation

The exercise of extraterritorial jurisdiction has the potential to give rise to conflicts of interest between the involved States and between the regulating State and the affected private parties. While the rules described above are capable of mitigating such risks, the mere design of a new framework will certainly not sway (in particular powerful) States away from conducting business-as-usual, seeing that they are by far the biggest beneficiaries of the cacophonous regime of State jurisdiction right now. One driver of change in this situation may be reciprocity, the concept that when one State abides by the rules of the game *vis-à-vis* another State, that other State may respond in kind. On the other hand, if one State regularly resorts to outrageous assertions of jurisdiction, it eventually risks to face a situation when the tables are turned. Thus, at least in the area of transnational anti-trust regulation, even though it was not possible to establish substantive standards, a number of Western States seemed to have enough appetite to establish at least a series of procedural obligations with

1113 Ibid., 167.
1114 See *Clarey v Gregg*, 138 F 3d 764, 766 (9th Cir 1998).

each other, including notification, consultation and goodwill to avoid conflict.[1115] There is thus reason to believe that the adoption of procedural safeguards may prove less political than the establishment of substantive standards, but that eventually, one may lead into another.[1116]

However, while it was the fear of reciprocal retaliation that drove the establishment of a consultation procedure between States, there are more fundamental values at stake that suggest the creation of procedural obligations. For one, low-level contact between domestic agencies and courts with their counterparts in other States may provide the necessary fine-tuning of the variables and tests developed above, which have been rather open to ensure their applicability across a wide range of areas. Thus, they may need more detailed configuration for each specific subject matter of extraterritorial regulation, a task which is arguably better in the hands of domestic regulators connected through international consultation. For the other, it has already been mentioned that procedural safeguards, which serve the upholding of the rule of law, provide another possible mechanism to compensate, at least to a certain degree, the democratic deficit of extraterritorial jurisdiction.[1117] This is particularly the case, when procedural obligations are not only established in the interstate relationship but also with regard to the affected private parties.

The improvement of legitimacy and accountability *vis-à-vis* the affected individuals thus poses certain requirements for the design of safeguards in relation to the exercise of extraterritorial jurisdiction. As already mentioned above, extraterritorial jurisdiction is by far not the only area of global governance, in which issues of legitimacy have arisen. Thus, the academic literature has already conceptualized a range of solutions, which improve rule of law standards and thus help to legitimize exercises of public authority. The emerging school of global administrative law in

---

1115 Agreement Regarding the Application of Competition Laws between the Government of the United States and the Commission of the European Communities, (1991) 4 CMLR 823; (1995) 30 ILM 1487, [1995] OJ L 132; see also already above at D.I.1. Alternative Approaches to Solve Concurrent Jurisdiction.

1116 This is also the position of Ryngaert, *Jurisdiction in International Law* (n 2), at 215 who believes 'that a *reasonable* exercise of jurisdiction could spontaneously spring from a network of transnational governance and judicial cooperation. States will inform other States – and relevant private actors – that they intend to exercise jurisdiction over a particular situation. Foreign nations will comment on the proposed assertions, and the asserting States will presumably take foreign concerns into account.'.

1117 See above at D.II.1c) Proximity, Community Interests and the Rule of Law.

particular has focused on process to mitigate issues of democratic legitimacy and accountability by highlighting standards of transparency, participation, reasoned decision, and legality.[1118] Similar procedural principles are imaginable in the context of extraterritorial regulation and would for instance allow affected private parties to participate in the rule-making process of legal acts with extraterritorial effects. While this proposal may sound ambitious, there are concrete examples, for instance with regard to the EU process of designing its conflict minerals regulations.[1119] Even when participation cannot be ensured, providing a thorough reasoning to decisions that factor in the possible interests of foreign private parties affected by a particular law, administrative act or judgment may already go a long way in creating mutual understanding and prevent conflicts.[1120] With regard to procedural safeguards, the possibility for foreigners to contest extraterritorial regulations and have them reviewed may also provide relief for affected individuals.

In relation to this last point, the restriction of US constitutional rights to persons who have come within US territory or developed substantial connections with this country proves to be particularly problematic. While extraterritorial US economic sanctions are adopted without any prior notification against foreign individuals with no connection to the United States, these individuals, at the same time, may not be able to have these sanctions reviewed by independent courts afterwards.[1121] This incongruence between, on the one hand, the exercise of public authority and, on the other hand, the lack of judicial accountability strongly suggests the illegitimacy of US extraterritorial sanctions in this particular instance and should be addressed through domestic legislation. Finally, from a practical perspective, adding procedural safeguards to extraterritorial sanctions may be more realistic than to abolish this kind of regulation altogether.

---

1118 Benedict Kingsbury, Nico Krisch and Richard B Stewart, 'The Emergence of Global Administrative Law' (2005) 68(3) Law and Contemporary Problems 15, 17; Battini (n 182), 75 – 80 also argues along these lines.

1119 See above at C.V.4b) Mandatory Supply Chain Regulation.

1120 Similar suggestions are made by Benvenisti (n 23) who grounds his 'minimum obligations' on the sovereignty of States, which he considers to entail a trusteeship not only for a State's own constituents, but also at some level for humanity at large.

1121 See on this already C.II.5. Protection of Individual Rights.

### 5. Application of the Framework in Practice

#### a) Market Access Regulation Conditioned on Extraterritorial Circumstances

The proposed conception of the abuse of rights test may prove useful in solving some of the jurisdictional conundrums identified in the analysis of actual practice of the United States and the EU, for instance, the weakness of the traditional doctrine to adequately deal with market access regulations conditioned on extraterritorial circumstances. As discussed above, States and academics have provided no coherent argument to assess these diverse measures, ranging from secondary boycotts such as the ISA, measures aimed at regulating climate change in the form of the Aviation Directive 2008/101/EC, or human rights conditionality in domestic procurement policies.[1122] According to the approach outlined above, there would be an abuse of rights if the connection relied upon, the access to domestic markets, does not justify exercising jurisdiction to pursue the particular regulatory interest.

A number of different situations should be distinguished here: In the first instance, if the interest pursued relates to the protection of domestic consumers, domestic territory or the domestic market from physical or economic harm, conditions imposed upon access should be deemed justified. In relation to these inward-looking measures, the domestic harm creates a particularly strong proximity between the regulating State and the private addressee. With regard to their own citizens and their own territory, States are principally free to determine the level of health, environmental or economic protection. Thus, merely establishing conditions to uphold these objectives and blocking access of products or conduct that undermine these objectives can hardly be construed as an abuse of rights.[1123] Though not determinative, this interpretation of the abuse of rights test also aligns well with a modern notion of the effects doctrine, which recognizes a basis for the exercise of jurisdiction to mitigate substantial adverse effects beyond traditional antitrust regulation.

Market access conditions that pursue outward-looking interests, where the subject matter or concern is located abroad, are harder to justify.

1122 See above at C.VI.1a) Market Access Regulation Conditioned on Extraterritorial Circumstances.

1123 For the protection of consumer health: Meyer (n 983), 216 – 218; for the protection of the domestic environment: Cooreman (n 38), 132 – 133.

According to the sliding scale principle, such measures would be unproblematic if they seek to 'enforce' a norm of universal recognition or otherwise a widely shared community interest. An example in this regard may be the EU Timber Regulation, which prohibits the placement into the internal market of illegally harvested timber. Illegal logging is a global cause to a variety of economic, environmental and social issues, as deforestation may negatively impact climate change and biodiversity.[1124] Thus, sustainable forest management has also been recognized as a concern in a number of international soft law documents, such as the Forest Principles[1125] and Chapter 11 on deforestation of Agenda 21.[1126] With regard to binding instruments, some timber species are listed under the appendices of CITES[1127] and forest management is also covered in the Convention on Biological Diversity.[1128] Thus, while there is no binding international consensus on illegal logging *per se*, the concern is hardly parochial and enjoys tremendous global support.[1129] In this regard, it should be noted that the EU, because of a lack of a universally accepted definition of illegal logging, chose instead to define the term according to the local law of the exporting country.[1130] Thus, it is convincing to argue that the EU, through the Timber Regulation, is indeed enforcing an interest that is both recognized at a global level and by the affected State itself.[1131] Finally, from the perspective of individual foreign operators, such trade restrictions create no additional compliance burden since the market access conditions are analogous to their domestic regulation, or, phrased in another way, the

1124 Cooreman (n 38), 249.

1125 United Nations Conference on Environment and Development, Non-Legally Binding Authoritative Statement of Principles for a Global Consensus on the Management, Conservation and Sustainable Development of All Types of Forests, A/CONF.151/26 (Vol. III).

1126 United Nations Conference on Environment and Development, Agenda 21.

1127 Convention on international trade in endangered species of wild fauna and flora (adopted 3 March 1973, entered into force 1 July 1975) 993 UNTS 243 ('CITES').

1128 Convention on Biological Diversity (adopted 5 June 1992, entered into force 29 December 1993) 1760 UNTS 79.

1129 Cooreman (n 38), 261.

1130 See above at B.II.2. Comity.

1131 Cedric Ryngaert, 'Whither Territoriality?: The European Union's Use of Territoriality to set Norms with Universal Effects' in Cedric Ryngaert and others (eds), *What's Wrong with International Law?: Liber amicorum A.H.A. Soons* (Nova et vetera iuris gentium. Brill Nijhoff 2015), at 439 raises some doubt whether exporting countries actually welcome the EU Timber Regulation despite its reference to local law.

regulated conduct is equally 'illegal' in both States. Thus, using market access as a connection to pursue a widely shared concern cannot be deemed an abuse of rights.

The most difficult cases are those instances, where market access is used to 'enforce' a unilateral or particular interest, such as in the case of the ISA. According to the considerations above, striking the right balance here depends on whether a relationship exists between the connections relied upon to regulate and the pursued regulatory interest so as to justify a particular kind of jurisdictional assertion. Legislation such as the ISA uses domestic economic benefits, such as the possibility to enter certain banking and property transactions with banks in the United States, as leverage. The purpose is to induce the (third country) addressees of the regulation to modify their business relationships with regard to the primary sanctions target according to US foreign policy preferences. In this case, the domestic benefits that may be withdrawn create proximity between the addressees of the regulation and the United States while disrupting business relationships with the primary sanctions target, and, more generally, the US policy of isolating certain governments, constitute the underlying regulatory interest. It would seem that there is no direct relationship between accessing the US market and upholding its foreign policy. Thus, provisions such as those in the ISA simply (ab)-use market access to compel a wholly unrelated conduct and should indeed be considered an abuse of rights.

However, the analysis may be different if, instead of isolating an allegedly hostile country, an interest is pursued that more closely relates to the connection relied upon. For instance, the United States uses regulations, which condition the maintenance of correspondent banking accounts by foreign banks in the United States on whether or not that foreign financial institution raises red flags with regard to the risk of money laundering.[1132] Here, it is possible to establish an inner relationship between the connection, the maintenance of banking accounts in the United States, and the regulatory interest, the prevention of money laundering. Furthermore, given the fungible nature of money one can well argue that banking transactions with money laundering institutions might compromise the domestic correspondent banking system, thus establishing an additional link between the connection relied upon and the subject matter of regulation. Given that, it could be argued that such a regulation would more likely pass an abuse of rights tests.

---

1132 USA PATRIOT Act of 2001 Pub. L. 107–56, § 311, codified at 31 U.S.C § 5318a.

### b) Parent-based Regulation of Multinational Corporations

Largely similar considerations guide the application of the proposed framework to solve the issues posed by another frequently adopted regulatory mechanism, which utilises corporate parent-subsidiary structures to achieve extraterritorial effects. Given the ubiquity of multinational corporations, it comes as no surprise that both the United States and European States have extensively practiced this technique in multiple regulatory areas. Parent-based mechanisms cover a wide range of different measures, among others the direct regulation of foreign subsidiaries, holding domestic corporate parents strictly liable for conduct by their foreign subsidiaries and establishing certain policies that demand group-wide compliance. Focusing largely on territoriality, conventional doctrine has had a hard time to adequately capture the nuanced approach in practice.[1133] According to the framework proposed in the preceding sections, the normative validity would depend on whether the specific parent-based regulations satisfy the abuse of rights and the proportionality tests.

The abuse of rights test asks whether the specific proximity between the regulating State and the addressee or the subject matter justifies the exercise of extraterritorial jurisdiction to pursue the objective at issue. A strong indication for an abuse of rights exists if the connection relied upon to exercise jurisdiction is completely detached from the regulatory interest, as in this case, it would seem arbitrary to burden the addressee with normative commands that do not arise out of the purposeful association of the private person with the State. According to this standard, regulations pertaining to the establishment of uniform accounting, disclosure or similar compliance policies throughout a corporate group would usually constitute no abuse of rights. The regulatory objective of these measures is precisely to protect the interests of domestic investors, consumers and the public at large, who usually regard the group as a single enterprise with regard to its economic, environmental and social performance. Thus, there is an evident inner relationship between the exercise of extraterritorial jurisdiction based on corporate affiliation and the regulatory interest.[1134]

---

1133 C.VI.1b) Parent-based Regulation of Multinational Corporations.

1134 This is also the position of the *Restatement (Third) of the Foreign Relations Law of the United States* (n 5), § 414.

The evaluation becomes more difficult in other cases. With regard to economic sanctions based on parent-subsidiary mechanisms,[1135] considerations similar to those, which led to a rejection of the ISA, may apply. There, it has been argued that while foreign companies that access the US market or receive other economic benefits undoubtedly enjoy a connection to the domestic territory, this connection does not seem to have any relationship with the business of the foreign company with other third States. Thus, such regulations may not pass the abuse of rights test. In the same vein, the parent-subsidiary structure does not immediately suggest that subsidiary companies abroad need to uphold the same unilateral foreign policy of the home State of the corporate parent. Rather, in this instance as well, there seems to be no necessary relationship between the connection relied upon to exercise extraterritorial jurisdiction and the regulatory interest at issue.

The situation may be somewhat different again with regard to parent-based regulations in the area of business and human rights. As discussed above, the abuse of rights test is also commonly satisfied when the regulatory interest itself is so weighty, so universally shared, that even minute contacts between the regulating State and the addressee or the conduct in question may legitimize an exercise of jurisdiction.[1136] This requirement seems to be generally satisfied with regard to recognized international human rights, although certain norms, such as those giving rise to universal criminal jurisdiction, may be considered particularly strong for this purpose. Thus, with regard to parent-based regulations in relation to the human rights obligations of foreign subsidiaries, the normative assessment may rather revolve around the question of proportionality. At this stage, it is necessary to examine the precise content of each regulatory measure, in particular, to which extent it requires the foreign addressee to adapt its conduct and to which degree it displaces the foreign subsidiary's home State of its regulatory authority. Thus, the more a regulation purports to directly target the foreign subsidiary without finding specific fault on the part of the domestic parent, the more intrusive this regulation is *vis-à-vis* both the norm addressee as well as the affected State and the more likely it is to be disproportionate. This may be the case for instance if the domestic parent is held strictly liable for subsidiary conduct or otherwise if the standard of supervision is so high that in practice, the domestic parent may

1135 See for such regulation for example, 31 C.F.R. § 560.215, above at C.II.2. The Extension of Personality-based Jurisdiction to Foreign Subsidiaries.

1136 D.II.3a) The Abuse of Rights Test.

not have recourse to a due diligence defence. So far, there is no indication in practice that courts in the United States or in Europe holding home State corporations liable for subsidiary conduct have crossed this high bar.[1137]

c) Regulation Based on Individual Consent of the Affected

The above analysis has shown that the individual consent of private parties to be subjected to a certain set of (State mandated) rules is gaining importance in the wider development of transnational regulation. The most controversial examples in this regard are certainly submissions concluded in the area of export controls, where the foreign importer of controlled goods regularly has to agree to be bound by the regulations of the original exporting State or to otherwise refrain from re-exporting the goods without prior administrative approval.[1138] While such extensions of State jurisdiction are now often tacitly accepted, they have once caused diplomatic uproar. Despite some scholarly debate on the topic, merging the role of individual consent into the traditional jurisdictional doctrine has been difficult.[1139] According to the here proposed framework, jurisdictional assertions based on private contractual submissions as well would have to satisfy the abuse of rights and the proportionality tests while recognizing the strength of individual interests to shape jurisdictional assertions.

As a starting point, it seems to make sense to divide cases of re-export control into two categories, depending on whether they refer to goods and technologies that are jointly listed through multilateral agreements, even if this happens through informal regimes such as the Wassenaar Arrangement, or those that are unilaterally controlled. The reason is that with regard to multilaterally regulated goods, the interest variable in the triangle framework becomes much weightier as both the original exporting country and the re-exporting country have a joint interest in suppressing the proliferation of the concerned goods. Thus, in light of the proportionality test, exercises of extraterritorial jurisdiction affecting multilaterally regulated re-export activities would usually fare better than with regard to export control of unilaterally listed items. In the former cases, the affected companies and individuals are in any case bound by a substantially similar

1137 See above at C.V.5c) Comparative Normative Analysis.
1138 See above at C.III.4c) Comparative Normative Analysis.
1139 See above at C.VI.2. The Restriction to Considerations of State Sovereignty.

rule in their forum State even without additional private consent. Thus, extraterritorial jurisdiction should not prove to be particularly intrusive and the existence of a contractual arrangement may further legitimize such exercises.

With regard to unilaterally controlled items, the question becomes whether the regulating State may refer exclusively to its contractual agreement to justify the exercise of jurisdiction *vis-à-vis* a foreign natural or juridical person. As elaborated above, consent of the private parties may mediate proximity between the regulating State and the re-export control matter in question.[1140] Moreover, it can be argued along the lines of the general principle of *volenti non fit iniuria* that no one may claim damages if he has knowingly and voluntarily consented into a certain act. Thus, the intrusiveness of regulatory measures in relation to the consenting individual is greatly diminished.[1141] It is true that measures based on private submission may still interfere with the regulatory choices of the forum State as was most clearly demonstrated in the *Pipeline* incident. However, as mentioned above, if the forum State fears that private submission by 'its' companies would displace its regulatory authority, there is nothing stopping the State to adopt measures, including blocking-statutes, limiting the possibility or authority of such contractual agreements.[1142] In general, therefore, the intrusiveness of extraterritorial measures based on consent should be rather minor in relation to both the State and the private party. Thus, such measures should usually pass the proportionality test and prove legitimate.[1143]

---

1140 See above at D.II.2a) Proximity and Substantial Connection.

1141 On a more theoretical level, one of the main arguments raised against extraterritorial jurisdiction is the fact that the affected were not possible in any way to participate in and influence the creation of the norm and thus that extraterritorial jurisdiction lack (democratic) legitimacy. However, one could argue that this deficiency does not pose a problem in the event of contractual submission, as there is undoubtedly an act of voluntary consent into the regulation. Thus, the lack of legitimacy is cured in these cases.

1142 See above at C.III.4c) Comparative Normative Analysis.

1143 The principle of consent may also provide additional insights to the problem of regulating along the corporate parent – subsidiary relationship. When a company incorporates under the laws of a certain State, the company accepts the applicability of the regulations of that State even if the company otherwise does no business at all there. When a company is incorporated under the laws of a certain legal system, all its rights and duties are derivative to the law of that State. Put differently, the company has explicitly consented to the application of the regulations of that State, see Brilmayer (n 998), at 1298. In the case of an independent subsidiary therefore, this legal person may be said to have

To be sure, the idea of private party submission has certain limitations. One the one hand, it must be reasonably possible for the participating private party to foresee what conduct is covered by the extraterritorial regulation. On the other hand, the party has to in fact consent into these specific matters. This was indeed one of the more critical issues during the *Pipeline* incident: European companies had already received the US controlled goods and technologies consenting to US regulations at a time when no export prohibitions were in place regarding the Soviet Union. However, when these regulations changed, the US sought to apply the new regulations based on the original agreements, which drew the criticism of retroactivity.[1144] This was particularly problematic because while some of these private contracts expressly contained provisions to also subject the private party to subsequent regulatory changes, the Pipeline orders were not limited to these instances.[1145] Thus, it could be argued that the original agreements did not cover these new regulations and that the extraterritorial jurisdictional assertions thus could not rely on consent.

Furthermore, as a general principle, for any consent to be legally valid, it has to be voluntary, which one can understand as to be free from duress, coercion or other undue influence. In the State – private party relationship, this might prove to be particularly difficult to assess, as private parties, sometimes even if they are large corporations, may not be able to resist a foreign State's command for submission. This may particularly be the case in relation to US export control where comprehensive contractual agreements may be the only way of obtaining the goods and technologies in question.[1146] Finally, as mentioned above, private party consent finds its limits in cases in which this very act would be contrary to domestic legislation, typically, when a blocking-statute or other mandatory national

explicitly consented to the regulation of the State of incorporation. In principle therefore, its relationship to the home State of the parent corporation has to defer to this new bond, see Meessen, 'Extraterritoriality of Export Control' (n 539), 103. Even the ICJ, in *Barcelona Traction,* explicitly refers to consent when the Court submits that the exercise of diplomatic protection with regard to a corporation may need to take into account whether incorporation in the host State was forced upon the company, hinting at the concept of a defective consent, see *Barcelona Traction Light and Power Co, Ltd. (Belgium v Spain)* (n 126).

1144 Meessen, 'Extraterritoriality of Export Control' (n 539), 97.

1145 Stanley Marcuss and Mathias Stephen, 'U.S. Foreign Policy Export Controls: Do They Pass Muster under International Law' (1984) 2 Berkeley Journal of International Law 1, 16 with footnote 86.

1146 Ziegenhain (n 59), 161.

regulations exist.[1147] This caveat strikes the needed balance between individual and State interests: In those cases in which they do not neatly align, the home State still possesses the tools to compel compliance.

### 6. Pre-empting Some Potential Objections

As with anything as fundamental as State jurisdiction, no framework will be anywhere near the perfect solution and the proposal just outlined certainly does not pretend to be. In the end, managing such a complex endeavour will always involve trade-offs, between flexibility and predictability as well as between practical applicability and theoretical ambitions. In this regard, keen readers may criticise that the above developed and advocated variables and tests do not even fulfil their very own ambition of practical applicability. They will have already observed that the new framework, not unlike traditional doctrine, does not manage to eliminate the possibility for concurrent jurisdiction. After all, it is not unconceivable that two or more States may exercise jurisdiction over the same subject matter because none of the regulations applied to the matter fail either the abuse of rights or the proportionality test. This is fair criticism.[1148] However, two aspects should be mentioned in this regard.

First, a diligent application of the abuse of rights and the proportionality tests should reduce the number of instances of permitted concurrent jurisdiction over time. It is predicted that in matters that can boast no internationally accepted regulatory interest, the framework will likely result in a primary regulatory competence of the States most proximate to a certain situation. This is because failing to advance a substantial connection, any assertion of jurisdiction by a State will face greater hurdles in relation to both the abuse of rights and the proportionality test. In practice therefore, this result may be similar to Ryngaert's principle of subsidiarity, according to which the State with the strongest nexus to a case should generally be given jurisdictional primacy over the matter.[1149] However, if the determination, which single State has the strongest nexus to a given case, proves

---

1147 See the conflict caused by individual consent that runs counter to mandatory domestic regulations in: Rice (n 563).

1148 Ryngaert makes the quest for a solution that prevents concurrent jurisdiction one of the centrepieces of his work, see Ryngaert, *Jurisdiction in International Law* (n 2), 142 – 144.

1149 Ibid., 219 – 228.

to be particularly difficult itself, then the proposed framework allows for more flexibility while at the same time offering effective tools to restrain exercises of exorbitant jurisdiction.[1150]

Second, concurrent jurisdiction does not lead to international controversies in nearly all situations in which the issue arises. Rather, certain cases are more conflict-prone then others, for instance if the underlying substantial regulations differ from State to State, leading to conflicting commands for individuals caught in the middle, or if the threatened punishment in one State is much harsher than in another State, or if the nexus relied upon is perceived as particularly illegitimate by another State. It is precisely with regard to these issues, that the proposed framework has been developed and thus, such particularly counterproductive frictions should be largely eliminated by a thorough application of the variables and tests outlined. On the other hand, when the exercise of jurisdiction by a State respects both the abuse of rights and the proportionality test, the legitimate interests of both affected States and individuals have already factored in, and the added flexibility may indeed be handy in relation to enforcement matters.

Critics may further argue that with regard to conduct about which there already exists an internationally accepted regulatory interest, the proposed framework could allow too many States, even those with only loose connections, to assert jurisdiction based of the concept of false conflicts elaborated above.[1151] One need to only imagine the regulatory chaos when all or the majority of States concern themselves with the same situation, even if the underlying rules are harmonized.[1152] While the argument is appealing on a theoretical level, the practical probability of this happening is quite low. The experience with universal jurisdiction and extraterritorial jurisdiction in the area of anti-corruption shows that even in areas of overwhelming consensus, under- and not over-enforcement remains the more urgent issue.[1153] Given the natural restraints on regulatory and investiga-

---

1150 See for instance the particularly contentious Microsoft Ireland case; while Microsoft is a US company, the data is stored in Ireland. Does an order compelling Microsoft to disclose the Irish data by a US law enforcement agency have a stronger nexus to the US or to Ireland? See above at B.I.4. Territoriality-based Jurisdiction and the Internet.

1151 See above at D.II.3b)bb) False Conflicts.

1152 This risk is also acknowledged by Gruson (n 389), 764.

1153 According to Transparency International, as of 2020, only four parties to the OECD Anti-Bribery Convention are considered active enforcers of the Convention, see Transparency International, 'Exporting Corruption' Progress

tive resources to exercise jurisdiction extraterritorially, over-enforcement may also not become an actual problem in the future. Of course, there still might be individual cases that attract transnational attention and where several States with harmonized legal frameworks wish to intervene. However, given that the States would be pursuing the same regulatory interest in these cases, it is not improbable that through the development of notice and other procedural requirements or through simple negotiations, these States may come to an accord.

A second strand of criticism may be less concerned with the practical consequences of concurrent jurisdiction, but rather with the technical difficulties of applying the framework in the first place. In particular, one might argue that the proposed tests are too vague and that, for instance, it is utterly impossible to objectively determine whether in light of a certain connection and regulatory interest, extraterritorial jurisdiction of the subject matter in question is too intrusive. This is a serious observation. However, it is also an observation that has been raised in relation to proportionality tests for decades if not centuries. Yet still, these principles have seen fruitful application by the courts and arbiters in domestic and international law settings to balance complex competing interests.[1154] At the very least, the above proposed variables and tests provide a common language in the analysis of extraterritorial jurisdiction, along which reasoning may take place. It forces States to stop hiding behind labels of 'territoriality' and spell out the actual underlying concerns for and against asserting jurisdiction over a particular subject matter. Over time, the repeated use of this language will translate into a sense of which instances are to be regarded as acceptable and which as disproportionate or abusive.

In relation to this argument, one may also point out that, ultimately, the quality of the variables and tests proposed above depends on the person who is going to administer them.[1155] Thus, one might ask who is going to decide on these variables and tests in practice and remark that unlike in domestic law, there is generally no final arbiter in international law. Without such an authority, however, States could abuse these malleable criteria according to their particular conceptions of fairness and justify even exor-

---

report 2020: Assessing enforcement of the OECD Anti-Bribery Convention, at 10, available at https://files.transparencycdn.org/images/A-slim-version-of-Exporting-Corruption-2020.pdf, last accessed on 13 April 2022.

1154 See already above at B.II.1c) Proportionality; For applications of this principle in international law, see also Peters, 'Verhältnismäßigkeit als globales Verfassungsprinzip' (n 226), 2 – 6.

1155 Svantesson (n 13), at 78 – 79 was faced with similar arguments.

bitant assertions of jurisdiction. There is no completely satisfying answer in this regard. The framework laid out in the previous sections remains silent on who is going to apply the variables and tests in practice. Thus, the task falls onto the same domestic and international institutions that decide right now whether an activity is territorial or not, such as domestic administrative agencies, courts or other dispute resolution bodies. It is true that these institutions may abuse the flexibility of the proposed framework and may succumb to a more parochial interpretation favouring their own political objectives at any certain time. However, this issue exists already in the present. As has been described extensively in previous chapters, US and European legislators, agencies and courts have often invoked territoriality as the jurisdictional basis when the actual connection to State territory has been marginal.[1156] Thus, there is no reason to believe that the abuse of rights and the proportionality tests are more prone to misinterpretation by States than are the territoriality, effects or protective principles. In a way, the lack of centralized authoritative decision mechanisms is a weak spot that afflicts large parts of international law and for which this study (unfortunately) offers no cure. However, one may still hope that over time, by adopting a common language of proximity, interests and proportionality and through procedural safeguards, a casuistry will develop that is able to guide the actions of States in the future.

If one does not subscribe to the belief that States are inherently prone to exploit international legal doctrines for their own benefit, one may still argue that even an impartial domestic judge may find it difficult to correctly apply these admittedly rather vague principles. This has been one of the most severe criticisms against the conception of reasonableness in the Third Restatement and it certainly is legitimate also in relation to the framework proposed above.[1157] However, in contrast to the criteria outlined by the Third Restatement, the variables and tests proposed above constitute *legal* standards that allow the determination of the appropriateness of jurisdictional assertions largely without recourse to political considerations. It is true that the proportionality test may have to also look at the interests of the affected State. However, this determination is to be made in general solely by referring to the existing regulatory framework of the affected State in place and how much its laws and standards differ from

1156 See above at C.VI.1c) Regulation of Conduct Based on Only Fleeting Territorial Connections or Based on Territorial 'Presence'.

1157 Meng, *Extraterritoriale Jurisdiktion im öffentlichen Wirtschaftsrecht* (n 43), 638 – 639; Ryngaert, *Jurisdiction in International Law* (n 2), 167.

the ones of the State exercising extraterritorial jurisdiction. Ultimately, the reduction of the reasonableness assessment of the Restatement (Third) to only three variables and the elaboration of the relationships between them through tests do significantly limit the discretionary freedom in applying these principles and serve as useful guidance to the arbiters.

One final possible criticism should be addressed and that is that the new framework is not ambitious enough. After all, it does not pretend to bring about a paradigm-shift.[1158] The three variables discussed above, proximity between the State and the subject matter in question, the regulatory interest or concern pursued and the intrusiveness of the measure *vis-à-vis* the affected States and individuals, these are all known criteria to assess exercises of jurisdiction. In this regard, there is nothing new under the sun. However, governments, legislators and courts are rarely famed for their agility and the more radical a proposed departure is from the existing system, the less chance it has to be actually employed in practice. It was the objective of this research to produce practical guidance[1159] while maintaining academic coherence. A complete break with the existing system of State jurisdiction was never envisioned. Rather, the new approach hopes to slowly steer practitioners away from a binary and futile argument of territoriality versus extraterritoriality to a more holistic assessment of State jurisdiction.

More importantly however, these criteria were not drawn out of thin air, but they do reflect weighty theoretical considerations of public law. Thus, even though they are not new in their own right, their interpretation has been brought into a new context of examining extraterritorial jurisdiction as a problem of exercises of public authority by individual States in international law. It has been elaborated that the three criteria should be read as factors both legitimizing and limiting extraterritorial regulation. Bearing this background in mind, the variables and tests offered above will gain a different meaning in delimiting spheres of regulatory competence, which will eventually also lead to different results than the application of the traditional doctrine. Finally, this new perspective on extraterritorial jurisdiction will decrease counterproductive conflicts between States and protect the legitimate interests of individuals.

---

1158 It is in any case debatable what this term exactly entails, see Svantesson (n 13), at 77 – 78.

1159 On this goal, see above at D.II.1. Practical Requirements and Objectives of the New Framework.

# E. Conclusion

This study was set out to explore the concept of extraterritorial jurisdiction in international law and has sought to answer whether the territoriality-based system of jurisdiction is capable of providing order in international relations by delimiting regulatory competences between States. Is it possible to define normatively consistent boundaries of territoriality to be respected by States? Or are States, in their pursuit of political goals, able to exploit and disregard the system? It was expected that the formal principles of the territoriality-based system would indeed fail to deliver on their promise of order. Therefore, the study also sought to answer how, in light of the necessary progressive development of the law, extraterritorial jurisdiction can be adequately reconceptualised so that it also accounts for essential interests apart from State sovereignty, such as individual rights and the interests of the international community at large.

There is much at stake. Globalization not only entails *de facto* developments such as the creation of powerful and interconnected economic operators and the ubiquity of modern communication technologies, but also a *de jure* process, by which powerful States advance particular domestic policies into the global arena through the use of unilateral regulation. Extraterritorial jurisdiction provides 'a procedural apparatus through which the future of transnationalism can be distilled'.[1160] It is a phenomenon that is not only going to stay, but is likely going to expand to other areas of law and to increasingly affect natural persons as bearers of rights and obligations. On the one hand, there has been a sharp decrease in the appetite of States to solve challenges through multilateralism, in particular, through the formalized procedures of international organizations. On the other hand, global interconnectedness is going to stay both as an economic and as a social reality. Currently however, the transnational regulatory space is akin to a lawless Wild West. Whether and how extraterritorial jurisdiction is regulated under international law will thus increasingly determine the development of international relations.

In answering the first of the two research questions, this study has found that the territoriality-based system does not adequately constrain States in their pursuit of particular political objectives through extraterritorial juris-

1160 Ireland-Piper, *Accountability in Extraterritoriality* (n 113), 1.

diction. If ever the boundaries of territoriality could have been determined in a normatively consistent way, it is not possible anymore. Part B of this study set out the rules of the currently dominant territoriality-based system of jurisdiction under international law. Assessed against these rules, this study found in part C that States resorted to a host of complex regulatory techniques to exploit and circumvent the formality of the system. In part C, it was observed that these regulatory techniques included (1), conditioning market access and other domestic benefits on circumstances abroad, (2), leveraging parent-based regulation of multinational corporations and (3), regulating essentially foreign conduct based on only fleeting territorial or other factual connections. Although all of these forms of regulations could nominally advance a territorial basis, they allowed States to unilaterally set regulations with a global reach contrary to the ordering purpose of the territoriality-based system of jurisdiction.

Moreover, States disregard the system: They promote or contest such measures not based on considerations of territoriality, but take into account other political and legal objectives and limits. This was demonstrated particularly by the stark differences in treatment of extraterritorial jurisdiction across and even within the examined subject areas, the regulation of economic sanctions and export control, transnational corporate bribery and the prevention of and redress for corporate violations of human rights: On the one hand, States accepted even exorbitant exercises of extraterritorial jurisdiction in the regulation of transnational corporate bribery, because the fight against this specific form of corruption was an objective almost universally accepted by all States. On the other hand, whether States contested the 'extraterritorial' extension of economic sanctions depended particularly on the content of the underlying substantive rules and the interests that were being 'enforced' through the sanctions. Finally, within the regulation of corporate violations of human rights, it was particularly the existence of rights and interests of the private victims that complicated the picture and led to inconsistent responses.

In answering the second of the two research questions, it was found that a more adequate conceptualisation of extraterritorial jurisdiction had to acknowledge its hybrid nature, in that it both concerns the sovereignty of States while at the same time also directly affects the rights and interests of individuals. The role of individual natural and juridical persons was particularly demonstrated through the analysis of the mechanism of private submissions in the area of extraterritorial export control regulation. It was found that the traditional principles of jurisdiction could not adequately include considerations beyond State sovereignty. This is lamentable, because extraterritorial jurisdiction also functions as an exercise of public authority. The legitimation and limitation of extraterritorial jurisdiction may thus be inspired by principles of domestic public law. Part D of the study identified (1), the proximity between the regulating State and the addressee or the conduct in question, (2), the realization of community interests and (3), the protection of individuals against State overreach as the cardinal aspects legitimizing and limiting extraterritorial jurisdiction. In a final step, this study translated these theoretical considerations into a practically applicable new framework based on the interaction between three concrete variables, the proximity between the State and the subject matter in question, the regulatory interest or concern pursued and the intrusiveness of the measure *vis-à-vis* the affected States and individuals.

In current scholarship, it is often implicitly assumed that there are clearly established limits to 'extraterritorial jurisdiction'. Thus, it is argued either that these limits should be upheld in order to constrain 'extraterritorial jurisdiction' as an antithesis to territorial sovereignty,[1161] or that these limits should be disregarded in order to endorse extraterritorial jurisdiction for the achievement of some higher objective, such as the protection of human rights.[1162] However, this research has noted that this premise may have to be rethought: It has found through a conclusive inquiry into the practice of States and the EU in four reference areas that the traditional system of jurisdiction is frequently unable to provide such consistent limits. Territoriality in particular is often like a checkbox, which formally needs to be ticked, but which says very little about the actual content of the claim. Certainly, this checkbox-mentality also somewhat reflects the practice of actual State decision-makers. In deciding whether or how to regulate an 'extraterritorial' situation, only the formal satisfaction of one of the bases of prescription is frequently considered.

---

1161 See to this end, in particular, the extensive argumentation by Parrish, 'Reclaiming International Law from Extraterritoriality' (n 10).

1162 Surya Deva, 'Corporate Human Rights Violations: A Case for Extraterritorial Regulation' in Christoph Luetge (ed), *Handbook of the Philosophical Foundations of Business Ethics* (Springer Netherlands 2013), 1087: 'It is high time that new legal principles are developed and invoked to respond to the modern forms of human rights abuses by companies that operate in disregard to geographical boundaries. In the area of extraterritoriality, such new principles should provide clearer and stronger basis for states to adopt extraterritorial measures in appropriate cases to promote a better realization of human rights.'.

This study, in part D, has offered an applicable three-part framework to mitigate this shortcoming of the territoriality-based system of jurisdiction in international law. It is the hope here that this framework may serve as a compass guiding future academic debate as well as actual State decisions. In this regard, there is also particular need for future research: the usefulness of the framework is somewhat limited by its high-level abstractness. It is therefore necessary to develop more concrete, subject-area specific solutions clarifying the precise contours of the principles both through academic discourse and case-law.[1163]

Perhaps even more radical however, this research advocates for a change in perspective. So far, international law scholars, addressing the topic of extraterritorial jurisdiction, have spent much energy on the 'extraterritorial' part. Marko Milanovic made the shrewd observation that '[i]ndeed, practically the entirety of the law of (prescriptive) jurisdiction is about the exceptions to territoriality'.[1164] This focus may have been misplaced. Despite the tremendous effort, the normative boundaries between 'extraterritorial' and 'territorial' are still muddied. Much less effort has gone into studying the second element of the concept, that of 'jurisdiction'. However, as this study has demonstrated, extraterritorial jurisdiction has a hybrid nature and paying more attention to this second part of 'extraterritorial jurisdiction' may indeed be a more promising route to innovation.

Writing on the history of (extra-)territorial jurisdiction, Richard Thompson Ford once came to this bleak conclusion:

> 'We may be doomed to reproduce the same tensions in different form, over and over again. The meaning of history may not be the heroic story of progress and perfection, nor the epic of decline, rebirth and redemption, but the blank tragedy of meaningless repetition.
>
> It is this realization that demands constant vigilance, with no guarantee of safety, that demands we make the effort and take the risk to find and nurture that which may be more noble than it is familiar.'[1165]

It is safe to say that the upheaval in the real world through processes such as globalization and the advent of the internet have not proven him wrong. Rather, we just seem to be producing the same tensions at a faster rate than ever. Indeed, this study has described how the territoriality-based

1163 This approach is also advocated by Svantesson (n 13), 59 – 62.
1164 Milanovic (n 27), 421.
1165 Ford (n 119), 930.

system of jurisdiction has, across different regulatory subject areas, repeatedly failed to satisfyingly balance the complex and deep interests at stake. It is neither a guarantor for State sovereignty and international order, nor is it an advocate for the marginalized voices of the individuals, nor is it the stern expert reminding us all of the common good.

I would, however, like to end on a more positive note. This study has taken the risk to find something that may be more noble than it is familiar: Extraterritorial jurisdiction is not only a technical inquiry relating legal acts to coordinates on a geographic map, but also an act driven by an actual purpose and having an effect on real persons. Extraterritorial jurisdiction, how could it be differently, concerns the exercise of public authority.

# Deutschsprachige Zusammenfassung

## *A. Einleitung*

Die Ausübung extraterritorialer Jurisdiktion unterliegt den Regeln des Völkerrechts. Die Grenzen staatlicher Befugnisse werden traditionell durch das Prinzip der souveränen Gleichheit der Staaten gezogen. Nach diesem Modell ist die Staatsgewalt in der Regel territorial begrenzt. Die Ausübung extraterritorialer Jurisdiktion als Ausnahme ist nur dann zulässig, wenn ein anderes Legitimationsprinzip des Völkerrechts erfüllt ist. Die Funktionalität dieses Systems hängt von zwei getrennten, aber miteinander verflochtenen Prämissen ab, die das Herzstück des Systems bilden: Die erste Prämisse ist, dass es möglich sein muss, exakt die Grenzen territorialer Hoheitsgewalt, d.h. die Grenze zwischen Territorialität und Extraterritorialität, zu bestimmen. Die zweite Prämisse ist, dass es möglich sein muss, solche weitere Prinzipien als Ausnahme zur Territorialität zu definieren, die vernünftigerweise die Ausübung extraterritorialer Jurisdiktion legitimieren.

Staaten wie auch Völkerrechtswissenschaftler waren sehr lange Zeit davon überzeugt, hinsichtlich beider Prämissen zufriedenstellende Antworten gefunden zu haben. Zwar wurden bestimmte Einzelheiten weiterhin kontrovers diskutiert. Insbesondere im Bereich des Strafrechts lassen sich die Auseinandersetzungen um die richtige geographische Reichweite des Rechts bis ins mittelalterliche Europa zurückverfolgen. Nichtsdestotrotz ist die völkerrechtliche Dogmatik zur Jurisdiktion erstaunlich widerstandsfähig geblieben und die ihr zugrundeliegenden Annahmen haben sich über die Jahre nur geringfügig verändert. Dies steht in einem krassen Widerspruch zu den grundlegenden Veränderungen in der realen Welt, die unter dem Schlagwort der „Globalisierung" zusammengefasst werden können. Globalisierung findet dabei insbesondere auch im Bereich der Regulierung statt, d.h., dass Staaten vermehrt versuchen, durch unilaterale Regulierung bestimmte innenpolitische oder moralische Werte und Ziele weltweit zur Geltung zu bringen.

Unter diesen Umständen setzt sich diese Arbeit die Beantwortung zweier Forschungsfragen zum Ziel: Erstens soll festgestellt werden, ob das auf dem Territorialitätsprinzip basierende System staatlicher Jurisdiktion noch in der Lage ist, durch eine klare Abgrenzung der Regelungskompetenz zwischen den Staaten die Ordnung in internationalen Beziehungen zu garantieren. Die Antwort auf diese Frage hängt davon ab, ob die erste Prämisse im Hinblick auf die Globalisierung noch zutrifft: Ist es möglich, normativ einheitliche Grenzen der Territorialität zu definieren, die von den Staaten respektiert werden? Oder können die Staaten bei der Verfolgung ihrer politischen und rechtlichen Ziele das System ausnutzen und missachten? Zweitens versucht diese Studie auch eine Antwort darauf zu geben, wie die extraterritoriale Jurisdiktion angesichts der notwendigen Rechtsfortentwicklung angemessen rekonzipiert werden kann, um der zunehmenden Bedeutung von Interessen jenseits der staatlichen Souveränität Rechnung zu tragen. Denn angesichts der normativen Umwälzungen, die die Globalisierung mit sich bringt, stellt diese Studie die Validität der zweiten, oben dargelegten Prämisse in Frage, dass die anerkannten Ausnahmen vom Territorialitätsprinzip in der Lage sind, die Ausübung extraterritorialer Jurisdiktion adäquat zu legitimieren.

Diese Arbeit argumentiert, dass das auf dem Territorialitätsprinzip basierende System der Jurisdiktion zwar auf dem ersten Blick eine logische Methode darstellt, um die Regulierungskompetenzen zwischen den Staaten zu verteilen, in der Praxis aber nun sein wichtigstes Versprechen nicht einlöst, nämlich zwischenstaatliche Ordnung zu garantieren. Es ist nicht möglich, konsistente, formale Grenzen zwischen Territorialität und Extraterritorialität zu definieren. Dies erlaub es Staaten, das System bei der Verfolgung politischer und rechtlicher Interessen auszunutzen oder es in seiner Gänze zu missachten. Die notwendige Weiterentwicklung des Rechts bietet jedoch die Chance, die extraterritoriale Jurisdiktion nicht nur als eine Funktion der staatlichen Souveränität, sondern im weiteren Sinne auch als eine Ausübung öffentlicher Gewalt zu begreifen, deren Legitimität auch von der Beziehung zwischen dem regulierenden Staat und dem Adressaten und der internationalen Gemeinschaft als Solche abhängt.

## *B. Die Regelungshoheit im Völkerrecht*

Dafür befasst sich diese Arbeit in ihrem Teil B zunächst mit den allgemeinen Zulässigkeitsvoraussetzungen für die Ausübung von Regelungsgewalt im Völkerrecht. Theoretisch vorstellbar sind insoweit zwei Ansätze, der *Lotus*-Ansatz, dass Staaten ihre Regelungsgewalt beliebig ausdehnen können, solange keine ausdrückliche völkerrechtliche Verbotsnorm dem entgegensteht, und der Ansatz, dass erst die Erfüllung bestimmter Jurisdiktionsprinzipien die Ausübung der Regelungsgewalt erlaubt. In der Theorie und Praxis durchgesetzt hat sich letztere Herangehensweise. Einen hinreichenden Anknüpfungspunkt zur Ausübung von Regelungsgewalt vermittelt dabei insbesondere das Territorialitätsprinzip. Als Ausnahmen hierzu kommen jedoch auch das aktive- und passive Personalitätsprinzip, das Schutzprinzip, das Universalitätsprinzip und das Wirkungsprinzip in Betracht. Das Territorialitätsprinzip und die weiteren Ausnahmen bilden die Basis für die normative Beurteilung von Jurisdiktionsausübungen und werden in Teil B, Kapitel I untersucht. Insbesondere werden dabei bestehende Kontroversen hinsichtlich der exakten Reichweite einzelner Prinzipien diskutiert.

Trotz der Erfüllung mindestens einer dieser Prinzipien, ist es möglich und auch völkerrechtlich zulässig, dass ein bestimmter Sachverhalt oder ein bestimmtes Verhalten einer Person in die konkurrierende Zuständigkeit mehrerer Staaten gleichzeitig fällt. Im Hinblick darauf geht Teil B, Kapitel II daher der Frage nach, ob Regeln des Völkergewohnheitsrechts oder sonst allgemeine Rechtsgrundsätze existieren, die die Ausübung staatlicher Hoheitsgewalt einschränken, obgleich eines der oben erwähnten Prinzipien eine Verbindung zwischen dem Staat und dem zu regelnden Sachverhalt vermittelt. Dabei fällt auf, dass es nicht an Vorschlägen in dieser Hinsicht mangelt. In Betracht kommen insbesondere das *genuine-link* Erfordernis, das Verbot des Rechtsmissbrauchs und der Grundsatz der Verhältnismäßigkeit, aber auch die speziell für das Problem der konkurrierenden Zuständigkeit entwickelten Prinzipien der *Comity* und der *Reasonableness*. In der Praxis konnte sich bisher jedoch keines dieser Ansätze durchsetzen, sodass eine Jurisdiktionsausübung, die sich auf eines der Jurisdiktionsprinzipien als Erlaubnistatbestand stützen kann, nicht noch weiteren Beschränkungen im Völkerrecht unterliegt.

## *C. Fallstudien zur Staatenpraxis*

Teil C der vorliegenden Arbeit argumentiert, dass die Anwendung der in Teil B hergeleiteten Jurisdiktionsprinzipien in der Praxis keine tauglichen, d.h. normativ klaren und einheitlichen, Ergebnisse liefert. Dafür untersucht dieser Teil der Arbeit die tatsächliche Staatenpraxis im Hinblick auf die Erfüllung des Territorialitätsprinzips oder einer der oben genannten Ausnahmetatbestände. Die Staatenpraxis selbst wird dabei festgestellt durch die Auswertung einer großen Zahl von offiziellen Dokumenten, die von Gesetzen, Verordnungen, Verwaltungsakten und Gerichtsentscheidungen über *Amicus-Curiae*-Stellungnahmen bis hin zu Protesten und Affirmationen durch diplomatische Mitteilungen reichen.

Es ist, selbstverständlich, kein Raum zur Berücksichtigung sämtlicher materiellen Rechtsbereiche, in denen es schon zur Ausübung extraterritorialer Jurisdiktion gekommen ist. Die vorliegende Arbeit beschränkt sich daher auf eine Auswahl von Forschungsbereichen, aus der sich allgemeine Schlussfolgerungen über den Zustand des auf dem Territorialitätsprinzip basierenden Jurisdiktionssystems ziehen lassen. Diese Studie hat sich auf Staatenpraxis im Bereich der Wirtschaftssanktionen (Kapitel II) und der Exportkontrolle (Kapitel III), der transnationalen Bestechung (Kapitel IV) und der Verhinderung und Wiedergutmachung von Menschenrechtsverletzungen durch Unternehmen (Kapitel V) konzentriert. Diesen Regelungsbereichen ist gemeinsam, dass Staaten hier häufig auf extraterritoriale Jurisdiktion zurückgreifen, um unilaterale Regelungen mit globaler Reichweite zu schaffen. Dies liegt daran, dass die Ziele und Interessen dieser Regelungsbereiche oft eine Außenorientierung haben, d.h., dass Staaten versuchen, ihre innerstaatlichen politischen Präferenzen oder Regulierungsstandards in Drittländer zu „exportieren“. Diese Arbeit erwartet, dass Staaten in diesen Bereichen stärker auf komplexe Regulierungsmechanismen zurückgreifen müssen, die das traditionelle Jurisdiktionssystem herausfordern.

Wie Teil C, Kapitel II zeigt, dominieren im Bereich der Wirtschaftssanktion die Vereinigten Staaten die Staatenpraxis hinsichtlich der Ausübung extraterritorialer Hoheitsgewalt. Andere Staaten haben sich bisher hauptsächlich darauf beschränkt, auf diese Jurisdiktionsausübungen zu reagieren. Der Gesetzgeber, die Regulierungsbehörden und die Gerichte in den Vereinigten Staaten erweitern den Anwendungsbereich ihrer Rechtsvorschriften durch verschiedene Ansätze. Dazu gehören die Kontrolltheorie, die auf der Kontrolle inländischer Mutterunternehmen über ausländische Tochtergesellschaften basiert, ein territorialer Ansatz, der auf dem spezifischen Mechanismus von US-Dollar-Transaktionen beruht, die technisch gesehen fast alle durch US-Banken abgewickelt werden, und schließlich sekundäre Handelsboykotte, die Wirtschaftssanktionen auch gegenüber Drittstaaten mit der Androhung möglicher Handelsbeschränkungen durchsetzen.

Europäische Staaten haben sehr uneinheitlich auf diese Jurisdiktionsausübungen durch die USA reagiert: Zum Beispiel akzeptierten sie stillschweigend die Verlängerung der Iran-Sanktionen in den Jahren 2010 und 2012 sowie die Verhängung extraterritorialer Sanktionen gegen Russland angesichts der Situation in der Ostukraine. Demgegenüber übten sie starke

Kritik an den strukturell identischen Maßnahmen der Vereinigten Staaten nach deren Rückzug aus dem Atomabkommen mit Iran. Diese Widersprüche in der Staatenpraxis tragen nicht gerade zur Feststellung des geltenden Rechts bei. Bei der Beurteilung der Praxis und der Reaktionen anderer Staaten hierauf kommt diese Arbeit zu dem Schluss, dass der völkerrechtliche Status dieser Regulierungsmechanismen weitgehend nicht geklärt ist. Es erscheint vertretbar, zu argumentieren, dass sie formal auf dem Territorialitätsprinzip beruhen, aber sie erlauben es den Vereinigten Staaten, unilaterale Regelungen mit globaler Reichweite zu treffen, die dem Ordnungsgedanken des Jurisdiktionssystems diametral zuwiderlaufen.

Andererseits zeigen auch die Reaktionen der Staaten auf die Hoheitsausübung der USA, dass den Jurisdiktionsprinzipien in der Praxis wenig Beachtung geschenkt wird. Tatsächlich lässt sich die uneinheitliche Reaktion insbesondere der europäischen Staaten am ehesten durch politische Zweckmäßigkeit erklären. Da aber Wirtschaftssanktionen als völkerrechtliche „Durchsetzungsinstrumente“ eine Vielzahl unterschiedlicher innenpolitischer Interessen bedienen können, fällt auch die Reaktion notwendigerweise je nach Interessenlage unterschiedlich aus.

Teil C, Kapitel III untersucht den Bereich der extraterritorialen Exportkontrolle. Obwohl sich verschiedene völkerrechtliche Verträge, rechtlich unverbindliche multilaterale Exportkontrollregime sowie die Resolution 1540 des UN-Sicherheitsrates zu diesem Regelungsbereich äußern, bietet keines dieser Instrumente eine rechtliche Grundlage für die Ausübung extraterritorialer Jurisdiktion. In der Praxis greifen Staaten daher insbesondere auf die innerstaatliche Reexportkontrolle zurück. Reexportkontrollen knüpfen entweder an die Herkunft der zu exportierenden Güter und Technologien an oder basieren auf der freiwilligen Unterwerfung des Importeurs, dass dieser die Güter nicht ohne vorherige Genehmigung des ursprünglichen Ausfuhrstaates weitergibt. Beide Regulierungsansätze spielten bereits im Pipeline-Zwischenfall von 1984 eine wichtige Rolle und wurden damals von der Europäischen Gemeinschaft vehement kritisiert.

Eine genauere Analyse kommt auch tatsächlich zu dem Schluss, dass es beiden Mechanismen an einer normativen Grundlage im geltenden Völkerrecht fehlt: Die Ausübung von Jurisdiktion über Personen als Inhaber der tatsächlichen Kontrolle über die exportierten Güter, wobei auf die Herkunft dieser Güter abgestellt wird, ist nach den derzeitigen Grundsätzen des Völkerrechts nicht zulässig. Das Personalitätsprinzip gilt nicht für Produkte oder Technologien und seien sie auch noch so sensibel, denn auf diese ist (selbstverständlich) nicht das Nationalitätsprinzip anwendbar. Solche Regulierungen sind auch nicht durch das Schutz- oder Wirkungsprinzip legitimiert. Ebenso sehen die traditionellen Jurisdiktionsprinzipien nicht die Möglichkeit vor, dass sich private Unternehmen der Regelungsgewalt eines anderen Staates unterwerfen können, weil die privatrechtliche Zustimmung angesichts der Souveränität des Importstaates irrelevant ist.

Im Gegensatz zu dieser Rechtslage steht jedoch die tatsächliche Staatenpraxis. Insoweit haben Staaten zwar nicht ausdrücklich herkunftsbezogene Exportkontrollen, wie sie durch die Vereinigten Staaten angewandt werden, akzeptiert, aber sie haben auch keine Proteste dagegen eingelegt und die Existenz einer solchen Praxis stillschweigend gebilligt. Noch deutlicher wird dieser Gegensatz jedoch im Hinblick auf die Reexportkontrolle, die auf privatrechtlicher Unterwerfung basiert. So verlangen fast alle Exportländer Endverbleibserklärungen oder ähnliche Dokumente, die die importierende Partei dazu verpflichten, hinsichtlich einer Weitergabe der Güter zunächst eine Genehmigung des Ursprungsstaates einzuholen. Diese Praxis zeigt, dass ein tatsächliches Bedürfnis für Reexportkontrollregelungen besteht. Das Völkerrecht lässt jedoch solche Mechanismen nicht zu. Die Rolle privater Vereinbarungen im Bereich der Exportkontrolle ist insoweit nur Ausdruck eines größeren Problems, nämlich, dass das auf dem Territorialitätsprinzip basierende Jurisdiktionssystem nicht in der Lage ist, Interessen zu berücksichtigen, die nicht mit der staatlichen Souveränität in Zusammenhang stehen.

Im Gegensatz zu extraterritorialen Wirtschaftssanktionen handelt es sich bei der in Teil C, Kapitel IV untersuchten Regulierung der transnationalen Korruption durch Unternehmen um einen Bereich, dessen Ziele von der internationalen Gemeinschaft nahezu universell akzeptiert werden. Transnationale Korruption ist heute als eines der drängendsten Folgeprobleme der Globalisierung anerkannt. Dies mündete in dem Abschluss von insgesamt sechs internationalen Übereinkommen zur Korruptionsbekämpfung sowie dem Erlass zahlreicher nationaler Rechtsvorschriften, die jeweils Bestimmungen mit weitreichender Extraterritorialität enthalten.

Vergleicht man die Gesetzgebung in den Vereinigten Staaten, im Vereinigten Königreich und in Frankreich, so zeigt sich, dass alle drei Staaten besonders darauf bedacht sind, das Verhalten ausländischer Tochtergesellschaften von inländischen Unternehmen zu regulieren. Dies soll sicherstellen, dass Anti-Korruptionsmaßnahmen nicht durch geschickte Unternehmensorganisation frustriert werden. Technisch wird dies entweder durch die Anordnung von konzernweiten Buchhaltungs- und Compliance-Maßnahmen zur Verhinderung oder Aufdeckung von Bestechung, oder durch die Schaffung von Haftungstatbeständen für das Mutterunternehmen, welches für das Verhalten seiner ausländischen Tochtergesellschaft einzustehen hat, oder durch die direkte Sanktionierung des Verhaltens der Tochtergesellschaft, erreicht. Letztere Maßnahmen sind unter dem geltenden Völkerrecht umstritten. Insoweit kann nämlich argumentiert werden, dass es sich bei dieser Form der Regulierung um eine Ausübung von Regelungsgewalt gegenüber der ausländischen Tochtergesellschaft anhand der Kontrolltheorie handelt, die im Bereich der Wirtschaftssanktionen starke negative Staatenreaktionen hervorgerufen hat.

Ebenso besteht im Bereich der Korruptionsbekämpfung die Tendenz, die Zuständigkeit gegenüber ausländischen Akteuren auf der Grundlage nur schwacher territorialer Verbindungen geltend zu machen. Insbesondere enthalten sowohl das britische *UK Bribery Act* als auch das französische *Sapin II* einen völlig neuartigen Anknüpfungspunkt, der die strafrechtliche Verfolgung von ausländischen Unternehmen ermöglicht, die nur einen begrenzten Teil ihrer wirtschaftlichen Tätigkeit im Inland ausüben. Im Hinblick auf diese Maßnahmen wird zwar vertreten, dass sie auf eine territoriale Verknüpfung beruhen. Dieser neuartige Anknüpfungspunkt kann aber auch als eine Erweiterung der Staatszugehörigkeit von Unternehmen interpretiert werden, für die es nach dem geltenden Völkerrecht keine Grundlage gibt. Ähnliche Schlussfolgerungen lassen sich auch für die auf Emittenten ausgerichteten Regelungen des amerikanischen *FCPA* ziehen.

Trotz dieser erheblichen völkerrechtlichen Bedenken ist nicht bekannt geworden, dass extraterritoriale Anti-Korruptionsregulierung zu zwischenstaatlichen Konflikten geführt hätte. Dies steht in einem beachtlichen Gegensatz zu der Situation bei (formal) sehr ähnlichen Maßnahmen im Bereich der Wirtschaftssanktionen. Es lässt sich damit argumentieren, dass die Staaten im Bereich der Korruptionsbekämpfung bereit sind, ein höheres Maß an Extraterritorialität zu akzeptieren, auch wenn die traditionellen Jurisdiktionsprinzipien bestimmte Ausübungen von Regelungsgewalt jedenfalls nicht eindeutig stützen. Dies könnte wiederum auf die bereits erwähnte Tatsache beruhen, dass Korruption überall auf der Welt als schädlich angesehen wird und insbesondere, dass der Kampf gegen transnationale Bestechung nicht nur als eine innenpolitische Priorität, sondern als ein globales Ziel anerkannt ist.

Daraus ergibt sich eine gewisse Vergleichbarkeit des Bereiches der Korruptionsbekämpfung mit der in Teil C, Kapitel V untersuchten Thematik der Verhinderung und Wiedergutmachung von Menschenrechtsverletzungen durch Unternehmen. Hier kommt allerdings noch eine weitere Dimension hinzu, nämlich, dass die Rechte und Interessen der Opfer von Menschenrechtsverletzungen, gleichsam in einem Dreiecksverhältnis, ebenfalls Beachtung zu finden haben. Bisher haben Staaten zwei weitgehend unabhängige Regulierungsmethoden eingesetzt, um das Verhalten von Unternehmen in Bezug auf Menschenrechte zu kontrollieren. Dies geschieht einerseits durch den Erlass von Gesetzen und anderen Vorschriften, die Menschenrechtsverpflichtungen für Unternehmen entlang von Konzern- oder Lieferantenbeziehungen etablieren, und andererseits durch die Ermöglichung von transnationalen Rechtsbehelfen für betroffene Opfer.

Im ersten Teilbereich wenden die Staaten zunehmend Handelsmaßnahmen, wie zum Beispiel Einfuhrbeschränkungen, oder *Due Diligence* Regelungen an, um Zwangs- und Kinderarbeit zu bekämpfen. Diese Maßnahmen werden im Hinblick auf ihre Extraterritorialität zumeist für unproblematisch gehalten, da sie stets auf eine inländische Verknüpfung zurückgreifen können, sei es der Zugang zu einem territorial abgegrenzten Markt oder der Sitz des Mutterunternehmens. Dieses Argument überzeugt jedoch nicht vollständig, denn diese Maßnahmen entsprechen von ihrer formalen Struktur den völkerrechtlich umstrittenen sekundären Wirtschaftssanktionen. Zwar gab es in der Tat trotz der starken extraterritorialen Auswirkungen keine Staatenproteste gegen Handelsmaßnahmen zur Verhütung von Menschenrechtsverletzungen. Dieser mangelnde Widerstand ist jedoch eher auf den Zweck dieser Maßnahmen, nämlich der Wahrung internationaler Menschenrechte, zurückzuführen. Wie im Bereich der Korruptionsbekämpfung sind Staaten also scheinbar auch hier bereit, eine weitergehende Extraterritorialität zu akzeptieren. Diese Feststellung bereitet aber dem traditionellen Jurisdiktionssystem Schwierigkeiten. Denn sie bedeutet ganz offenbar, dass die rechtliche Akzeptanz extraterritorialer Jurisdiktion nicht nur von formalen Kriterien abhängt, sondern dass diese durchaus auch mit dem materiellen Inhalt jeder Regelung variiert.

Transnationale Gerichtsverfahren wegen Menschenrechtsverletzungen durch Unternehmen können wiederum in zwei Kategorien unterteilt werden, nämlich Rechtsstreitigkeiten gegen Unternehmen mit Sitz im Forumstaat und Rechtsstreitigkeiten gegen Unternehmen aus Drittstaaten. Umstritten sind insbesondere letztere Verfahren. Während die Vereinigten Staaten mit dem *Alien Tort Statute* gleichsam das Universalitätsprinzip auf zivilrechtliche Streitigkeiten übertragen, hat in Europa zunehmend die Lehre vom *forum necessitatis* Beachtung gefunden. Beide Konzepte werfen schwierige normative Fragen auf. Sowohl die Übertragung des Universalitätsprinzips auf zivilrechtliche Streitigkeiten wie auch der Gerichtsstand des *forum necessitatis* werden nicht allgemein akzeptiert. Dies ist insbesondere im Hinblick auf *forum necessitatis* bedauerlich, bei dem es im Wesentlichen um die Abwägung zweier konkurrierender Werte des Völkerrechts geht und bei dem eine Jurisdiktionsausübung auch ohne eine sonstige substantielle Verknüpfung legitim sein kann. Bisher kann jedoch das auf dem Territorialitätsprinzip basierende Jurisdiktionssystem dieser besonderen Situation nicht gerecht werden.

Die in Teil C, Kapitel I – V dargelegte Staatenpraxis zeigt eindrucksvoll, dass das traditionelle Jurisdiktionssystem, welches seine Grundlage im Territorialitätsprinzip findet, auf zwei Arten herausgefordert wird.

Erstens ist dieses System nicht in der Lage, die Ordnung in internationalen Beziehungen zu garantieren, weil keine normativ konsistenten Grenzen der Territorialität existieren: Nach der traditionellen Dogmatik würde die Beantwortung der Frage, ob bestimmte Formen der Regulierung als territorial oder extraterritorial zu betrachten sind, in einem Zweischritt erfolgen. Zunächst, wird dabei der territoriale Teil des Verhaltens oder der Situation identifiziert und dann beurteilt, ob dieser Teil in einem normativen Sinne „relevant" ist, sodass eine Anknüpfung daran die Jurisdiktionsausübung legitimiert. Die Antworten auf diese Fragen sind jedoch keineswegs eindeutig. In der Praxis können Staaten diese Unklarheiten daher ausnutzen, und, indem sie sich nominell auf territoriale Verbindungen berufen, einseitige Regelungen mit globaler Reichweite treffen. Das auf dem Territorialitätsprinzip basierende Jurisdiktionssystem ist also, im Gegensatz zu seiner Zielsetzung, keineswegs in der Lage, die Regelungskompetenzen der Staaten zu begrenzen.

Zweitens lässt das System keine Erwägungen zu, die nicht in der Souveränität der Staaten verankert sind, obwohl sie die Legitimität von Jurisdiktionsausübungen beeinflussen sollten. Einerseits haben wir beobachtet, dass die Akzeptanz oder Ablehnung von Jurisdiktionsausübungen durch andere Staaten auch von den darin betroffenen materiellen politischen oder rechtlichen Interessen abhängt. So sind Staaten weniger geneigt, gegen bestimmte extraterritoriale Regelungen zu protestieren, wenn diese Regelungen die Erfüllung von Interessen der internationalen Gemeinschaft zum Zweck haben. Andererseits besteht im Hinblick auf die Jurisdiktionsausübung aufgrund privatrechtlicher Unterwerfung und das Prinzip des *forum necessitatis* das reale Bedürfnis, dass Staaten die Rechte und die Autonomie von natürlichen und juristischen Personen berücksichtigen können sollten.

## *D. Ein neuer Ansatz*

Da das auf dem Territorialitätsprinzip basierende Jurisdiktionssystem somit an verschiedenen Unzulänglichkeiten leidet, bietet Teil D der Arbeit eine alternative Konzeption der extraterritorialen Jurisdiktion an. Dieser Teil der Arbeit schlägt vor, dass die Ausübung extraterritorialer Jurisdiktion funktional der Ausübung inländischer öffentlicher Gewalt gegenüber Individuen gleichzusetzen ist. Daher sollten Staaten, die extraterritoriale Jurisdiktion nach dem Völkerrecht ausüben, nicht nur die souveräne Gleichheit der Staaten respektieren, sondern auch Aspekte sowohl der Legitimation als auch der Begrenzung von Hoheitsgewalt berücksichtigen, insbesondere die Beziehung zwischen dem regulierenden Staat und dem Adressaten und der internationalen Gemeinschaft als solche.

Teil D, Kapitel I begründet diesen Ansatz näher. Es widerlegt dabei zunächst das Argument, die Untersuchung neuer Ansätze zur extraterritorialen Jurisdiktion könnte im Hinblick auf weitere zwischenstaatliche Rechtsharmonisierung und verstärkte internationale Zusammenarbeit obsolet werden. Es räumt weiterhin mit dem Mythos auf, dass ein auf dem Territorialitätsprinzip beruhendes Jurisdiktionssystem gleichsam unvermeidbar ist. Insbesondere demonstriert Teil D, Kapitel I, dass die Territorialität eine relativ neue historische Entwicklung darstellt. Drittens wird diskutiert, ob nicht die Weiterentwicklung bestehender völkerrechtlicher Prinzipien, insbesondere das Prinzip der Nichteinmischung, bereits genügt, um die ermittelten Defizite des Jurisdiktionssystems zu überwinden.

Allerdings ist das Phänomen der extraterritorialen Jurisdiktion tatsächlich in dieser Hinsicht einzigartig, dass es einen Regelungsraum zwischen klar definiertem innerstaatlichen Recht und internationalem Recht einnimmt. Dieser hybride Charakter zeigt sich insbesondere darin, dass es auch Zweck der Ausübung extraterritorialer Jurisdiktion ist, das Verhalten der betroffenen Person direkt und unmittelbar zu „beherrschen". Die Ausübung extraterritorialer Jurisdiktion ist daher vergleichbar mit der Ausübung inländischer öffentlicher Gewalt, die innerstaatlich dem öffentlichen Recht unterliegen würde. Dessen Aufgabe ist es sowohl, öffentliche Gewalt zu legitimieren, d.h. die Situationen zu definieren, in denen staatlicher Zwang zulässig ist, als auch die Ausübung der öffentlichen Gewalt zu begrenzen. Richtigerweise muss daher auch die Ausübung extraterritorialer Jurisdiktion im Völkerrecht neben der souveränen Gleichheit der Staaten auch diese weiteren Dimensionen der öffentlichen Gewalt beachten.

Teil D, Kapitel II konkretisiert diesen Ansatz hinsichtlich der Legitimation und der Begrenzung der Ausübung extraterritorialer Jurisdiktion. Zu diesem Zweck untersucht dieses Kapitel verschiedene Legitimationsgründe, die zur Rechtfertigung von Jurisdiktionsausübungen auf der Grundlage traditioneller Prinzipien wie Territorialität, Nationalität und Universalität angeführt werden. Darin zeigt sich, dass selbst diese weithin akzeptierten Jurisdiktionsprinzipien nicht vollständig auf demokratische Legitimation zurückgreifen können. Vielmehr ergeben sich aus der Analyse drei kardinale Prinzipien, die die Ausübung (extra-)territorialer Hoheitsgewalt legitimieren und beschränken, nämlich (1), die Nähe zwischen dem regelnden Staat und dem Adressaten oder dem zu regulierenden Verhalten, (2), die Verwirklichung von Interessen der internationalen Gemeinschaft und (3), die Wahrung individueller Rechte und Interessen als Teil der Rechtsstaatlichkeit. Diesem letzten Aspekt widmet dieses Kapitel sodann besondere Aufmerksamkeit: Insoweit wird argumentiert, dass bereits jetzt Individualinteressen eine wachsende Rolle bei der Gestaltung der Reichweite staatlicher Jurisdiktion spielen, entweder durch die Möglichkeit, die Ausübung von Jurisdiktion durch Parteiautonomie zu bestimmen, oder als ein Prinzip, das die Ausübung exorbitanter Jurisdiktion einschränkt, oder als ein Recht, das die Staaten in besonderen Situationen dazu verpflichtet, extraterritoriale Jurisdiktion zum Schutz von Privaten auszuüben.

Teil D, Kapitel III demonstriert, dass die bereits erwähnten drei Prinzipien, die die Ausübung (extra-)territorialer Hoheitsgewalt legitimieren und beschränken, nicht nur eine gute theoretische Grundlage bieten, sondern dass sie auch praxistauglich sind. Es stellt daher ein neues praktisches Gerüst für die Ausübung extraterritorialer Hoheitsgewalt bereit. Dafür stellt Teil D, Kapitel III zunächst Erwägungen dahingehend an, welchen tatsächlichen Herausforderungen dieses neue Gerüst gerecht werden muss. Basierend auf diesen Erwägungen schlägt dieses Kapitel drei praxistaugliche Variablen, nämlich die Nähe zwischen dem Staat und dem betreffenden Gegenstand, das verfolgte Regulierungsinteresse oder der Regulierungszweck und die Eingriffsschwere der Maßnahme gegenüber den betroffenen Staaten und Einzelpersonen, als Grundlage des Gerüsts vor.

Diese Variablen stehen dabei nicht nebeneinander, sondern ihre Beziehung zueinander ist gleitend: Je näher der Staat und der Gegenstand der Regulierung beieinanderliegen, desto partikulärer darf das verfolgte Regulierungsinteresse sein. Umgekehrt darf die Verbindung umso schwächer sein, je mehr die Regulierung auf einer international anerkannten Norm beruht. Ausübungen von extraterritorialer Regelungsgewalt, die diese Voraussetzung nicht erfüllen, sind rechtsmissbräuchlich. Ähnliche

Überlegungen gelten in Bezug auf die Eingriffsschwere der Maßnahme: Größere Nähe oder gewichtige gemeinsame Interessen erlauben Regelungen, die die Rechte und Interessen der Betroffenen stärker beeinträchtigen, während Regelungen, die sich auf flüchtige Verbindungen stützen oder partikuläre Interessen verfolgen, weniger schwerwiegend eingreifend sein müssen. Ausübungen von extraterritorialer Regelungsgewalt, die diese Voraussetzung nicht erfüllen, sind unverhältnismäßig.

## *E. Ausblick*

Die Völkerrechtswissenschaft, die sich mit dem Konzept der extraterritorialen Jurisdiktion befasst, hat bisher viel Energie auf den Teil „extraterritorial" aufgewandt. Praktisch die Gesamtheit des Rechts der Regelungsgewalt dreht sich um die Ausnahmen zur Territorialität. Dieser Schwerpunkt ist fehlplatziert. Trotz der enormen unternommenen Anstrengungen sind die normativen Grenzen zwischen „extraterritorialer" und „territorialer" Jurisdiktion immer noch verwischt. Das zweite Element dieses Konzepts, das der „Jurisdiktion", wurde mit viel weniger Engagement untersucht. Wie diese Arbeit jedoch gezeigt hat, besitzt die extraterritoriale Jurisdiktion einen hybriden Charakter, und die stärkere Beachtung dieses zweiten Teils des Konzeptes könnte in der Tat ein vielversprechenderer Weg zu weiterer Innovation sein. Extraterritoriale Jurisdiktion kann nicht durch eine mechanische Untersuchung, indem bestimmte Regelungsakte mit den Koordinaten auf einer geographischen Karte in Beziehung gebracht werden, erfasst werden. Sie ist vielmehr auch ein Akt, der von einem tatsächlichen Zweck getrieben wird und der sich auf reale Personen auswirkt. Extraterritoriale Jurisdiktion, wie könnte es also anders sein, betrifft die Ausübung der öffentlichen Gewalt.

# Table of Cases

## ***Permanent Court of International Justice***

*Certain German Interests in Polish Upper Silesia (Germany v Poland)* (Merits) [1926] PCIJ Reports Series A No 7

*Free Zones of Upper Savoy and the District of Gex, Second Phase (France v Switzerland)* [1930] PCIJ Reports Series A No 24

*S.S. Lotus (France v Turkey)* [1927] PCIJ Reports Series A No 10

## ***International Court of Justice***

*Arrest Warrant of 11 April 2000 (Democratic Republic of the Congo v Belgium)* [2002] ICJ Rep 3

*Barcelona Traction Light and Power Co, Ltd. (Belgium v Spain)* [1970] ICJ Rep 3

*Case concerning military and paramilitary activities in and against Nicaragua (Nicaragua v United States of America)* [1986] ICJ Rep 14

*North Sea Continental Shelf Cases (Fed Rep of Germany v Netherlands)* [1969] ICJ Rep 3

*Nottebohm, Second Phase (Liechtenstein v Guatemala)* [1955] ICJ Rep 4

## ***Human Rights Committee***

*Länsmann v Finland* (1994), Communication No 511/1992, U.N. Doc. CCPR/C/52/D/511/1992

## ***International Criminal Tribunal for the former Yugoslavia***

*Furundzija Case* (Judgment), No IT-95–15/1-T, Trial Chamber (10 December 1998)

*Prosecutor v Tadic* (Jurisdiction), No IT-94–1-AR72, (2 October 1995), 35 ILM (1996)

## ***International Criminal Tribunal for Rwanda***

*Akayesu Case* (Judgement), No ICTR-96–4-T, Trial Chamber (2 September 1998)

## ***African Commission on Human and People's Rights***

*Social and Economic Rights Action Center (SERAC) and Center for Economic and Social Rights (CESR) v Nigeria* [2001] No 155/96

## European Court of Human Rights

*Banković and others v Belgium and others*, App No 52207/99, Decision of 12 December 2001

*Handyside v United Kingdom*, App No 5493/72, Judgment of 7 December 1976

*K.U. v Finland*, App No 2872/02, Judgment of 2 December 2008

*Kovačić and Others v Slovenia*, App No 44574/98, 45133/98 and 48316/99, Decision of 1 April 2004

*Loizidou v Turkey*, Preliminary Objections, App No 15318/89, Judgment of 23 March 1995

*López Ostra v Spain*, App No 16798/90, Judgment of 9 December 1994

*Nait-Liman v Switzerland* App No 51357/07, Judgment of 15 March 2018

## Inter-American Commission on Human Rights

*Maya indigenous community of the Toledo District v Belize* [2004] Case 12.053, Report No 40/04

*Victor Saldano v Argentina* [1999] Report No 38/99

## Inter-American Court of Human Rights

*Velásquez Rodríguez v Honduras* [1988] Series C No 4

## Court of Justice of the European Union

Case C-281/02, *Owusu v Jackson* [2005] ECR I-01383

Case C-366/10, *Air Transport Association of America and Others v Secretary of State for Energy and Climate* Change [2011] ECR I-13755

Case C-402/05 P, *Kadi and Al Barakaat International Foundation v Council and Commission* [2008] ECR I-06351

Case C-413/14 P, *Intel Corp. v European Commission*, [2017] ECLI:EU:C:2017:632

Case C-48/69, *Imperial Chemical Industries Ltd. v Commission of the European Communities* [1972] ECR 619

Case C-584/10 P, *Commission and Others v Kadi*, [2013] ECLI:EU:C:2013:518

Case C-89/85, *Ahlström Osakeyhtiö and others v Commission of the European Communities* [1988] ECR 5193

Case T-35/10, *Bank Melli Iran v Council of the European Union* [2013] ECLI:EU:T:2013:397

Case T-496/10, *Bank Mellat v Council* [2013] ECLI:EU:T:2013:39

## European Commission

*Dyestuffs*, (Case IV/26278) Commission Decision 69/243/EEC [1969], OJ L 195/11

### *WTO Appellate Body and WTO Panel*

WTO Appellate Body, *United States – Import Prohibition of Certain Shrimp and Shrimp Products*, WTO Doc WT/DS58/AB/R (1998)

WTO, Decision by the Arbitrators, *EC – Regime for the importation, sale and distribution of bananas, Recourse to arbitration by the EC under Article 22.6 of the DSU*, WT/DS27/ARB (1999)

### *US Supreme Court*

*American Banana Co. v United Fruit Co.*, 213 US 347 (1909)

*Boumediene v Bush*, 553 US 723 (2008)

*Crosby v National Foreign Trade Council* 530 US 363

*EEOC v Arabian American Oil Co.*, 499 US 244, 248 (1991)

*Goodyear Dunlop Tires Operations, S. A. v Brown*, 564 US 915 (2011)

*Hartford Fire Ins. Co. v California* 509 US 764, (1993)

*Hilton v Guyot*, 159 US 113 (1895)

*International Shoe Co. v Washington*, 326 US 310 (1945)

*J. McIntyre Mach., Ltd. v Nicastro*, 564 US 873 (2011)

*Jesner v Arab Bank, PLC*, 138 S Ct 1386 (2018)

*Kiobel v Royal Dutch Petroleum Co.*, 569 US 108, 113 (2013)

*Morrison v National Australia Bank Ltd.*, 561 US 247 (2010)

*Murray v Schooner Charming Betsy*, 6 US 2 Cranch 64

*Nestlé United States, Inc. v. Doe.* 141 S Ct 1931 (2021)

*RJR Nabisco, Inc. v European Community*, 136 S Ct 2090 (2016)

*Societe Internationale pour Participations Industrielles et Commerciales, S.A. v Rogers* 357 US 197, 211 (1958)

*Sosa v Alvarez-Machain*, 542 US 692, 724 (2004)

*United States v Microsoft Corp.*, 138 S Ct 1186 (2018)

*United States v Verdugo-Urquidez* 494 US 259, 271(1990)

### *US Federal Appeals Court*

*Al Shimari v CACI Premier Tech., Inc.*, 758 F 3d 516, 530 (4th Cir 2014)

*Allen v Lloyd's of London*, 94 F 3d 923, 930 – 932 (4th Cir 1996)

*Clarey v Gregg*, 138 F 3d 764, 766 (9th Cir 1998)

*Filartiga v Pena-Irala*, 630 F 2d 876, 887 (2d Cir 1980)

*Ibrahim v Department of Homeland Security*, 669 F 3d 983 (9th Cir 2012)

*In re Arab Bank, PLC Alien Tort Statute Litigation*, 808 F 3d 144 (2d Cir 2015)

*In re Terrorist Attacks on September 11*, 2001, 538 F 3d 71 (2d Cir 2008)

*In re Warrant to Search a Certain E-Mail Account Controlled and Maintained by Microsoft Corp*, 829 F 3d 197, 221 (2 Cir 2016)

*Iran Air v Kugelman*, 996 F 2d 1253, 1257–59 (DC Cir. 1993)
*Kadic v Karadžić*, 70 F 3d 232, 239 (2d Cir 1995)
*Licci v Lebanese Canadian Bank*, No 15–1580 (2d Cir 2016)
*Mannington Mills v Congoleum Corp*, 595 F 2d 1287 (3d Cir 1979)
*Mujica v AirScan Inc.*, 771 F 3d 580, 594 (9th Cir 2014)
*National Ass'n of Manufacturers v SEC*, 800 F 3d 518 (DC Cir 2015)
*Nat'l Council of Resistance of Iran v Dep't of State*, 251 F 3d 192, 201 (DC Cir 2001)
*Pakootas v Teck Cominco Metals, Ltd.*, 452 F 3d 1066 (9th Cir 2006)
*People's Mojahedin Org. of Iran v U.S. Dep't of State*, 182 F 3d 17, 22 (DC Cir 1999)
*Riley v Kingsley Underwriting Agencies*, Ltd, 969 F 2d 953, 957 – 958 (10th Cir 1992)
*Roby v Corporation of Lloyd's*, 996 F 2d 1353, 1366 (2d Cir 1993)
*Timberlane Lumber Co. v Bank of America NT & SA*, 549 F 2d 597 (9th Cir 1976)
*United States v Aluminum Corp of America*, 148 F 2d 416, 443 (2d Cir 1945)
*United States v Cardales*, 168 F 3d 548, 553 (1st Cir 1999)
*United States v Gonzales*, 776 F 2d 931 (11th Cir 1985)
*United States v Hoskins*, 902 F 3d 69, 85 (2d Cir 2018)
*United States v Peterson*, 812 F 2d 486, 493 – 494 (9th Cir 1987)
*United States v Yousef*, 327 F 3d 56 (2d Cir 2003)

### US Federal District Court

*Al-Aqeel v Paulson*, 568 F Supp 2d 64 (DDC 2008)
*Chase Manhattan Bank v State of Iran*, 484 F Supp 832 (SDNY 1980)
*Doe I v Unocal Corp* 963 F Supp 880, 891 – 892 (CD Cal 1997)
*Dooley v United Technologies Corp.*, 803 F Supp 428, 439 (DDC 1992)
*Kadi v Paulson*, Civil Action No. 2009–0108 (DDC 2012)
*In re Terrorist Attacks on September 11*, 2001, 740 F Supp 2d 494, 507–08 (SDNY 2010)
*In re Search Warrant No. 16–1061-M to Google*, 232 F Supp 3d 708, 712 (ED Pa 2017)
*In re Warrant to Search a Certain E-Mail Account Controlled and Maintained by Microsoft Corp*, 15 F Supp 3d 466, 475 – 476 (SDNY 2014)
*National Foreign Trade Council v Baker*, 26 F Supp 2d 287 (D Mass 1998)
*Pakootas v Teck Cominco Metals, Ltd.*, CV-04–256-AAM, 2004 WL 2578982 (ED Wash. 8 November 2004)
*SEC v Sharef et al.*, No. 1:2011cv09073 at 15 (SDNY 2013)
*SEC v Straub*, 921 F Supp 2d 244 (SDNY 2013)
*SEC v Straub*, No. 11 Civ. 9645 (RJS) (SDNY 2016)
*Sud v Costco Wholesale Corp. et al*, No. 15-cv-03783-JSW (ND Cal 2017)
*United States v Angola*, 514 F Supp 933, 935 – 936 (SD Florida 1981)

*United States v Evans*, 667 F Supp 974, 980 – 981 (SDNY 1987)

*US v Hoskins*, Ruling on Defendant's Rule 29(C) and Rule 33 Motions, 3:12-cr-00238 (D Conn 2020)

*United States v Kozeny*, 582 F Supp 2d 535, 539 (SDNY 2008)

*United States v Zarrab*, No. 15-cr-867, 2016 WL 6820737 (SDNY 2016)

*Yahoo! Inc v La Ligue Contre Le Racisme et l'Antisémitisme*, 169 F Supp 2d 1181, 1186 (ND Cal 2001)

## US State Courts

*People v World Interactive Gaming Corp*, 714 NYS 2d, 844 (1999)

## Other US Case Documents

Complaint, *SEC v Schering-Plough Corp.*, No 1:04cv00945 (DDC 2004)

Criminal Complaint, *United States v Dandong Hongxiang Industrial Development Co. Ltd. et al* (DNJ 2016)

Criminal Complaint, *United States v Robert Kraaipoel et al* (DDC 2007)

Criminal Information, *United States v DPC (Tianjin) Co. Ltd.*, No 05-cr-482 (CD Cal 2005)

Criminal Information, *United States v Hewlett-Packard Polska, SP Z O.O.*, No 14-cr-202 EJD (ND Cal 2014)

Criminal Information, *United States v JGC Corporation*, No 11-cr-260 (SD Texas 2011)

Criminal Information, *United States v Odebrecht S.A.*, No 16-cr-643 (EDNY 2016)

Criminal Information, *United States v ZAO Hewlett-Packard A.O.*, No 5:14-cr-201 DLJ (ND Cal 2014)

Department of Commerce, *In the Matter of McWane International Sales Company*, Order of 24 September 2014, Case No 14.06

Department of Commerce, *In the Matter of Zhongxing Telecommunications Equipment et al*, Order of 15 April 2018 Activating Suspended Denial Order relating to Zhongxing Telecommunications Equipment Corporation and ZTE Kangxun Telecommunications Ltd

Department of Commerce, *In the Matter of Zhongxing Telecommunications Equipment et al*, Order Terminating Denial Order Issued on April 15, 2018, Against Zhongxing Telecommunications Equipment Corporation and ZTE Kangxun Telecommunications Ltd., 83 Fed. Reg. 34825

Department of Justice, Plea Agreement between the DoJ and BNP Paribas, Letter of 27 July 2014

Department of the Treasury, Settlement Agreement between OFAC and BNP Paribas SA of 30 June 2014, COMPL-2013–193659

Factual Resume, *United States v ZTE Corporation*, 3–17-cr-120k (ND Texas 2017)

Indictment, *United States v Schneider et al,* No 09-cr-10.03.4 (D Mass 2009)

New York State Department of Financial Services, *In the matter of Commerzbank AG and Commerzbank AG New York Branch*, Consent Order of 12 March 2015

Plea Agreement of 20 June 2019, *United States v WMT Brasilia S.a.r.l.*, Criminal No. 1:19cr192

SEC, *In the Matter of Aloca Inc.*, Order of 9 January 2014, Administrative Proceeding File No 3–15673

SEC, *In the Matter of Diagnostics Products Corporation*, Order of 20 May 2005, Administrative Proceeding File No 3–11933

SEC, *In the Matter of Hewlett-Packard Co.*, Order of 9 April 2014, Administrative Proceeding File No. 3–15832

Superseding Indictment, *United States v Goncalves et al.*, No 1:09-cr-00335-RJL (DDC 2009)

Superseding Indictment, *United States v Zarrab*, No 15-cr-867, (SDNY 2016)

## British Cases

*AAA & Others v Unilever PLC and Unilever Tea Kenya Limited* [2018] EWCA Civ 1532

*Chandler v Cape Plc*, [2012] EWCA Civ 525

*Director of the Serious Fraud Office v Airbus SE* [2020] Case No U20200108

*Director of the Serious Fraud Office (SFO) v Eurasian Natural Resources Corporation Ltd* [2017] EWHC 1017 (QB) (08 May 2017)

*Her Majesty's Advocate v Abdelbaset Ali Mohmed Al Megrahi and Al Amin Khalifa Fhimah* High Court of the Justiciary at Camp Zeist, (Case No. 1475/99), Opinion of 31 January 2001

*Lamesa Investments Ltd v Cynergy Bank Ltd* [2019] EWHC 1877 (Comm)

*Libyan Arab Foreign Bank v Bankers Trust Co* [1989] 1 QB 728

*Lubbe v Cape Plc* [2000] UKHL 4

*Okpabi and others v Royal Dutch Shell Plc and another* [2018] EWCA Civ 191

*Okpabi & Others v Royal Dutch Shell plc & Anor* [2021] UKSC 3

*R v Perrin* (2002) EWCA Crim. 747 (22 March 2002)

*Serious Fraud Office v Standard Bank plc* [2014] Case No U20150854

*Thompson v The Renwick Group plc* [2014] EWCA Civ 635

*Vedanta Resources Plc and Konkola Copper Mines Plc v Lungowe and Others* [2019] UKSC 20

## German Cases

BGH, Judgment of 12 December 2000, 1 StR 184/00, reported in NJW 2001, 624 (*Töben*)

BGH, Judgment of 21 December 1960, VIII ZR 1/60, reported in BGHZ 34, 169

BGH, Order of 23 April 2010, AK 2/10, reported in BGHSt 55, 94

BGH, Order of 26 March 2009, StB 20/08, reported in NJW 2010, 385

Kammergericht, Order of 1 July 1983, Kart. 16/82, reported in WuW/E OLG 3051 (*Philip Morris Inc. v Bundeskartellamt*)

LG Hamburg, Judgment of 3 December 2014, 401 HKO 7/14

OLG Frankfurt am Main, Judgment of 9 May 2011, 23 U 30/10

OLG Rostock, Order of 29 February 2008, I Ws 60/08

## French Cases

Conseil constitutionnel, 23 March 2017, Decision no. 2017–750 DC

Cour d'appel de Paris, 22 May 1965, *Société Fruehauf Corp. v Massardy*, 1968 DS Jur 147, 1965, 5 ILM 476 (1966)

Cour d'appel de Paris (pole 6, ch 2), 20 June 2013, No 12/08935

Cour d'appel de Paris (pole 5, ch 4), 25 February 2015, No 12/23757

Cour de Cassation, civile, Chambre Sociale, 28 January 2015, 13–22.994, 13–22.995, 13–23.003, 13–23.004, 13–23.005, 13–23.006

Tribunal de Grande Instance de Paris, Ordonnance de référé, 22 May 2000, *UEJF et Licra v Yahoo! Inc. et Yahoo France*,

Tribunal de Grande Instance de Paris, Ordonnance de référé, 20 November 2000, *UEJF et Licra v Yahoo! Inc. et Yahoo France*,

## Dutch Cases

*Akpan v Shell* (18 December 2015) ECLI:NL:GHDHA:2015:3587

*Compagnie européenne des Pétroles S.A. v Sensor Nederland B.V.*, The Hague District Court (17 September 1982) 22 ILM (1983) 66

*El-Hojouj v Unnamed Libyan Officials*, The Hague District Court (21 March 2012) LJN: BV9748

*Oguru-Efanga v Shell* (18 December 2015), ECLI:NL:GHDHA:2015:3588

## Israeli Cases

*Israel v Eichmann*, 36 International Law Reports 277, 289 – 304, Isr. S. Ct. (1962)

## Hong Kong Cases

*American President Lines Ltd v China Mutual Trading Co Ltd.*, Supreme Court of Hong Kong, 1953 American Maritime Cases 1510

# Bibliography

Abbott KW, 'Defining the Extraterritorial Reach of American Export Controls: Congress as Catalyst' (1984) 17 Cornell International Law Journal 79.

Achilleas P, 'Introduction Export Control' in Dai Tamada and Philippe Achilleas (eds), *Theory and Practice of Export Control: Balancing International Security and International Economic Relations* (SpringerBriefs in Economics. Springer 2017).

Addo MK and Martin J, 'The Evolving Business and Society Landscape: Can Human Rights Make a Difference?' in Jena Martin and Karen E Bravo (eds), *The Business and Human Rights Landscape: Moving Forward, Looking Back* (Cambridge University Press 2015).

Akehurst MB, 'Jurisdiction in International Law' (1972–73) 46 BYIL 145.

Alldridge P, 'The U.K. Bribery Act: "The Caffeinated Younger Sibling of the FCPA"' (2012) 73 Ohio State Law Journal 1181.

Allwörden Sv, *US-Terrorlisten im deutschen Privatrecht: Zur kollisions- und sachrechtlichen Problematik drittstaatlicher Sperrlisten mit extraterritorialer Wirkung* (Studien zum ausländischen und internationalen Privatrecht v.313, Mohr Siebeck 2014).

Arcuri A and Violi F, 'Reconfiguring Territoriality in International Economic Law' in Martin Kuijer and Wouter Werner (eds), *Netherlands Yearbook of International Law 2016* (T.M.C. Asser Press 2017).

Asada M, 'The Role of the Security Council in WMD-Related Export Control: Synergy Between Resolution 1540 (2004) and Sanctions Resolutions' in Dai Tamada and Philippe Achilleas (eds), *Theory and Practice of Export Control: Balancing International Security and International Economic Relations* (SpringerBriefs in Economics. Springer 2017).

Ashe DP, 'The Lengthening Anti-Bribery Lasso of the United States: The Recent Extraterritorial Application of the U.S. Foreign Corrupt Practices Act' (2005) 73(6) FordhamLR 2897.

Augenstein D and Jägers N, 'Judicial Remedies: The Issue of Jurisdiction' in Juan J Álvarez Rubio and Katerina Yiannibas (eds), *Human Rights in Business: Removal of Barriers to Access to Justice in the European Union* (Routledge 2017).

Augenstein D and Kinley D, 'When Human Rights "Responsibilities" become "Duties": the Extra-Territorial Obligations of States that Bind Corporations' in Surya Deva and David Bilchitz (eds), *Human Rights Obligations of Business: Beyond the Corporate Responsibility to Respect?* (Cambridge University Press 2013).

Avi-Yonah RS, 'National Regulation of Multinational Enterprises: An Essay on Comity, Extraterritoriality, and Harmonization' (2003) 42(1) Columbia Journal of Transnational Law 5.

Backer LC, 'Multinational Corporations, Transnational Law: The United Nation's Norms on the Responsibilities of Transnational Corporations as a Harbinger of Corporate Social Responsibility in International Law' (2006) 37(2) Columbia Human Rights Law Review 287.

Bantekas I, 'Criminal Jurisdiction of States under International Law' in R. Wolfrum (ed), *The Max Planck Encyclopedia of Public International Law* (Oxford University Press).

—— 'Corruption as an International Crime and Crime against Humanity: An Outline of Supplementary Criminal Justice Policies' (2006) 4(3) JICJ 466.

Barnes R, 'United States Sanctions: Delisting Applications, Judicial Review and Secret Evidence' in Matthew Happold and Paul Eden (eds), *Economic Sanctions and International Law* (Studies in international law volume 62. Hart Publishing 2016).

Bartels L, 'Article XX of GATT and the Problem of Extraterritorial Jurisdiction: The Case of Trade Measures for the Protection of Human Rights' (2002) 36(2) Journal of World Trade 353.

—— 'The EU's Human Rights Obligations in Relation to Policies with Extraterritorial Effects' (2014) 25(4) EJIL 1071.

Battini S, 'Globalisation and Extraterritorial Regulation: An Unexceptional Exception' in Gordon Anthony, Jean-Bernard Auby and Morison John (eds), *Values in Global Administrative Law* (Hart 2011).

Bauer S, 'Internationale Entwicklungen in der Exportkontrolle' in Arnold Wallraff, Dirk Ehlers and Hans-Michael Wolffgang (eds), *Recht der Exportkontrolle: Bestandsaufnahme und Perspektiven: Handbuch zum Exportkontrollrecht.* zugleich Festgabe für Dr. Arnold Wallraff zum 65. Geburtstag (Schriften zum Aussenwirtschaftsrecht 2015).

Beaucillon C, 'Practice Makes Perfect, Eventually? Unilateral State Sanctions and the Extraterritorial Effects of National Legislation' in Natalino Ronzitti (ed), *Coercive Diplomacy, Sanctions and International Law* (Brill Nijhoff 2016).

Bechky PS, 'Sanctions and the Blurred Boundaries of International Economic Law' (2018) 83 Missouri Law Review 1.

Benvenisti E, 'Sovereigns as Trustees of Humanity: On the Accountability of States to Foreign Stakeholders' (2013) 107(2) AJIL 295.

Berman PS, 'The Globalization of Jurisdiction' (2002) 151 University of Pennsylvania Law Review.

—— 'Global Legal Pluralism' (2007) 80 Southern California Law Review.

—— *Global Legal Pluralism: A Jurisprudence of Law beyond Border* (1. publ, Cambridge Univ. Press 2012).

—— 'Legal Jurisdiction and the Deterritorialization of Data' (2018) 71 Vanderbilt Law Review 11.

Bernaz N, 'Enhancing Corporate Accountability for Human Rights Violations: Is Extraterritoriality the Magic Potion?' (2013) 117(3) JOBE 493.

—— *Business and human rights: History, Law and Policy – Bridging the Accountability Gap* (Human rights and international law, Routledge 2017).

Bianchi A, 'Comment to Professor Maier' in Karl M Meessen (ed), *Extraterritorial Jurisdiction in Theory and Practice* (Kluwer Law Internat 1996).

Bingham T, 'The Rule Of Law' (2007) 66 CLJ 67.

Blakesley C, 'Extraterritorial Jurisdiction' in M. C Bassioni (ed), *International Criminal Law* (3rd ed. Martinus Nijhoff Publishers 2008).

Bloom B, 'Criminalizing Kleptocracy?: The ICC as a Viable Tool in the Fight against Corruption' (2014) 29(3) American University International Law Review 627.

Bogdandy A von, 'Supranationale Union als neuer Herrschaftstypus: Entstaatlichung und Vergemeinschaftung in staatstheoretischer Perspektive' (1993) 16 Integration: Vierteljahreszeitschrift des Instituts für Europäische Politik in Zusammenarbeit mit dem Arbeitskreis Europäische Integration 210.

Bogdandy A von, Dann P and Goldmann M, 'Völkerrecht als öffentliches Recht: Konturen eines rechtlichen Rahmens für Global Governance' (2010) 49(1) Der Staat 23.

Bogdandy A von, Goldmann M and Venzke I, 'From Public International to International Public Law: Translating World Public Opinion into International Public Authority' (2017) 28(1) EJIL 115.

Bossuyt M, 'The Adverse Consequences of Economic Sanctions on the Enjoyment of Human Rights' (2000).

Bothe M, 'Proliferation of Weapons of Mass Destruction: A Problem of Extra-Territoriality' in Günther Handl, Joachim Zekoll and Peer Zumbansen (eds), *Beyond Territoriality: Transnational Legal Authority in an Age of Globalization* (Queen Mary studies in international law. Martinus Nijhofff Publishers 2012).

Bowman G, 'A Prescription for Curing U.S. Export Controls' (2014) 97(3) Marquette Law Review 599.

Bradford A, 'The Brussels Effect: The Rise of a Regulatory Superstate in Europe' (2012) 107 Northwestern University Law Review 1.

Bradley J, 'The Legality of Executive Orders 13628 and 13645: A Bipartite Analysis' (2015) 29 Emory International Law Review 705.

Braithwaite J and Drahos P, *Global Business Regulation* (Cambridge Univ. Press 2000).

Brennan BA, 'The Foreign Corrupt Practices Act Amendments of 1998: Death of a Law' (1990) 15 North Carolina Journal of International Law and Commercial Regulation 229.

Brilmayer L, 'Rights, Fairness, and Choice of Law' (1989) 98 YaleLJ 1277.

Bruin E de, 'Export Control Regimes—Present-Day Challenges and Opportunities' in Robert Beeres and others (eds), *NL ARMS Netherlands Annual Review of Military Studies 2021* (NL ARMS. T.M.C. Asser Press 2022).

Buxbaum HL, 'Territory, Territoriality, and the Resolution of Jurisdictional Conflict' (2009) 57(3) AJCL.

Cameron I, 'UN Targeted Sanctions, Legal Safeguards and the European Convention on Human Rights' (2003) 72(2) Nordic Journal of International Law 159.

Campos NF, Dimova R and Saleh A, 'Whither Corruption?: A Quantitative Survey of the Literature on Corruption and Growth' (Bonn 2010). IZA Discussion Paper 5334, http://ftp.iza.org/dp5334.pdf.

Carroll AB and Shabana KM, 'The Business Case for Corporate Social Responsibility: A Review of Concepts, Research and Practice' (2010) 12(1) IJMR 85.

Carter BE, 'Economic Sanctions' in R. Wolfrum (ed), *The Max Planck Encyclopedia of Public International Law* (Oxford University Press).

Carter BE and Farha RM, 'Overview and Operation of the Evolving U.S. Financial Sanctions, Including the Example of Iran' (2013) 44(3) Georgetown Journal of International Law 903.

Casey-Maslen S and others, *The Arms Trade Treaty: A commentary* (Oxford commentaries on international law, First edition, Oxford University Press 2016).

Chambers R, 'An Evaluation of Two Key Extraterritorial Techniques to Bring Human Rights Standards to Bear on Corporate Misconduct: Jurisdictional Dilemma Raised/Created by the Use of the Extraterritorial Techniques' (2018) 14(2) ULR 22.

Chapman B, *Export Controls: A Contemporary History* (University Press of America 2013).

Chehtman A, 'The Extraterritorial Scope of the Right to Punish' (2010) 29(2) Law and Philos 127.

Chesterman S, 'Globalisation and Public law: A Global Administrative Law' in Jeremy M Farrall and Kim Rubenstein (eds), *Sanctions, Accountability and Governance in a Globalised World* (Connecting international law with public law. Cambridge University Press 2009).

Chimni BS, 'The international law of jurisdiction: A TWAIL perspective' (2022) 35(1) Leiden Journal of International Law 29.

Choi SJ and Guzman AT, 'Portable Reciprocity – Rethinking the International Reach of Securities Regulation' 1997 Southern California Law Review 903.

Clark HL, 'Dealing with U.S. Extraterritorial Sanctions and Foreign Countermeasures' (1999) 20 University of Pennsylvania Journal of International Economic Law.

Cleveland SH, 'Norm Internalization and U.S. Economic Sanctions' (2001) 26(1) YaleJIntLaw 1.

Colangelo AJ, 'A Unified Approach to Extraterritoriality' (2011) 97 Virginia Law Review 1019.

—— 'Spatial Legality' (2012) 107 Northwestern University Law Review 69.

Coleman S, 'Foreign Corrupt Practices Act' (2017) 54 American Criminal Law Review 1381.

Coomans F and Kamminga MT, 'Comparative Introductory Comments on the Extraterritorial Application of Human Rights Treaties' in Fons Coomans and Menno T Kamminga (eds), *Extraterritorial Application of Human Rights Treaties* (Intersentia 2004).

Cooreman B, *Global Environmental Protection through Trade: A Systematic Approach to Extraterritoriality* (Edward Elgar Publishing 2017).

Cossart S, Chaplier J and Beau de Lomenie T, 'The French Law on Duty of Care: A Historic Step Towards Making Globalization Work for All' (2017) 2(2) Business and Human Rights Journal 317.

Coughlan SG and others, *Law Beyond Borders: Extraterritorial Jurisdiction in an Age of Globalization* (Irwin Law; Canadian Electronic Library 2014).

Crawford J and Brownlie I, *Brownlie's Principles of Public International Law* (Eighth edition, Oxford University Press 2012).

Criminal Division of the U.S. Department of Justice and the Enforcement Division of the U.S. Securities and Exchange Commission, 'A Resource Guide to the U.S. Foreign Corrupt Practices Act: Second Edition' (2020).

Currie RJ, 'Cross-Border Evidence Gathering in Transnational Criminal Investigation: Is the Microsoft Ireland Case the "Next Frontier"?' (2017) 54 Canadian Yearbook of international Law/ 63.

de la Torre, Mateo J. 'The Foreign Corrupt Practices Act: Imposing an American Definition of Corruption on Global Markets' (2016) 49 Cornell International Law Journal 469.

De Schutter O, 'Extraterritorial Jurisdiction as a Tool for Improving the Human Rights Accountability of Transnational Corporations' (2006).

Deva S, 'Corporate Human Rights Violations: A Case for Extraterritorial Regulation' in Christoph Luetge (ed), *Handbook of the Philosophical Foundations of Business Ethics* (Springer Netherlands 2013).

Diamant MS, Sullivan CW and Smith Jason H. 'FCPA Enforcement Against U.S. and Non-U.S. Companies' (2019) 8 Michigan Business & Entrepreneurial Law Review 353.

Dietrich T, *Die Erstreckung der Strafbarkeit auf Auslandssachverhalte nach § 35 AWG: Die Vereinbarkeit von § 35 AWG mit dem Völkerrecht* (Zugl.: München, Univ. Diss. 2013. Schriftenreihe Studien zum Völker- und Europarecht vol 121, Kovač 2014).

Dimant E and Schulte Thorben, 'The Nature of Corruption: An Interdisciplinary Perspective' (2016) 17(1) German Law Journal 53.

Dobson NL and Ryngaert C, 'Provocative Climate Protection: EU "Extraterritorial" Regulation of Maritime Emissions' (2017) 66(02) ICLQ 295.

Donovan DF and Roberts A, 'The Emerging Recognition of Universal Civil Jurisdiction' (2006) 100 AJIL 142.

Drobak J, 'Personal Jurisdiction in a Global World: The Impact of the Supreme Court's Decisions in Goodyear Dunlop Tires and Nicastro' (2013) 90 Washington University Law Review 1707.

Eckert S, 'The Business Transparency on Trafficking and Slavery Act: Fighting Forced Labor in Complex Global Supply Chains' (2013) 12(2) Journal of International Business and Law.

Edoardo Varisco A, Brockmann K and Robin L, 'Post-shipment Control Measures: European Approaches to On-site Inspections of Exported Military Materiel' (2020), https://www.sipri.org/sites/default/files/2020-12/bp_2012_post-shipment_controls.pdf.

Elagab OY, *The Legality of Non-Forcible Counter-Measures in International Law* (Oxford Monographs in International Law, Clarendon Press 1988).

Emmenegger S, 'Extraterritorial Economic Sanctions and Their Foundation in International Law' (2016) 33 Arizona Journal of International & Comparative Law 631.

Engelhart M, 'Der britische Bribery Act 2010' (2016) 128(3) Zeitschrift für die gesamte Strafrechtswissenschaft.

Enneking LFH, *Foreign Direct Liability and Beyond: Exploring the Role of Tort Law in Promoting International Corporate Social Responsibility and Accountability* (Zugl.: Utrecht, Univ. Diss. 2012, Eleven Internat. Publ 2012).

Erman E, 'Global Political Legitimacy beyond Justice and Democracy?' (2016) 8(1) Int Theory 29.

Fassbender B, 'Targeted Sanctions Imposed by the UN Security Council and Due Process Rights' (2006) 3 International Organizations Law Review 437.

Faure M and Zhang X, 'Towards an Extraterritorial Application of the Chinese Anti-Monopoly Law that Avoids Trade Conflicts' (2013) 45 The George Washington International Law Review 101.

Ford RT, 'Law's Territory (a History of Jurisdiction)' (1999) 97 Michigan Law Review 843.

Fornara C, 'Plutarch and the Megarian Decree' in Donald Kagan (ed), *Studies in the Greek historians: In memory of Adam Parry* (Yale classical studies vol 24. Cambridge University Press 1975).

Forwick C, *Extraterritoriale US-amerikanische Exportkontrollen: Folgen für die Vertragsgestaltung* (Abhandlungen zum Recht der Internationalen Wirtschaft vol 25, Verlag Recht und Wirtschaft (c)1992).

Friedberg J, 'The Arab League Boycott of Israel: Warring Histories, International Trade, and Human Rights' in Jena Martin and Karen E Bravo (eds), *The Business and Human Rights Landscape: Moving Forward, Looking Back* (Cambridge University Press 2015).

Genard Q, 'European Union Response to Extraterritorial Claims by the United States: Lessons from Trade Control Cases' [2014] Non-Proliferation Papers 1.

George E, 'Influencing the Impact of Business on Human Rights: Corporate Social Responsibility through Transparency and Reporting' in Lara Blecher, Nancy K Stafford and Gretchen C Bellamy (eds), *Corporate Responsibility for Human Rights Impacts: New Expectations and Paradigms* (American Bar Association 2014).

Gerber DJ, 'The Extraterritorial Application of the German Antitrust Laws' (1983) 77(4) AJIL 756.

Gibney MP, 'The Extraterritorial Application of U.S. Law: The Perversion of Democratic Governance, the Reversal of Institutional Roles, and the Imperative of Establishing Normative Principles' (1996) 19(2) Boston College International and Comparative Law Review 297.

Goldhaber MD, 'Corporate Human Rights Litigation in Non-U.S. Courts: A Comparative Scorecard (Human Rights Litigation in State Courts and Under State Laws)' (2013) 3 University of California Irvine Law Review 127.

Goldsmith JL, 'Against Cyberanarchy' (1998) 65(4) The University of Chicago Law Review 1199.

Grossfeld B and Rogers CP, 'A Shared Values Approach to Jurisdictional Conflicts in International Economic Law' (1983) 32(4) ICLQ 931.

Grosswald Curran V, 'Harmonizing Multinational Parent Company Liability for Foreign Subsidiary Human Rights Violations' (2016) 17 Chicago Journal of Interanational Law 403.

Grosswald Curran V and Sloss D, 'Reviving Human Rights Litigation After Kiobel' (2013) 107 AJIL 858.

Gruson M, 'The U.S. Jurisdiction over Transfers of U.S. Dollars between Foreigners and over Ownership of U.S. Dollar Accounts in Foreign Banks' [2004] Columbia Business Law Review 721.

Handl G, 'Extra-Territoriality and Transnational Legal Authority' in Günther Handl, Joachim Zekoll and Peer Zumbansen (eds), *Beyond Territoriality: Transnational Legal Authority in an Age of Globalization* (Queen Mary studies in international law. Martinus Nijhofff Publishers 2012).

Happold M, 'Economic Sanctions and International Law: An Introduction' in Matthew Happold and Paul Eden (eds), *Economic Sanctions and International Law* (Studies in international law volume 62. Hart Publishing 2016).

Harris KD, 'The California Transparency in Supply Chains Act: A Resource Guide'.

'Harvard Research Draft Convention on Jurisdiction with Respect to Crime' (1935) 29 Supp AJIL 439.

Hatcher SL, 'Circuit Board Jurisdiction: Electronic Payments and the Presumption against Extraterritoriality' (2020) 48 Georgia Journal of International and Comparative Law 591.

Hertogen A, 'Sovereignty as Decisional Independence over Domestic Affairs: The Dispute over Aviation in the EU Emissions Trading System' (2012) 1(02) TEL 281.

—— 'Letting Lotus Bloom' (2015) 26(4) EJIL 901.

Hills L, 'Universal Anti-Bribery Legislation Can Save International Business: A Comparison of the FCPA and the UKBA in an Attempt to Create Universal Legislation to Combat Bribery around the Globe' (2014) 13 Richmond Journal of Global Law and Business 469.

Hocke E and others, *Außenwirtschaftsrecht* (Heidelberger Kommentar, C.F. Müller 2017).

Hoffman PL, 'Kiobel v. Royal Dutch Petroleum Co: First Impressions' [2013] Columbia Journal of Transnational Law 28.

Holthausen D, 'Die Strafbarkeit von Auslandstaten Deutscher und das völkerrechtliche Interventionsverbot' [1992] NJW 214.

Hovell D, 'The Authority of Universal Jurisdiction' (2018) 29(2) EJIL 427.

Huntington SP, *Political Order in Changing Societies* (11. printing, Yale Univ. Press 1976).

Illingworth P, 'Global Need: Rethinking Business Norms' in Jena Martin and Karen E Bravo (eds), *The Business and Human Rights Landscape: Moving Forward, Looking Back* (Cambridge University Press 2015).

International Bar Association, *Report of the Task Force on Extraterritorial Jurisdiction* (International Bar Association 2008).

International Law Commission, *Report of the International Law Commission on the Work of its Fifty-eighth Session* (UN Doc A 61/10, 2006).

Ireland-Piper D, 'Prosecutions of Extraterritorial Criminal Conduct and the Abuse of Rights Doctrine' (2013) 9(4) ULR 68.

—— *Accountability in Extraterritoriality: A Comparative and International Law Perspective* (Edward Elgar Publishing 2017).

Jackson JH, 'Sovereignty – Modern: A new Approach to an Outdated Concept' (2003) 97(4) AJIL 782.

Jankowitsch-Prevor O and Michel Q (eds), *European Dual-Use Trade Controls: Beyond Materiality and Borders* (Peter Lang 2014).

Johnson DR and Post D, 'Law and Borders: The Rise of Law in Cyberspace' (1996) 48 Stanford Law Review 1367.

Joyner DH, 'International Legal Limits on the Ability of States to Lawfully Impose International Economic/Financial Sanctions' in Ali Z Marossi and Marisa R Bassett (eds), *Economic Sanctions under International Law* (T.M.C. Asser Press 2015).

Kaeb C and Scheffer DJ, 'The Paradox of "Kiobel" in Europe' (2013) 107 AJIL 852.

Kämmerer JA, 'Comity' in R. Wolfrum (ed), *The Max Planck Encyclopedia of Public International Law* (Oxford University Press).

Kamminga MT, 'Extraterritoriality' in R. Wolfrum (ed), *The Max Planck Encyclopedia of Public International Law* (Oxford University Press).

Kappel J and Lagodny O, 'Der UK Bribery Act – Ein Strafgesetz erobert die Welt: Ein kritischer Diskussionsanstoß' [2012] StV 695.

Kassan S, 'Extraterritorial Jurisdiction in the Ancient World' (1935) 29 AJIL 237.

Katz Cogan J, 'The Regulatory Turn in International Law' (2011) 52(2) HarvIntlLJ 322.

Katzenstein S, 'Dollar Unilateralism: The New Frontline of National Security' (2015) 90 Indiana Law Journal 293.

Kelsen H, *Principles of international law* (Rinehart and Co 1952).

Kingsbury B, Krisch N and Stewart RB, 'The Emergence of Global Administrative Law' (2005) 68(3) Law and Contemporary Problems 15.

Kinley D and Chambers R, 'The UN Human Rights Norms for Corporations: The Private Implications of Public International Law' (2006) 6(3) HRLRev 447.

Kiss A, 'Abuse of Rights' in R. Wolfrum (ed), *The Max Planck Encyclopedia of Public International Law* (Oxford University Press).

Koehler M, 'The Facade of FCPA Enforcement' (2010) 41 Georgetown Journal of International Law 907.

—— 'The Foreign Corrupt Practices Act under the Microscope' (2012) 15 University of Pennsylvania Journal of Business Law 1.

Kohl U, 'Corporate Human Rights Accountability: The Objections Of Western Governments To The Alien Tort Statute' (2014) 63(03) ICLQ 665.

—— 'Jurisdiction in Cyberspace' in Nikolaos K Tsagourias and Russell Buchan (eds), *Research Handbook on International Law and Cyberspace* (Research handbooks in international law, Paperback edition 2017. Edward Elgar Publishing 2015).

Kokott J and Sobotta C, 'The Kadi Case – Constitutional core values and international law – finding the balance?' (2013) 23(4) EJIL 1015–1014.

Koskenniemi M, 'What Use for Sovereignty Today?' (2011) 1(1) Asian Journal of International Law 61.

Krisch N, 'The Decay of Consent: International Law in an Age of Global Public Goods' (2014) 108 AJIL 1.

Krisch N and Kingsbury B, 'Introduction: Global Governance and Global Administrative Law in the International Legal Order' (2006) 17(1) EJIL 1.

Layton A and Parry AM, 'Extraterritorial Jurisdiction: European Responses' (2004) 26 Houston Journal of International Law 309.

Leff NH, 'Economic Development Through Bureaucratic Corruption' (1964) 8(3) American Behavioral Scientist 8.

Leibold A, 'Extraterritorial Application of the FCPA under International Law' (2015) 51 Willemette Law Review 223.

Letzien C, *Internationale Korruption und Jurisdiktionskonflikte: Die Sanktionierung von Unternehmen im Fall der Bestechung ausländischer Amtsträger* (Juridicum – Schriftenreihe zum Strafrecht, Springer Fachmedien Wiesbaden 2018).

Liivoja R, 'Review of "Jurisdiction in International Law" by Cedric Ryngaert' (2008) 19 Finnish Yearbook of International Law 397.

Loomis W, 'The Responsibility of Parent Corporations for the Human Rights Violations of their Subsidiaries' in Michael K Addo (ed), *Human rights standards and the responsibility of transnational corporations* (Kluwer 1999).

Lordi JA, 'The U.K. Bribery Act: Endless Jurisdictional Liability on Corporate Violaters' (2012) 44 Case Western Reserve Journal of International Law 955.

Lowe A, 'Blocking Extraterritorial Jurisdiction: The British Protection of Trading Interests Act, 1980' (1981) 75 AJIL 257.

Lowe V, 'US Extraterritorial Jurisdiction: The Helms-Burton and d'Amato Acts' (1997) 46 ICLQ 378.

Lowe V and Staker C, 'Jurisdiction' in Malcolm D Evans (ed), *International Law* (5th ed. Oxford University Press 2018).

Lowenfeld AF, *International Economic Law* (International Economic Law Series, 2nd ed. Oxford University Press 2008).

Luo W, 'Research Guide to Export Control and WMD Nonproliferation Law' (2007) 35 International Journal of Legal Information 447.

Magnuson W, 'International Corporate Bribery and Unilateral Enforcement' (2013) 51(2) Columbia Journal of Transnational Law 360.

—— 'Unilateral Corporate Regulation' (2016) 17 Chicago Journal of Interanational Law 521.

Maier HG, 'Jurisdictional Rules in Customary International Law' in Karl M Meessen (ed), *Extraterritorial Jurisdiction in Theory and Practice* (Kluwer Law Internat 1996).

Maine HS, *Ancient Law: Its Connection with the Early History of Society, and its Relation to Modern Ideas* (3rd American, from 5th London ed. H. Holt 1873).

Mann FA, 'The Doctrine of Jurisdiction in International Law' (1964) 111 Recueil des Cours 1.

Marauhn T, 'Global Governance of Dual-Use Trade: The Contribution of International Law' in Oliver Meier (ed), *Technology Transfers and Non-Proliferation: Between Control and Cooperation* (Routledge global security studies. Routledge/ Taylor & Francis Group 2014).

Marceau JF, 'A Little Less Conversation, A Little More Action: Evaluating and Forecasting the Trend of More Frequent and Severe Prosecutions Under the Foreign Corrupt Practices Act' (2007) 12 Fordham Journal of Corporate & Finance Law 285.

Marcuss S, 'Jurisdiction with Respect to Foreign Branches and Subsidiaries: Judicial Power in the Foreign Affairs Context under Section 414 of the Foreign Relations Restatement' (1992) 26 The International Lawyer 1.

Marcuss S and Mathias Stephen, 'U.S. Foreign Policy Export Controls: Do They Pass Muster under International Law' (1984) 2 Berkeley Journal of International Law 1.

Martyniszyn M, 'Japanese Approaches to Extraterritoriality in Competition Law' (2017) 66(03) ICLQ 747.

Massey DB, 'How the American Law Institute Influences Customary Law: The Reasonableness Requirement of the Restatement of Foreign Relations Law' (1997) 22 YaleJIntLaw 419.

Massoud S, *Menschenrechtsverletzungen im Zusammenhang mit wirtschaftlichen Aktivitäten von transnationalen Unternehmen* (Interdisziplinäre Studien zu Menschenrechten vol 2, 1. Auflage 2018, Springer Berlin; Springer 2018).

Mauro P, 'Corruption and Growth' (1995) 110(3) The Quarterly Journal of Economics 681.

McCorquodale R, 'Corporate Social Responsibility and International Human Rights Law' (2009) 87 (2009) JOBE 385.

—— 'International Human Rights Law Perspectives on the UN Framework and Guiding Principles on Business and Human Rights' in Lara Blecher, Nancy K Stafford and Gretchen C Bellamy (eds), *Corporate Responsibility for Human Rights Impacts: New Expectations and Paradigms* (American Bar Association 2014).

Meeran R, 'Access to Remedy: the United Kingdom Experience of MNC Tort Litigation for Human Rights Violations' in Surya Deva and David Bilchitz (eds), *Human Rights Obligations of Business: Beyond the Corporate Responsibility to Respect?* (Cambridge University Press 2013).

—— 'Multinational Human Rights Litigation in the UK: A Retrospective' (2021) 6(2) Business and Human Rights Journal 255.

Meessen KM, 'Antitrust Jurisdiction under Customary International Law' (1984) 78 AJIL 783.

—— 'Extraterritoriality of Export Control: A German Lawyer Analysis of the Pipeline Case' (1985) 27 German Yearbook of International Law 97.

Mehle B and Mehle V, 'Die notwendige Einhaltung von EU-Embargoregelungen durch Unternehmen mit Sitz in Drittstaaten' (2015) 61(7) Recht der internationalen Wirtschaft 397.

Meier O, 'Dual-Use Technology Transfers and the Legitimacy of Non-Proliferation Regimes' in Oliver Meier (ed), *Technology Transfers and Non-Proliferation: Between Control and Cooperation* (Routledge global security studies. Routledge/ Taylor & Francis Group 2014).

Meijer H, *Trading with the Enemy: The Making of US Export Control Policy toward the People's Republic of China* (First edition, Oxford University Press 2016).

Meng W, *Extraterritoriale Jurisdiktion im öffentlichen Wirtschaftsrecht: Extraterritorial Jurisdiction in Public Economic Law* (Beiträge zum ausländischen öffentlichen Recht und Völkerrecht vol 119, Springer 1994).

—— 'Wirtschaftssanktionen und staatliche Jurisdiktion – Grauzonen im Völkerrecht' (1997) 47 ZaöRV 269.

Mestral AL de and Gruchalla-Wesierski T, *Extraterritorial application of export control legislation: Canada and the USA* (Research study/ Canadian Council of International Law vol 1, Nijhoff 1990).

Meyer JA, 'Second Thoughts on Secondary Sanctions' (2009) 30(3) University of Pennsylvania Journal of International Law 905.

—— 'Dual Illegality and Geoambiguous Law: A New Rule for Extraterritorial Application of U.S. Law' (2010) 95 Minnesota Law Review 110.

Meyer K, *Grenzen und Entwicklungsmöglichkeiten des Souveränitätsprinzips in transnationalen Handelsbeziehungen: Zur Legitimation grenzüberschreitender Verwaltungszusammenarbeit am Beispiel des Lebensmittelhandels zwischen der Europäischen Union und Drittstaaten* (Jus Internationale et Europaeum, 1. Auflage, Mohr Siebeck 2018).

Milanovic M, 'From Compromise to Principle: Clarifying the Concept of State Jurisdiction in Human Rights Treaties' (2008) 8(3) HRLRev 411.

Mills A, 'Rethinking Jurisdiction in International Law' (2014) 84 BYIL 187.

Ministry of Justice, 'The Bribery Act 2010: Guidance about Procedures which Relevant Commercial Organisations Can Put into Place to Prevent Persons Associated with them from Bribing (Section 9 of the Bribery Act 2010)' (2011).

Mora PD, 'The Alien Tort Statute After Kiobel: The Possibility For Unlawful Assertions Of Universal Civil Jurisdiction Still Remains' (2014) 63(03) ICLQ 699.

Moreno-Lax V and Costello C, 'The Extraterritorial Application of the EU Charter of Fundamental Rights: From Territoriality to Facticity, the Effectiveness Model', *The EU Charter of Fundamental Rights: A Commentary* (Hart Publishing 2014).

Nash JR, 'The Curious Legal Landscape of the Extraterritoriality of US Environmental Laws' in Günther Handl, Joachim Zekoll and Peer Zumbansen (eds), *Beyond Territoriality: Transnational Legal Authority in an Age of Globalization* (Queen Mary studies in international law. Martinus Nijhofff Publishers 2012).

Niestedt M, 'Die Geltung des EU-Sanktionsrechts für Tochtergesellschaften und Niederlassungen' in Arnold Wallraff, Dirk Ehlers and Hans-Michael Wolffgang (eds), *Recht der Exportkontrolle: Bestandsaufnahme und Perspektiven: Handbuch zum Exportkontrollrecht.* zugleich Festgabe für Dr. Arnold Wallraff zum 65. Geburtstag (Schriften zum Aussenwirtschaftsrecht 2015).

Nolan J, 'From Principles to Practice: Implementing Corporate Responsibility for Human Rights' in Jena Martin and Karen E Bravo (eds), *The Business and Human Rights Landscape: Moving Forward, Looking Back* (Cambridge University Press 2015).

Note, 'Developments in the Law – Extraterritoriality' (2011) 124 HarvLRev 1226.

—— 'Clarifying Kiobel's "Touch and Concern" Test' (2017) 130 HarvLRev 1902.

Nowrot K, 'Steuerungssubjekt und -mechanismen im Internationalen Wirtschaftsrecht (einschließlich regionale Wirtschaftsintegration)' in Christian Tietje (ed), *Internationales Wirtschaftsrecht* (2. Aufl. De Gruyter 2015).

Nuyts A, 'Study on Residual Jurisdiction: Review of the Member States' Rules concerning the "Residual Jurisdiction" of their Courts in Civil and Commercial Matters pursuant to the Brussels I and II Regulations' (2007).

Nwapi C, 'A Necessary Look at Necessity Jurisdiction' (2014) 47 UBC Law Review 211.

Obidairo S, *Transnational Corruption and Corporations: Regulating Bribery through Corporate Liability* (Taylor and Francis 2016).

O'Brien CM, 'The Home State Duty to Regulate TNCs Abroad' (2016).

O'Brien CM, Vander Meulen N and Mehra A, 'Public Procurement and Human Rights: A Survey of Twenty Jurisdictions' (2016).

O'Keefe R, 'Universal Jurisdiction: Clarifying the Basic Concept' (2004) 2(3) JICJ 735.

Oxman BH, 'Jurisdiction of States' in R. Wolfrum (ed), *The Max Planck Encyclopedia of Public International Law* (Oxford University Press).

Pantaleo L, 'Sanctions Cases in the European Courts' in Matthew Happold and Paul Eden (eds), *Economic Sanctions and International Law* (Studies in international law volume 62. Hart Publishing 2016).

Parrish AL, 'The Effects Test: Extraterritoriality's Fifth Business' (2008) 61 Vanderbilt Law Review 1455.

—— 'Reclaiming International Law from Extraterritoriality' (2009) 93 Minnesota Law Review 815.

—— 'Evading Legislative Jurisdiction' (2012) 87 Notre Dame Law Review 1673.

Peters A, *Jenseits der Menschenrechte: Die Rechtsstellung des Individuums im Völkerrecht* (Jus Internationale et Europaeum vol 88, Mohr Siebeck 2014).

—— 'Verhältnismäßigkeit als globales Verfassungsprinzip' in Björnstjern Baade and others (eds), *Verhältnismässigkeit im Völkerrecht* (Jus Internationale et Europaeum vol 116. Mohr Siebeck 2016).

Pieth M, Low LA and Bonucci N, *The OECD Convention on Bribery: A Commentary on the Convention on Combating Bribery of Foreign Public Officials in International Business Transactions of 21 November 1997* (2. ed. Cambridge University Press 2014).

Planitzer J, 'Trafficking in Human Beings for the Purpose of Labour Exploitation: Can Obligatory Reporting by Corporations Prevent Trafficking?' (2016) 34(4) Netherlands Quarterly of Human Rights 318.

Posadas A, 'Corruption under International Law' (2000) 10 Duke Journal of Comparative and International Law 345.

Pottmeyer K, 'Die Strafbarkeit von Auslandstaten nach dem Kriegswaffenkontroll- und dem Außenwirtschaftsrecht' [1992] Neue Zeitschrift für Strafrecht 57.

Prete L, 'On Implementation and Effects: The Recent Case-law on the Territorial (or Extraterritorial?) Application of EU Competition Rules' [2018] Journal of European Competition Law & Practice 1.

Putnam TL, *Courts without Borders: Law, Politics, and U.S. Extraterritoriality* (Cambridge University Press 2016).

Ramasastry A, 'Closing the Governance Gap in the Business and Human Rights Arena: lessons from the anti-corruption movement' in Surya Deva and David Bilchitz (eds), *Human Rights Obligations of Business: Beyond the Corporate Responsibility to Respect?* (Cambridge University Press 2013).

Rathbone M, Jeydel P and Lentz A, 'Sanctions, sanctions everywhere: Forging a path through complex transnational sanctions laws' (2013) 44(3) Georgetown Journal of International Law 1055.

Raustiala K, 'The Geography of Justice' (2005) 73 FordhamLR 101.

—— *Does the Constitution Follow the Flag?: The Evolution of Territory in American law* (Oxford University Press 2009).

Rehbinder E, 'Extra-Territoriality of Pollution Control Laws from a European Perspective' in Günther Handl, Joachim Zekoll and Peer Zumbansen (eds), *Beyond Territoriality: Transnational Legal Authority in an Age of Globalization* (Queen Mary studies in international law. Martinus Nijhofff Publishers 2012).

Reinisch A, 'Human Rights Extraterritoriality: Controlling Companies Abroad' in Eyal Benvenisti and Georg Nolte (eds), *Community Interests Across International Law* (First edition. Oxford University Press 2018).

Reisman M and Stevick DL, 'The Applicability of International Law Standards to United Nations Economic Sanctions Programmes' (1998) 9 EJIL 86.

Rennack DE, 'Iran: U.S. Economic Sanctions and the Authority to Lift Restrictions' (May 2018), https://fas.org/sgp/crs/mideast/R43311.pdf.

Rensmann T, 'Völkerrechtliche Grenzen extraterritorialer Wirtschaftssanktionen' in Arnold Wallraff, Dirk Ehlers and Hans-Michael Wolffgang (eds), *Recht der Exportkontrolle: Bestandsaufnahme und Perspektiven: Handbuch zum Exportkontrollrecht.* zugleich Festgabe für Dr. Arnold Wallraff zum 65. Geburtstag (Schriften zum Aussenwirtschaftsrecht 2015).

*Restatement (Fourth) of the Foreign Relations Law of the United States* (American Law Inst. Publ 2018).

*Restatement (Third) of the Foreign Relations Law of the United States* (American Law Inst. Publ 1987).

Rice S, 'Discriminating for World Peace' in Jeremy M Farrall and Kim Rubenstein (eds), *Sanctions, Accountability and Governance in a Globalised World* (Connecting international law with public law. Cambridge University Press 2009).

Ronzitti N, 'Sanctions as Instruments of Coercive Diplomacy: An International Law Perspective' in Natalino Ronzitti (ed), *Coercive Diplomacy, Sanctions and International Law* (Brill Nijhoff 2016).

Rose C, *International Anti-Corruption Norms: Their Creation and Influence on Domestic Legal Systems* (Oxford University Press 2015).

Rose-Ackerman S and Palifka BJ, *Corruption and Government: Causes, Consequences, and Reform* (Second edition, Cambridge University Press 2016).

Ruggie JG, *Just business: Multinational corporations and human rights* (Amnesty international global ethics series, First edition, W.W. Norton & Company 2013).

Ruys T and Ryngaert C, 'Secondary Sanctions: A Weapon out of Control? The International Legality of, and European Responses to, US Secondary Sanctions' [2020] BYIL.

Ryngaert C, *Jurisdiction in International Law* (Oxford Monographs in International Law, Second edition.).

—— 'Extraterritorial Export Controls (Secondary Boycotts)' (2008) 7 Chinese Journal of International Law 625.

—— *Unilateral Jurisdiction and Global Values: Oratie in verkorte vorm uitgesproken bij de aanvaarding van het ambt van hoogleraar Internationaal Publiekrecht aan de Faculteit Recht, Economie, Bestuur en Organisatie van de Univ. Utrecht op maandag 30 maart 2015* (Eleven International 2015).

—— 'Whither Territoriality?: The European Union's Use of Territoriality to set Norms with Universal Effects' in Cedric Ryngaert and others (eds), *What's Wrong with International Law?: Liber amicorum A.H.A. Soons* (Nova et vetera iuris gentium. Brill Nijhoff 2015).

—— 'From Universal Civil Jurisdiction To Forum Of Necessity: Reflections On The Judgment Of The European Court Of Human Rights In Nait-Liman' [2017] Rivista di Diritto Internazionale 782.

—— *Selfless intervention: Exercising jurisdiction in the common interest* (Oxford scholarship online, First edition, Oxford University Press 2020).

Ryngaert C and Koekkoek M, 'Extraterritorial Regulation of Natural Resources: a Functional Approach' in Jan Wouters and others (eds), *Global Governance through Trade: EU Policies and Approaches* (Leuven Global Governance. Edward Elgar Publishing 2015).

Ryngaert C and Ringbom H, 'Introduction: Port State Jurisdiction: Challenges and Potential' (2016) 31(3) The International Journal of Marine and Coastal Law 379.

Sagafi-nejad T and Dunning JH, *The UN and Transnational Corporations: From Code of Conduct to Global Compact* (United Nations Intellectual History Project, Indiana University Press 2008).

Salbu SR, 'Extraterritorial Restriction of Bribery: A Premature Evocation of the Normative Global Village' (1999) 24(1) YaleJIntLaw 223.

Sarfaty GA, 'Shining Light on Global Supply Chains' (2015) 56 HarvIntlLJ 419.

Schaefer ME, 'Should a Parent Company Be Liable for the Misdeeds of Its Subsidiary?: Agency Theories Under the Foreign Corrupt Practices Act' (2019) 94 New York University Law Review 1654.

Schalber R, *Der UK Bribery Act und seine Bedeutung im Rahmen von Criminal Compliance* (Schriften zu Compliance v.13, 1st ed. Nomos Verlagsgesellschaft 2018).

Schmahl S, 'Zwischenstaatliche Kompetenzabgrenzung im Cyberspace' (2009) 47 Archiv des Völkerrechts 284.

Schöppner T, *Wirtschaftssanktionen durch Bereitstellungsverbote* (Zugl.: Münster, Univ. Diss, 2013. Schriftenreihe des Europäischen Forums für Aussenwirtschaft, Verbrauchsteuern und Zoll e.V. an der Westfälischen Wilhelms-Universität Münster vol 51, Mendel 2013).

Schultz T, 'Carving up the Internet: Jurisdiction, Legal Orders, and the Private/Public International Law Interface' (2008) 19(4) EJIL 799.

Schuster G, *Die internationale Anwendung des Börsenrechts* (Beiträge zum ausländischen öffentlichen Recht und Völkerrecht, Springer 1996).

Scott C, 'Analysing Regulatory Space: Fragmented Resources and Institutional Design' [2001] PL 329.

Scott J, 'Extraterritoriality and Territorial Extension in EU Law' (2013) 62 AJCL 87.

Scully EP, *Bargaining with the State from Afar: American Citizenship in Treaty Port China, 1844–1942* (Columbia University Press 2012).

Second Annual International Business Law Symposium, 'Trading with Cuba: The Cuban Democracy Act and Export Rules' (1993) 8 Florida Journal of International Law 335.

Sève M, 'Sapin II: Is the Era of Compliance and Criminal Settlements upon France?' [2017] RTDF 2.

Simma B, 'From Bilateralism to Community Interest in International Law' (1994) 250 Recueil des Cours 217.

Skinner G, 'Rethinking Limited Liability of Parent Corporations for Foreign Subsidiaries' Violations of International Human Rights Law' (2015) 72 Washington and Lee Law Review 1769.

Spiro PJ, 'Perfecting Political Diaspora' (2006) 81(1) New York University Law Review 207.

Stephens B, 'The Amorality of Profit: Transnational Corporations and Human Rights' (2002) 20 Berkeley Journal of International Law 45.

Stigall DE, 'International Law and Limitations on the Exercise of Extraterritorial Jurisdiction in U. S. Domestic Law' (2012) 35 Hastings International and Comparative Law Review 323.

Stilz A, 'Why do States have Territorial Rights?' (2009) 1(2) Int Theory 185.

Svantesson DJB, *Solving the Internet Jurisdiction Puzzle* (Oxford University Press 2017).

Sweet AS and Mathews J, 'Proportionality Balancing and Global Constitutionalism' (2008) 47(1) Columbia Journal of Transnational Law 72.

Thoms A, 'Offenlegungspflichten für Konfliktmineralien in den USA und der EU' in Arnold Wallraff, Dirk Ehlers and Hans-Michael Wolffgang (eds), *Recht der Exportkontrolle: Bestandsaufnahme und Perspektiven: Handbuch zum Exportkontrollrecht.* zugleich Festgabe für Dr. Arnold Wallraff zum 65. Geburtstag (Schriften zum Aussenwirtschaftsrecht 2015).

Thorhauer NI, *Jurisdiktionskonflikte im Rahmen transnationaler Kriminalität* (Nomos Verlagsgesellschaft mbH & Co. KG 2019).

Turner R, 'Transnational Supply Chain Regulation: Extraterritorial Regulation as Corporate Law's new Frontier' (2016) 17 MelbJIntLaw 1.

Uecker P, *Extraterritoriale Regelungshoheit im Datenschutzrecht* (Frankfurter Studien zum Datenschutz vol 52, 1. Auflage, Nomos 2017).

Vagts DF, 'Extraterritoriality and the Corporate Governance Law' (2003) 97(2) AJIL 289.

Vázquez CM, 'Trade Sanctions and Human Rights: Past, Present and Future' (2003) 6 JIEL 797.

Verdier P-H, 'Transnational Regulatory Networks and their Limits' (2009) 34(1) YaleJIntLaw 113.

Volz M, *Extraterritoriale Terrorismusbekämpfung* (Tübinger Schriften zum internationalen und europäischen Recht Bd. 86, Duncker & Humblot 2007).

Wade R, 'The System of Administrative and Political Corruption: Canal Irrigation in South India' (1982) 18(3) The Journal of Development Studies 287.

Wagner-von Papp F, 'Competition Law and Extraterritoriality' in Ariel Ezrachi (ed), *Research handbook on international competition law* (Elgar 2012).

Wallace CD, *The Multinational Enterprise and Legal Control: Host State Sovereignty in an Era of Economic Globalization* ([2. ed.], Martinus Nijhoff 2002).

Walter C, 'Grundlagen und Rahmenbedingungen für die Steuerungskraft des Völkerrechts' (2016) 76(2) ZaöRV 363.

Weissbrodt DS and Kruger M, 'Norms on the Responsibilities of Transnational Corporations and Other Business Enterprises with Regard to Human Rights' (2003) 97 AJIL 901–922.

Whang C, 'The Challenges of Enforcing International Military-Use Technology Export Control Regimes: An Analysis of the United Nations Arms Trade Treaty' (2015) 33(1) Wisconsin international law journal 114.

White ND and Abass A, 'Countermeasures and Sanctions' in Malcolm D Evans (ed), *International Law* (5th ed. Oxford University Press 2018).

Wilson N, 'Pushing the Limits of Jurisdiction Over Foreign Actors Under the Foreign Corrupt Practices Act' (2014) 91 Washington University Law Review 1063.

Windholz EL, *Governing through Regulation: Public Policy, Regulation and the Law* (Routledge critical studies in public management, Routledge Taylor & Francis Group 2018).

Woody KE, 'Conflict Minerals Legislation: The SEC's New Role as Diplomatic and Humanitarian Watchdog' (2013) 81 FordhamLR 1315.

—— 'No Smoke and no Fire: The Rise of internal Controls absent anti-bribery Violations in FCPA Enforcement' (2017) 38 Cardozo Law Review 1727.

Wouters J, Ryngaert C and Cloots AS, 'The International Legal Framework against Corruption: Achievements and Challenges' (2013) 14 MelbJIntLaw 1–76.

Wu Z, 'Perspectives on the Chinese Anti-Monopoly Law' (2008) 75(1) Antitrust Law Journal 73.

Yee S, 'Universal Jurisdiction: Concept, Logic, and Reality' (2011) 10(3) Chinese Journal of International Law 503.

Yihdego Z, *The Arms Trade and International Law* (Studies in international law vol. 15, Hart Pub 2007).

Yilmaz Vastardis A and Chambers R, 'Overcoming the Corporate Veil Challenge: Could Investment Law Inspire the Proposed Business and Human Rights Treaty?' (2018) 67(02) ICLQ 389.

Zagaris B, *International White Collar Crime: Cases and Materials* (2. ed. Cambridge University Press 2015).

Zerk JA, *Extraterritorial Jurisdiction: Lessons for the Business and Human Rights Sphere from Six Regulatory Areas* (A Report for the Harvard Corporate Social Responsibility Initiative to Help Inform the Mandate of the Unsg's Special Representative on Business and Human Rights. Working paper/ Corporate Social Responsibility Initiative vol 59, Harvard University, John F. Kennedy School of Government 2010).

Ziegenhain H-J, *Extraterritoriale Rechtsanwendung und die Bedeutung des Genuine-Link-Erfordernisses: Eine Darstellung der deutschen und amerikanischen Staatenpraxis* (Zugl.: München, Univ. Diss. 1991/92. Münchener Universitätsschriften Reihe der Juristischen Fakultät vol 92, Beck 1992).